Reading the Early Modern Passions

Reading the Early Modern Passions

Essays in the Cultural History of Emotion

Edited by Gail Kern Paster,
Katherine Rowe, and
Mary Floyd-Wilson

PENN

University of Pennsylvania Press
Philadelphia

10   9   8   7   6   5   4   3   2   1

Published by
University of Pennsylvania Press
Philadelphia, Pennsylvania 19104-4011

Library of Congress Cataloging-in-Publication Data

Reading the early modern passions : essays in the cultural history of emotion /edited by
Gail Kern Paster, Katherine Rowe, and Mary Floyd-Wilson.
  p.   cm.
  ISBN 0-8122-3760-9 (alk. paper); ISBN 0-8122-1872-8 (pbk. : alk. paper)
  Includes bibliographical references and index.
    1. European literature—Renaissance, 1450–1600—Histroy and criticism.
2. European literature—17th century—History and criticism.
3. Emotions in literature. I. Paster, Gail Kern. II. Rowe, Katherine.
III. Floyd-Wilson, Mary.
PH715 .R43   2004
809'.93353—dc22   *2003065786*

Contents

Introduction:
Reading the Early Modern Passions

The title of this volume should properly be phrased as a question. Are there early modern passions? Do the emotions in the period and place we now designate, however unsatisfyingly, as "early modern Europe" have a character and distinctive profile—an "emotional universe"—such as anthropologists describe for the societies under their professional gaze?[1] The essays gathered here explore this possibility, implicitly or explicitly, from different points of view. Our contributors find textual evidence for what might constitute the early modern emotional universe in English lyric poems and Italian tragicomedies; in a beloved but misunderstood painting; in a selection of musical examples from "Greensleeves" to Monteverdi; in particular political events of the French and English civil wars. They address specific emotions—sadness, courage, compassion—as experienced by the individual and interrogate the emotions spread throughout a particular society by fears of tyrannical rule or popular disturbance. They investigate early modern anxieties about the overwhelming power of emotions in general or of women characters in particular—as well as the relation of emotions to the public good and their role in promoting an individual subject's relation to God, to monarch, to fellow human beings, and to other creatures besides. In bringing these essays together, it is our assertion that students and scholars of early modern creative expression—poetry, drama, painting, music, the fields represented in this collection—bring a crucial perspective to the study of emotion more generally. Their insights into the early modern taxonomies of emotion suggest not only how these differ from our current categories, but also how they continue to script our debates about emotions as objects of study in the humanities, sciences, and social sciences. The three sections of this volume, "Early Modern Emotion Scripts," "Historical Phenomenology," and "Disciplinary Boundaries," represent three different kinds of contributions our authors make to this larger conversation.

As scholars with an interest in cultural history, we gravitate towards the differences between early modern and modern representations of emotions. While there is important evidence—some of it summarized below— that the emotions have broad similarities across both cultures and time periods, historical narratives of the kind provided here are obliged to explain difference by focusing on what is particular to any given moment in time—including representation of the salient emotions. Furthermore, while similarities in emotional experience argue strongly for the biological basis of human emotion, the insistence on universality can be too dismissive of the variousness of emotional expression and experience—and thus sharply limited in its explanatory potential. One index of these differences is lexical variants. How translatable is the language of emotion? What connotations have faded over time? Steven Mullaney has observed that the word "emotion" did not become a term for feeling until about 1660, around the time that "individual" took "on its modern meaning."[2] The Renaissance words that most closely approximated what we call emotion were "passion" and "affection." That we now tend to associate both these terms with amorous or fond feelings hints at an unfamiliar emotional terrain, where hope and sadness were "passions" together with love and desire, and where one's "affections" could run in a different direction from love. As Claudius remarks of Hamlet after witnessing his outbursts to Ophelia in the nunnery scene, "Love? his affections do not that way tend" (3.1.162).[3] Moreover, even early modern writers who studied the passions provided different maps of this terrain. There were competing taxonomies of passions: a range of ancient categories were available, and these vie for dominance not only with each other but with Christian classifications in early modern passions discourse. Where Cicero claimed that there were only four passions— fear, desire, distress, and pleasure—Thomas Aquinas's popular classificatory scheme identified eleven fundamental passions—the concupiscible passions of love, hate, desire, aversion, pleasure, and sadness and the irascible passions of hope, despair, fear, courage, and anger.[4] Even more basically, some early modern writers treated "passions" and "affections" as synonyms, whereas others drew careful distinctions between the two terms.[5]

In their varied approaches, our contributors do not always employ the same vocabulary of the emotions, sometimes preferring the early modern "passions" but also introducing a variety of modern affect terms borrowed from philosophy, psychology, anthropology, and social science. Nor are all of them equally interested in the project of historical phenomenology— imagining how emotions might have been experienced differently by early modern subjects. And though lexical and taxonomic questions about emotion have always haunted the topic, some of our essays eschew these issues as well. What all our contributors do assume in common is that the emotions require no justification as a subject in their own right because writing about the emotions tells a long and complex story involving the history of rhetoric, the history of science and religion, the social role of the arts, and the aesthetic role of pleasure, and employing a variety of discourses from the medical to the religious to the aesthetic.

Despite this shared starting point, however, some justification of the terms of our project seems to us required by a topic that does not exist in terms recognizable from one academic discipline to another. For some influential thinkers, indeed, "emotion" as a category may not exist at all. It is this profound lack of consensus about the object under discussion that causes Amélie Rorty to write emphatically, "Emotions do not form a natural class," because they cannot "be shepherded together under one set of classifications as active or passive; thought-generated and thought-defined or physiologically determined; voluntary or nonvoluntary; functional or malfunctional; corrigible or not corrigible by a change of beliefs."[6] Philosopher Paul E. Griffiths maintains that, if empirical science has no place in the study of emotions—if emotions cannot be quantified, measured, or otherwise studied objectively—then emotions by definition cannot form a natural kind and "there is an important sense in which the emotions do not really exist."[7] Both philosophers are reacting here to the fact that, when it comes to the emotions, a working vocabulary common to the disciplines involved in their study has yet to develop. There is little agreement on what constitutes the cardinal or core emotions, on how to rank emotions on a scale of complexity, on which creatures experience them, or on whether emotions are more pan-cultural than they are local and culturally specific.

One insight afforded by the essays in this volume is that such questions remain hard to settle precisely because of the divided spheres of knowledge and experience the emotions straddle, a legacy of disciplinary divisions that sharpened in the early modern period. To understand the force of this legacy, it is useful first to sketch out the current debates about emotion in different spheres of Western scholarship. Scientists, for example, diverge strongly over what part of the body is most involved in the expression of emotion, with evolutionary psychologists focused on heart rates and brain waves, cognitive scientists interested in emotional change after lesions to the brain, and behavioral psychologists such as Paul Ekman attracted to the face and its musculature as the central site and means of emotional expression.[8]

Cultural anthropologists, by contrast, define the whole body as a site of emotional expression and social symbolism, with posture and other cultur-ally specific gestures understood to signify greatly in the display rules gov-erning expression of such emotions as shame or anger.[9] There is also so little overlap in basic assumptions about what constitutes an emotion that one discipline will rule out of contention the very objects of study that another discipline defines as central.[10] The contest most crucial to the de-bate has been waged by behavioral and evolutionary psychologists, on the one hand, and cultural anthropologists on the other. The one discipline is committed to a universalist premise about objectively measurable emo-tional output, while the other focuses on emotional variation and the value of culture-specific reports as transmitted from within a single culture by a trained, linguistically competent observer in the field.[11]

Evolutionary psychologists, for example, are characteristically disinter-ested in defining the emotion process to include any feeling-state that could be perceived and reported by an individual, let alone a society. One reason for this disinclination is the desire—shared by empirical and many social scientists—to escape from the indeterminacy and lexical circularity of lan-guage and to affirm the universality of their discoveries by doing so. Tax-onomies of emotions do not track or translate across cultures or historical periods—as many essays in this volume will demonstrate. For students of the emotions, language—affect-laden and highly variant—can seem to be either a prison-house or a house of mirrors, revealing not what the emo-tions "really" are but only what people have believed about them at differ-ent times and places. And such descriptions of emotion may themselves vary from "collective pretenses about how people do behave" to highly pre-scriptive accounts of how people should or want to behave.[12]

Another reason for some empiricists' lack of interest in conscious emo-tions is that, if emotions are defined as a body's hard-wired neurochemical responses to external stimuli, then emotions work much the same across all the vertebrate species. By the time a person consciously experiences an emotion—feels angry or fearful, perceives his heart to be racing or his face to be flushed—the physiological response triggered in his brain has already occurred. For some evolutionary psychologists, this means that the "emo-tion" has already occurred. They are thus little interested in a person's (belated) report about an emotion—a "feeling"—when it has reached con-sciousness and more concerned with tracking the underlying neurological mechanism that caused it. And because this mechanism works much the same in animals and people, having evolved over eons "as behavioral and physiological specializations, bodily responses controlled by the brain, that allowed ancestral organisms to survive in hostile environments and procreate," studying emotion in these terms need not involve people at all.[13] As Joseph LeDoux concludes, "If we do not need conscious feelings to explain what *we would call* emotional behavior in some animals, then we do not need them to explain the same behavior in humans."[14] But here too the power of definition operates to exclude what cannot be explained; what LeDoux "would call" emotional behaviors are the short-term, stereotypical responses common to all animals under threat rather than the highly variant, fine-grained, conscious behaviors of human beings feeling shamed, angry, jealous, or sad for reasons that may not be intelligible from one culture to another. If LeDoux's approach has the self-evident merit of studying what is objectively measurable, its explanatory powers are limited because, as Griffiths expresses it, "it overestimates the heuristic value of evolutionary theory" in accounting for behavior.[15] This is because the emotional range describable by evolutionary psychology is quite narrow, in large part because the physiological responses open to this kind of observation and measurement do not vary greatly from one kind of stimulus to another. Such work rules conscious emotions out of court even though, as the biologist Charles Birch declares rather grandly, "Feelings are what matter most in life."[16]

Amélie Rorty's response to the massive lexical problems involved in studying the emotions is to pronounce research in the subject too immature to support a unified theory: it is even "too early for a single interdisciplinary account of the approaches whose contributions are required to explain the range of emotional conditions."[17] Jon Elster would agree: he dates the scientific study of the emotions from the publication of Darwin's *Expression of the Emotions in Man and Animals* (1872) and William James's paper, "What Is an Emotion?" (1884). But he tries to solve the disciplinary problem by classifying emotions as those that are eligible for scientific study and those that are not. In this way, he can place a high value on Aristotle, arguing that the ancient Greek polymath "anticipated the key elements of the modern theories and, moreover, had important insights that have not yet been rediscovered."[18] And he can distinguish hierarchically between basic emotions such as "anger, fear, disgust," available for empirical analysis, and the subtler emotional "subset" into which he places regret, relief, hope, disappointment, shame, guilt, and a host of other emotions of interest to poets, moralists, and novelists. Clearly his distinction is based on the common practice of ranking the emotions on a scale of complexity presumed to mirror the ethical complexity of their causation and the biological complexity of the experiencing subject: "no one to my knowledge," Elster writes, "has suggested that rats are capable of feeling malice or regret," though he is not confident that primates are similarly untouched by such emotions.[19] These disciplinary reassignments will not—and probably should not—satisfy rigorous thinkers such as Rorty, Griffiths, or LeDoux.[20] Indeed Rorty's response to the disciplinary problems besetting the study of emotion is to insist on the need for philosophers and other humanists to inform themselves of "relevant empirical investigations" and on the need of empirical researchers to become more self-conscious "about the assumptions built into their conceptual apparatus." She is particularly critical of attempts on the part of any discipline to preempt the field of study.[21]

Cultural historians are typically less apprehensive about this taxonomic morass than philosophers, psychologists of all stripes, or even social theorists such as Elster, because we see it as providing data to be analyzed rather than noise to be filtered. In turn, we tend to be more anxious about the motivations and methodologies behind the universalist aspirations of these rival disciplines. Darwin was clearly a pioneer of scientific methodology in the study of emotional expression—sending out questionnaires all over the British Empire, asking test subjects to interpret uncontextualized photographs of subjects' faces, observing physical behaviors of threat or submission across species from cats to dogs to monkeys to people. Moreover, by defining his topic as the study of the expression of emotion rather than of emotion itself, he limited himself to what was observable—if still not quantifiable. But his methods—still influential among psychologists—are nevertheless open to serious question: in order to produce certain facial expressions, he stimulated muscle reaction in one old man's face through electric wires applied to his skin; he assumed the universality of emotions in humans rather than making that question part of his program; and he regarded the expression of emotion in children, "savage races," and the insane to be more genuine and spontaneous—less culturally encoded—than that of adults in modern European societies.[22] Certainly he was far from unbiased in his goals, being determined at the outset to find similarities in the emotional behaviors of animals and people and to use that similarity to prove the continuity of species and thus the truth of evolution.[23]

For contemporary psychologists such as Paul Ekman, Darwin's work remains highly influential. As Griffiths notes, Darwin's detailed accounts of facial expressions and the muscles involved in producing them in expressions of fear, surprise, anger, disgust, sadness, and happiness "are very similar to those accepted today."[24] Ekman emulates Darwin in his use of photographs to record facial expressions, in his privileging of subjects from isolated cultures, and in his interest in cross-cultural interpretation of those photographs. But he departs from Darwin in widening both the scope of and the claims for his investigation, reducing emotion to facial expression in order to break down the prismatic effects of language.[25] Yet Ekman's photographs are not themselves clear evidence of what he most wants to claim for them—proof of the universality of emotions—in part because taking photographic evidence of what might count as "natural" or spontaneous emotion in a situation controlled enough to interpret it reliably is very diffi-cult, as Darwin certainly knew and as Ekman himself acknowledges.[26] This is why, for example, Ekman asked photographic subjects from the South Fore people of New Guinea to imagine an affect-laden situation—your child has died, you are angry and about to fight, you see a dead pig that has been lying there a long time—and then to express it facially.[27] But such facial expressions, far from representing spontaneous emotion, are in fact the fictional product of theatrical framing: the situations intended to pro-duce expressions of grief, anger, or disgust are entirely hypothetical and the test subject's goal must be to communicate clearly the "look" of an emotion without actually feeling it.[28] The result is not the photographic portrait of emotion, but the photographic portrait of acting—often bad acting. If, with his photographs and 100,000 feet of film, Ekman proved that there are no unfamiliar or new facial expressions, he did so by erasing the line between feeling and the simulation of feeling—a line that seems to us important to recognize. At such fictional moments, psychological experiment becomes theater, the psychologist becomes a director eliciting now one emotion, now another, and the subject becomes a highly self-conscious actor in the presence of an acknowledged, emotionally receptive audience. The results of such experimentation may support the general recognizability of strong emotions across cultural boundaries, though as James Russell points out "we have no cross-cultural studies of recognition of emotion from sponta-neous facial expression"[29] And there is still reason to be suspicious of a methodology that does not distinguish between emotional experience and its simulation and refuses to accept the role of language and the body more generally in the communication of emotion.

Certainly Darwin's book is now at enough of a temporal remove for us to recognize the historical embeddedness of his scientific program, a recog-nition harder to achieve in scientific writing like Ekman's closer to us in time and seemingly more self-aware of its potential for bias. But Darwin's desire to escape from language through such "objective" devices as photographs and to prove the universality of emotions by privileging the emotions of animals over those of people does align him with his disciplinary descendants among psychologists, behaviorist and evolutionary ones alike. And the methodology Darwin pioneered offers cultural historians the opportunity to distinguish their brand of disciplinary self-consciousness from that of other students of the emotions. It seems appropriate for example to return to Amélie Rorty's long list of binarisms in order to ask why these terms—"active or passive; thought-generated and thought-defined or physiologically determined; voluntary or involuntary; functional or malfunctional; corrigible or not corrigible by a set of beliefs"—should present themselves to her as obstacles to the study of emotions rather than as a potentially useful framework, within which we can explore the nuances and complexities of emotional experience. Certainly her list of terms evokes the discursive history of the emotions from ancient times forward. Certainly too her list is a good example of the tendency to think in dualistic terms about the emotions rather than looking within the interstices of those terms for equally useful terms for generating accounts of emotion. In order to be a natural class, must emotions be either voluntary or involuntary? Or involve thought to the exclusion of the bodily? How easy is it to distinguish between what is active and what is passive in the experience of emotion? How easy is it to distinguish between the functional and the malfunctional for emotions as complex as regret, grief, or jealousy? And functional or malfunctional for whom?

The terms Rorty invokes are part of the intellectual history of the emotions that this volume aims to outline. They carry associations weighted heavily towards different sets of interests in the contest over authority and taxonomic privilege on the subject. Thus active/passive is the adjectival variant of a binary with overarching importance for the premodern history of the emotions. As Susan James has recently written, "We tend to forget that philosophers of this era worked within an intellectual milieu in which the passions were regarded as an overbearing and inescapable element of human nature, liable to disrupt any civilized order, philosophy included, unless they were tamed, outwitted, overruled, or seduced."[30] So, too, the binary of voluntary/involuntary silently elides a long and complex theological history about the nature and status of free will as the hallmark of the human. It rests upon a time-honored division of the mind into rational and emotional sectors, a division that has been set aside by newer connectionist, cognitive models of the brain. Furthermore, it begs the question of cultural determinism, an intellectual stance that offers the possibility that some emotions may owe their very existence—and certainly their names—to cultures that encourage or discourage their expression. Finally, Rorty's list self-consciously displays the tendency in Western culture to organize important cultural binaries hierarchically, with active usually valued over passive, voluntary over involuntary, thought over physiology, and corrigible emotions over the incorrigible ones.[31] This tendency, along with the desire to break through past language, is itself symptomatic of the larger cultural problem, a problem in which the discoveries of science as part of the history of thought are deeply implicated. In the case of the emotions, this desire and this history stretch very far back in time.

Cultural Scripts

We agree with Paul Griffiths that empirical science and cultural studies ought to create more space for each other in their conceptual nesting grounds. However, the findings of evolutionary psychology, taken by themselves, seem to us to offer limited resources for the study of human emotions as plastic biological phenomena, culturally selected for and shaped by language. We agree, with Griffiths and others, that some emotions are probably pan-cultural and some are highly determinate, though whether that distinction correlates to a division between core and secondary emotions is not yet clear. For this reason and others, we are dissatisfied with the linguistic inadvertence of philosophers and psychologists who wish—in vain, we think—to break through the veil of language to prior or nonlinguistic truth about the emotions. The research program of a cultural linguist such as Anna Wierzbicka seems to us to offer a promising bridge between the competing methods at impasse here, because Wierzbicka wants to reconcile the philosophical desire for translinguistic study of emotional expression with a recognition of language's constitutive role in any culture's emotional universe. That is, Wierzbicka refuses to accept the incommensurability of cultural expressions of emotion and wishes to enlist language in support of "emotional universals."[32] While acknowledging the undeniable fact that many emotion words as well as the semantics and grammar of emotion are language- and culture-specific, she nevertheless hazards a basic translinguistic vocabulary that includes such words as GOOD, BAD, THINK, KNOW, WANT, FEEL.[33] She uses such words (capitalized), and their equivalents in other tongues, to create a semantic metalanguage that seeks to describe the particular flavor of emotion words in any language—and the rules of the road for using them. By doing so, she may discover a cultural matrix which locates primary emotions—the emotions that every culture needs to find linguistic expression for—and what we might then confidently call secondary emotions.[34] The ambition and promise of this model, for cultural historians, is that it may allow us to study emotion both synchronically and diachronically, as affect terms and emotional scenarios either change or remain much the same over time. Primary and secondary emotions might not be distinguished from one another on the basis of complexity—however we might wish to define complexity in this context—but on the basis of something resembling a measurable range of cultural selection. Some emotions will recur with reliable frequency in various languages. Other "outlier" emotions will find particular expression in response to semantic changes over time in a given language or to historical events in a given society.[35]

By identifying the cognitive scenarios that feature particular emotions, however they may be expressed, Wierzbicka can compare the linguistic and social rules for emotion in different cultures. The cognitive scenarios she sketches with her core terms reflect the normative "emotion scripts" that govern affective expression and exchange. Illustrating the concept of emotion scripts, Wierzbicka describes a familiar scenario: the enthusiastic American greeting "You look great!" The high premium Americans place on this ubiquitous routine reflects a social investment in cheerfulness which Wierzbicka and others attribute to the pressures of middle-class mobility. The norm of friendliness, they explain, involves a cultural script: "I feel something good toward everyone." That script became increasingly important as "one autonomous individual had to deal with other autonomous individuals in situations where one's self-esteem and prospects depended on one's ability to impress and negotiate."[36]

Cheerfulness is an emotion that ought intuitively to travel well. Indeed, Wierzbicka's assessment of its premium in American culture has much to do with social success in increasingly mobile populations. However, the significance of this affect varies considerably from one culture to another. Wierzbicka notes the absence of similar norms for "good feelings" in modern Polish and Australian cultures. Europeans, she observes, may be nonplussed by the American tendency towards frequent compliments.[37] Australians may respond to hyperbolic Americanisms even more strongly, with deadpan understatements that stress the indiscriminacy of American friendliness.[38] In either case, one cultural script elicits responses in another cultural idiom in a way that highlights the different values informing each. Such encounters emphasize how easily one set of cultural interests may translate to counterproductive affects away from home.[39]

Scholars interested in reading emotions transhistorically need to question the match between their own normative scripts for emotion and those of the culture whose affects they explore. An awareness of Wierzbicka's work across languages helps us refine our claims about emotional transformation or continuity across time periods in this way. To see how a mismatch might play out in a scholarly context, we might try a thought experiment with Ekman's photographic study. The situations he conjures for his photographic subjects assume an intrinsic value to the *expression* of feeling. To be useful, his scenarios must produce legible changes in the muscles of his subject's face. In other words, his samples necessarily exclude emotions that a culture requires to be censored for public expression. It would be silly to conclude that systematically unexpressed emotions cannot, by definition, constitute significant or core emotions in a given culture.[40] At least one of Ekman's core emotions, grief, makes an obvious counterexample. The scenario for grief that Ekman chooses, the death of a child, has historical roots that call into question the value of expressing and even experiencing strong feeling. The death of a child is a commonplace test for *apathia*, dating back to classical philosophy.[41] This test sits at the heart of competing strains of thought about emotional expression and control. Stoic and anti-Stoic arguments revived in the Renaissance debated the value of—and even the distinction between—corrigible and incorrigible emotions. Had Ekman used early modern subjects—any gentleman reader of a manual such as Thomas Wright's *Passions of the Minde in Generall* (1604)—he would have been as likely to photograph stony faces as visibly sorrowful ones. Moreover, that apparent lack of affect would communicate powerfully. As a topos, in other words, the death of a child carries with it specific standards for emotional expression. In this case, those expressive standards (Western and classical) are vexed: part of a long-running debate about the virtues of emotional expression in which Ekman's experiments unwittingly take a side. The historical thought experiment may not apply to the emotion norms of subjects from New Guinea. It does apply to Ekman's norms, illustrating the usefulness of a comparatist analysis of the questions a discipline or period allows itself to ask.

Modern readers tend to misread early modern emotion codes along specific lines, often parsing emotional control as a lack of feeling and privileging spontaneous and passionate expressions as evidence of authentic experience.[42] Lawrence Stone's notorious assessment of Renaissance England as a culture of cold feelings—lacking in strong affections and attachments—illustrates just such a mismatch of modern and early modern emotion scripts.[43] In the first section of this volume, Richard Strier, Michael Schoenfeldt, Zirka Filipczak, and John Staines demonstrate that our current tendency to separate reason from passion, for example, or to privilege individual experiences as more authentic than culturally sanctioned ones, has dimmed our capacity to perceive less familiar Renaissance valuations of the passions. And several of the early modern emotion scripts that our contributors discover bring us back to the historical legacy of Rorty's binaries of active and passive, voluntary and involuntary. We may recall that for the early moderns the verb *patior* "combines the idea of passivity with that of suffering, a sense nowhere more vividly conveyed than in the story of Christ's Passion," while *pathe* invokes the more active sense of perturbations.[44] Certainly, a significant number of early moderns subscribed to the neo-Stoic sense of passions as perturbations, or perilous forces that acted on the suffering body. Yet it was Christ's suffering, the theologians argued, that made him human, and to imitate Christ was to identify with his Passion and to combat anger and revenge with love.[45] Hence, rather than seeking to quell emotions in the Stoic sense, many Renaissance writers appealed instead to the classical tradition of controlling affections with other affections.[46] In this way, they translated the passivity of Christian suffering, or the passivity of perturbations that act upon the body, into a willful redirection of the very "motions" that constituted the feeling self.

Taken together, the essays by Schoenfeldt and Strier provide a gloss on these seeming paradoxes, for their scholarship reveals how varied and conflicted classical and Christian conceptions of the passionate self were. In his earlier work *Bodies and Selves*, Schoenfeldt demonstrated that it was the Stoic disciplining of emotional disruptions that helped produce the early modern sense of an autonomous self. In this volume, Schoenfeldt points up the equivocal status of seventeenth-century passions, arguing that the seemingly dangerous "commotion" of Adam's love for Eve is, in fact, what makes Milton's Eden paradisal. Identifying the anti-Stoic strain of early modern humanism and reformist theology, Strier maintains that Shakespeare and George Herbert may have valued emotional vulnerability over and above the "autonomous, unmoved, always detached" Stoic self.[47]

But as the essays by Filipczak and Staines make clear, a too persistent focus on the passionate *individual* may also overshadow the early modern investment in emotional expression as either a generic marker of social status or the sentient matter of communal bonds. Filipczak helps us see that our romantic fascination with Mona Lisa's smile (which may signify her husband's name, "Giacondo" or "cheerful") has distracted us from the portrait's participation in an early modern system of emotional cataloging, wherein group identity determines affect display, if not affect itself. Staines reveals that the rhetorical battles fought before the English Civil War depended on a conception of the public sphere defined by the contagion of compassion. Staines and Filipczak make clear that our modern inclination to script passions as individual and proprietary (Hamlet's melancholy or Mona Lisa's smile) leads us to miss those feelings that come from the outside. Perhaps the most contested issue that this volume illuminates is the current privileging of emotions as inward rather than social phenomena, a privilege reflected in Rorty's dualist categories, Wierzbicka's universal grammar ("X feels something"), and Ekman's tendency to ignore rhetorical occasion. Do our norms for handling inwardness, our attitudes toward it, and our communication strategies associated with it, match those of Renaissance Europe? It is our aim in what follows to venture an answer to this question.

Historical Phenomenology

The critical questions we ask about emotion—even the emotions we select as objects of study—are themselves coded expressions, scripted by normative attitudes.[48] Sadness, for example, takes center stage in both Wierzbicka's and Ekman's studies, as it has in modern studies of Renaissance affects. That emphasis arguably reflects the discursive privilege of melancholy in Western philosophy, which Juliana Schiesari traces from Aristotle through the Renaissance to Freud.[49] Schiesari's work on melancholia further attests to the continuing power of psychoanalysis as an interpretive model for scholars interested in early modern affects. Psychoanalytic approaches pay off for this topic in part because they understand emotions as coded expressions, as evidence of psychic events rather than the events themselves, and as symbolic processes. Yet, an ongoing challenge for psychoanalytical readings of early modern affect has been the essentialist logic that governs interpretation of that evidence: for example, the patriarchal hierarchies Freud naturalized in divisions of emotional labor or Lacan's gendered terms for subjectivity that feminist scholarship has sought to redress.[50]

The essays in this volume provide a wider framework for those, like

Schiesari, who are committed to comparatist analysis of psychological categories.[51] They also offer a fruitful context for scholars interested in historicizing the procedures of psychoanalysis. Schiesari, for example, has positioned Freud not only as the "historical end of that great era of Cartesian selfhood," but also as the inheritor of a Renaissance discourse of melancholia as an elite affliction of men of genius.[52] Debora Shuger has noted that Calvinist theories of mind inform the Freudian "allegory of id, ego, and superego."[53] David Hillman has reflected on the ways in which Freudian ego-identity resembles post-Cartesian skepticism.[54] If we read these scholarly insights through Wierzbicka's lens, we can see them as a variety of early modern emotion scripts drawn together under the rubric of Freudian inwardness. Thus Freud's psychic economy, with its attention to managing the boundary between inner and outer, might be seen to internalize neo-Stoic practices. The Freudian subject arguably translates such neo-Stoic boundary policing to a dominant interpretive mode—in which, Sarah Winter observes, "every event is interpreted as a psychodynamic scenario, however personalized, impelled by desires defined as arising from within the individual and the mind."[55]

Framed by the essays in this volume, the particular, disciplinary inflection of Freud's work shows clearly: the way he resituates within the psyche events and processes previously considered to be external. As Winter describes it, the constitution of a subject that precedes social and cultural formation is a central aspect of Freud's drive to institutionalize psychoanalysis as a discipline. To the extent that Freud's project defines emotional knowledge as *inaccessibly* inward, such knowledge is situated beyond the explanatory reach of the educational, social, and cultural practices that—as our essayists show—emotion scripts belonged to in the early modern period. Thus, for example, the distinctive procedures of the talking cure might be seen to adapt basic principles of emotion management from early modern classical education. The sixteenth-century educator Richard Mulcaster recommends *vociferatio* (rhetorical expression) as a means to purge ill humors.[56] Yet educational practice and the corrigible body it belongs to drop from Freud's intimate scene of individual analyst and patient. In this context, we might press Hillman's observation even more strongly. Psychoanalysis does not so much resemble late seventeenth-century skepticism as adopt it in a way that increases its own explanatory power. To read Freud's writings exclusively through the lens of his drive to institutionalize a new field is, of course, to tell only part of the story. For scholars like Schiesari and Lynn Enterline, Lacanian psychoanalysis provides an important revision to the disciplinary priority accorded psychological inwardness by restoring cultural formation to subject development in fruitful ways and supporting historically comparatist readings of psychological states like melancholia.[57]

Recent work in the history of the subject has argued that the discourse of psychological inwardness gains its present urgency in the early modern period, as a legacy of late seventeenth-century religious, philosophical, and political theory.[58] Charles Taylor's influential *Sources of the Self* describes the rise of inwardness as a radical departure from earlier Renaissance theories of the self. According to Taylor's history, Cartesian, Lockean, and Calvinist philosophies of mind shared a common drive to disengage consciousness from the body, reason from emotion, and the self from its physical and social environment.[59] Taylor's account of this epistemic shift has been strongly critiqued by scholars, such as William Ian Miller, who maintain that the vocabulary and experience of a "deep inner life" has long been a crucial component of Western psychology, dating back at least to Icelandic saga. What changes, Miller argues, is not the experience of inwardness as such, but the values placed on it and the norms for handling and communicating it.[60] In other words, Taylor's epistemic model totalizes what would better be understood as continuous but uneven developments in Western emotion concepts, in which the norms for handling feelings described in one discourse (the discourse of honor, say) may remain much the same, while undergoing significant transformation in others. Like Norbert Elias's theory of progressive emotional containment (similarly influential and similarly critiqued), Taylor's "grand narrative" privileges one emotion script among others, the value of each of which rises and falls over time in describable ways.[61]

Indeed, early modern psychology only partially shares the priority we place on inwardness, alongside very different conceptions of emotions as physical, environmental, and external phenomena.[62] For seventeenth-century England, John Sutton has argued, the dualist disengagement Taylor traces involved a systematic revision of the material psychology derived from classical and medieval theory. Writers such as Descartes and Locke reimagined the body as separate from its environment: what earlier theorists described as a porous, labile arena of contesting fluids, began to be reconfigured as "a static, solid container, only rarely breached, in principle autonomous from culture and environment, tampered with only by diseases and experts."[63] In keeping with this trend, late Renaissance neurophilosophy revised Galenic models of emotion, refashioning the more volatile Galenic body into an arena of self-possession, volition, and executive control.[64] Sutton's analysis explains why early modern texts may prove so fruitful for post-structuralist scholars who wish to estrange and reflect critically on Freudian essentialism, and why these texts suit the more plastic body theorized by Lacanian psychology. The very structure of essentialist logic works in fundamentally different ways in the humoral model. Elaine Scarry defines what we think of as modern essentialism: an appeal to the "sheer material factualness of the human body," that lends a given cultural construction "the aura of realness and certainty."[65] By contrast, the early modern body that grounds social facts is radically labile, prone to biological alterations and lapses from the temperate mean of civility. In this respect it lacks the certain fixedness we are used to in essentialist appeals. Early modern subjects experienced strong passions as self-alteration: being moved measurably "besides" oneself, as experts like Levinus Lemnius describe it in *The Secret Miracles of Nature* (1658).[66]

Reminding us that early modern Europeans had not yet separated the mind from this changeable body, or the body from the world, a significant number of our contributors take a phenomenological approach to exploring how pre-Cartesian psychophysiology may have affected early modern self-experience. By putting pressure on the fact that the period's most categorically "scientific" discourses on the passions are in themselves not only socially invested representations but also cultural scripts, Gail Kern Paster, Katherine Rowe, Mary Floyd-Wilson, Bruce Smith, and Gary Tomlinson all imply that the very language of physiology—from Galenic humoralism to Ficinian cosmology to Cartesian categories to modern cognitive science— helps determine phenomenology. The way we describe the workings of our bodies and minds, and how we characterize our habitation in the world, may shape and color our emotional experiences. Thus, we are asked to imagine an emotional existence where one can, for example, hear green, suffer the melancholy of cats, become infected with fear, transform the environment with valor, or experience in song the "unbroken continuity" of the "material and immaterial realms."[67] One tactic for engaging our modern imagination in this way is to keep in mind, as Gail Kern Paster has urged, the "materiality of the passions," or to literalize those locutions that we have long presumed to be figurative.[68] In observing the gap between the language of the past and present, Maurice Pope explains: "when we describe somebody as having hot blood or a cold heart or a dry wit we realize that we are talking metaphorically whereas in the past we would have believed ourselves to have been talking about physical qualities."[69]

The relationship between the body and metaphorical language is a pressing question in linguistics. Observing that emotion language seems to rely cross-culturally on similar metaphors (English: "Billy's a hothead"; Japanese: "My head got hot," etc.) the linguist Zoltán Kövecses maintains that these figurative tropes are not only culturally constructed but also arise from our universally shared and "real" physiology.[70] Since anger does appear to increase skin temperature and blood pressure, the argument goes, we are inclined to produce heat analogies to express it verbally.[71] Countering Kövecses, Dirk Geeraerts and Stefan Grondelaers contend that much of our current emotional vocabulary in the West is "part of the lexical legacy of the theory of the four humors."[72] Providing a crucial diachronic dimension to the cultural study of emotion, Geeraerts and Grondelaers contend, with Pope, that humoral "expressions that were once taken literally" linger in our current metaphors.[73] Yet Geeaerts and Grondelaers resist locating the origin of emotional language strictly in the body by entertaining the notion that humoral theory itself may have been motivated by a prior metaphorical understanding of a physiological experience, along the lines of "anger as fire."[74]

Many of our contributors refer to the diachronic linguistic process described above—the post-Cartesian movement "towards abstraction and dematerialization."[75] But they also question whether the binary of literal versus metaphorical prohibits our understanding of the way language and emotion functioned in the early modern period. In his essay "Hearing Green," Bruce R. Smith, for example, suggests that phonetic linguistics may help us imagine a pre-Cartesian reception of sound in which the "passions 'hear' sensations before reason does."[76] Paster's essay aids us in thinking beyond the humoral body to the "analogical network of early modern ontology."[77] Here, the early modern "simile" should remind us that bodies felt, sympathetically, their generic and fixed sameness with the correspondingly sensible world. Thus, felt passions situated humans within a connected web of "sympathies" and "correspondences," while also, paradoxically, distinguishing them from the world—an emotional experience that would seem to collapse our modern distinction between the literal and metaphorical.

Indeed, the dominant "metaphorical" link between humans and the world—the relation between microcosm and macrocosm—should be understood, simultaneously, as a rhetorical figure and the "very substance" of creation.[78] We are accustomed to viewing, for example, the meteorological analogy that likens sighs and tears to winds and storms as one-sided: human emotional expressions are analogous to the weather. But the correspondences ran both ways: the weather is correspondent with human emotions. Though it may not surprise us to learn that the "assumed parallelism" between the body and the world led William Harvey to discover the circulation of blood, we should also take note of the fact that Harvey's discovery inspired Renaissance geologists to search for "some central fire in the earth that performed a role analogous to that of the heart of man."[79] As Paster, Katherine Rowe, and Mary Floyd-Wilson stress, the passions are not "internal objects," or even "bodily states":[80] they comprise, instead, an ecology or a transaction.[81] For these contributors, passions characterize the microcosm's shifting interaction with a continuously changing macrocosm. Indeed, the liminality of early modern emotions (literal and metaphorical; internal and external) seems evident in the in-between status they possess in certain taxonomies. Not only are they categorized as one of the predominantly environmental "non-naturals," (which include air, exercise and rest, sleep and waking, food and drink, repletion and excretion), but they also act as internal messengers or porters—vehicles that transverse the Cartesian division between physiology and psychology.[82]

Disciplinary Boundaries

While our first group of essays seeks to demonstrate how modern narratives concerning the development and status of emotions fail to match entirely the twists and turns of early modern emotion scripts, the second group of essays invites us to imagine the early modern embodiment of emotion in terms that challenge post-Cartesian divisions between thought, soma, and world. The third and final group offers a critical context for understanding the methodological differences among the scholarly fields that currently claim emotion as their expertise. Emotion, as a topic, does not exist in terms recognizable from one discipline to another in part because the very formation of distinct disciplines (and bounded bodies) erased the interstices that had formerly comprised emotion. As the essays by Victoria Kahn, Timothy Hampton, Douglas Trevor, and Jane Tylus all provocatively suggest, the history of emotion is also a history of fixing aesthetic or disciplinary boundaries. Early modern emotions resist the dualist categories that underwrite the formation of separate fields of study: literal and metaphorical, physiological and spiritual, inner and outer, passive and active, affect and affectation.

As cultural historians, our contributors are keenly aware that the representation of affect resides at the very heart of artistic production. In his essay Gary Tomlinson contends that the artistic representation of the world and the soul "assumed a new power" when spaces opened "between tone and word, singer and listener, soul and bodily expression of emotion."[83] To put this argument in linguistic terms, the gradual movement towards abstraction and dematerialization in this period necessarily reshaped the relationship between emotion and language. As a case in point, Timothy Hampton's close attention to the altering meaning of "alteration" in the sixteenth century suggests that literature played a special role in the reconfiguration of this relationship. Literary authors in the period repeatedly responded to scenes of "emotional or physiological *alteration* by redefining the term itself, through a pun or a misreading"—a linguistic abstraction that succeeded in affirming the "agency of the self beyond the physiology of passion."[84] In a similar vein, Douglas Trevor contends that Edmund Spenser "marshaled a litany of imagistic, lexical, and allegorical strategies" to preserve Christian feeling from the corporeality of early modern passions.[85]

Ironically, this same movement towards the abstraction of emotion also seems to parallel an increasing sense of what Jane Tylus terms literature's "ethical uselessness"—and even, more radically, the separation of the expressive arts from other spheres of experience and knowledge.[86] Jane Tylus argues, for example, that it is the private inaccessibility of Gertrude's emotions in *Hamlet* that marks the end of the humanist confidence that drama can rehabilitate unruly passions in the service of the state. Victoria Kahn contends that Renaissance romance and the debates over the autonomy of art helped produce a "new prudent and calculating subject, as well as a new sense of affect."[87] No longer physiologically influenced or ethically persuaded by the depiction of passions, this new, proto-capitalist spectator gained, instead, a detached understanding of the manipulative power of aesthetic representations. In all four of these essays, artistic work trades an expansive set of interests—endangering, altering, or reforming individuals and communities—for its status as a privileged venue of affective expression and play. This trade-off has shaped the way different disciplines approach their cardinal questions about emotion, apportioning some emotions and emotion work (including dispassion) to the arena of scientific inquiry and others to aesthetics.[88]

The essays in this volume contribute to a broader account of these boundary shifts, the emotion scripts that inform them, and the methodological challenges such shifts generate for scholars interested in the study of emotion—including the apparently unsystematic impressionism of our modern vocabularies of feeling. Emotions emerge as "part of historical perception" in the essays that follow.[89] Historically conditioned perception, in turn, emerges as a critical component of the study of emotion. As a collection, these studies help us understand that the Western discourse of emotion remains meaningful—present and powerful to us—to the extent that it is also archaic.

PART I

Early Modern Emotion Scripts

Chapter 1
Against the Rule of Reason:
Praise of Passion from Petrarch to Luther
to Shakespeare to Herbert

Richard Strier

It is often taken as a basic truth about the whole "Western Tradition" that the control of "passion" by "reason" is its fundamental ethical-
psychological ideal. Passion, especially strong or uncontrolled passion, is
the villain of this story, and is often seen as linked to that other, perhaps
even more reprehensible villain, the body. The trouble with this view is
not only that it distorts intellectual history in its positive claims—equating
virtually all classical philosophy with a fairly severe version of a Socratic
or Stoic position—but that it also obscures another strand in "the tradition": the praise of passion. The Aristotelian tradition, understood as anti-
Stoic as well as anti-Socratic, has a place for this, since the "mean" is a
conceptual and situational, not an arithmetic or fixed conception; the "right
amount" of emotion for a circumstance need not be a moderate amount—
though there is much confusion about this point.[1] Even more important,
the Judaeo-Christian tradition, insofar as it is biblical, is a tradition that
allows for strong, even uncontrolled emotion. The Psalms are an important
case in point, as is the behavior of Jesus and the apostles in the gospels,
and the passions of St. Paul in his letters. None of this is sufficiently widely
recognized.

The Renaissance revived anti-Stoicism as well as Stoicism. The two
strands exist in opposition and complex interaction throughout the period.[2]
But insofar as self-consciously "Renaissance" figures defined themselves as
committed to rhetoric over against "mere" philosophy or logic, they were
committed to stressing the importance of the emotional and affective in
life.[3] In Petrarch's little book on the state of learning in his time ("On his
own Ignorance, and that of Many Others"), he explains his preference for

Cicero over Aristotle. Aristotle, Petrarch concedes, defines and distinguishes the virtues and vices with great insight. Yet, Petrarch reports, "when I learn all this, I know a little bit more than I knew before, but mind and will remain the same as they were, and I myself remain the same" (*tamen est animus qui fuerat, voluntasque eadem, idem ego*).[4] He then goes on to make a key distinction, one that Plato, for instance, would not make, and one that explains the centrality of rhetoric:

It is one thing to know, another to love; one thing to understand, another to will. He [Aristotle] teaches what virtue is, I do not deny that; but his lesson lacks the words that sting and set afire and urge toward love of virtue and hatred of vice, or has only the smallest amount (*paucissimos*) of such power.[5]

Petrarch conceives of the ethical life primarily in affective terms, and knowledge is seen as insufficient to produce affect: "what is the use of knowing what virtue is if it is not loved when it is known?" It is not the concepts alone but the words in which they are expressed "that sting and set afire and urge." The most important authors, therefore, from an ethical point of view, are those like Cicero, who "stamp and drive deep into the heart the sharpest and most ardent stings of speech" (*acutissimos atque ardentissimos orationis aculeos precordiis admovent infliguntque*).[6] The violence of this imagery is intentional. Effort and violence are required to penetrate what is clearly seen as the object of ethical teaching: the heart.[7]

This stress on the centrality of affectivity is crucial not only to the humanist defense of rhetoric, but also (and this is a closely related theme) to the defense of the active life, of life within rather than outside of the ordinary political and social world. Coluccio Salutati's letter to Peregrino Zambeccari (1398) appears to concede the greater sublimity, delight, and self-sufficiency of the contemplative life, but Salutati (Chancellor of the Florentine republic from 1375–1406) insists that though the active life is "inferior," it is, nonetheless, "many times to be preferred."[8] Part of the work of the letter is to blur the distinction between the kinds of life. Salutati suggests that not bodily placement but state of mind is determinative. In a certain state of mind, "the city will be to you a kind of hermitage"; and, on the other hand, one can be distracted and tempted in solitude (108). But Salutati's major thesis is that detachment from the world is not, in fact, a good thing, especially with regard to one's feelings. The most surprising (and passionate) part of the letter is its attack on detachment.

The focus of the issue is the appropriateness of grief. Imagining (as is inevitable in the context) the would-be contemplative as a male householder, Salutati begins at the personal level, asking, "Will he be a contemplative so completely devoted to God that disaster befalling a dear one, or the death of relations will not affect him?" (112). What is being imagined here, though not named as such, is the state of Stoic *apathia*. What ordinary folk take to be occasions for grief (or for anger) are the tests for the achievement of *apathia*. In the *Tusculan Disputations*, the ideal Stoic is presented as receiving the news of the death of his child with the words, "I was already aware that I had begotten a mortal."[9] Salutati's initial position is not that this response is impossible, but that it is undesirable. He adds to his list of disasters that should move a person a case that transcends the personal, a case that represents the ultimate disaster to a civic humanist and republican patriot: "the destruction of his homeland." None, Salutati implies, should not be moved—to grief, and perhaps to anger—at this.

Salutati is, in fact, skeptical about the possibility of such an unmoved person, but his deeper point is that such a being would not be a person:

> If there were such a person, and he related to other people like this, he would show himself not a man but a tree trunk, a useless piece of wood, a hard rock and obdurate stone.

Human beings, for Salutati, are defined by their affections, and these affections are seen as fundamental to social life: "If there were such a person . . . *and he related to other people like this*." Sociality and affectivity are seen as defining the human, and as inextricably linked. The Stoic sage—autonomous, unmoved, always detached—is seen as "useless" at best, and destructive at worst. Aristotle saw the person who had no need for a polis as either "a poor sort of being," or "a being higher than man."[10] Salutati discounts the second possibility.

The final point that Salutati makes about such a creature is perhaps the most interesting and historically significant. Zambeccari, in planning to give up the cares and commitments of civic life, and to detach himself from disquieting passions, clearly sees himself as following a religious, and especially a Christian path (see his letter to Salutati quoted in Salutati's response [101]). Salutati's answer to this is his trump card. Not only would the detachment that Zambeccari imagines be a betrayal of the fundamental nature of his humanity, such detachment would also not be Christian. Were Zambeccari to succeed in becoming a contemplative unmoved by any human situations, Peregrino would not thereby "imitate the mediator of God and man, who represents the highest perfection" (112). For Salutati, *imitatio Christi* means precisely to be passionate and moved:

For Christ wept over Lazarus, and cried abundantly over Jerusalem, in these things as in others, leaving us an example to follow.

Through this appeal to the Gospels, Salutati sharply distinguishes the Christian from the Stoic tradition—indeed, from the entire tradition of the classical sage.[11]

A text in which it might be said that the humanist critique of Stoicism culminates is Erasmus's *Praise of Folly* (1511–16). Obviously, this is a tricky work and has multiple rhetorical modes. For much of the text, the praise of folly is ironic; sometimes the critique of contemporary practices (especially with regard to war and religion) does not even maintain the fiction of praise. As Folly says, sometimes she seems "to be composing a satire rather than delivering an encomium."[12] In the richest and most interesting parts of the text, however, the praise of folly is either semi- or fully serious, and it is in these moments that the text is most anti-Stoical.[13] When Folly is arguing for her special relation to happiness and pleasure, she accepts "the Stoic definition" according to which "wisdom consists in nothing but being led by reason," and, conversely, "folly is defined as being swept along at the whim of emotion" (28). Folly is pleased with this definition, since it seems to cede so much of human life (that guided by emotion) to her. Erasmus cannot seriously be praising "being swept along," but the sense that human life would be very limited were it restricted to the nonaffective may not be entirely tongue-in-cheek ("in order to keep human life from being dreary and gloomy, what proportion did Jupiter establish between reason and emotion?"). The texture of the argument gets more complex when Folly moves from the defense of pastimes to more major features of social life. She notes that those who scorn pastimes insist that, in social life, friendship "takes precedence over everything else" (31). She presents the Stoic sage as incapable of lasting friendship through an incapacity to overlook faults:

if it should happen that some of these severe wisemen should become friendly with each other, their friendship is hardly stable or long-lasting, because they are so sour and sharp-sighted that they detect their friends' faults with an eagle eye. (32)

Folly's praise of (as Swift put it later) "being well-deceived" is, again, not fully serious, but it is also not—as it is in Swift—fully ironized.[14] As Erasmus presents the phenomenon, even through Dame Folly, this state is uncomfortably akin to a recognizable conception of charity (which, for instance, "suffereth long" and "covers a multitude of sins").

The opposition between Stoic wisdom and social life is continued, in a mostly unserious vein, a few pages later—"Bring a wiseman to a party: he will disrupt it either by his gloomy silence or his tedious cavils" (39)—but the argument about the need to adapt to circumstances (44) is as unsettled here as it is in the first Book of More's *Utopia*, the companion text to *Folly*.[15] Folly says that "true prudence," as opposed to the rigidity of the sage, "recognizes human limitations and does not strive to leap beyond them." Such "prudence" is willing to overlook faults tolerantly or, and here the irony reemerges, "to share them in a friendly spirit." But this, of course, is folly, as Folly happily concedes—as long as her philosophical opponents "will reciprocate by admitting that this is exactly what it means to perform the play of life" (44).

At this point of complex irony and non-irony, the issue of emotion surfaces again. "First of all," says Folly, beginning yet again, "everyone admits that emotions all belong to Folly" (45). This is why, she explains (again with complete accuracy), "the Stoics eliminate from their wiseman all emotional perturbations as if they were diseases."[16] Folly, however, in an uncharacteristically sober moment, straightforwardly endorses the alternative classical

Figure 1.1. Albrecht Dürer's "Fool Preaching," from the *Ship of Fools* (1594). Photo courtesy of Spaightwood Galleries.

position: "But actually the emotions not only function as guides to those who are hastening to the haven of wisdom, but also, in the whole range of virtuous action, they operate like spurs or goads, as it were, encouraging the performance of good deeds." This returns us to Petrarch's "ardent stings." Regaining something closer to her own voice, Folly states that she knows that "that died-in-the-wool Stoic, Seneca," strenuously denies this conception (of emotions as "spurs" to virtue), "removing all emotion whatever from his wiseman." Here Folly's critique joins Salutati's. Seneca is Folly's representative Stoic; she claims that in denying emotion to his wiseman, Seneca

is left with something that cannot even be called human; he fabricates some new sort of divinity that never existed and never will . . . he sets up a marble statue of a man, utterly unfeeling and quite impervious to all human emotion. (45)

Returning to the issue of normal social life, Folly asks:

Who would not flee in horror from such a man, as he would from a monster . . . a man who is completely deaf to all human sentiment . . . no more moved by love or pity than a chunk of flint . . . who never misses anything, never makes a mistake, who sees through everything . . . never forgives anything, who is uniquely self-satisfied, who thinks he alone is rich, he alone is healthy, regal, free. (45–46)

This is a brilliant characterization of Stoic autonomy ("uniquely self-satisfied"), and also brilliantly echoes the Stoic practice of paradoxically redefining the normal terms of social life ("he alone is rich," etc.).[17] It is also a devastating critique, and it is hard to see that there is much undercutting of Folly here.

In the peroration of the *Encomium*, the praise of Folly is unmistakably sincere. Echoes of the Pauline praise of "foolishness" over against the wisdom of the world are sounded (127–29), but the most lyrical and exultant section of the text is the final movement, which begins (again), "First of all, Christians essentially agree with Platonists" (133). As in Salutati, Christianity is seen as essentially affective. But Erasmus is not defending normal emotional reactions here. The affection that he defends is not grief but, as the reference to Plato would suggest, a version of love. Plato is praised for asserting that "the madness of lovers is the height of happiness" (136). Unlike Salutati, Erasmus does not connect the turn to the bible with the critique of Stoicism, but it is clear that his vision of Christianity has affect at its center. In the polarity between Stoicism and Augustinianism in Renaissance thought, Erasmus clearly stands (with Folly) squarely in the Augustinian camp.[18]

Although the critique of Stoicism is, as we have seen, an important strand in the humanist tradition, the pull of Stoicism—and of dualism, and even of asceticism—remained strong among the humanists as well.[19] Even the Epicurean Utopians, who primarily value the mental pleasures but who also accept bodily pleasure gratefully, think of the celibate and ascetic among their priests as less sensible but holier (*sanctiores*) than the nonascetic ones.[20] It is only in the Reformation tradition that the attack on Stoicism and asceticism is freed from ambivalence.[21] We must turn to the Reformers, and especially to Luther, for the most full-throated defenses of passion and of imperfection in the period. Luther gives Folly's horror theological underpinnings.

One of the great paradoxes of Reformation theology is that it is the doctrine of total depravity that yields such humane and comforting consequences. Luther rejected the idea that sin primarily concerns or emanates from the body. He insisted (probably correctly) that "flesh" and "spirit" in the Pauline epistles were not used in the Platonic sense—were not equivalent, in other words, to body and soul. Luther held that flesh, according to St. Paul, "means everything that is born of the flesh, i.e. the entire self, body and soul, including our reason. "[22] Fleshliness or carnality, from this point of view, is fundamentally the condition of egotism or self-regard—the condition of being, as Luther wonderfully put it in Latin, "*incurvatus in se*" ("curved in upon oneself").[23] Being "spiritual," from this point of view, would be a matter of being turned away from self-regard. Beware, warned Luther, "of all teachers who use these terms differently, no matter whom they may be, whether Jerome, Augustine, Ambrose, Origen, or their like, or even," he somewhat mysteriously adds—perhaps with Erasmus in mind—"persons even more eminent than they."[24]

Luther's reinterpretation of the central terms of Christian and philosophical anthropology had, as he well knew, profound and far-reaching implications. The theology of grace is necessitated by it, as is the entire Reformation rethinking of sanctity. The doctrine of grace flows from the reinterpretation of "flesh" and "spirit" because it seems truly impossible to imagine the self willing itself out of self-regard. All sorts of other things are possible. To do great works of charity or (for instance) patriotism in order either to attain glory or to lay up treasures in heaven seemed, to Luther, simply elaborate and particularly dangerous forms of self-regard, of working "in order to attain some benefit, whether temporal or eternal."[25] Only a force from outside the self can change so fundamental and natural an orientation. Grace, as the gift of faith, effects this by convincing the person that he or she already has the ultimate good for which he or she was striving through works. The psychological impact of this conviction is what Luther meant by the "freedom" of a Christian. Already having the goal— beyond what one could ever have earned—takes away the need for self-interest and allows works to be done "out of pure liberty and freedom," seeking "neither benefit nor salvation" (70).

When this conception of the impossibility and non-necessity of merit is put together with the conception of sin as not primarily concerned with the body, the whole rationale for asceticism and renunciation of the world disappears. Salutati's suggestion (also present at times in Erasmus) that holiness is a state of mind rather than a particular set of activities comes to fruition here.[26] Every believer, for Luther, is a saint. He insists that we must reject "this foolish and wicked opinion concerning the name of saints (which once we thought to pertain only to the saints which are in heaven, and in earth to the hermits and monks which did certain great and strange works)." Let us learn, he continues, "that all they which faithfully believe in Christ are saints."[27] Luther is suspicious of the famous monks and ascetics. He sees the ascetic life as full of superstitions, and, most of all, as an induce-ment to pride:

those which lurk in caves and dens, which make their bodies lean with fasting, which wear hair [shirts], and do other like things, [do so] with this persuasion and trust, that they shall have a singular reward in heaven above all other Christians. (161)

Among those to whom the word "saint" was wrongly restricted, Luther much prefers those, like Augustine and Ambrose, "which lived not so strait and severe a life," but rather

were conversant among men, and did eat common meats, drank wine, and used cleanly and comely apparel, so that in a manner there was no difference between them and other honest men as touching the common custom, and the use of things necessary to this life. (161)

According to Luther, the ascetic ideal encouraged not only pride in its practitioners but also a false and psychologically dangerous moral and spir-itual perfectionism. In the 1531 commentary on Galatians, Luther noted: "When I was a monk, I thought I was utterly cast away, if at any time I felt the concupiscence of the flesh" (148). By *concupiscentia*, he does not mean primarily sexuality (he acknowledges this as one of its meanings, but one that the schoolmen mistakenly took as definitive).[28] He immediately ex-plains what he means by the term: "that is to say, if at any time, I felt any

evil motion, fleshly lust, wrath, hatred, or envy against any brother." He dili-
gently employed all prescribed and recommended penitential and devotional practices, but was "continually vexed" with one sort of "evil motion"
or another.[29] This led Luther to misery and desperation. He knew he would
never be perfect. And he despaired. Only when he came to recognize the
true depth of human sinfulness, and consequently the need for grace to
come "from without," was he freed from torment of conscience.[30] Grace
"from without" transforms the recipient's relation to God and to "works"; it
allows the graced person to experience God as loving and giving rather than
as judging and demanding. The "righteousness" that is required for salvation is *imputed to* the believer; it is not literally and actually imparted to him
or achieved by him.[31] What this means is that the regenerate, the saints, are,
like St. Paul, "simul justus et peccator" ("at once righteous and a sinner").[32]
They are not free from sin and they are not free from passion: "the holiest
that live have not yet a full and continual joy in God, but have their sundry
passions" (127). To say that the saints are not "without all feeling of temptations or sins" is to say, Luther insists, that they are not "very stocks and
stones" (158). This is what makes their examples religiously and humanly
valuable: "Assuredly Mary felt great grief and sorrow of heart when she
missed her son"; David in the psalms "complaineth that he is almost swal-
lowed up with excessive sorrow of the greatness of his temptations and
sins." Luther has only scorn for what he calls (in the Elizabethan translation) the "imagination" that "the monks and schoolmen had of their saints,
as though they had been very senseless blocks, and without all affections"
(158). He makes the key connection: "the saints of the Papists are like to the
Stoics, who imagined such wise men as in the world as were never yet to be
found." And if they were to be found, Luther agrees with Folly that they
would be "monsters" (159, 162).

This view was not unique to Luther. It could not have been so, since it
was central to the Protestant redefinition of sanctity. The Psalms, with all
their passionate complaints to and rebukes of God, were made easily available—in every European vernacular (and in print)—as models of piety.
Luther loved the psalms for their sincerity and naked emotionality.[33] Calvin
felt the same. He made a rare allusion to his own conversion experience in
the Preface to his commentary on the Psalms, and he alerted the reader that
"in unfolding the internal affections both of David and of others, I discourse upon them as matters of which I have familiar experience."[34] Calvin
is particularly keen to explain the piety of the opening of Psalm 22, the verse
that Jesus quoted on the cross ("My God, my God, why hast thou forsaken

me?"). Calvin argues that a crucial feature of this question and others like it in the bible is that, while the question is certainly a complaint and even a rebuke, it is a complaint addressed to God—and therefore an act of faith. "What point would there be in crying out to him," Calvin asks, "if they hoped for no solace from him?"[35] Calvin discusses Christian patience at length, and is more invested in this notion than Luther is, but Calvin nonetheless insists that patiently to bear the cross "is not to be utterly stupefied" (*Institutes* III.viii.9). Like Luther, Calvin notes that "among the Christians there are also new Stoics, who count it depraved not only to groan and weep but also to be sad and care-ridden." Calvin's rejection of this is as strong as Luther's: "we have nothing to do with this iron philosophy." Calvin makes the same point that Salutati did about what "imitating Christ" means. The "iron philosophy"

> our Lord and Master has condemned not only by His word, but also by His example. For He groaned and wept over both his own and others misfortunes. And he taught his disciples in the same way.

The point of recognizing this, Calvin notes, is to recall "godly minds" from despair at their own continuing and unavoidable imperfection (*Institutes* 3.8.10).

It should now be clear that both the humanist and the Reformation traditions provided powerful defenses of the validity and even the desirability of ordinary human emotions and passions. Texts from both traditions expressing such a view were widely available (Erasmus, Luther, Calvin, etc.) The rest of this essay will be devoted to showing some of the ways that the Renaissance and Reformation defenses of passion entered into English vernacular literature in the sixteenth and seventeenth centuries. Examples will be drawn from both the secular and the religious spheres: from two plays of Shakespeare and from the religious lyric.

The Comedy of Errors is keenly aware of both humanist and Reformation traditions. The play begins on a moment of Stoic resignation—"proceed, Solinus, to procure my fall, / And by the doom of death end woes and all"— but its most striking thematic, thoroughly enacted in its dramaturgy, is its low estimate of human intellectual capacity. Every assertion of such capacity in the play is ironized. Bertrand Evans notes that *The Comedy of Errors* is unique in the Shakespearean corpus "in the universal depth of the participants' ignorance."[36] Intellectual impotence is thematized in the play. Antipholus of Syracuse (the stranger Antipholus) has exceedingly little faith in the powers of the human mind. He believes in "dark-working sorcerers that change the mind" (1.2.99); he is unsure whether sleeping and waking can be distinguished (2.2.181–83); he speaks of his "earthy gross conceit / Smother'd in errors, feeble, shallow, weak" (3.2.34–35); and he thinks that only a benign transcendental force can keep him (and all of us?) from wandering "in illusions"—"Some blessed power deliver us from hence" (4.3.41–42).[37] But while the play is extremely skeptical about human intellectual capacity, it has no doubt about the human capacity for feeling—in both senses of the term, physical and emotional. This leads to a series of remarkable jokes. Each of these jokes simultaneously demeans human intellectual capacity and asserts the capacity for feeling. Moreover, as we shall see, it is highly significant that these jokes are always made by social inferiors who are being, or have been, assaulted.

Dromio of Ephesus, having just encountered the uncomprehending and then angry Antipholus of Syracuse, responds to Adriana's questions about her husband (the other Antipholus)—"Didst thou speak with him? knowst thou his mind?"—with this: "Ay, ay, he told his mind upon mine ear." Communication, in other words, failed on one level (the semantic) but succeeded on another (the somatic). Adriana picks up the conceit—"Spoke he so doubtfully, thou couldst not feel his meaning?"—and Dromio responds: "Nay, he struck so plainly I could too well feel his blows; and withal so doubtfully, I could scarce understand them" (2.1.47–54). The pain, if nothing else, is clear. This is not an isolated moment. Similar sets of jokes occur in the scene that follows. Dromio of Syracuse says that he cannot locate his "wit," since his head is being batted about as a mere physical object, but he raises a question that truly arises from a sensible being (in both meanings, rational and sensate): "sir, why, am I beaten?" (2.2.39). Yet another form of the joke occurs in the scene following this when Dromio of Ephesus, claiming (wrongly) to know what he knows, gives another example of "sensible" inscribing:

If [my] skin were parchment and the blows you gave were ink,
Your own handwriting would tell you what I think. (3.1.13–14)

What he "thinks" is what he has felt.

This emphasis on the reality of suffering, apart from comprehension, leads to a major motif in the play: the critique of patience. In another set of puns equating social with bodily phenomena, Dromio of Ephesus responds to a question about Antipholus of Syracuse's "thousand marks" (of money) with a reference to bearing "some marks" of his master's beatings upon (of course) his "pate." And here Dromio cogently adds, "If I should pay your worship those again, / Perchance you will not bear it patiently" (1.2.81–86). The issue of patient bearing arises most powerfully in the play, however, in the context of another relationship of subordination, that of wife to husband. Shakespeare invents a character, the wife's sister, to provide a love interest for Antipholus of Syracuse, but Luciana's first role is to contend intellectually with her sister on precisely this matter of patience. When Adriana expresses annoyance that Antipholus (of Ephesus) has not come home for dinner, Luciana tells her to "be patient" (II.i.9). Adriana, however, refuses, asking, as Dromio of Syracuse did, the "why" question (which is, in these contexts, an act of protest rather than a demand for explanation): "Why should their [men's] liberties than ours be more?" Adriana rejects the idea that she should meekly allow herself to be "bridled" by her husband: "There's none but asses will be bridled so." At this point, Luciana rolls out the big gun of conservative Elizabethan ideology, the Chain of Being. Female subordination is a cosmic principle, one that should be especially true in creatures, says Luciana, "Indued with intellectual sense and souls." We have already noted the status of "intellectual sense" in the play, especially in regard to males, and the speech equivocates between "homo" and "vir" in its claims about "man," but Adriana's response takes a different tack. She first presents marital subordination as demeaning—"This servitude makes you to keep unwed"—but then returns to the issue of patience, of not being moved to anger or complaint. In posing the case of a wife who has been betrayed, Adriana denies the idea that her unmarried sister has any right to speak:

Patience unmov'd! no marvel though she pause;
They can be meek that have no other cause.

Adriana's next lines are a remarkably powerful defense of her critique of counsels to patience:

A wretched soul bruis'd with adversity,
We bid it quiet when we hear it cry;
But were we burden'd with like weight of pain,
As much, or more, we should ourselves complain. (2.1.34–37)

Dromio of Ephesus made a similar point about "bearing," but Adriana remains the key spokesperson for the critique of patience. The most complex interaction concerning this theme involves her. After the Syracusan Antipholus avoids danger by running into a "priory," the figure of the

Abbess enters the play. She attempts to take control of the situation and tricks Adriana into presenting herself as a shrew. When the Abbess makes a speech denouncing Adriana, a remarkable moment occurs. Luciana, heretofore the spokesperson for patience and meek obedience, speaks up when Adriana is silent, and asks: "Why bear you these rebukes and answer not?" (5.1.89). Suddenly Luciana is the spokesperson for not going quietly. And Adriana does not do so. When the Abbess invokes (medieval, Catholic) religious privilege ("He took this place for sanctuary") and tells Adriana again to "Be patient" and leave her (supposed) husband in the priory, Adriana will not.[38] She challenges not only the Abbess' ideal of patience but her ideal of holiness—"ill it doth beseem your holiness / To separate the husband and the wife" (V.i.110–11).[39] The newly nonconservative Luciana suggests that secular authority is the relevant one here: "Complain unto the Duke of this indignity" (113). When Adriana cries "Justice, most *sacred* Duke" (133), it is even clearer that two conceptions of sanctity are in conflict here. The Duke assumes authority over the Abbess (166–67), but the conflict between the ascetic and the Protestant ideal is resolved by the plot rather than by direct assertion, and it is resolved in favor of the noncloistered life. When the Abbess is revealed to be Egeon's long lost wife, she immediately assumes her familial identity, and the abbey becomes the site not of religious separation but of a secular reunion conceived as holy—"After so long grief, such Nativity" (406).[40]

Moreover, the play has a final word on the subject of preaching patience. Shortly after the Duke appears and takes control of the action, an unnamed servant of Antipholus of Ephesus enters to announce that his supposedly mad master has broken loose. Dr. Pinch, a Catholic exorcist, had been called in to deal with Antipholus of Ephesus' supposed condition (madness caused by demonic possession), but now, instead of the "madman" being (properly) "bound and laid in some dark room" (4.4.92), the Antipholus and the Dromio of Ephesus have

> bound the doctor,
> Whose beard they have sing'd off with brands of fire,
> And ever as it blaz'd, they threw on him
> Great pails of puddled mire to quench the hair
> . . .
> His man with scissors nicks him like a fool. (5.1.170–75)[41]

And while all this is going on, says the messenger, "My master preaches patience to him" (174).

King Lear is (among other things) Shakespeare's most extended meditation on the problematics of patience.[42] I cannot treat the play at length
here, but I will try to offer an initial sketch of some of the ways it does (and
does not) participate in the humanist and Reformation critiques of being
"unmoved." Clearly the play is aware of the cost of irrational rage. Lear can
never undo the effects of his initial act of rage. Yet, as the play develops, and
Lear becomes a character who is, arguably, "More sinned against than sin-
ning" (3.2.60), the moral status of rage in the play undergoes a transformation.[43] The villains in the play tend to be the spokespersons for calm and for
decorum. This begins at the end of the opening scene, when Regan (in the
Quarto) or Goneril (in the Folio) tells Cordelia, with self-satisfaction and
obvious correctness of a sort, "You have obedience scanted" (1.1.267/278).[44]
This motif, as part of the discourse of the villains, continues in the wicked
daughters' insistence that Lear behave himself with "discretion" and decorum. Goneril's first major assaults on Lear are attacks on license, insolence,
"riots," and disorder in the name of "a wholesome weal" and of the decorum
proper to a great (or graced) palace (1.4.188–201/174–87; 223–39/206–21).
Regan admonishes Lear, "I pray, sir, take patience" (2.4.113/127), and speaks
of herself and Goneril as "those that mingle reason with your passion"
(2.4.204/223). Lear, with his beloved Fool, is a figure of folly, while Goneril,
Regan, and company stand for "wisdom" (2.4.261/280; 276/296).[45]

The culmination of this development in the play is Lear's great protest
against common sense and prudence, "O reason not the need" (2.4.234/253).
The speech is a call for generosity, for the rejection of calculation in the face
of "need." It echoes the Reformation critique of giving alms for "reasons"—
in relation, that is, either to one's own salvation or to the "merit" of the
object (Luther notes that "a joyful, willing, and free mind serves one's neighbor willingly, and takes no account of gratitude or ingratitude, of praise or
blame, of gain or loss").[46] And Lear's speech rejects discretion as well as
calculation. It picks up a notion developed earlier in the Act through the
plain-spoken figure ("Caius") that Kent becomes in disguise. This figure is
startlingly badly behaved. He cannot contain his contempt for Oswald and
he insults everyone around (and over) him. When the Duke of Cornwall
speaks for decorum, and questions whether Caius has any proper "reverence" for authority and social position, Kent replies, "Yes sir, but anger hath
a privilege" (2.2.63/66). Lear is attempting to claim this "privilege" in his
speech on need.[47] He rejects meekness, urging the gods to "fool me not so
much" as to let him bear his situation "tamely" (2.4.246/265).[48] He wants

to be touched with "noble anger" (245–46/264–65)—the anger that is connected to honor and to heroic (or merely integral) identity.[49]

Yet even in this speech, the situation is more complex. Just before he asks for "noble anger," Lear asks the heavens to "give me that patience," and insists, "patience I need." How can he follow the prayer for patience with a prayer for anger? The answer might seem to be that Lear imagines that "noble anger" might be compatible with or enabled by patience, that such anger is not a form of excess or madness. Yet the speech itself undercuts this fantasy. The prayer for "noble anger" turns into a vision of "revenges," and the vision of "revenges" turns into the rant of madness: "I will do such things, / What they are, yet I know not; but they shall be / The terrors of the earth." The play accepts the Stoic equation of anger with madness. When Kent asks Lear, "where is the patience now / That you so oft have boasted to retain" (3.6.54–55/17–18), Kent is trying to keep Lear from going mad. Seneca saw the connection of anger to madness as the strongest argument for the sage not to indulge in anger, since "never will the wise man cease to be angry, if once he begins" because the world is so full of injustices and vices.[50] *Lear* can be seen as accepting the Stoic equation (anger leads the perceptive to madness), but rejecting the Stoic conclusion (anger is therefore to be avoided). The play may well present madness as the price that must be paid for a certain kind of wisdom rather than seeing the inevitability of madness as the reason why the wise man must renounce anger. Part of what makes the play a tragedy is its acceptance of the Stoic equation, its awareness that "noble anger" is indeed a fantasy, an unstable category.[51] Yet the play commits itself to anger nonetheless. Lear's apocalyptic rage, his dialogue with the elements, are borrowed from Senecan tragedy, and are clearly on the verge of madness.[52] Yet the passion that animates Lear's rage at how he has been treated is also seen as enabling his newfound sympathy for all the victims of injustice. Madness and "noble anger" do indeed go together in the play. The idea of the mighty and powerful willingly exposing themselves "to feel what wretches feel" is a mad idea, but it has an undeniable moral grandeur—just as Lear's own attempt at enacting this fantasy (through stripping) has both dimensions.[53]

The obvious contrast to Lear's response to injustice is Gloucester's. Gloucester rises to moral heroism—"Though I die for't, as no less is threatened me, the King, my old master, must be relieved" (Q 3.3.16–17)—and he suffers horribly for it, yet he would rather die than lose his patience toward the gods. He chooses (as he believes) suicide in order not to "fall / To quarrel with your [the gods'] great opposeless wills" (4.6/5.38). He takes the posited objective reality of "opposeless" (not being alterable by opposition) to imply the subjective condition (and moral necessity) of not opposing.[54] He articulates a Stoic, perhaps especially Senecan, conception of suicide as moral freedom and political resistance, idealizing a time "When misery could beguile the tyrant's rage / And frustrate his proud will" (4.6/5.63–64).[55] Even after Edgar has contrived the apparent miracle for Gloucester and presented suicide as a demonic temptation and the gods as benign, Gloucester is still eager to die quietly. When Oswald appears, chortling with delighted opportunism, and announcing rather grandly to Gloucester that "The sword is out / That must destroy thee," Gloucester too takes this moment as a happy one: "Now let thy friendly hand / Put strength enough to't" (4.6.215–20/5.220–25). This renewed urge toward suicide is probably to be seen as produced by the encounter with the mad Lear; Gloucester responds to Lear's person and his madness with admirable pity and affection. But Gloucester does not respond to Lear's savage indignation. Gloucester never responds to the picture of universal injustice and wickedness that Seneca said would drive the wise man mad if he were once to allow himself to be moved by it, the picture that does drive Lear mad (Seneca mentions the judge "who will condemn the same deeds that he himself has committed" and insists that there is no place in society not filled with "crime and vice").[56] When Lear finally does bring himself to acknowledge Gloucester calmly, Lear knows what Gloucester needs and wants to hear: "I know thee well enough; thy name is Gloucester. / Thou must be patient" (165–66/170–71).[57]

Gloucester dies a lovely, quiet death, in which "two extremes of passion, joy and grief" (that is, pity) simultaneously assert themselves and cancel themselves out, so that his heart "burst smilingly" (5.3.192–93/190–91). The play would seem to present this as a sort of ideal, one connected, perhaps, to Edgar's conception of "ripeness." But Lear does not go quietly, and his death cannot be assimilated to any conception of "ripeness," whether Stoic or Christian.[58] The play refuses to wrap up when it should, and insists on presenting us with the body of Cordelia, murdered through a piece of bad timing ("Great thing of us forgot!" [5.3.230/211]). After having had his "great rage" cured earlier—by a medical practitioner in the Quarto—Lear regains the "great rage" here.[59] Entering, as the early printed versions identically specify, with the corpse of Cordelia in his arms, Lear insists on the opposite of patience:

Howl, howl, howl, howl! O you are men of stones.
Had I your tongues and eyes, I would use them so
That heaven's vault should crack. (Q 5.3.250–52)

We are back to the "privilege" of anger—cosmologized, so that it truly knows "no reverence." The "men of stones," here, are statues, of course, mere simulacra of persons, but they are also, as Folly and others would remind us, Stoic sages.

It may seem odd to approach the devotional poetry of George Herbert immediately after contemplating the supreme blasphemy of *Lear*, but Herbert, in his context, is as radical in his defense of unfettered emotion as Shakespeare is in his. Herbert is the great spokesman, in English poetry, for the Reformation defense of passion.[60] His lyrics are modeled on the psalms, which he clearly saw, as Luther did, as expressions of the full range of emotions of the human heart in dialogue with God. Herbert saw Jesus' words on the cross in just the way Calvin did, as words spoken from the heart—in agony, in sincerity, and as part of a dialogue. In "Longing," Herbert wrote:

My throat, my soul is hoarse;
My heart is wither'd like a ground
Which thou dost curse.
My thoughts turn round,
And make me giddie; Lord, I fall,
Yet call. (7–12)[61]

At times Herbert felt the pull of Stoic equanimity—"the pliant minde, whose gentle measure / Complies and suits with all estates" ("Content," lines 13–14); and at times he felt the pull of Stoic *apathia*, as in "Constancie," when the "honest man" is to "treat / With sick folks, women, those whom passions sway," he "Allows for that, and keeps his constant way" (lines 26–28). Yet Herbert's most distinctive and important poetry is poetry of passion— poetry that, in the seventeenth century and beyond, was, in fact, extremely important to "sick folks, women, those whom passions sway."[62] Herbert knew that the priority that he gave to unvarnished and unbridled emotion might seem odd, might seem to contradict the claims of both art and decorum. But he took this priority to be God's. In "Sion," one of a whole set of ironic architectural poems in *The Temple*, Herbert explains why God has given up wanting to be served as He was (on His own command) in

Solomon's temple with magnificent materials and elaborate art ("most things were of burnished gold" and the whole structure was "embellished / With flowers and carvings, mysticall and rare"). It turns out, as Herbert puts it with typically audacious and humorous understatement, that "all this glorie, all this pomp and state" did not "affect" God much (7–8). What does "affect" Him, apparently, is precisely affect. In place of all the pomp and state, God has chosen to inhabit the intimate and peculiar world of human emotionality:

> There thou art struggling with a peevish heart,
> Which sometimes crosseth thee, thou sometimes it:
> > The fight is hard on either part.
> > Great God doth fight, he doth submit. (13–16)

The couplet of the stanza sums up the account of God's preferences:

> All Solomons sea of brasse and world of stone
> Is not so deare to thee as one good grone. (17–18)[63]

Why God should condescend to do this, why He should wish to deal with something so apparently unattractive as "a peevish heart" (childish, petulant, irritably demanding), why He should place such a value on "one good grone"—these odd preferences have been recorded, but they have not been explained. The final stanza provides the "explanation":

> And truly brasse and stones are heavie things,
> Tombes for the dead, not temples fit for thee:
> > But grones are quick, and full of wings,
> > And all their motions upward be;
> And ever as they mount, like larks they sing;
> Their note is sad, yet musick for a King. (19–24)

The final line alludes directly to the psalms (with David as singer), but the "King" here is not David but God. Why the struggling heart is a better temple for God than a great building is explained by the contrast between "dead" and living things (compare "O you are men of stones"). "Quick" is the crucial word here. Groans are products of human emotional responsiveness; they have "wings" because of their "motions upward," their expression of desire for succor, relief, and love. "Man groaning for grace" was the essential picture of piety for Luther and Calvin.[64] The kind of king that God is values heartfeltness—sincerity—more than anything else.

Herbert knows that this is as strange a picture of divinity as it is of kingship. He knows that this conception of the "music" God enjoys is as far from a traditional picture of heavenly decorum as the complaining speaker of "Longing" is from some models of "saintly" behavior. "Gratefulnesse" is another exploration and celebration of the oddness of God's preferences. It imagines the impact of human neediness on a traditional picture of heaven. God does not reason the need or worry about his great (or graced) palace:

Perpetuall knockings at thy doore.
Tears sullying thy transparent rooms,
Gift upon gift, much would have more,
                    And comes. (13–16)

After explaining, once again, that God "didst allow us all our noise" and has "made a sigh and grone" His joys (lines 18–20), Herbert acknowledges the full oddness of this, and provides a whimsical explanation. God is one of those Renaissance aristocrats who likes folk-music (recall Orsino's special preference for songs that are rural, old, and plain):

Not that thou hast not still above
Much better tunes than grones can make;
But that these countrey-aires thy love
                    Did take. (21–24)[65]

What all this serves for is to license Herbert to express his longing with a full, unabashed, and relentless infantile intensity. In Lear's terms, he "howls":

Wherefore I crie, and crie again;
And in no quiet canst thou be,
Till I a thankfull heart obtain
                    Of thee. (25–28)

Perhaps the clearest expression of the privileged status of emotion in Herbert is in the poem entitled "The Storm." The first stanza of this poem postulates a situation that would make one of Lear's storm fantasies true. Lear asks that the Gods make the storm affect the consciences of sinners and criminals: ("Close pent-up guilts, / Rive your concealèd centres" [Q 3.2.57–58]). Herbert asserts that "tempestuous times / Amaze poore mortals, and object their crimes" (lines 5–6). But, here again, what Herbert is interested in is not human moral and psychological vulnerability but the extraordinary power of this vulnerability to have the effect of successful rhetoric (as the Renaissance conceived it) on God—to "move / And much affect thee" (lines 4–5). The body of this poem gives the most powerful account in English of the "privileged" religious status of human psychological and moral need. Again Herbert praises importunate knocking:

A throbbing conscience spurred by remorse
                    Hath a strange force:
It quits the earth, and mounting more and more
Dares to assault thee, and besiege thy doore. (9–12)

What "Sion" presents as "music," what "Gratefulnesse" first presents as "noise" but then presents as "countrey-aires," is here presented in its most raw, unaesthetic, and indecorous form—"There it stands knocking, to thy musick's wrong, / And drowns the song." And the status of this painfully sincere and visceral ("throbbing") human longing is truly privileged:

Glorie and honour are set by, till it
                    An answer get. (15–16)

What all this should serve to show is that the next time one hears some pundit explaining that the "Western tradition" has always valued order, reason, self-control, and decorum above all else, one should remember Petrarch, Salutati, Folly, Luther, and their followers.

Chapter 2
"Commotion Strange":
Passion in Paradise Lost

Michael Schoenfeldt

A fascinating thing happens in Book 8 of *Paradise Lost* when the unfallen Adam describes to Raphael the powerful feelings that Eve arouses in him—Adam discovers that his own vocabulary, although capable of accurately naming every creature on the earth, is far less precise when it comes to articulating the nuances of emotion. Adam feels that Eve very literally moves something within him, and struggles to explain to Raphael the delicious and disturbing power of this internal agitation. Other Edenic pleasures, he concedes, are delightful, "but [are] such / As us'd or not, works in the mind no change, / Nor vehement desire."[1] But with Eve, Adam discovers an inner turbulence so strong that it seems to move and alter him:

> here
> Farr otherwise, transported I behold,
> Transported touch; here passion first I felt,
> Commotion strange, in all enjoyments else
> Superiour and unmov'd, here onely weake
> Against the charm of Beauties powerful glance. (8.523–33)

Adam here gropes for a terminology that would describe the dangerous and delicious pleasures of being moved by another being. The pleasure is particularly delicious because it is endowed with paradisal intensity, and it is particularly dangerous because it seems to change him, and any variation from paradisal perfection might entail degradation. He experiences this feeling of movement in the presence of Eve as a kind of internal transport that makes him susceptible, even "weake," to the "charm" that inheres in her beauty, as if only a language imbued with magic could depict the mysterious power that Eve, the purportedly secondary being, holds over him.

Most cogently, Adam describes the internal churning he feels in the

Figure 2.1. Carlotta Petrina, frontispiece for Book 9 of *Paradise Lost* (San Francisco: Limited Editions Club, 1936). Special Collections Library, University of Michigan. Reproduced by permission of Limited Editions Club and University of Michigan.

presence of Eve as a "commotion," a term like our own "emotion" which is etymologically linked to the visceral motion Adam describes. According to the *Oxford English Dictionary*, a *commotion* is a "physical disturbance, more or less violent; tumultuous agitation of the parts of particles of any thing." Its earliest uses apply to public disturbance or disorder—Jack Cade's rebellion in Shakespeare's *2 Henry VI*, for example (3.1.358), or Achilles's murderous rage in *Troilus and Cressida* (2.3.175).[2] Milton, moreover, uses the term earlier in *Paradise Lost,* to describe the destructive tumult possible if Satan and Gabriel had squared off in paradise: "now dreadful deeds / Might have ensu'd, nor onely Paradise / In this *commotion,* but the Starrie Cope / Of Heav'n perhaps, or all the Elements / At least had gon to rack" (4.992; emphasis mine). *Commotion,* then, is a surprisingly violent and unruly term for an unfallen creature to use to describe its interior state. As such, it seems to be another of those myriad moments when Milton teases us with a fallen lexicon that adumbrates the ultimate fate of Adam and Eve.

Indeed, Roy Flannagan's notes to Book 8 in *The Riverside Milton* emphasize the moral peril implicit in Adam's lexicon of emotion: "Being transported is a potentially dangerous experience, since it suggests not only being rendered ecstatic but being put in exile. The chain of associated words, 'transported' (repeated for emphasis), 'touch,' 'passion,' 'Commotion,' 'strange,' and 'passion' is also ominous."[3] Yet this ominous vocabulary, I hope to show, was part of the common coin of discussions of the passions. It is not so much that Milton here intends to show the peril of Adam's passion for Eve as that Milton's deep investment in the importance of affective relations to paradisal existence draws him into this volatile vocabulary.

Fascinatingly, Milton refuses for the most part to replicate in his epic one of the standard accounts of the status of emotion in relation to sexual difference. The Galenic physiology of the period argued that because women were cooler and wetter than men, they were also more susceptible to extreme emotion, and less capable of the rational wisdom required properly to regulate their emotions.[4] In Milton's redaction, though, it is not so much the first woman's inability to control her passions as the unruly passions she stirs in the first man that threatens the stability of prelapsarian humanity. By having two males deliberate the ethical status of passion, then, Milton refuses to make passion simply a symptom of feminine weakness; rather, he locates passion, with all of its disturbing and delicious pleasures, at the center of male and female paradisal experience. He courts rather than dampens the volatility that his culture attaches to the phenomena of passion by mapping it against the story of the Fall.

Passions indeed occupy an unsettled status in early modern culture, at once dangerous and necessary to ethical and physical health. Not just the range of quotidian desires and disgusts that render for us the vagaries of human character and motivation, the early modern passions were powerful affective impulses that the individual was thought to suffer (thus the etymology from the Latin *passus*, to suffer). In this essay I will explore the status of passion in Milton's *Paradise Lost.* I hope to show that Milton's attitude to passion is equivocal, and situational, and represents the radical inconsistency with which early modern culture confronted the phenomenon of passion. While Milton prizes the capacity of rightly directed emotion to move one to virtuous action, he also fears the loss of rational control passion can entail. His work at times values emotion, and at others endorses the Stoic self-control that would banish such emotion from the well-regulated subject. Both *Paradise Regained* and *Comus* connect the performance of virtue to the proto-Stoic effort to be "not mov'd," even though *Paradise Regained* mocks Stoicism's perfectionism while Comus the character ridicules the Lady's arguments as worthy of "those budge doctors of the *Stoick* Furr" (*Paradise Regained*, 2.407, 4.420, and 4.561; *Comus*, 707). *Samson Agonistes*, though, seems to find a stable, unmoved place only after a violent homeopathic expenditure of extreme emotion precipitated by Samson's ineffable experience of "Some rouzing motions in me"; the closet drama concludes with "Calm of mind, all passion spent" (1382; 1758). Milton's prose repeatedly attacks the "stoic apathy" of his political opponents, and endorses the idea that "each radicall humor and passion wrought upon and corrected as it ought, might be the proper mold and foundation of every mans peculiar gifts and virtues."[5] Yet Milton praises Cromwell in *Defensio Secunda* as a Stoic who, "whatever enemy lay within—vain hopes, fear, desires—he had either previously destroyed within himself or had long since reduced to subjection."[6]

It is in *Paradise Lost*, though, where the investment in the emotions is richest and also most troubling. In the epic, Milton carefully tracks the disturbingly constitutive status of emotion both before and after the Fall. Passion, I hope to show, is at once what makes Milton's paradise paradisal and what undoes it. Looking closely at the ways that passion suffuses pre- and postlapsarian subjects, I will show how the conversation between Adam and Raphael over the role of passion in prelapsarian erotic life can be seen as a debate between incommensurable but legitimate views of passion that course throughout Milton's career, and throughout early modern culture. The paradisal setting, and Milton's rigorous exploration of prelapsarian psychology, only throws into relief the radical instability of early modern attitudes to the passions.

Extreme passion certainly seems to take on a particularly demonic tinge early in the epic. Our first view of Satan manifests an emotionally tortured physiognomy that betrays his spiritually altered state: "round he throws his baleful eyes / That witness'd huge affliction and dismay / Mixt with obdurate pride and stedfast hate" (1.56–58). After his first speech, Satan is "rackt with deep despare" (1.126). His oration awaking the fallen angels produces passion among them; it makes them "abasht" (1.331). When he tries to address the assembled throng, "Thrice he assayd, and thrice in spight of scorn, / Tears such as Angels weep, burst forth" (1.619–20). The phrase "tears such as Angels weep" at once delineates a continuum between human and angelic emotion, and demarcates their qualitative difference. Milton adopts a particularly circuitous syntax to embody the tornadic passions that suffuse Satan:

> from despair
> Thus high uplifted beyond hope, aspires
> Beyond thus high, insatiate to pursue
> Vain Warr with Heav'n. (2.6–9)

Even a kind of perverse joy is available to the fallen angels. After Beelzebub's proposal that they send someone to corrupt earth, "joy / Sparkl'd in all thir eyes" (2.387–88). When Satan accepts the perilous voyage to earth, the fallen hordes "Ended rejoycing in thir matchless Chief" (2.487). God's account of Satan's fantastic voyage, moreover, puns wickedly on the kinetic power of emotion: "Onely begotten Son, seest thou what rage / Transports our adversarie" (3.80–81). It is fascinating that God uses for Satan's passionate voyage exactly the same verb—transport—that Adam uses to describe to Raphael his internal agitation when in the presence of Eve.

The rebellion in heaven begins, moreover, in passion; it is "envie against the Son of God" that precipitates the entry of sin into the world (5.662). Satan's poignant address to the sun is prefaced by a whirlwind of emotions: the ideas are "rowling" as his dire attempt . . . / "boiles in his tumultuous brest" while "horror and doubt distract / His troubl'd thoughts, and from the bottom stirr / The Hell within him" (4.16–20). Milton here suggests that Hell is not a place but rather an emotional state; a seething cauldron of extreme passions, Satan is his own Hell. After the remarkable speech, we learn that

Thus while he spake, each passion dimm'd his face
Thrice chang'd with pale, ire, envie and despair,
Which marrd his borrow'd visage . . .
                Whereof hee soon aware,
Each perturbation smooth'd with outward calme. (4.114–20)

Satan's disguise as an inferior angel is in fact broken by these perturbations, the physical manifestations of his inner passions. The angel Uriel indeed spots Satan amid this passionate outburst of "gestures fierce" and "mad demeanor," and knows that he is "Alien from Heav'n, with passions foul obscur'd" (4.571). By obscuring the placidity that apparently characterizes heavenly bearing, passions betray the demonic interiority of Satan.

Passions, of course, play a central role in the Temptation. Just before he begins his verbal assault, Satan is briefly drained of passion when viewing Eve; he is made "Stupidly good, of enmitie disarmd, / Of guile, of hate, of envie, of revenge" (9.465–66). During the temptation, he forcefully exploits the persuasive power of theatricalized passion, acting

    With shew of Zeal and Love
To Man, and indignation at his wrong
New part puts on, and as to passion mov'd,
Fluctuats disturbd, yet comely. (9.665–68)

Punning on Satan's gesticulations and the way these movements move Eve, Milton describes how Satan, like a classical orator,

Stood in himself collected, while each part,
Motion, each act won audience ere the tongue . . .
So standing, moving, or to highth upgrown
The Tempter all impassioned thus began. (9.673–78)

Satan, then, is marked both by the deliberate passions of the orator, moving himself in order to move others, and by the fierce gestures of the tortured soul. His primary vehicle for influencing Eve is ontologically related to the very feelings that draw Adam and Eve to each other—the capacity of one human being to move another.

The pull between two beings, then, is at once valued and viewed with suspicion. In a recent exploration of the creative and demonic aspects of sympathy in Milton's universe, Kevis Goodman has demonstrated that "Sympathy is not, in *Paradise Lost*, or elsewhere in Milton's poetry, an instinct generally to be trusted."[7] Indeed, some of the most troubling moments in the epic parade under the unexpected rubric of sympathy. Eve tells Adam that her reflection responded to her with "answering looks / Of sympathie and love" (4.464–65)—a response she initially finds superior to whatever Adam offers. After the Fall, moreover, Sin feels herself drawn to earth by "sympathie, or som connatural force / Powerful at greatest distance to unite / With secret amity things of like kinde / By secretest conveyance" (10.246– 50). The repetition of "secret" emphasizes the mysterious invisibility of this inner prompting. Sin describes herself as able to navigate the universe confidently based on this powerful feeling, a kind of compass of compassion: "Nor can I miss the way, so strongly drawn / By this new felt attraction and instinct" (10.262–63). Sin, moreover, tells Satan, that her "Heart . . . by a secret harmonie / Still moves with thine, join'd in connexion sweet" (10.358–59).

Yet this covert telepathy linking fallen beings is akin to the heavenly compassion that the Son exudes: "in his face / Divine compassion visibly appeerd, / Love without end, and without measure Grace" (3.140–42). This compassion, moreover, offers a celestial manifestation of the commotion Adam experiences; both are ways that one being is moved to action through feeling for another. In the case of the Son, though, it is all the more stunning because the feeling bridges heaven and earth, just as Sin's "connatural force" leads her from Hell to earth. The Son's "meek aspect / Silent yet spake, and breath'd immortal love / To mortal men" (3.266–68). The Son, moreover, concludes his offer to be a sacrifice for humanity—what will of course come to be called "the Passion"—with the hope that after death he will

> returne,
> Father, to see thy face, wherein no cloud
> Of anger shall remain, but peace assur'd,
> And reconcilement; wrauth shall be no more
> Thenceforth, but in thy presence Joy entire. (3.261–65)

The Son, then, is not only the primary locus of heavenly compassion but also deeply attentive to the emotional state of the Father. Indeed, he hopes that his own Passion will purge a particular passion—wrath—from the Father, moving him instead to joy.

While God's words frequently convey the anger the Son wishes to placate, the narrative voice is careful not to attribute such irritability directly to him. The Father does feel "pittie" towards his soon-to-be-fallen creatures as they work in the Garden (5.220), and laughs in derision at the "tumults vain" of Satan and the fallen angels (5.737). Unsurprisingly, the predominant angelic emotion is unmitigated joy. When word of the Fall reaches Heaven, the angels do experience a kind of sadness, but in decidedly attenuated form:

> Soon as th'unwelcome news
> From Earth arriv'd at Heaven Gate, displeas'd
> All were who heard, dim sadness did not spare
> That time Celestial visages, yet mixt
> With pitie, violated not thir bliss. (10.21–25)

Even angelic sadness born of pity for fallen humanity does not threaten their bliss. The Father, moreover, discourages such feelings of sadness: "be not dismaid, / Nor troubl'd at these tidings from the Earth" (10.35–36). Both the range and the extent of heavenly passion, then, seem severely attenuated when compared with the sweeping spectrum of hellish emotion. It as if the purer matter of heavenly beings was preternaturally immune to the internal compulsions of extreme emotion.

This makes Adam's words to Raphael about his powerful feelings for Eve before the Fall all the more unsettling. But careful attention to the early modern discourse of passion helps us understand Milton's remarkable portrait of the turbulent passion of love in paradise. As Adam's terminology of "commotion" indicates, passions were understood to be something that could move and alter the person who experiences them. Both a product of and alien to the creature they inhabit, the passions were officially listed among the non-naturals in the faculty psychology of the time, those curiously named external influences on health and behavior. These include air, food and drink, exercise and rest, sleep and wakefulness, and elimination and retention. The passions involved any feeling by which the mind is powerfully affected or moved; they entailed a vehement, commanding, or overpowering force, whose power is to be feared. Feelings are in this paradigm something one endures rather than something one produces. Aristotle had divided the passions into the concupiscible and the irascible passions. The concupiscible passions cause us to move towards what is pleasurable and necessary, and to turn away from what is harmful or repulsive. Aquinas identified six such passions, a scheme that still holds much power in the Renaissance; these are three pairs of opposites, love and hatred, desire and aversion, and joy and sadness. The irascible passions include two pairs of opposites—hope and despair, and fear and boldness—as well as a fifth passion that has no direct opposite—anger. The irascible passions entailed motivations and states that could aid one in the accomplishment of the concupiscible passions.

Like contemporary neurophysiologists, Renaissance natural philosophers were fascinated and troubled by the mysterious conduit between bodily condition and emotional state. Of particular interest is the way that
health affects emotion, and emotion affects health.[8] In *The Passions of the
Minde*, a popular work for which Ben Jonson composed a dedicatory sonnet, Thomas Wright sees the passions as inextricably bound up with the
humors, the fluids whose excess was thought to cause most diseases: "Passions ingender Humours," he writes, "and humours breed Passions."[9] In a
1650 work entitled the *Via Recta ad Vitam Longam. Or, A Treatise Wherein
the Right Way and Best Manner of Living for Attaining a Long and Healthfull
Life, is Clearly Demonstrated*, Thomas Venner elaborated the critical link
between emotion and health:

seeing that the affections and perturbations of the mind are of such force for the
overthrowing of the health and welfare of the body, I advise all such as are respective of their health, to bridle all irrational motions of the mind, by the reason and
understanding and labour by all means to observe a mediocrity, in their passion,
wherein consisteth the tranquillity both of mind and body.[10]

Venner suggests that moderating the passions is absolutely necessary for
mental as well as physical health. Passions were manifested by the physiological changes they could cause in the body of the person experiencing
them. They were thought capable of harming, and even killing someone.

Because they were so dangerous, many writers had followed the Stoic
philosophers in banishing the passions from the well-regulated ethical
life. Seneca had observed: "It is often asked whether it is better to have
moderate passions or none. Our people [the Stoics] drive out the passions
altogether [expellunt]; the Peripatetics moderate them."[11] Cicero likewise
advises the person suffering from passion:

There is only one method of cure: one must say nothing about what kind of thing
disturbs the soul but must address the disturbance itself. Thus first of all in dealing
with an actual desire, since it matters only that it be eradicated, one must not inquire
whether that which incites the desire is good or not, but one must eradicate the
desire itself . . . even if it is an over-ardent desire for virtue itself.[12]

To the Stoic, passions are pathological disturbances, painfully experienced,
in Martha Nussbaum's terms, as "geological upheavals of thought."[13] Mental and moral health for the Stoic is produced by a state of deliberate apathy, whereby the turbulent, corrosive, and alienating internal phenomena
known as passions have been purged completely.

Other thinkers, though, wanted not so much to banish the passions as to manage them carefully, redirecting them in virtuous directions. Plato, Aristotle, and Augustine all assume the central importance of the passions, and consider ethical activity to lie not in their eviction but in their proper orientation. In *A Treatise of the Passions and Faculties of the Soule of Man,* Bishop Edward Reynolds disagrees with those Stoics who would make

Passion in generall to be *Aegritudo Animi*, a Sicknesse and Perturbation, and would therefore reduce the Mind to a senseless Apathie, condemning all Life of Passion, as Waves, which serve onely to tosse and trouble Reason. An Opinion, which, while it goeth about to give unto Man an absolute government over himselfe, leaveth scarce any things in him, which he may command and governe. . . . there is more honour, in the having Affections subdued, than having none at all; the businesse of a wise man, is not to be *without* them, but to be *above* them.[14]

If the self is indeed a little kingdom, as the Stoics were wont to declare, the person who has banished the passions has nothing left to rule. This is a point that the Milton who wrote the *Areopagitica* would loudly endorse; there he asks: "Wherefore did [God] creat passions within us, pleasures round about us, but that these rightly temper'd are the very ingredients of vertu?"[15] For Milton, the passions are absolutely necessary to ethical existence, divinely sanctioned by the order of creation. A being without passions to regulate would be like the "meer artificiall *Adam,* such an *Adam* as he is in the motions," that Milton censures in his attack on censorship (*Areopagitica*, 1010).

Reynolds develops a telling comparison to depict the blend of danger and necessity that the passions entail:

as Fire (though it be of all other creatures, one of the most comfortable and usefull, while it abides in the place ordained for it;) yet, when it once exceeds those limits, and get to the house-top, it is most mercilesse and over-running: So Passion (though of excellent service in Man, for the heating and enlivening of Vertue, for adding spirit and edge to all good undertakings, and blessing them with an happier issue, than they could alone have attained unto) yet if once they flye out beyond their bounds, and become subject onely to their owne Lawes, and encroach upon Reasons right, there is nothing more tumultuous and tyrannicall . . . They [the passions] are the best Servants, but the worst Masters, which our Nature can have. Like the Winds, which being moderate, carry the Ship; but drowne it, being tempestuous.[16]

For Reynolds, the passions animate human virtue, giving spirit and edge to its undertakings. It is critical that the human subject experience passion, and it is equally critical that that subject not allow the passions to rule.

Reynolds even argues that it is the transporting activity of the passions—an activity the Stoics, with their emphasis on the moral qualities of constancy, find so disturbing—that discloses the importance of the passions to health:

Those imputations therefore which Tully [Cicero] and Seneca, and other Stoicall Philosophers make against Passions, are but light and emptie, when they call them diseases and perturbations of the Mind; which requireth in all its actions both health and serenitie, a strong and a cleare judgement; both which properties, they say, are impaired by the distempers of Passion: For it is absurd to thinke, that all manner of rest is either healthfull or cleare; or on the other side, all motion diseased and troublesome: for what water more sweet than that of a Spring, or what more thick or lothsome, than that which standeth in a puddle, corrupting it selfe.[17]

Stoic apathy is for Reynolds not a state of mental calm and moral constancy but rather a cesspool of fetid muck; it is by contrast the subject suffused by vigorous desires who is clear, quick, fresh, and healthy, like a mountain stream.

In a wonderful essay, William Bouwsma has identified what he terms the two faces of Renaissance Humanism: Stoicism and Augustinianism.[18] These two strains center on the moral status of the emotions. Where the Stoic aspires to banish all feeling from the properly regulated subject, idealizing a kind of deliberate apathy, the Augustinian argues that it is the direction and decorous proportion of emotion that determines the ethical status of the subject. Fascinatingly, Milton absorbs this central Renaissance debate about the respective claims of reason and passion into the foolish behavior of the fallen angels. He imagines them in Hell disputing about "Passion and Apathie, and glory and shame, / Vain wisdom all, and false Philosophie" (2.564–65). I want to suggest that Milton continues to stage attitudes present in these two strains in the argument between Raphael and Adam in Book 8, and throughout the rest of *Paradise Lost*. Where the angel articulates a blend of Stoic and Neoplatonic attitudes to passion, wishing to banish its transporting affects from prelapsarian interiority while sublimating it to divine subjects, Adam struggles to legitimate the mighty passion he feels toward his unfallen, god–given mate. Adam wonders if the unique ontology of Eve's creation would explain this powerful feeling of movement within him, since a piece of him was taken to form Eve; either

Nature faild in mee, and left some part
Not proof enough such Object to sustain

Or from my side subducting, took perhaps
More then enough. (8.534–37)

Adam's ontological speculation is an attempt to explain the puzzling disso-
ciation he feels between his overwhelming love for Eve and the masculinist
hierarchy that he has been repeatedly told derives from his prior creation.
This hierarchy, moreover, frequently imagined female inferiority as exemplified by women's greater susceptibility to just the kinds of extreme passion
that Adam here displays.

Adam certainly knows that he is supposed to translate his own ontological priority into a principle of hierarchical superiority, but he also
knows that his emotional experience of Eve belies this principle:

For well I understand in the prime end
Of Nature her th' inferiour . . .
        yet when I approach
Her loveliness, so absolute she seems
And in her self compleat, so well to know
Her own, that what she wills to do or say,
Seems wisest, vertuousest, discreetest, best;
All higher knowledge in her presence falls
Degraded, Wisdom in discourse with her
Looses discount'nanc't, and like folly shewes;
Authority and Reason on her waite,
As one intended first, not after made
Occasionally. (8.540–56)

Raphael responds to Adam's account of his experience of passion with the
"contracted brow" of Angelic censure (8.560). Raphael suggests that Adam
is only describing a particular fondness for sexual passion, "the sense of
touch whereby mankind / Is propagated" (8.579–80). Raphael recommends
that Adam remember that there is nothing uniquely human about such
pleasure, "think the same vouchsaf't / To Cattel and each Beast" (8.581–82).
He translates Adam's experience of inner movement in front of Eve into a
Neoplatonic opposition between terrestrial passion and heavenly love:

What higher in her societie thou findst
Attractive, human, rational, love still;
In loving thou dost well, in passion not,
Wherein true Love consists not; love refines
The thoughts, and heart enlarges, hath his seat
In Reason, and is judicious, is the scale

By which to heav'nly Love thou maist ascend,
Not sunk in carnal pleasure. (8.586–93)

Raphael indicates that Adam should sublimate his bewildering internal commotion into an external motion aimed exclusively at heaven. Raphael, then, wishes to cast the exuberant sexuality of paradise as an ethical descent rather than the devout act of worship that it is for Milton. Raphael's words here resemble those of the "hypocrites" that the narrative voice condemns in Book 4 as Adam and Eve retire to perform "the Rites / Mysterious of connubial Love":

Whatever Hypocrites austerely talk
Of puritie and place and innocence,
Defaming as impure what God declares
Pure, and commands to som, leaves free to all.
Our Maker bids increase, who bids abstain
But our destroyer, foe to God and Man? (4.742–49)

Curiously, Raphael's words demeaning passion produce the glimmers of a comparatively new passion in Adam; he is "half abash't." This is a prelapsarian version of the effect that Satan's stirring words have on the fallen angels. Yet this comparatively innocent embarrassment does not prevent Adam from asserting that Raphael has misstated Adam's position, that Adam is not talking exclusively about sex but instead about that fully incarnated blend of admiration and desire that is love. Adam proclaims that he is moved not by "her out-side formd so fair, nor aught / In procreation common to all kindes" but rather by

        those graceful acts,
Those thousand decencies that daily flow
From all her words and actions mixt with Love
And sweet compliance, which declare unfeign'd
Union of Mind, or in us both one Soule;
Harmonie to behold in wedded pair
More grateful then harmonious sound to the eare. (8.596–606)

Adam here wishes to affiliate his powerful feelings for Eve with heavenly harmony, not with beastly passion. Adam argues for a marriage of true minds to which Raphael would admit impediments. Like Reynolds, Raphael argues that the powerful passions Adam describes entail a kind of playing with fire; but Raphael asks Adam to separate the fire from the flame. For

Raphael, passions constitute a fire that will burn any who give them reign; for Adam, these passions comprise a fire that warms and comforts and completes paradise.

Most commentators on this passage have tended to side with the angel, assuming that his higher ontological status produces superior knowledge of moral philosophy as well as of terrestrial sexuality. In his annotations on this passage, for example, Alastair Fowler suggests that "According to generally received doctrine, passion was never experienced until after the Fall. Raphael's frown, therefore, is entirely understandable."[19] In fact, there was a long-established theological and philosophical debate over whether unfallen humans experienced passion in paradise. Attention to this debate allows us to comprehend the possible legitimacy of Adam's defense of his prelapsarian passion. In the *Summa Theologica*, for example, Aquinas asks "Whether in the State of Innocence Man would have been passible," that is, capable of feeling passion. He understands Passion in two senses:

First, in its proper sense, [where] a thing is said to suffer when changed from its natural disposition. . . . Secondly passion can be taken in a general sense for any kind of change, even if belonging to the perfection of nature . . . In this second sense, man was passible in the state of innocence, and was passive both in soul and body. In the first sense man was impassible, both in soul and body, as he was likewise immortal.[20]

Humans, in other words, could not be changed or corrupted before the fall, but they certainly were subject to the transporting nature of passion. Aquinas imagines that humans could experience prelapsarian passion, but wants to segregate the experience of that passion from the corrupting and unhealthy nature of postlapsarian passion. This opinion derives in part from his generally approbatory attitude to postlapsarian passion; elsewhere in the *Summa*, he argues that the "passions of the soul, in so far as they are contrary to the order of reason, incline us to sin; but in so far as they are controlled by reason, they pertain to virtue."[21]

In his *Treatise of the Passions*, Bishop Reynolds likewise observes that:

as long as Man continued intire and incorrupt [in Paradise], there was a sweet harmonie between all his Faculties, and such an happie subordination of them each to other, as that every Motion of the Inferiour Power was directed and governed . . . But, when once Man had tasted of that murthering Fruit, and poyson'd him and all his Posteritie; then began those Swellings, and inward Rebellions, which made him as lame in his Naturall, as dead in his Spirituall Condition. Whence Passions are become, now in the state of Corruption, Beastly and Sensual, which were before, by Creation, Reasonable and Humane.[22]

Reynolds:

For Reynolds, humans experience before the Fall a benign but profound version of the passions that suffuse postlapsarian subjects.

Milton would I think agree. Yet Milton makes this issue of prelapsarian passion even more complicated, by allowing Satan to enter Paradise and plant a dangerously subversive dream in the ear of the sleeping Eve. Here Milton, in a scene with no biblical precedent, puts immense pressure on the question of whether humans could be predisposed to corruption through their passions before the Fall. "Squat like a Toad, close at the eare of *Eve*," Satan is

> Assaying by his Devilish art to reach
> The Organs of her Fancie, and with them forge
> Illusions as he list, Phantasms and Dreams,
> Or if, inspiring venom, he might taint
> Th' animal Spirits that from pure blood arise
> Like gentle breaths from Rivers pure, thence raise
> At least distemperd, discontented thoughts,
> Vaine hopes, vaine aimes, inordinate desires
> Blown up with high conceits ingendring pride. (4.801–9)

Milton here imagines that Satan can literally influence, or flow into, Eve's prelapsarian body and mind. "Organs of her Fancie" is a wonderful phrase, encapsulating the tense blend of psychology and physiology that subtends early modern moral philosophy. Likewise, the yoking of "distemperd" and "discontented" fuses perfectly the physiological and the psychological. The language here endorses a materialist account of prelapsarian behavior, suggesting that Eve's being is in some sense altered by the words that Satan plants in her ear. Satan's "Devilish art" here offers a demonic correlative to the "charm of Beauties powerful glance" whose power over him Adam confesses to Raphael.

At stake, then, is the question of whether this dream alters Eve, just as Adam's experience of passion moves and transports him.[23] In the *Summa Theologica*, Aquinas argued that a demon "can change the inferior powers of man, in a certain degree: by which powers, though the will cannot be forced, it can nevertheless be inclined" (1.111.2.3). A demon, he argues, can work on humans in two ways: "Firstly, from within; in this way a demon can work on man's imagination and even on his corporeal sense . . . Secondly, from without: for just as he can from the air form a body of any form and shape, and assume it so as to appear in it visibly: so in the same way he can clothe any corporeal things with any corporeal form, so as to appear therein"

(1.111.4.2). In Book 4, Satan adopts the first method, secretly working on the organs of Eve's fancy, while in Book 9, Satan adopts the second, appealing to her in the guise of a serpent.

In *The Touchstone of Complexions*, Levinus Lemnius, an influential sixteenth-century Dutch physician, argued that "good and ill Angels, which being intermingled with the humours and spirits, cause sondry changes and mutations in mens myndes."[24] "As Spirites be without bodyes," Lemnius continues, "they fitly and secretly glyde into the bodye of man, even much like a fulsom stench, or as a noysome and ill ayre, is inwardly drawen into the bodye."[25] In Book 9, Milton imagines Satan sneaking into the garden "through each Thicket Danck or Drie, / Like a black mist low creeping" (9.179–80), as if he has just this passage in mind. For both Lemnius and Milton, it is the comparatively immaterial nature of demons that allows them to be so successful at insinuating themselves into the comparatively material substance of human motive. According to Stuart Clark, whose recent *Thinking with Demons* is the fullest account we have of the role of the supernatural in early modern psychology, the devil "suggests ideas to the imagination which induce love or hatred or other mental disturbances. For the purpose of causing bodily infirmities he distils a spirituous substance from the blood itself, purifies it of all base matter, and uses it as the aptest, most efficacious, and swiftest weapon against human life." The devil, Clark argues, "had full power over all the spirits and humours of the body to displace them, weaken or excite them, or otherwise disable them from working properly. He could produce anger, vengefulness, violence, and murder by flooding the heart with blood, awaken venereal lust by inflaming the male sperm and genitals, and cause unbearable heaviness by acting on the melancholic humour."[26]

Disturbingly, this is exactly what Milton imagines the devil doing before the Fall. But is Eve morally responsible for, or contaminated by, this dream of disobedience that Satan plants in her ear? Dream theorists of the period would suggest that she is not morally responsible for its content, since its origins are demonic, but that she is affected by it. She emerges from it "With Tresses discompos'd, and glowing Cheek," displaying in her physiology and demeanor the unruly passions that have surged within her (5.10). Innocent of the dream's demonic origins, Adam argues that Eve is neither responsible for it nor tainted by it. Yet this leads him to theorize the emergence of evil within an unfallen creature. Adam says he does not

> like
> This uncouth dream, of evil sprung I fear;

Yet evil whence? in thee can harbour none,
Created pure. But know that in the Soule
Are many lesser Faculties that serve
Reason as chief; among these Fansie next
Her office holds; of all external things,
Which the five watchful Senses represent,
She forms Imaginations, Aerie shapes,
Which Reason joyning or disjoyning, frames
All what we affirm or what deny, and call
Our knowledge or opinion; then retires
Into her private Cell when Nature rests.
Oft in her absence mimic Fansie wakes
To imitate her; but misjoyning shapes,
Wilde work produces oft, and most in dreams,
Ill matching words and deeds long past or late. (5.97–113)

The lesson is correct, as far as Renaissance faculty psychology understood it, accounting for the capacity of the Fancy to produce original images
unfettered by Reason or Nature in sleep. But the lesson is also inapposite,
since it cannot address the central fact of the dream—that it was inspired by
Satan, who serves as its demonic muse. Adam is more to the point, but on
thinner theological ice, when he attempts to cheer up Eve by asserting that

Evil into the mind of God or Man
May come and go, so unapprov'd, and leave
No spot or blame behind: Which gives me hope
That what in sleep thou didst abhorr to dream,
Waking thou never wilt consent to do. (5.117–21)

It is true that Eve has not yet consented with her full rational faculties to
eating the forbidden fruit. But Adam's words belie the elaborate description
that Milton gives to the operation of Satan's words on the organs of her
fancy, and also fly in the face of much contemporaneous theorizing about
the transformative power of demonic interventions. Satan's capacity to
forge illusions in Eve's imagination, to taint with venom her animal spirits,
challenges Adam's wistful description of the non-stick coating given to the
interior walls of prelapsarian moral consciousness.

As if not fully comforted by Adam's philosophical explanation, Eve

silently a gentle tear let fall
From either eye, and wip'd them with her haire;
Two other precious drops that ready stood,
Each in thir chrystal sluce, hee ere they fell

Kiss'd as the gracious signs of sweet remorse
And pious awe, that feard to have offended.
So all was cleard. (5.130–36)

Because tears were thought in contemporaneous physiology to be "an excrementitious humiditie of the braine" of humors normally voided by the palate and the nose, perhaps Eve in crying purges her animal spirits of Satan's stain.[27] The narrative voice declares that all was cleared, partially endorsing Adam's theory that evil can pass harmlessly through the mind of God or man. This tender scene entails a prelapsarian version of the passionately repentant Magdalene, but the adjective *sweet* must work overtime to remove the postlapsarian taint from the remorse it modifies.

The physical manifestations of the passions become more pronounced, and more threatening, at the Fall. When Adam first sees the "Countnance blithe" of the newly fallen Eve, he notes that "in her Cheek distemper flushing glowd" (9.886–87). He is stunned at this demeanor, so different from Raphael's blush, and his own physiology manifests in turn the powerful emotions that course through him:

On th' other side, *Adam*, soon as he heard
The fatal Trespass don by *Eve*, amaz'd,
Astonied stood and Blank, while horror chill
Ran through his veins, and all his joynts relax'd;
From his slack hand the Garland wreath'd for *Eve*
Down drop'd, and all the faded Roses shed:
Speechless he stood and pale. (9.888–94)

Adam's stunned pallor makes a cogent contrast with Eve's passionately glowing cheeks; both demonstrate how physiology betrays internal emotion. Lodowick Bryskett suggests that blushing was thought to be caused by "the minde finding that what is to be reprehended in us, commeth from abroade, it seeketh to hide the fault committed, and to avoide the reproach thereof, by setting that colour on our face as a maske to defend us withal." Blanching in turn was the result of the imagination

Looking about for meanes of defense, it calleth al the bloud into the innermost parts, specially to the heart, as the chiefe fort or castle; whereby the exterior parts being abandoned and deprived of heate, and that colour which it had from the bloud and the spirits, there remaineth nothing but palenesse.[28]

Both blanching and blushing entail efforts to defend inwardness, then, but in the process they also reveal the inner emotional state of the subject. Adam's prelapsarian pallor and Eve's postlapsarian blush show how passions suffuse the human subject before and after the Fall. Milton, of course, concludes Book 8 with a striking glimpse of angelic passion: the blush that Raphael musters in response to Adam's question about the practices of angelic sex. Raphael's "smile that glow'd / Celestial rosie red, Loves proper hue" provides a licit and benign version of the passion of shame that marks the moral descent of humans at the Fall (8.618–19). Fascinatingly, Milton here takes a primary signifier of postlapsarian erotic meaning—the (largely female) blush that is at once an exhibition of reticence designed to elicit passion and a manifestation of desire—and asks it to represent an angelic physiological response to a decidedly innocent question. He imagines that the bodies of angels, of prelapsarian humans, and of postlapsarian humans all perform a deed which is, in the words of Mary Ann O'Farrell, "a somatic act of confession."[29] He is fascinated by such moments because they are occasions when the body registers emotion fully and instinctively.

As the unfallen Adam stares in horror at the fallen, blushing Eve, moreover, he must restage internally the debate between the claims of passion and reason. Adam, that is, could have rejected the pull of his emotional connection to Eve, as a Stoic would be urged to do. As the great defender of divorce on the grounds of spiritual incompatibility, moreover, Milton had ample arguments at hand for severing their relationship at this moment, since it is difficult to imagine a spiritual incompatibility greater than Fallen and Unfallen. But Adam's emotional attachment to Eve is so profound that he cannot imagine life without her:

So forcible within my heart I feel
The Bond of Nature draw me to my owne,
My own in thee, for what thou art is mine;
Our State cannot be severd, we are one,
One Flesh; to loose thee were to loose my self. (9.955–59)

Adam describes here a kind of physiological determinism that abrogates his rational processes, and for this he has been censured, surrendering his autonomy to the forces that issue from his heart, the seat of his passions.[30] But it is also difficult to determine what our attitude might be to the moral automaton who could pass with flying colors what Eve only half-perversely terms a "glorious trial of exceeding Love." Adam, we are told, "scrupl'd not to eat / Against his better knowledge, not deceav'd, / But fondly overcome with Femal charm" (9.961, 997–99). Whereas in Book 8, Adam had described in fastidious detail to Raphael his unsettling experience of "the charm of Beauties powerful glance," in Book 9 the power of that charm is woven into a facile misogynist explanation of the Fall. Milton, then, makes the Fall a product of sympathetic engagement. As Eve was moved by Satan, so Adam is moved by Eve. We are torn, I think, between admiring the vigorous constancy of Adam's emotional bond with Eve and lamenting a decision based on emotion rather than reason that introduces misery, disease, and death into the world.

One of the many effects of the fruit seems to be to amplify the benign but bewildering passions of prelapsarian existence. Immediately after the Fall, Adam and Eve do what they have done frequently in Paradise—they have sex. But as many commentators have noted, their sex assumes a very different tone, filled with salacious wordplay about the lustful passions they now experience. Adam feels his sense "enflame[d] . . . With ardor" (9.1031–32). When they awake from their post-coital nap—a nap disturbed by the "unkindly fumes" that the fruit's "exhilarating vapour bland" produced "About thir spirits"—they find only a bitterly ironic version of the enhanced vision promised by the fruit:

> up they rose
> As from unrest, and each the other viewing,
> Soon found thir Eyes how op'nd, and thir minds
> How dark'nd. (9.1047–54)

Here they discover a physiological lesson that Edward Reynolds explains in *A Treatise of the Passions and Faculties of the Soule of Man*: "Passion, in opposition to Reason, is like an Humour, which falling from the Head to the Eyes, darkeneth the Sight thereof." [31] This must have been a medical and moral lesson that the blind John Milton took to heart.

We have seen Eve cry tears of sweet remorse before the Fall. After the Fall human tears assume a representative rather than a purgative function, revealing but not clearing the storms of passion within:

> They sate them down to weep, nor onely Teares
> Raind at thir Eyes, but high Winds worse within
> Began to rise, high Passions, Anger, Hate,
> Mistrust, Suspicion, Discord, and shook sore
> Thir inward State of Mind, calm Region once
> And full of Peace, now tost and turbulent:
> For Understanding rul'd not, and the Will
> Heard not her lore, both in subjection now

To sensual Appetite, who from beneathe
Usurping over sovran Reason claimd
Superior sway. (9.1121–31)

These "high Passions" disturb the delicate microclimates of the postlapsarian subject.[32] At the Fall, Adam and Eve enter the morally and meteorologi-
cally roiled world described by numerous early modern moral philosophers.
In *The Passions of the Minde in Generall*, for example, Thomas Wright
describes the agonistic relationship that mortals share with their emotions:

The flesh molesteth us in the service of God, with an army of unruly Passions, for
the most part, withdrawing from goodnes, and haling to ilnesse, they toss and turmoile our miserable soulls, as tempests & waves the Ocean sea, the which never
standeth quiet, but either in ebbing or flowing, either winds doe buz about it, or
raines alter it, or earthquakes shake, or stormes tyrannize over it: even so our soules
are puffed up with selfelove; shaken with feare: now they be flowing with concupis-
cences and desires, and presently ebbing with desperation & sadnesse: joy altereth
the mind, and ire tyrannizeth and consumeth both body and mind.[33]

The world of blame and exculpation—a world many of us know all too
well—becomes the external domestic version of this tortuous internal agitation. When Adam addresses Eve, it is from "distemperd brest," as the rule
of excess passions inaugurates the physiological and moral disease of distemper (9.1131).

    Even the moral tools that one might use to control these rebellious and
unhealthy passions are dulled and disabled by the Fall. Discovering the
proper course of virtuous action and following it—a process that the prelapsarian Adam and Eve had failed—becomes far more demanding after
the Fall. As the archangel Michael tells Adam,

Since thy original lapse, true Libertie
Is lost, which always with right Reason dwells
Twinn'd, and from her hath no dividual being:
Reason in man obscur'd, or not obeyd,
Immediately inordinate desires
And upstart Passions catch the Government
From Reason, and to servitude reduce
Man till then free. (12.83–90)

Humans at the Fall suffer an internal revolt among their appetites and
passions; this revolt entails a microcosmic and physiological version of the

disobedience they have performed. The passions that should obey right reason instead assault it, blurring the very capacities that would be necessary to apprehend even a partial truth, much less to act upon it. For Milton, the failure to sustain this internal subordination of the passions to reason is the prime reason that God allowed the political affliction called monarchy to emerge. As Michael relates,

> since [man] permits
> Within himself unworthie Powers to reign
> Over free Reason, God in Judgement just
> Subjects him from without to violent Lords;
> Who oft as undeservedly enthrall
> His outward freedom. (12.90–95)

The internal battle between right reason and inordinate passions becomes for the late Milton the central site of political action and of heroic virtue.[34] As the Son declares to Satan in *Paradise Regain'd* in response to the temptation of earthly rule: "he who reigns within himself, and rules / Passions, Desires, and Fears is more a King; / Which every wise and vertuous man attains" (2.466–68). The only authentic site of moral command is internal; one should aspire to control not other human beings but rather "Anarchy within, / Or lawless passions" (*Paradise Regain'd*, 2.471–72).

After the Fall, passion becomes both the locus of mortal suffering and the medium of redemption. Contemplation of the consequences of the Fall throws Adam into despair; he is "To sorrow abandond, but worse felt within, / And in a troubl'd Sea of passion tost" (10.717–18). His soliloquies explore the "Abyss of fears / And horrors" that constitute postlapsarian subjectivity (10.842–43). Though "sad" and "Desolate" herself, Eve attempts to console Adam, addressing "Soft words to his fierce passion" (10.863–65). His fierce passion, though, is not allayed; instead, Adam responds with a bilious stream of antifeminist invective intended to devastate Eve. At the end of Adam's querulous diatribe, he turns from her in disgust, but Eve, in a pose that becomes the postlapsarian version of her prelapsarian remorse after her dream,

> with Tears that ceas'd not flowing,
> And tresses all disorderd, at his feet
> Fell humble, and imbracing them, besaught
> His peace. (10.910–13)

Eve's subsequent speech, in which she seeks peace with Adam by describing her own misery at having sinned "against God and thee," concludes with her "weeping" (10.923, 931, 937). As she cries tears such as humans weep, Eve's display of passion has a powerful effect on Adam. Her words "in *Adam* wraught / Commiseration; soon his heart relented . . . As one disarm'd, his anger all he lost" (10.939–45). Where Eve had before the Fall uninten-tionally produced commotion in Adam, after the Fall her speech engenders commiseration, as her "soft words" mollify his "fierce passion." Eve's speech, argues Kevis Goodman, "initiates a new if fragile structure of human rela-tionships after the destruction of all relations brought on by the Fall."[35] The abject posture and extreme passion of the repentant Magdalene achieve the consummately heroic act of disarming another. Milton here focuses his epic on the magical power of emotional speech to stir emotion in another human being—to generate, in other words, that particular variant of pas-sion called compassion. He wishes, moreover, to give such passion an epic, even heroic dimension, by emphasizing its capacity to *disarm* Adam and so to enable the crucial reconciliation of Adam and Eve, a reconciliation nec-essary for the survival of humanity. In the invocation to Book 9, Milton announces his intention deliberately to displace the traditional epic passion of anger for "the better fortitude / Of Patience and Heroic Martyrdom / Unsung" (9.31–33). Neither the murderous "wrauth / Of stern *Achilles*" nor the jealous "rage / Of *Turnus*" nor "*Neptun's* ire or *Juno's*," he argues, suit the "Sad task" of true epic composition (9.13–18). Rather, Milton's epic at this critical moment pivots on the mollifying sorrow of repentant Eve. Where before the Fall Eve's capacity to move Adam had precipitated a genial argument with an angel, here Eve's capacity to move Adam breaks their lethal cycle of factious quarreling.

The emotional muddle of postlapsarian moral existence is marked by the vast range and contradictory trajectories of extreme passion that tra-verse Adam's being in the last two books of the epic. When told that he must leave Paradise, Adam is "Heart-strook with chilling gripe," a "cold sudden damp" which severely depresses his spirits (11.265–66). This is in Judeo-Christian history literally the first case of depression. After the grisly image of the Lazar house encompassing all forms of corporeal suffering in Book 11, Adam experiences extreme grief born of compassion for the suffering of others:

Sight so deform what heart of Rock could long
Drie-ey'd behold? *Adam* could not, but wept,
Though not of Woman born; compassion quell'd
His best of Man, and gave him up to tears
A space, till firmer thoughts restraind excess. (11.494–98)

Milton goes out of his way here to approve in the first man a mode of conduct traditionally licit only to women—shedding tears of intense grief. Indeed, as the tragedy of early human history unfolds, Milton even imagines the stern archangel Michael moved at the horrible scenario of Cain killing Abel—"hee also mov'd," Milton tells us of the narrating angel (11.453). As a spectator at the tragicomedy of human history, Adam in the last two books of *Paradise Lost* reels from despair at his first vision of death, to false joy at the union of the Sons of Seth with the "Beavie of fair Women" (11.582), to tearful sadness at the story of Enoch, to despair at the Flood, to rejoicing at the survival of Noah and his family, to disgust at the political pretensions of Nimrod, the first monarch, to delight at Moses, to overwhelming jubilation at the story of Jesus:

> *Adam* with such joy
> Surcharg'd, as had like grief bin dew'd in tears,
> Without the vent of words. (12.372–74)

After the full story of Jesus, Adam is "Replete with joy and wonder" (12.468). Fascinatingly, the excruciating Passion of Jesus—a subject in which Milton shows comparatively little interest throughout his career—permits humans to know again the passion of unmitigated joy.[36] Indeed, Michael assures Adam that if he will

> add
> Deeds to thy knowledge answerable, add Faith,
> Add vertue, Patience, Temperance, add Love,
> By name to come call'd Charitie, the soul
> Of all the rest: then wilt thou not be loath
> To leave this Paradise, but shalt possess
> A paradise within thee, happier farr. (12.581–87)

Even as Adam and Eve are forced to leave paradise, then, the performance of virtue, and in particular the virtue emerging from the affection that binds them together, will give them the capacity to manifest in their inner emotional state the experiential essence of that joyous geographical place. As Eve says in the epic's final speech, "with thee to goe, / Is to stay here" (12.615–16). If Satan's exorbitant passions express his inner hell, Adam and Eve retain the potential to reproduce paradise in their passionate attachment to each other.

Eve's final speech to Adam as she wakes up from the dreams God has given her is uttered "with words not sad" (12.609). As Adam and Eve leave Paradise, "Som natural tears they drop'd, but wip'd them soon" (12.645);

tears have become "natural" to humanity, a part of their nature. Even as they mirror Eve's prelapsarian tears after her demonic dream, these tears measure the critical distance between those two states. After the Fall, Adam and Eve and their progeny spend an inordinate amount of time consumed by the passion of weeping.[37]

For all of its emphasis on temperate self-regulation, then, the epic is operatically passionate to its core. Its announced goal, we need to remember, is to sing the origin of the predominant emotional state of postlapsarian humanity—"all our woe." For Milton, the passions were intimately linked with poetry. In *Of Education*, Milton described his ideal poetry as "simple, sensuous, and passionate." In *The Reason of Church Government*, Milton praised the power of poetry to convey "whatsoever hath passion or admiration in all the changes of that which is call'd fortune from without, or the wily suttleties and refluxes of mans thoughts from within."[38] Early modern discussions of the passions provided Milton with a remarkably precise vocabulary for locating the "wily suttleties" and internal "refluxes" of human passion amid a series of corporeal sensations available to all. The epic, I would argue, moves us in part because of Milton's fastidious attention to these internal motions. For Milton, the cathartic power of poetry was inextricably linked to the kinetic activity of passion. In *The Reason of Church Government*, Milton praises the ability of poetry to "allay the perturbations of the mind, and set the affections in right tune."[39] His remarkable capacity to set the central events of Judeo-Christian history in the resonant chords of human passion invites us to attend to an earlier disposition of the relation of personality to emotion, one where passion was not yet an intrinsic element of personality but rather an external force that needed to be tamed and subjugated for the human subject to live well. For Milton, the passions are necessary disturbances, ethical irritants that produce the pearls of virtue. Committed at once to the power of rational choice and to a materialist psychology and predestinarian theology that would seem to abrogate that power, Milton's epic eloquently performs the fruitful incoherence of early modern attitudes to the passions. Endorsing both the rigorous self-control promised by classical ethics and the sacrificial compassion at the core of Christian affect, Milton in *Paradise Lost* explores with lucid uncertainty the specific gravity of human relationships, the invisible lines of force that bond one human with another, for better and for worse. His bold redefinition of epic heroism in terms of the ability to feel and to stir compassion makes the emotional state of the individual a region where Paradise might indeed be regained.

Chapter 3

Poses and Passions:
Mona Lisa's "Closely Folded" Hands

Zirka Z. Filipczak

The best-known pair of hands belongs to the woman known as Mona Lisa, whose portrait Leonardo da Vinci began to paint around 1504 (Figure 3.1). To early modern viewers the position of her hands described a state of feeling as clearly as the expression on her face, but modern writers have usually neglected her hands to focus on her smile as the key to the portrait's supposed mystery.[1] The reason for this discrepancy lies in different assumptions about what kinds of feelings would likely be recorded in a portrait from ca. 1504 and how they can be recognized.

Why Mona Lisa smiles has been explained in diverse ways, especially since the late nineteenth century. In his biographies of artists published in 1550 Giorgio Vasari discussed the smile, which he probably knew through one of the copies that remained in Italy after Leonardo took the reportedly unfinished original to France with him. Vasari (who could have talked with Mona Lisa, a fellow Florentine still alive during the writing of the biographies) explained the "peaceful" smile as a solution to a problem in portraiture. Leonardo hired musicians to play during the lengthy posing sessions to "take away the look of melancholy which is so often seen in portraits."[2] No writer found her smile to be enigmatic until the late nineteenth century, as George Boas has pointed out.[3] Since then interpretations have proliferated that posited an emotional mystery at the heart of the painting and attempted to explain it by deciphering the smile. For Walter Pater, for instance, the "unfathomable smile" manifested her femme fatale mentality by containing "a touch of something sinister." For Sigmund Freud it symbolized the smile that the illegitimate Leonardo remembered on the face of his own birth mother, whom he lost by being raised within his father's household. For Kurt Eissler it recorded a fleeting smile on the melancholy face of Mona Lisa, whose daughter had died five years earlier. By keeping a smile

Figure 3.1. Leonardo da Vinci, *Mona Lisa*. Musée National du Louvre, Paris. Reproduced by permission of Réunion des Musées Nationaux / Art Resource, NY.

permanently on her face, Leonardo symbolically returned a smile to the face of the mother he himself had lost.[4]

Popular texts continue to describe the smile as enigmatic, but Paul Barolsky has plausibly reinterpreted it as evidence of a social relationship rather than a personal feeling. Mona Lisa's husband, a Florentine nobleman, was named Francesco del Giacondo. "Giacondo" means "jocund, merry, glad, joyous," and it is the smile that memorably identified her as his wife. Leonardo had introduced a visual reference to the name of a sitter, or the identity of a male partner, in two previous portraits of women, and so Mona Lisa would be the third and subtlest example.[5] The faintness of her smile would not have puzzled contemporaries. No respectable adult smiled so broadly as to display teeth, since that would simultaneously reveal one's vulgarity.

Could Leonardo also have used the smile to characterize Mona Lisa herself as having a sanguine temperament? Classifying people as belonging to one of the four temperaments remained standard practice, but portraits cannot be separated into four groups using physiognomy as the criterion. Portraitists did not identify the dominant temperament of sitters by varying their facial expressions to look distinctly happier (sanguine), fiercer (choleric), blander (phlegmatic), or dourer (melancholic). Instead, if portraits described a sitter's temperament, they did so through props and settings, color, and especially the positioning of the body. For instance, when melancholy became fashionable, some men were portrayed as melancholics through the dominance of a black hue or shadows, or through poses previously absent from portraiture (the head supported by a hand, a traditional sign of melancholy, or crossed arms), but not through clear sadness on the face.[6] If contemporary viewers recognized a reference to Mona Lisa's dominant temperament in the portrait, it would be in the configuration of her hands and not in her smile.

Gestures "by which we can penetrate by careful observation into the most guarded thoughts"

Leonardo described the accepted relationship of gestures and poses to passions in several oft-quoted passages about painting, for example, "that figure is most worthy of praise which by its action best expressed the passion which animates it."[7] Non-artists also paid close attention to what is now known as body language. The Venetian nobleman and humanist Francesco Barbaro warned wives in his *On Wifely Duties* to be careful about their "faces, countenances, and gestures (by which we can penetrate by careful observation into the most guarded thoughts)." [8] Even second-hand evidence could be used for this purpose. Inquiring about another potential spouse, for example, Henry VIII of England wanted information about her "answers, gestures, and her countenance" since all three could provide useful information about her.[9]

Although Leonardo placed Mona Lisa's hands prominently in the foreground, they have been neglected in publications about the portrait. The eclipsing effect of the smile and the strange setting (which length precludes discussing here) contributed to the neglect, but so did the very familiarity of the placid pose, which has remained a commonplace in women's portraits to this day. Precisely the conventionality of the pose, however, provides access to the meanings it carried for early modern viewers.

As has been well established, even bodily positions and actions that seem natural, such as walking or sitting, were shaped by cultural conventions. Manuals of civility and other contemporary texts document part of this material, and thus have been the basis for scholarly work on the early modern language of the body.[10] Without the help of such historical reconstruction, even otherwise knowledgeable viewers today have only a roughly fifty-fifty chance of assigning the same psychological meaning to a depicted pose that it carried originally. A case in point involves the positioning of a neck. Whereas manuals of civility from the sixteenth and seventeenth centuries interpreted a neck inclined sideways as a sign of "hypocrisy" or "unmanly faintheartedness," a book about Renaissance portraits published in 1990 concluded that it made the sitter "either attentive or languorous." By contrast, a neck bent backward retained the same meaning across time, with a sixteenth-century text interpreting it as "a sign of conceit to bend the body backward" and the 1990 text as producing an "impression of haughtiness."[11] The danger of misreading is greatest with portraits, especially formal, commissioned examples. Early modern viewers expected psychological indicators appropriate to the sitter's class, profession, or gender. By contrast, modern writers more often read the same indicators as clues to personal, even spontaneous emotions.[12]

The positions and movements of the body loomed so important because they were believed to influence emotions, not just reveal them. Prescribing body language thus served as a way of regulating the passions, especially of women, who were considered easily swayed by their feelings. Although biographies as well as fictional narratives testify that contemporaries accepted some flexibility in gender roles, stereotyped views of masculinity and femininity prevailed in the manuals of civility and other guides to proper conduct. In describing appropriate body language, such texts gravitated to a binary approach. For instance, although a speaker in Baldasarre Castiglione's widely read *The Book of the Courtier* (first published in 1528) accepted that male and female courtiers needed some of the same qualities, he contradictingly insisted that almost all aspects of behavior, including gestures, be gendered. "Above all, I hold that a woman should in no way resemble a man as regards her ways, manners, words, gestures, and bearing." Deviation from the recommended guidelines, especially by women, could meet with vigorous disapproval. "For it is a monstrous and naughtye thing, to see a young Gyrle use suche libertye and boldnesse in her Gesture, lookes, and talke, as is proper to men."[13] Stefano Guazzo added classical authority to this opinion by attributing it to Cicero.[14] Because portraits remained permanently visible, they could serve as models of a proper stance, in addition to their other functions.

Mona Lisa dates to the early history of Italian portraits with hands. Only since the second half of the fifteenth century did patrons increasingly commission independent portraits that extended below the face and chest. In the developing repertoire, some gestures and poses remained unusual, but others recurred often enough to become recognized conventions. The relationship of props to the conventional poses seems to have been the following. Hand positions that proved equally acceptable for both men and women, such as placing a hand on one's chest, relied on props (e.g., scholarly books, a hunting dog for men; a prayer book, a lap dog for women), to add any desired gender distinctions not made by clothing. By contrast, poses restricted to, or preferred for one gender needed no help from props to associate the sitter with masculine or feminine characteristics; props might exist, but they were not a necessary accompaniment. The placement of Mona Lisa's hands belongs to this category.

Leonardo chose a conventional pose that he and others specifically recommended for women. *Décor puellarum*, a handbook for maidens published in Venice in 1461, gave exceptionally detailed and rigid instructions: "Whether you are standing still or walking, your right hand must always rest upon your left, in front of you, on the level of your girdle."[15] *Décor puellarum* probably specified that the right hand remain uppermost because it performed the important role in any significant action. A comparable folding pose resulted, however, irrespective of which hand remained on top. Consistent with Leonardo's more generalized advice that women be depicted with "their arms closely folded," he interchanged left and right in portraying contemporary women with their hands joined together.[16] From the fifteenth century on, so did other portraitists (e.g., Figure 3.2). They also did not limit placement to belt level but rather referred to that general area "in front of you," as exemplified in Filippo Lippi's *Portrait of a Man and a Woman at a Casement* from around 1435–40 (Figure 3.3).

That a single pose could even be recommended for a woman in all situations highlights the contrast in prevailing attitudes towards women's and men's bodies and feelings. In actuality, of course, practical considerations would have precluded women from keeping their hands always folded in front of them, and even in formal portraits hand positions vary, though far less than men's. The recommendation of a single pose implied that women's bodies needed to be regulated in a singleminded, clear manner. Sexual desire loomed as the crucial passion to be kept under control, and it could be disciplined by promoting a feeling of modesty through the right positioning of the body. Mona Lisa has that pose.

Leonardo noted without elaboration in his journal what "intention of the soul" the pose of folded hands represented: "Women must be represented in modest attitudes (atti vergogniosi), their legs close together, their arms closely folded."[17] Although *Décor puellarum* insisted on this pose for women who are "virtuous" and Leonardo recommended it for the "modest," no real difference existed between these two terms, which functioned as synonyms when applied to women. A feeling of modesty implied and supported the virtue of chastity, and the value assigned to a woman's chastity cannot be exaggerated. Early modern authors described it as so essential that its absence made all of a woman's other virtues meaningless. "First let her understand that chastity is the principal virtue of a woman and outbalances all the rest."[18] *Mona Lisa* is only the best-known early modern portrait in which folded hands testify to the woman's modesty (e.g., Figures 3.3, 3.4). Deliberate refusal to take this pose went hand in hand with rejection of other conventions respected by a morally proper woman. An anonymous English publication from 1620, *Haec Vir; or The Womanish Man*, features a female speaker who has adopted some masculine freedoms, as her hybrid name of Hic Mulier suggests. In her description of what she has cast off she starts with this pose: "Because I stand not with my hands on my belly . . . am I therefor barbarous or shamelesse?" The error, she concludes, lies not in her behavior, but "in the fashion, in the custom."[19]

If Leonardo had portrayed Mona Lisa full-length, he probably would have followed his own recommendation that "women must be represented in modest attitudes, their legs close together, their hands closely folded."[20]

Figure 3.2. Anthony van Dyck, *Marie Anne Schotten*. Museum of Fine Arts, Boston, Isaac Sweeten Fund and Contributions. Reproduced by permission of the Museum of Fine Arts, Boston.

Figure 3.3. Fra Filippo Lippi, *Portrait of a Man and a Woman at a Casement*, fifteenth century. Metropolitan Museum of Art, New York, Marquand Collection, Gift of Henry G. Marquand, 1889. Reproduced by permission of the Metropolitan Museum of Art.

Figure 3.4. Raphael, *Portrait of Maddalena Doni.* Galleria Palatina, Palazzo Pitti, Florence. Reproduced by permission of the Ministero per i Beni e le Attivita Culturali.

This remained the standard guideline, and a century later in the Netherlands Karel van Mander gave the same advice to fellow artists. "Indeed, to make the feet of a woman stand or lie too far apart, particularly stand, is done contrary to dignity, which requires that the feet be placed close together according to the demands of modesty."[21] Since floor-length skirts largely masked women's legs, hands carried the main message of modesty even in full-length portraits.

Complicating the Picture

Why did modesty become identified with placing folded hands at roughly "the girdle," and was this pose absent from men's portraits? Location mattered, and joining the hands at waist level placed them over the uterus. In narrative scenes resting one hand there served as a straightforward reference to pregnancy (e.g., Francesco Penni, *Visitation*, Prado, Madrid). When the same gesture occurred in a woman's portrait, it probably also referred to childbearing (e.g., Figure 3.5), which would explain why artists often gave this pose to women but virtually never to men. The physician and medical historian Kenneth Keele even interpreted the *Mona Lisa* as a record of actualized fertility, diagnosing the sitter as being at an advanced stage of pregnancy.[22] Francesco del Giocondo apparently had lost one or both of his previous wives to childbirth before he married Lisa, daughter of Antonmaria di Noldo Gherardini, in 1495. No evidence exists for a pregnancy around 1504, but the fact that Mona Lisa had successfully given birth to two sons who survived, the second being born at the end of 1502, warranted recognition.[23]

Drawing attention to the uterus area produced a mixed subtext, however, for although a desirable wife had an "aptitude for bearing and giving birth to many fine children," many contemporaries still regarded the uterus as a troublesome source of lust. Its desires could wreak havoc with a woman's otherwise "natural" and socially mandated chastity.[24] Folding a woman's hands merged a psychological indicator of modesty with a physical reference to fertility, and the pose's visual effect reinforced that combination. The arc formed by joining the hands directs attention to the uterus area yet also seems to protect and fence it in.

Variations that complicate or contradict the established meaning of a pose or gesture can only be introduced after it has become conventional.[25] Folded hands were a well-established convention for women by the time

Figure 3.5. Giovanni Antonio Fasolo, *Family Group Portrait*, sixteenth century. Fine Arts Museums of San Francisco, Gift of Mortimer Leventritt in memory of his parents, Marion and Frances Leventritt, 1937.9. Reproduced by permission of the Fine Arts Museums of San Francisco.

Leonardo used this pose—and introduced a subtle variation. He rested Mona Lisa's hands on a chair, and acknowledged its presence by her fingers around its arm. This act modified the traditional pose, for although Mona Lisa's hands still visually overlap her uterus area, they no longer touch her body directly. To include a chair in a portrait was highly unusual around 1504.[26] Its presence created a more relaxed effect, and perhaps also served a symbolic purpose. Just the previous year Francesco del Giocondo had purchased a new house near the one in which he had been living, apparently with his extended family. The move would have involved the acquisition of new furniture and decorations, which might have prompted him to commission a portrait of his wife. In turn, Leonardo may have introduced the chair as a reference to the new family residence. (The mountainous setting hardly looks like the countryside near Florence, however.)

Hands could suggest modesty without alluding to fertility. The *Venus pudica* pose (so named because it derived from classical sculptures of Venus surprised after her bath) placed a woman's hands at her body yet spaced far apart, with one hand covering the breasts, the other the genitals. Too sexually explicit for use in portraits of real women, this pose played a dual role in narrative images by illustrating both the feeling of modesty and, if contextualized to do so, of sexual shame. For example, when Massaccio pictured the first couple being cast out of Paradise, he expressed Eve's shame by giving her the *Venus pudica* pose, Adam's by covering his face while leaving the rest of his body exposed (Brancacci Chapel, Florence).[27]

Early modern writers did not view shame as the feeling resulting from imagined or actual transgression, but as a prerequisite for female modesty even for virtuous women in proper situations. "Shame is the key that opens and closes the treasure of female modesty," wrote Annibale Pocaterra in 1592 in the first book-length publication devoted to the subject of shame, which he described as "part feeling and part virtue."[28] In fact, a specific English term existed for the feeling of modesty combined with shame, namely, "shamefastness," as in "let the women's faces be . . . closed and covered with shamefastnes."[29] By contrast, guides to behavior advised men not to reveal a sense of shame outwardly, and if wrongdoing elicited that feeling, it "should be internal rather than apparent."[30] For instance, James Cleland advised boys "against a foolish shamefastness in hanging down the head, and blushing at every light word."[31] The physical manifestations of shame mentioned by Pocaterra and others involved blushing and a lowered head. The absence of any mention of folded hands in this context, suggests they had no specific association with shame.

Silence

Manuals of civility recommended silence for women as second only to chastity; in fact, they linked the two states. Francesco Barbaro, for instance, considered speech to be "in general alien to the chastity, discretion, and constancy of the matron."[32] Even Baldasarre Castiglione 's recommendation that women at court be able to hold a "fluent, and extremely reserved, decent, and charming" conversation did not change the prevailing opinion, which had its counterpart in portraits.[33] Fire destroyed the most important exception, a group portrait of Sir Thomas More and his family by Hans Holbein the Younger, and only a preparatory drawing and painted copies survive. Holbein pictured the highly educated daughters with books, and even gave the youngest, Cecily Heron, the rhetorical pose of disputation.[34] In fact, of the ten men and women shown gathered together, she alone had a speaking hand, and one indicative of serious discourse. That gesture is still absent from the detailed preparatory drawing (Oeffentliche Kunstsamm-lung, Basel) that Holbein would have submitted for approval, which sug-gests he only included it after consulting his patron.[35]

In portraits as in public life, speech remained the prerogative of men. To convey the presence of speech visually, portraitists occasionally gave men the same gestures that rhetoricians and preachers used to strengthen the effect of their words. For instance, Cardinal Pietro Bembo had written on rhetoric, and Titian portrayed him with the gesture that Quintilian recom-mended for beginning a speech and Leonardo characterized as a gesture of argument (Figure 3.6).[36] By contrast, portraits of women, including the *Mona Lisa*, remained devoid of such speaking gestures, considered inappro-priate for them. "To her neither the intricacies of debate nor the oratical artifices of action and delivery are of the least practical use, if indeed they are not positively unbecoming."[37]

Bernardo Bellincioni's sonnet praising Leonardo's portrait of Cecilia Gallerani (*Lady with an Ermine*, Czartoryski Museum, Cracow) exempli-fies to what extent the passivity of silence prevailed as the interpretative norm for women's portraits.[38] Leonardo depicted this young noblewoman with a reputation for intellectual brilliance looking calmly to the side, but Bellincioni described her as listening passively. "In his painting he [Leonardo] makes her seem to listen, without speaking." Yet writers praised portraits of men, including ones devoid of a speaking gesture, such as Raphael's *Portrait of Baldassare Castiglione* (Figure 3.7), for seeming about to speak without being addressed by the viewer.[39]

Figure 3.6. Titian, *Cardinal Pietro Bembo*, c. 1540. National Gallery of Art, Washington, D.C., Samuel H. Kress Collection. Reproduced by permission of the National Gallery of Art.

Figure 3.7. Raphael, *Portrait of Balthasar Castiglione*. Musée National du Louvre, Paris. Photo: Alinari/Art Resource, NY.

A Phlegmatic Temperament

Women's folded hands also conveyed their dominant temperament. The idea that passivity remained women's natural state belonged to the theory of humors inherited from classical antiquity and still commonly accepted through the mid-seventeenth century. According to humoral theory, women's passivity resulted from their innate cold wetness. From the moment of conception men stayed hotter and drier, which made them more active and thus superior to women.[40] Custom shaped gestures, stance, and even the act of walking to convey men's more active nature. For instance, Giovanni della Casa advised the male readers of his *Il Galateo* (1558) "not to run like a lackey, or walk as slowly as women." In order to walk slowly women had to keep their legs close together, which also maintained their modesty.[41] Similar advice about the speed of motion extended to hands. Leonardo owned a manuscript copy of Matteo Palmieri's *On Civil Life* (1493) in which that Florentine writer encouraged men to manage their hands differently than women. "The hands should . . . not be uncouth, or rigid, or soft and drooping, or still like those of a woman."[42] Rules of decorum stilled woman's hands by recommending they always remain folded. By itself, this overdetermined pose thus characterized women as modest, fertile, silent, and phlegmatic in temperament, in short, as contemporaries expected a woman to be.

Favored Gestures in Men's Portraits

Men preferred one pose above all others, namely, the elbow akimbo (e.g., Figures 3.5, 3.8). The projecting elbow crossed class lines, appearing in images of kings and nobles, mercenary soldiers, and even peasants. Unlike women's folded hands, however, this was not a pose specifically recommended for men, and in fact, it had been discouraged. Yet despite initial complaints about the aggressive and prideful connotations of sharply angling one's elbow into the surrounding space, the elbow akimbo became swiftly established as the favored male stance even in portraits, as Joaneath Spicer has discussed.[43] It was as if men, being naturally active, could not help taking the pose. By its spatial assertiveness a projecting elbow proclaimed a man to be physically vigorous and to possess bravery, the virtue and feeling deemed as essential for men as chastity was for women. In short, the pose epitomized admired masculinity. The father in Figure 3.5 holds one arm akimbo while his other hand grasps a sword.

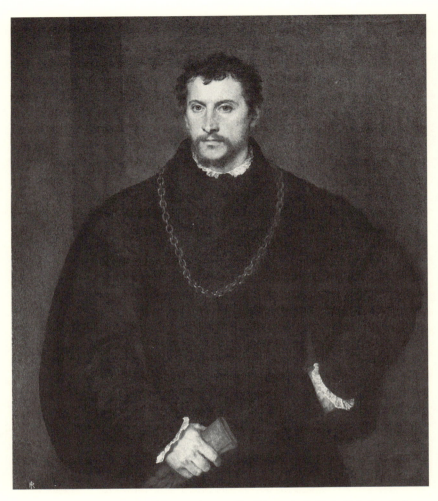

Figure 3.8. Titian, *Portrait of a Man (Young Englishman)*. Galleria Palatina, Palazzo Pitti, Florence. Reproduced by permission of the Ministero per i Beni e le Attivita Culturali.

Despite the explicit identification of folded hands with modest women, some men allowed themselves, or chose to be portrayed in this restrained position. They included men particularly attuned to the implications of body language, such as Albrecht Dürer (*Self-Portrait*, Madrid, Prado, 1498) and Baldasarre Castiglione (Figure 3.7), which suggests such examples should not be dismissed as unimportant exceptions.

A pose did not retain a fixed meaning, but shifted with a change in context, especially in the sex of the body taking that pose. For instance, a woman atypically pictured with an elbow akimbo, especially in narrative images, implied she was or might be a virago. In a context suggestive of a positive or neutral intention (e.g., a self-portrait), the projecting elbow identified her with a masculine role or profession.[44] Portraying a man with folded hands would not have associated him with chastity since that ranked as a man's least important virtue. Moreover, the area at his waist had no association with sexuality. In fact, men's joined hands tend to project into the surrounding space, in contrast to the enclosing placement of women's hands within the silhouette of the torso.

Because the pose locked both hands into inactivity it carried some class implications, suggesting the sitter did not need to work manually for a living.[45] Albrecht Dürer may have wished to distance himself from the demeaning manual aspects of his professional activity as printmaker and painter by presenting himself as a well-traveled gentleman with elegant clothes and inactive hands. Disassociation from manual work would not, however, explain the use of this pose for men who hardly needed to persuade viewers that their income did not derive from manual work, such as Baldasarre Castiglione, a courtier from an aristocratic family.

No text of the time, to my knowledge, discussed the significance of folding a man's hands, but some of the pose's implications can be gauged by comparison with other male poses, especially the favored projecting elbow. Seen in relation to each other, these two poses functioned as gestural synechdoches for the two main modes of life admired in men. The elbow akimbo stood for the *vita activa* usually associated with military action, whereas folded hands evoked the *vita contemplativa*, with its stilling of the body to privilege the activity of the mind. Folded hands thus did not serve as an effeminate, demeaning contrast to the favored elbow akimbo; rather, through body language alone they conveyed a respected alternative to what the spatially aggressive elbow symbolized.[46] Although contemporaries described the two life styles as opposites, they believed both depended on men's ample supply of heat to generate the requisite physical or mental activity. Thus, although Castiglione's folded hands resemble Mona Lisa's, they carried different associations. Even without such props as books, the pose in and of itself evoked his choice of a contemplative mode of life. By contrast, Mona Lisa's folded hands represented the only socially respected option available to a woman.

Different Folding Actions for Different Emotions

Hands could vary in the specifics of their joining, not just their distance from the torso. For example, intertwined fingers rarely appeared in portraits because they functioned as a traditional sign of grief.[47] Leonardo used that gesture in the *Last Supper* (Milan, Sta. Maria delle Grazie) to convey St. John's sorrow at Christ's announcement that he would be betrayed. Simultaneously, St. John's tightly interlocked fingers foreshadow the future, when he stood mourning with the holy women at the Crucifixion.

The significant variation in Mona Lisa's case involves the wrist, for one of her hands rests on the wrist of the other. That pose had carried undesirable connotations for at least four hundred years by the time Leonardo painted the *Mona Lisa*. During the Middle Ages, standing with crossed hands in the presence of a social superior expressed awareness of one's subordinate position and lesser power, but this usage seems not to have survived into the early modern period. Tracing the pose's medieval usage also leads into courts of law. In legal practice, holding the wrist of one hand with the other declared the person's incapacity for action in the situation under discussion, and seeing the defendant in this pose imprinted the declaration of incapacity on the visual memory of witnesses. Medieval and Renaissance artists used crossed hands to illustrate the powerlessness of prisoners and future prisoners, mourners or spectators overcome with grief, and corpses.[48]

When the motif of crossed hands migrated into portraiture it obviously no longer identified the depicted person as incapacitated. Nevertheless, traces of an association with the state of restraint may have clung to the pose, given that artists employed crossed hands in many more portraits of women than men. The decorum of modesty, in fact, incapacitated a complying woman's activity, her gestures as well as her walk, talk, and glance.[49] Constraint is hardly the overall effect of the *Mona Lisa*, however. The portrait carries a mixed, even contradictory message. The pose stands for restraint, whereas the forms, especially the smooth rhythms and softened, full surfaces, suggest only ease. In earlier portraits women's hands joined in a stiffer, tighter way to confirm their modesty (e.g., Figure 3.3), but Mona Lisa's come together with the apparent effortlessness of behavior that Castiglione would soon recommend in *The Book of the Courtier*. A similarly complex, mixed effect results from the relationship of Mona Lisa's folded hands to the rest of her body. Although the hands stand for a passive female state, her body seems gently animated because the head turns more than the torso, and the eyes more than the head. By 1500 this type of implied mobility had become part of the Italian portrait tradition for men, but it was still novel for a woman. Though traditional, the pose of *Mona Lisa* eludes a straightforward classification.

Passions, Class, and Gender

As manuals of civility document, posture became increasingly important during the early modern period, first to distinguish nobility from everyone else, and gradually to distinguish any civil person from the lower classes, especially from peasants. An upright bearing demonstrated control both of body and passions, and images of hunched, slouching peasants symbolized the unmanaged lower-class body and its attendant psychological and moral failings. As mentioned earlier, attention focused on how the head sat on the neck because, as Willem Goeree wrote in 1682, "by moving our heads we reveal many states of our feelings." Although a head tilted sideways disclosed "unmanly faintheartedness," or according to some manuals, including Erasmus's, "hypocrisy," such undesirable connotations evaporated when the tilted neck belonged to a woman.[50] Then the meaning became neutral or even positive, as when Goeree added that a slightly slanting neck only enhanced a woman's gracefulness and gentleness. Leonardo had also noted that a modest woman's head should be "inclined and somewhat on the side." A tilted neck identified a woman as possessed of such feminine qualities as gentleness, cowardice (a natural and thus excusable weakness in women) and most important, modesty. Contrary to his own advice, nevertheless, Leonardo did not incline Mona Lisa's head. Despite turning, it remains upright—and so do the necks of almost all women in early modern portraits.[51] Only Mona Lisa's slightly averted glance reinforces the modesty conveyed by her hands. [52]

Necks demonstrate that gender was not the sole determinant of body posture in early modern portraits. Whereas in narrative paintings artists used a variety of neck positions, in portraits necks do not distinguish among sitters. Straight carriage remained the norm even for women, and in fact, anyone who could afford to commission a portrait would usually be pictured with neck erect. A servant has the only inclined neck in a family portrait from the mid-sixteenth century (Figure 3.5). Good posture served as the firm armature of class distinction on which the artist could arrange gestures and add props appropriate to the sitter's gender and, especially with men, to professional and personal interests. If Leonardo had illustrated Mona Lisa's feminine modesty more insistently by inclining her neck, he would have undermined the main bodily indicator of her upper-class standing.

Socially Shaped Feelings

To summarize, consistent with standard practice, the indicators of feeling that Leonardo included in his portrait of Mona Lisa affirm her social identity, not her personal emotions. The unusual smile probably referred to Francesco del Giacondo's surname, thereby identifying her as his wife. Upright posture confirmed the control of both body and passions associated with the upper class to which she belonged. And despite Leonardo's contradictory heightening of the symbolism of restraint as well as the air of ease, her folded hands still functioned as a familiar sign of modesty, the crucial feeling and virtue expected of all women.

Leonardo's influential variation on the traditional female pose filtered down to subsequent portraitists, who, significantly, intensified its conventional form, and thereby content. For instance, although the young Raphael based Maddalena Doni's pose (Figure 3.4) exceptionally closely on the recently started portrait by Leonardo, he introduced slight but significant changes. Lessening the turn of her torso and loosening her hold on the armrest, Raphael shifted his sitter's hands closer to the area at her "girdle," a more traditional placement appropriate to her recent marriage and the childbearing expectations inscribed on the back of the portrait.[53] Such adjustments suggest that contemporaries recognized the core of conventional feminine meaning, both psychological and physical, carried by Mona Lisa's pose.

While women continued to be urged to fold their hands in a restricting, static position, the upper classes increasingly prized behavior that looked effortless. Widely admired, the portrait of Mona Lisa met these contradictory social expectations through the easy grace with which her restrained hands display the feeling of modesty.

Chapter 4

Compassion in the Public Sphere of Milton and King Charles

John Staines

If to command and rule ore others be
The thing desir'd above all worldly pelf,
How great a Prince, how great a Monarch's he,
Who govern can, who can command Himself?
If you unto so great a Pow'r aspire,
This Book will teach how you may it acquire.
—Henry Carey, Earl of Monmouth, on his translation of
J.-F. Senault's The Use of Passions *(London, 1649), sig. b6*

The analogy between governing one's own body and governing the bodies of others is certainly not surprising to anyone familiar with early modern images of the body politic. Yet in 1649 Monmouth's readers would have immediately felt some radical dissonance: although their country had no shortage of men who desired "to command and rule ore others," it did lack a prince and monarch. Why would Monmouth produce a treatise on the passions, one translated from the work of a French Catholic prelate and royal counselor, just months after the execution of King Charles? On the face of it, *The Use of Passions* is not at all a topical work: it turns away from the public, "worldly" realm to address the "Pow'r" to "command" the private self. Nonetheless, we should be skeptical of Monmouth's claim to be turning away from any interest in public power. The frontispiece for the work, engraved by William Marshall, is an allegory of Reason enslaving the Passions, imagery whose political overtones are by no means subtle (Figure 4.1). Marshall, moreover, had just produced another, more famous engraving for *Eikon Basilike*, the royalist bestseller that purports to give the tear-soaked meditations of the late king (Figure 4.2).[1] There, King Charles appears in his private chamber, weeping over the sins of his nation. In the text, Charles claims that once Parliament had moved against him, he had only "Prayers and Tears" to "use against [his] Persecutors."[2] Nonetheless, despite his appeals to the passions, Charles claims to be defending his "Reason and Conscience," which he makes synonymous with his absolute royal

The VSE of
PASSIONS
Written in French by
J. F. Senault.
And
put into English
by
Henry Earle of
Monmouth
1649.

Divine Grace

Reason

Joy

Feare

Despaire

Sorrow

Choller

Hope

Boldnesse

Love

Eschewing

Hatred

Desire

W.M. sculp:

Passions araing'd by Reason here you see,
As shee's Advis'd therein by Grace Divine:
(But this, (yow'll say)'s but in Effigie!
Peruse this Booke, and you in ev'ry line
Thereof will finde this truth so prov'd, that yow
Must Reason contradict, or grant it True.

Figure 4.1. Reason enslaving the passions, frontispiece to Henry, Earl of Monmouth, *The Use of Passions* (1649). Beinecke Rare Book and Manuscript Library, Yale University. Reproduced by permission of Yale University.

authority.[3] In *Eikonoklastes* Milton gives an angry response: "Was the King-dom then at all that cost of blood to remove from him none but Praiers and Teares?"[4] He treats the king's challenge to Parliament's authority with con-tempt, "the reason, conscience, humour, passion, fansie, folly, obstinancie, or other ends of one man, whose sole word and will shall baffle and unmake what all the wisdom of a Parlament hath bin deliberately framing."[5] Milton collapses Charles's reason and conscience into not just humor and passion but fancy and folly and, finally, the obstinacy and self-interest of one man's will over the nation.

The confluence of these three works, a royalist translation of a Catholic treatise on the passions, a volume demonstrating the king's compassion for his people, and Milton's angry denunciation of the deceptions of the royalist's

Figure 4.2. Charles I in his solitude and sufferings, *Eikon Basilike* (1648/49). Beinecke Rare Book and Manuscript Library, Yale University. Reproduced by permission of Yale University.

pathetic rhetoric, raises questions about the political roles the passions played in the seventeenth century. Early modern understandings of political rhetoric began with an understanding of the passions and how they spread from body to body; thus the shared passion of *compassion*—known also as *mercy*, *pity*, or *sympathy*—was one model for public politics. My investigation into this public politics begins in its broad outlines with Jürgen Habermas's configuration of the modern public sphere as a realm of rational debate. In its ideal form, Habermas writes, "rational-critical public debate" gives rise to a legitimate and authoritative public opinion; what replaces the secret, authoritative conscience of the king is not, as some like Rousseau would have it, a truth "anchored in the hearts of the citizens" but public discussion and the give and take of competing ideas.[6] However, a reading of these three texts against the background of early modern writings on rhetoric and the passions will suggest several revisions to this model of the public sphere in the early modern period: (1) that passion played a role alongside reason in the early public sphere; (2) that compassion served as an ideal for political order and political debate; (3) that compassion also served as a rhetorical tool to sway audiences, thus becoming a target for doubts about the place of passion and rhetoric in the public sphere; and (4) that in this debate over compassion can be found clues to the divisions that gave rise to a public sphere in the seventeenth century, as well as to the ultimate (if temporary) failure of that public sphere in the English Revolution.

In his theories about the institutions of modern democratic society, Habermas argues that the modern public sphere developed into a challenge to the older aristocratic order by utilizing and legitimizing the "medium" of "people's public use of their reason."[7] In such a system (at least in its ideal form), authority comes not from one's birth but from one's ability to argue through reason. The persuasive role that early modern rhetoric gives to the passions complicates Habermas's idealized conception of reason in the modern public sphere. Indeed, in several decades of writing, Habermas himself has refined his understanding of the public sphere and his celebration of a reason engaged in political action by paying attention to problems raised by the study of language and rhetoric. He has come to defend a conception of reason as "communicative action," the social use of language where "the actions of the agents involved are coordinated not through egocentric calculations of success but through acts of reaching understanding."[8] He calls for a "paradigm of mutual understanding between subjects capable of speech and action," identifying the "irony" of modernity in the fact that the "communicative potential of reason first had to be released in the patterns of modern lifeworlds" for there to be any modernity at all but that this reason was ultimately suppressed by "the unfettered imperatives of the economic and administrative subsystems" of the modern world itself.[9] To achieve mutual understanding, reason needs to be free of its bondage to the economic and bureaucratic imperatives of modern institutions; that is, it needs to be free to be critical of those institutions, their aims, and their supporting ideologies. Moreover, reason, properly conceived, does not stand as an abstraction outside and above the everyday world; we instead should "conceive of rational practice as reason concretized in history, society, body, and language."[10] The conditions of such a reason "necessitate its branching out into the dimensions of historical time, social space, and body-centered experiences."[11] Reason, we might say, must include the passions.

There is no space here for a detailed account of the strengths and limitations of Habermas's defense of reason as communication; as a way to advance this volume's investigation into the place of the passions in early modern experience, Habermas's reconfiguration of reason as a communicative practice will (ironically) serve to put the passions back at the center of communication and persuasion. As Victoria Kahn notes, "Habermas's ideal of 'unconstrained communication' runs the danger of isolating reason from rhetoric and imitation altogether," creating a reason so idealized that it stands outside human language.[12] We can avoid the problem of an idealized reason if we think of communication as including not just a narrowly defined reason but also emotion and experiences commonly thought of as "bodily" as opposed to "mental" or "spiritual."[13] This conception of reason and emotion as part of the full experience of thought and communication very much reflects early modern notions of how reason and passion work together in deliberations both private and public. We should, of course, be wary of confusing Habermas's notion of a reason understood as the communicative practices of everyday life with early modern or ancient investigations into persuasion's role in the civil polity.[14] But as David Norbrook points out, Habermas can awaken us to "our need for a history of the citizen as well as of the bourgeois."[15] This essay will give part of that history, the role of rhetoric and the passions in the public sphere, for to understand early modern culture's communicative practice—its rhetoric and politics— we need to consider reason and passion not as antithetical but as part of a single practice.

In this development of a theory and practice of rhetoric that makes room for the proper use of both reason and passion, Thomas Wright's *Passions of the Minde in Generall*, first published in 1601 and revised and expanded in 1604, is an archetypal text. Wright, it is important to emphasize, did not write as a purely disinterested academic theoretician. His interest in the passions and their use stemmed from his work as a Catholic missionary, preaching in the Protestant England of Elizabeth and James and engaging in print controversies on behalf of his faith.[16] Wright renounced his Jesuit vows in order to undertake a personal mission to England, serving openly as a priest and declaring the compatibility of loyalty to the papacy with loyalty to the English crown. Other priests and Jesuits had gone to the scaffold, tortured and killed in gruesome spectacles that proclaimed the Protestant government's resistance to traitors, yet Wright claimed that he was loyal and that his religion and rhetoric were not treasonous.[17] Ironically, he wrote the earliest drafts of his *Treatise* while in prison for debating religious questions publicly.

It is against this political background that we should read *The Passions of the Minde in Generall*. Near the beginning of his work, Wright explains the purpose of his treatise by appealing in part to its utility to orators and preachers: "The Christian Orator (I meane the godly Preacher) perfectly vnderstanding the natures and properties of mens passions, questionlesse may effectuate strange matters in the mindes of his Auditors." What he calls "the Art of mouing the affections of those auditors" is "strange" and works "maruellously," but it is a "power" that one can attain through "perfectly vnderstanding the natures and properties of mens passions." This is the justification for his book. He then gives as an example one Italian preacher, presumably a Catholic priest from one of the preaching orders:

I remember a Preacher in *Italy*, who had such power ouer his Auditors affections, that when it pleased him he could cause them shedd abundance of teares, yea and with teares dropping downe their cheekes, presently turne their sorrow into laughter: and the reason was, because hee himselfe being extremely passionate, knowing moreouer the Art of mouing the affections of those auditors, and besides that, the most part were women that heard him (whose passions are most vehement and mutable) therefore he might haue perswaded them what hee listed.[18]

This man is an effective orator both because he has a naturally emotional character ("hee himselfe being extremely passionate") and because he has studied and gained a technical skill ("knowing moreouer the Art of mouing the affections of those auditors"). Wright concludes by declaring the usefulness of his work to "whosoeuer would perswade a multitude," giving at this point a marginal note, "See *Aristotles* Rhetorickes."

This persuasive practice is identified not with logic but with the moving of the passions.[19] Wright describes persuasion as in part a passive experience: "because, if once they can stirre a Passion or Affection in their Hearers, then they have almost halfe perswaded them, for that the forces of strong Passions maruellously allure and draw the wit & will to iudge and consent vnto that they are moued."[20] Orators "stirre" passions, and those passions "allure and draw the wit & will," which is to say that wit and will "are moued" towards a position and thus prepared to come to the active choice of "iudg[ing] and consent[ing]." This passive process is, not surprisingly, gendered as female, and this Italian preacher has his greatest success with his female audience, "whose passions are most vehement and mutable." Wright soon leaves behind this hint of disapproval, however, for his conception of how the mind operates posits a mixture of active and passive motions, of stereotypically "male" and "female" principles, of reason and passion. Such ambivalence is a constant tension in Wright's treatise. On the one hand, the passions make league with sense against reason, "like two naughtie servants, who oft-times beare more love one to an other, than they are obedient to their Maister."[21] On the other hand, passions "may by vertue be guided, and many good men so moderate and mortifie them, that they rather serve them for instruments of vertue, than foments of vice, and as an occasion of victory, than a cause of foyle."[22] Handled properly, passions may lead not to "foyle" and pollution but to virtue. This virtue plays a role not just in personal ethics but in public politics.

Wright's political mission, though, was largely a failure. About a year after publishing the second edition of *The Passions of the Minde*, Wright was called upon by James's government to interrogate the conspirators in the Gunpowder Plot.[23] This sign of loyalty may have saved his own life, but the Catholic community came out of the plot under an ever-darker cloud of suspicion. Catholics did not earn toleration, and, if anything, the subversive activities of the more radical missionaries and zealots made English Protestants associate Catholic religious beliefs even more closely with treason; indeed, this popular association of Catholic beliefs with subversive treason would have disastrous consequences for the Stuarts themselves and lead, in part, to revolution.[24] No public sphere of free religious debate opened in Wright's lifetime: besides *The Passions of the Minde*, all of Wright's other works appeared in England only in clandestine editions. Despite Wright's political failure, however, in his manual for a rhetorical practice of the passions we can see one of the origins of the modern public sphere: as the preacher appeals to the masses and seeks to persuade them to choose and give their loyalty to one of two competing churches, he is participating in the gradual creation of private consciences that frequently stand at odds against the official public sphere that was, till this time, constituted solely in the sovereign and his (or her) government.

Habermas himself largely ignores the effects of the Reformation, arguing that secularization is the necessary condition of the public sphere, that "Hobbes's devaluation of religious conviction actually led to an upward evaluation of all private convictions."[25] Hobbes, though, only devalued the religious conscience as a way to contain and limit the political conflicts created when the Reformation opened up belief to the questions of a prying conscience; he responded to the Civil War by arguing that the state should control public actions but leave private consciences largely alone.[26] Although Wright himself claimed not to challenge the sovereign and the state church, the practical effect of the Reformation was to open a space for controversy that spread from questions of religion to questions of politics—in any case, a more or less meaningless distinction in the period since religion was not then relegated to the private sphere. Individual consciences making practical judgments about the rhetorical performances presented before them: this was the condition of the humanist public sphere of the Reformation.[27]

Habermas places such developments largely in eighteenth-century Britain, but others, including Alexandra Halasz and David Zaret, have traced the roots of the modern public sphere in the print controversies of the sixteenth and seventeenth centuries.[28] Habermas argues that in Restoration and eighteenth-century Britain, coffee houses and salons "were centers of criticism—literary at first, then also political—in which began to emerge, between aristocratic society and bourgeois intellectuals, a certain parity of the educated."[29] In these elite and largely secular institutions, a public engaged in literary criticism became a public engaged in political criticism; rational, critical skills rather than social status determined the course and outcome of these arguments. In the sixteenth and seventeenth centuries, by contrast, a public engaged in religious criticism was becoming a public engaged (likewise) in political criticism. Habermas defines the "political public sphere" as existing "when the public discussions concern objects connected with the practice of the state."[30] In a political system in which there is, at least in theory, a nearly complete identification of church and state, as there is in England after Henry's break with Rome, the distinction between religious and political criticism soon breaks down. The institutions that made up this sphere of religious criticism, such as the sermon and the printed text, reached all social strata of society, from the elite to the common laborer, who all had consciences that needed to make a choice of belief.[31] This criticism prepared the way for revolution.[32]

Early modern readers educated in the schools and universities experienced this public realm of debate and argument through their study of rhetoric, the realm of, in Aristotelian terms, *praxis* and *phronesis*, practice and prudence.[33] They turned to Aristotle and ancient rhetoric in order to understand the practice of language, for ways of judging with prudence rhetorical performances and their effects upon the civil polity. The humanist Juan Luis Vives, for example, recommends Aristotle's *Rhetoric* because, unlike other rhetorical treatises that give merely random advice on style and ornament, this book teaches that to understand persuasion one must understand "the arts, customs, laws, affections, and the conduct of civil and human life."[34] In other words, Aristotle teaches that to understand how an audience is persuaded, one must undertake a political, psychological, and even (to use an anachronistic term) anthropological study of a people.[35] Aristotle and his heirs thus placed rhetoric, the art of persuasion, at the center of public life. Since they recognized that the emotions have an important role to play in persuasion, they carved a role alongside reason for the passions to play in public debate and deliberation.[36] By turning to ancient writers on rhetoric and civic life, early modern writers likewise brought the passions into their own developing sense of public life.[37]

In the ancient world, the question of the validity of rhetoric frequently turned on the place of the passions, and early modern writers thus carried those debates back into their conceptualization of the public use of passions. Wright, for instance, looks to Aristotle, who sees passion as preparing the mind for persuasion. In his *Rhetoric*, Aristotle answers Plato's objections by offering a conception of reason and passion working together in a persuasive argument.[38] Although the passions are not rational and cannot be eliminated by reason (as the Stoics would argue), they can be shaped and directed by reason. In Aristotle's theories of the mind and in his ethics, a person has an emotional response to an object and that response involves, as Alexander Nehemas has shown, "a value judgment"; the sum of these responses comprise our character or *ethos*, which is thus partially nonrational.[39] We can educate our passions and thus our character by considering the objects to which we attach emotions, and this Aristotelian notion of ethical education underlies the projects of writers like Wright and Senault.[40]

As Susan James has shown, early modern accounts of thought portray making a decision as both an active and a passive process: the mind can both act and be acted upon.[41] Passions are both passive and active: they are caused by some stimulus, yet themselves cause bodily motions, thoughts, volitions, and even other passions. The rational mind can control passions but is also controlled by passions, and writers will emphasize one power or the other depending upon their sense of human nature or upon their theological or political leanings. Deliberation is an act of will that is driven by both passion and reason, and persuasion thus involves both passion and reason; reason by itself, in the opinion of many writers, is unpersuasive.[42]

Pity, Aristotle's *eleos*, works in just this way: we see an object, in this case another person's suffering, and feel "a certain pain at an apparently destructive or painful evil happening to one who does not deserve it and which a person might expect himself or one of his own to suffer, and this when it seems close at hand."[43] The passion is immediate: the effect of sympathy, of imagining the other's suffering as my own, fades when it is not an object in my direct view, which is why an orator's performance must make the evil vivid and directly present to the imagination of the audience, "by making it appear before [our] eyes either as something about to happen or as something that has happened."[44] When describing the similar effect of the passion of love, the French Jesuit writer Nicholas Caussin uses an auditory metaphor: "Our passions resemble ecchoes: Do you not see that ecchoes the further you go from them, the less repercussion there is, they lessening and loosing themselves in the air."[45] But more important to Aristotle's account of the passions is the way that this response implies a series of ethical judgments: I decide both that someone "does not deserve" this suffering and that I can identify with this person's suffering because he or she could be me or one of my family and friends, the members of my community. This passion is at its root self-reflexive and even selfish—"And they pity those like themselves in age, in character, in habits, in rank, in birth; . . . people pity things happening to others in so far as they fear for themselves"—but also implies a sense of community united by the passion.[46]

The idea that a feeling might play a central role in ethics and politics meets with resistance from a variety of commentators, especially the Stoics.[47] In his treatise *De clementia*, Seneca argues that a ruler must make a reasoned decision of when to punish and when to grant clemency. The ruler should never feel the emotion of mercy or pity, which he terms *misericordia*, but should choose when it is useful to the common good to give *clementia* (clemency). *Clementia* is a rational consideration of a case, while *misericordia* merely "looks at" (*spectat*) a sad situation and responds emotionally; it is not a virtue but a "vice of a weak mind," which he contemptuously genders as female, belonging to "old ladies and wretched women (*anus et mulierculae*)."[48] For Seneca, *clementia* is the best of virtues, for "none is more human (*humanior*)," a position that follows from the Stoic conviction that "the human is a social animal, born for the common good"—though he adds that it would be so even for those like the Epicureans for whom "every word and deed looks to their own *utilitates*, to their own profit or use."[49] Clemency thus is necessary for the good of society; it holds everyone together and works for the common good, or for the good of each individual.

Seneca's *clementia*, however, does not fit a Christian notion of the human. Calvin, in his commentary on *De clementia*, counters Seneca's attack on the feeling of mercy by asserting that a man who does not feel pity is "certainly not human."[50] This attack upon the Stoic notion of clemency, that it is not even human, is a common theme in early modern writings on the passions, whether Protestant or Catholic. In his *Table of the Humane Passions*, for example, the Catholic bishop Nicolas Coeffeteau writes, "Let vs then leaue this inhumaine *Philosophy* which makes men rather stupid then constant, & to become insensible of the miseries of this life; and let vs consider more exactly of the true nature of this *Passion*, which giues vs a commendable feeling."[51] Although Christian writers frequently admire Seneca's moral teachings and even his advice on when it is wise to remit punishment, they cannot accept his dismissal of a passionate mercy—"this inhumaine *Philosophy*"—since that passion is at the heart of their conception of Christ's incarnation and sacrifice. As Senault, citing Augustine, proclaims near the end of his *Use of Passions*, "who dares blame a Passion, to which we ow our Innocence? . . . and shall not we adore a Vertue, which *Jesus Christ* hath pleased to consecrate in his own person?"[52] This sense of an incarnate God who must feel love, even *be* love, shapes how they conceive of the human person and human society: because God is love and chooses to take on our human form, he feels grief for our suffering. *Mercy* or *compassion* is the name given to this shared grief.

Mercy thus remains important to Christian conceptions of social order even when given over fully to the passions. In his introduction, Wright defends his project by calling upon the example of compassion: "Passions, are not only, not wholy to be extinguished (as the Stoicks seemed to affirme) but sometimes to be moued, & stirred vp for the seruice of vertue, as learnedly *Plutarch* teacheth: for mercie and compassion will moue vs often to pitty, as it did *Iob*, *Quia ab infantia mea mecum creuit miseratio*, Compassion grew with me from my infancy, and it cam with me out of my mothers womb."[53] He goes on to list how the other passions can serve wisdom and virtue, but this example of mercy and compassion, bolstered by classical and biblical authorities, is the keystone of his defense. A passion is to be moved in order to move a person to act virtuously: the passive emotion becomes active, spurring on a virtue. Not only is pity a virtue, but the feeling of mercy and compassion is to be "stirred up," as by an orator. The experience of this passion is frequently expressed in theatrical and rhetorical imagery. As Coeffeteau explains, we feel compassion for those whose ends are "lamentable and tragicall," moved most of all when "our eyes are spectators."[54]

Senault likewise celebrates how compassion moves men and women to act for one another's good: "Mercy is a sanctified Contagion, which makes us sensible of our Neighbors sufferings; we ayd him to comfort our selves: and we help him at his need, to free our selves from the Grief we feel."[55] The grief of compassion is good and holy because, as it touches each person— in the root sense of *contagion*, contact—it spreads virtuous behavior. This contact spreads what is, in effect, a physiological disease, but it is a "sanctified" infection. Nonetheless, this "contagion" remains problematic for the very reason that the spectacle touches the viewer in such an immediate and powerful way.

Nicholas Caussin, the Jesuit confessor of King Louis XIII who was sent into exile after opposing the policies of Cardinal Richelieu, spent his years out of power writing, revising, and expanding a lengthy vision of public and private virtues, his *Cour Sainte* or *Holy Court*.[56] At the heart of his moral teachings are concerns about the balance between passion and reason and about how the two shape the "motives" that "stir up" or "excite" men and women to "Christian perfection."[57] When he describes *compassion*, Caussin captures the immediacy of this experience by using the term "the bowels of compassion" and "the bowels of mercy."[58] He takes this striking image from the New Testament, where it is used to describe the love of God and Christ. The Vulgate uses the phrases "viscera misericordiae Dei nostri" (Luke 1:78), "cupiam omnes vos in visceribus Iesu Christi" (Phil. 1:8), "viscera miserationis" (Phil. 2:1), and even just "viscera sua" (1 John 3:17). English Protestant translators like William Tyndale seem uncomfortable with this physical image: the Geneva Bible translates "the tender mercie of our God," "compassion and mercie," "I long after you all from the verie heart rote in Iesus Christ," and "his compassion." In each of these passages, by contrast, the Catholic Douay-Rheims remains faithful to the Vulgate's vision of "the bowels of the mercy of our God" (Luke 1: 78).[59] David Hillman suggestively links the bowels of compassion with the problem of knowledge and skepticism:

How do we know and hence share what another person's body feels? Radical doubt results in the rejection of mercy.[60] He notes that this metonymy is "everywhere" in the period, particularly in the moving sermons of the apostate Catholic Donne,[61] but I would argue that its omission from the more radically Protestant Bibles like Tyndale's points to a growing anxiety within Christian moral thought. Hillman tends to collapse Catholic and Protestant examples, most problematically when he generalizes from the Catholic doctrine of the Eucharist.[62] The Protestant rejection of the mass and the real presence of Christ's body and blood in the bread and wine was the primary marker of the Tudor church's break with Rome.[63] The rejection of a miracle of body, spirit, and material substance paralleled the growing distrust of the visceral notion of compassion. The expression "bowels of compassion" encapsulated an intense experience, the direct witnessing of an event (or a narrative) that moved the entire body and soul of a spectator. And it was a *political* experience, as Wright, the Catholic missionary who sought to serve his Protestant queen, and Senault, Coeffeteau, and Caussin, all Catholic clergymen who held high political offices in the French government, each knew from firsthand experience. The contagion of compassion was the bond that held their society together, and any questions about the nature and effects of compassion thus hit at their conceptions of the nature of society.

The most intense public scene in the seventeenth century of the stirring up of compassion was the execution of Charles I. The spectacle of Charles being killed in the name of the people could move the crowd either to cheers or to tears. The feeling of grief, of compassion for the dead king, soon became the greatest argument in favor of monarchy. It was against the background of this crisis that the royalist Henry Carey, Earl of Monmouth, published his translation of Jean-François Senault's *The Use of Passions*.[64] Monmouth translates Senault's "Epistle Dedicatory to Our Saviour Jesus Christ,"

and that I may bring all men to observe, how *Passions* are *raised* in them, how they *rebel* against *Reason*, how they seduce the *Vnderstanding*, and what sleights they use to *enslave* the *will:* After I have known the *Malady*, teach me the *Remedy*, that I may cure it; teach me how a *Passion* is to be *stifled* in its *birth*; what *means* I must use to subdue a *Passion*.[65]

In dedicating his *Use of Passions* to Jesus Christ, Senault prays to him for the power to teach readers to conquer their passions. His imagery is violent and political: since the passions are rebels against reason who come "to enslave the will," they must be killed, smothered as soon as they are born. William

Marshall's frontispiece for the English translation provides a visual image for what Senault hopes his book can teach his readers (Figure 4.1). The rebellious Passions are enslaved by Reason, herself under the tutelage of a superior Divine Grace. The Passions are held in place by Reason's chains and watched over by a leashed dog. Reason's rod of correction points towards the scepter of Divine Grace: this is the true authoritarian order that God has ordained.

In his verses "To the Reader," Monmouth echoes Senault's imagery of the treasonous passions:

How harmless Joy we may Fore-runner make,
    Of that Eternal never-ending Bliss,
Whereof the Saints in Heaven do partake;
    And how our earthly Sorrow nothing is,
    But a sharp Corrosive, which, handled well,
    Will prove an Antidote to th'pains in Hell.
Thus, Rebels unto Loyalty are brought,
And Traytors true Allegeance are taught.[66]

Command transforms Joy—pictured in the frontispiece with a jug of wine, offering an intoxicating drink—into "harmless Joy" and, ultimately, "that Eternal never-ending Bliss." Monmouth contrasts "the Saints in Heaven" with "our earthly Sorrow." The "Saints" are emphatically "in Heaven," not the self-proclaimed Saints who were leading the revolution in England. When put in chains and "handled well," the "sharp Corrosive" of painful earthly passions becomes an "Antidote" giving immunity from the greater sufferings of hell. Active control makes productive use of the passive experiences of suffering.

It is easy to treat Monmouth's closing lines—"Thus, Rebels unto Loyalty are brought, / And Traytors true Allegeance are taught"—merely as the sort of platitude that reinforces power and obedience in early modern England. We could at this point be tempted to assent to a reading of the frontispiece, and Monmouth's entire book, as an allegory of power masquerading as knowledge: Reason is the name for the modern techniques of violence that discipline and suppress the bodies of passion; passions are reason's other, the body's emotions suppressed by the modern empire of reason. When we recognize Monmouth's royalism, however, this simple dichotomy between reason and passion, where reason disciplines passion and puts it in chains, becomes more complicated. We need to remember that Monmouth is *out* of power, writing as one exiled from the political realm by men he considers traitors. Monmouth wants his treatise to provide a way to contain conflict: the disorderly passions become mirrors for political disorders, and only through the control of passions and the rhetoric that moves them can there be an end to political conflict.

Wright also draws the analogy from subjects rising up in "ciuill broyles" against their King to the passions "rebell[ing] against Reason their Lord and King, or oppos[ing] themselues against another."[67] However, Wright's declaration against rebellion reflects his own defense of true persuasion as loyal: he wants to create a space for rhetoric and persuasion that is not rebellious, that influences and changes the public but does not destroy or overthrow its main institutions. At heart, Wright's is a vision of modern politics as a realm of debate and discussion. Monmouth's image, by contrast, contains a sharp protest against modern politics. The royalist has just witnessed the victory of rebels and traitors in the execution of the king, who, in the political world, once sat upon a throne analogous to Reason's. Monmouth makes his protest sharper in "The Translator to the Reader," through a *preteritio* where he explains why the book has no dedication. Since Senault had dedicated his book to Jesus Christ, Monmouth originally found it appropriate to dedicate the translation to the Church, but, he continues, "when upon second thoughts (which are, or ought to be the best,) I called to minde the many Rivals she hath in these days, which might peradventure cause both me and her to suffer, should I say any thing of her, or undertake her quarrel (me, by doing it; her, by my so ill doing it:) I resolved to pass over all Dedications."[68] The vacated space where the dedication should be reflects the hole left in the state by the destruction of the established church, by the death of its king, by the destruction of authority and reason. Monmouth puts in its place a protest. He figures the English Revolution as the death of a realm of rational argument or (so to speak) communicative reason—while at the same time, his insistence upon a truth enslaving all other opinions does not leave much room for a public sphere of reason and debate.

Monmouth rejects an innovation, the irruption of rebellious passions into an order of Grace and Reason. Yet his text, like the texts of his contemporaries, does not reject the passions, and the way in which we should "govern" the passions is never completely secure.[69] Senault rejects the Stoics, who argue "that to be a slave to Passion, is to live under tyranny, and that a man must renounce his liberty, if he obey such insolent Masters."[70] He counters that "there is no Passion which is not serviceable to vertue, when they are governed by reason, and those who have so cryed them down, make us see they never knew their use, nor worth."[71] In translating this treatise, Monmouth therefore admits the place of the passions and, implicitly, rhetoric, and sets out to prove their "use." Nonetheless, he struggles to erase the conflicts that the passions will move. This is the great problem of the public sphere of rhetoric: how to admit into the practice of private and public deliberation the full range of responses to language. It is important to notice that Senault's conclusion "that there is no Passion in our Soul, which may not profitably be husbanded by Reason, and by Grace," follows immediately upon his celebration of the passion of mercy and compassion: "provided she agree with Justice, a man must be Barbarous, not to reverence her, when she helps the poor, and pardons the guilty."[72] This caveat, "provided she agree with Justice," is, granted, a large one, though not one that Senault or Monmouth takes time to explain.

How to judge the balance between compassion and justice, however, was the unresolved issue of 1649. Monmouth's "earthly Sorrow" is the death of King Charles, whose book *Eikon Basilike, or the Pourtraicture of His Sacred Majestie in His Solitudes and Sufferings* was at that time London's greatest bestseller, going into thirty-five editions in 1649 alone.[73] The book, whose title means "The Royal Image," claimed to be Charles's own defense of his conduct during the civil war, even though it was secretly written by a ghostwriter from some of the king's papers.[74] The instant popularity of the book created a beloved new image for the king that challenged the new republican government to hold onto the affection and loyalty of the nation. The apocalyptic tone of the final stanza of Monmouth's introduction points not only to the victory of the righteous in heaven but also to the punishment of treason in this world, to the ultimate defeat of his enemies. Similarly, Charles pens a prayer for reason against disorder:

make us unpassionately to see the light of Reason, and Religion, and with all order, and gravity to follow it, as it becomes Men and Christians. . . .
Set bounds to our passions by Reason, to our errours by Truth, to our seditions by Lawes duely executed, and to our schimes by Charity, that we may be, as thy Jerusalem, a City at unity in it selfe.[75]

Charles, like Monmouth, envisions Reason putting the passions under control. Reason, Truth, Laws, and Charity become near synonyms, opposed to passions, errors, seditions, and schemes. The unity of the divine city of Jerusalem can be brought about in this world by order and discipline. Nonetheless, even as both Monmouth and Charles's texts gesture towards a rejection of worldly sorrow, they turn from the city of God to the city of this world.

Indeed, even the writers of Monmouth's party did not wish to see an order of complete reason. The title of Charles's book, after all, claims to give a portrait not of his reason, but of his "solitudes and sufferings." Marshall's engraving for *Eikon Basilike*, completed within a few months of the one he did for Monmouth's book, is in many ways a study of passion. The portrait of Charles on his knees, his face twisted with passion and tears, praying for deliverance like Christ in the Garden of Gethsemane, became the most enduring image of the Stuart tragedy, a rallying point for royalists against the republican regime (Figure 4.2).[76] Marshall astutely picked up on the way the text of *Eikon Basilike* affects its readers. In a series of personal reflections and meditations, the book presents the private side of the king, a man of deep passion who has become a martyr for his people. It creates a character for the king, a man of deep passion, full of tears for the sufferings of his people, who looks upon his enemies "as Christ did sometime over *Jerusalem*, as objects of my prayers and teares, with compassionate griefe."[77] His life is a tragedy of a people's senseless conflict against a loving king: "It is a hard and disputable choice for a King, that loves his People, and desires their love, either to kill his owne Subjects, or to be killed by them."[78] Charles battles not with the arms of war but with his image of sanctity and passion: "My chiefest Armes left Me, were those only, which the Ancient Christians were wont to use against their Persecutors, Prayers and Teares. These may serve a good mans turne, if not to Conquer as a Souldier, yet to suffer as a Martyr."[79] His prayers for reason notwithstanding, Charles's great appeal to the nation is his passion, the word for emotion punning both on the Latin word for "suffering" and on *the* Passion, Christ's sacrificial death. Marshall's engraving even evokes the pose of Christ in the Garden of Gethsemane, praying for deliverance the night before his Passion and martyrdom.[80] Charles's martyrdom is by definition a tearful suffering for which the witnesses (should) shed tears of compassion: "The teares they have denied Me in My saddest condition, give them grace to bestow upon themselves, who the lesse they were for Me, the more cause they have to weep for themselves. . . . But thou, O Lord, canst, and wilt (as thou didst My Redeemer) both exalt and perfect Me by My sufferings, which have more in them of thy mercy, than of mans cruelty or thy owne justice."[81] Charles claims to be, like Christ, an instrument of God's mercy and compassion. The people who do not shed tears for the dead king break a divine social covenant. Likewise, in weeping for the royal martyr, the reading public restores the bonds of compassion that unite the monarchic state and thus prepares the ground for a royal restoration.

The king's book was such an astonishing success in raising sympathy for the royalist cause—for pity for a man quickly becomes sympathy for a political cause—that the Commonwealth was forced to respond. The Council of State ordered Milton to answer the book, and in the fall of 1649 Milton published his *Eikonoklastes* ("The Image-Breaker"), attacking the portrait of the king as sympathetic martyr.[82] Milton angrily identifies the source of *Eikon Basilike*'s power, drawing an analogy to Mark Antony's speech at Caesar's funeral to attack the publication for "stirring up the people to bring him that honour, that affection, and by consequence, that revenge to his dead Corps."[83] That is, the reader identifies in his or her imagination with Charles's "Solitudes and Sufferings," then is moved or *stirred up* to compassion or sympathy for him, and thereby is moved to sympathize with his political position: the reader is thus stirred up by these passions to an action, to political allegiance with the dead king and his party. Milton argues that this practice of rhetoric, all passion and no reason, destroys public debate.

Milton claims that the king's book fails "to stirr the constancie and solid firmness of any wise Man, or to unsettle the conscience of any knowing Christian."[84] If *Eikon Basilike* is a work aimed at using reason and passion to stir, persuade, and move the conscience of a "wise" and "knowing" audience, Milton labels it unsuccessful rhetoric or even bad rhetoric. In evoking *conscience* here, Milton is responding to one of Charles's great themes, that his battle with Parliament was fought to defend "the liberty of our Reason, and Conscience," proclaiming, "I know no resolutions more worthy a Christian King, then to prefer His Conscience before His Kingdomes."[85] The royal conscience has authority that transcends the conscience of the kingdom; the former is truth, the latter mere opinion.[86] Charles prays to God, "Thou knowest the chief designe of this Warre is, either to destroy My Person, or force My Judgment, and to make me renege my Conscience and thy Truth."[87] To Charles's equation of his conscience with God's truth, Milton replies that this is "the hideous rashness of accusing God before Men to know that for truth, which all Men know to be most fals."[88] Charles's sin is to claim that God knows a truth that all men know to be an untruth: the conscience of the nation (of "all Men") bears witness to the falsehood of the king's conscience.

Milton defends the nation's conscience, essentially its "public opinion"—an admittedly anachronistic term, though a concept that (as Habermas has shown) developed out of seventeenth-century discussions of the private conscience.[89] Nonetheless, Milton's defense runs into trouble as he attempts to combat a work that has been successful in swaying the con-sciences of so many members of the reading public.[90] As he reaches his conclusion, Milton angrily reflects upon the fact that the king's rhetoric has been able "to catch the worthless approbation of an inconstant, irrational, and Image-doting rabble."[91] The consciences of the rabble have been stirred, Milton charges, leading them to a false opinion; *Eikon Basilike* works by stirring the passions of those who do not reflect upon its deeper signifi-cance, who reflexively fall back into their traditional affection for the royal image. Milton expanded his famous attack upon the mob in his second edi-tion, drawing attention to (among other things) how they respond to a rhetoric that plays upon their passions and their emotional attachment to the old, corrupt institutions of monarchy: they "hold out both thir eares with such delight and ravishment to be stigmatiz'd and board through in witness of their own voluntary and beloved baseness."[92] Unlike the wise men who are not moved, whose minds are not troubled or stirred by the repre-sentation of the royal image, the king's rhetoric and all the trappings of roy-alty give the people the lowest of pleasures; as their passions are moved and ravished, the people are moved to choose subjugation. They give up their active minds to be made slaves tied up in bonds of compassion.

   This slavery to the persuasive force of appeals to the passions points back to that problem raised by Aristotle and his followers: what is the proper place for the passions in rhetoric, and hence what is the place for rhetoric in the public sphere. In his third book, "Wherein are deliuered the meanes to know, and mortifie Passions: what prudence and policie may be practised in them," Wright cautions against being "induced to any thing by act, that is, by a tale well told in Rhetoricall manner, flexibility of voice, ges-tures, action, or other oratoricall perswasions."[93] Wright admits the danger-ous power of a rhetorical performance (an act or *actio*), whose sights and sounds result in the movement of the passions and the will. Nonetheless, he does not proceed from this point to reject all rhetoric: "Yet I would not by this condemne the faculty of eloquence, which I confesse, if it be well vsed, to bee most profitable for the Church and Common-weale." Since there are valid religious and political uses of rhetoric, he urges, essentially, a hermeneutics of suspicion: a spectator should step back, "suspend his iudge-ment, and not to permit [that] his will follow too farre his motion, more artificiall than naturall, grounded upon affection rather than reason."[94] The spectator needs to check where his emotions, created artificially by the ora-tor, are leading his will; such movements of the will are dangerous because they arise out of artful manipulation, not out of one's own nature, and are grounded in the emotion one feels for this artful performance, not in the reason the orator demonstrates. Much of the remainder of the third book and the entire fourth book thus concern understanding and "examin[ing] the Orators reasons."[95] He writes, "For that we cannot enter into a mans heart, and view the passions or inclinations which there reside & lie hidden," we must make judgments by external signs, "words and deeds, speech and action."[96] Essentially, the exercise of reasoned judgment serves to counteract the contagious nature of compassion, the way that the passion passes immediately from body to body via the media of sight and sound, as in a rhetorical performance.

In examining the hidden reasons of the publishers of *Eikon Basilike*, Milton follows this suspicion of rhetoric, going even further: "For in words which admitt of various sense, the libertie is ours to choose that interpretation which may best minde us of what our restless enemies endeavor, and what wee are timely to prevent."[97] Instead of responding with compassion or fellow feeling to the rhetoric of his opponents, Milton feels only distrust: because his enemies are abusing rhetoric and the passions, he claims complete liberty to impute the darkest meanings to their words. Milton's paranoid suspicion here reflects the crisis of a revolution that had gone beyond what its public could support. Such a public sphere was doomed to destroy itself since there were no grounds on which to build "a paradigm of mutual understanding."

This exchange between Milton and the writer of *Eikon Basilike* reflects a deep ambivalence among humanist intellectuals about the nature of a realm of public debate. A conflict employing reason and the passions has value since it can lead to a consensus of truth; nonetheless, they fear the consequences of the conflict itself.[98] A stable public sphere requires some shared ground on which to build "mutual understanding." Ironically, by ending the royal censorship regime, the Civil War made possible the first (nearly) free sphere of print and debate, yet the multiplicity of incommensurable ideas soon led the revolutionaries to feel the need to restrict print in order to save their own revolution. Those tensions became apparent as early as 1644, when Parliament sought to reestablish censorship in the form of the license. Milton responded in *Areopagitica* by envisioning a public sphere of competing religious ideas—save for Catholic ideas, which he sees as antagonistic to the public sphere:[99]

I mean not tolerated Popery, and open superstition, which as it extirpats all religions and civill supremacies, so it self should be extirpat, provided first that all charitable and compassionat means be us'd to win and regain the weak and the misled . . . but those neighboring differences, or rather indifferences, are what I speak of, whether in some point of doctrine or of discipline, which though they may be many, yet need not interrupt the *unity of spirit,* if we could but find among us the *bond of peace.*[100]

What is so striking about Milton's restriction of Catholic beliefs and writings is his simultaneous plea for compassion, unity, and peace even in a realm of diversity and dissent. Charity and compassion are models of persuasion operating in the civil polity. All that is necessary to maintain "the *unity of spirit,*" Milton suggests, is some grounds on which to found "*the bond of peace.*" As the civil war continued, this ideal realm of debate never found grounds for peace and unity, and Milton himself took the government post of licensor. No consensus appeared on which to form such a social bond. Compassion for the royal suffering, however, could produce a consensus—but one that would lead to a Restoration regime that sought to shut down the public sphere of questions and criticism.

Milton argues that the emotional manipulation of *Eikon Basilike* is not a true rhetoric, which is to say that it is not true, since truth for Milton is rhetorical, understood and experienced as persuasive, deliberative, and moving.[101] A true rhetoric is a passionate reason that moves the public towards the truth. Yet, like the Catholics who were excluded from the public sphere envisioned in *Areopagitica*, *Eikon Basilike* must be silenced because its compassion is aimed at unifying a public against the public sphere and, hence, against the body that is debating and searching for the truth. Both Monmouth and Milton, ironically, attack the public rhetoric of their opponents on the grounds of passion and irrationality, but neither does so to exclude passion from reason. They want to find a passion that will be public, rational, and persuasive in an ethical way, though each define their ethics differently and each sets a different limit to the amount of political debate and conflict he can stomach.

Nonetheless, much as Wright's mission to win toleration for Catholics failed, so too did the attempt to forge a public sphere out of the English Civil War fail, at least in the short term. The grounds for productive conflict and mutual understanding were not found, and the revolution soon lapsed into reaction and restoration. The execution of Charles I marked a rupture in the ancient ideology that held English government together. With the king and monarchy dead, the challenge for the republicans was to establish, in essence, a new "paradigm of mutual understanding" in which something approaching democratic debate could lead to some sense of political unity. Habermas argues that such a public sphere of political criticism only came about in Britain as an outgrowth of capitalism, of the conflict of classes and economic interests.[102] Following Milton, I want to entertain an alternative notion. Milton attacks pity in *Eikon Basilike* because the compassion one feels for Charles destroys the public sphere of debate: it submits the people's free consciences to the conscience of the king and thus, to borrow a phrase from *Areopagitica,* "it extirpats all religions and civill supremacies." Feeling compassion is an infectious pleasure that brings one, as Samson says, "to love Bondage more than Liberty, / Bondage with ease than strenuous liberty."[103] What Milton leaves unexplored in *Eikonoklastes'* attack upon compassion is the question of whether there really is a communal, shared passion that, if reflected upon strenuously and critically, can help us form meaningful, noncoercive social bonds, a "bond of peace" that would sustain a "unity of spirit." This is the promise of early modern writings about compassion, but one that, as Milton points out, too often serves the interests of an unfree ideology: the bonds of compassion become the bonds of slavery. If we allow ourselves to feel those bonds, yet always remain critical of the powers that those contagious passions draw us to, perhaps we can, "hand in hand with wand'ring steps and slow," find freedom in compassion.[104]

PART II

Historical Phenomenology

Chapter 5
Melancholy Cats, Lugged Bears, and Early Modern Cosmology: Reading Shakespeare's Psychological Materialism Across the Species Barrier

Gail Kern Paster

Among the unsavory similes uttered by Prince Hal and Falstaff in their opening conversation in *1 Henry IV* occurs a thematically trivial but phenomenologically important exchange. Hal has proposed that Falstaff serve as hangman when he becomes king, to which the old knight responds with the declaration that he is melancholy, indeed proverbially so:

FALSTAFF. Well, Hal, well, and in some sort it jumps with my humor as well as wait-
    ing in the court, I can tell you.
PRINCE. For obtaining of suits?
FALSTAFF. Yea, for obtaining of suits, whereof the hangman hath no lean wardrobe.
    'Sblood, I am as melancholy as a gib cat or a lugg'd bear.
PRINCE. Or an old lion, or a lover's lute.
FALSTAFF. Yea, or the drone of a Lincolnshire bagpipe.
PRINCE. What sayest thou to a hare, or the melancholy of Moor-ditch?
FALSTAFF. Thou hast the most unsavory [similes] and art indeed the most compar-
    ative, rascalliest, sweet young prince. (1.2.69–81)[1]

Thanks to Harry Berger's pioneering work on the concealed and self-concealed motives complexly at work in the speech acts of these two characters, we find signs in this exchange of the intersubjective conspiracy between them as they begin to work their way towards the final rejection of Falstaff.[2] Each strives here to specify the quality of Falstaff's humor with a series of references to animals, sounds, and urban topography—the waste water of a city ditch. To apply Berger's terms, Falstaff makes a semi-serious, hence rhetorically and psychologically defended bid for Harry's sympathetic

Figure 5.1. Melancholy cat from Edward Topsell, *Historie of the Foure-Footed Beasts* (London, 1607). Reproduced by permission of the Folger Shakespeare Library.

attention to his needy state of mind and body by calling it melancholy and expanding its meaning through the implied narratives of pathetic similes.

In a sense, there should be nothing noteworthy about Falstaff's report of a low mood, either as predictable response to the prospect of such a degrading post as executioner (even with its benefit of hanged men's clothing) or as a prognostication of aging. In Galenic humoralism, old men were expected to be melancholy because the aging process lowered the body's heat and evaporated its radical moisture, producing the coldness and dryness associated with the melancholic humor.[3] But Falstaff seeks notice by likening himself not just proverbially to a cat but to a (probably) gelded one, perhaps as a sign of sexual loss or injury.[4] He adds the baited bear, perhaps as a sign of anxiety about future persecution at the hands of authority, since the bear is being lugged—pulled—to the baiting ring.[5] Hal initially accedes to Falstaff's attempt at pathos with his complementary additions of the old lion, the lover's lute, and the hare—all objects, editors suggest, proverbially associated with melancholy.[6] But the prince's final rhetorical turn to the differentiating undifference of excrement seems meant to be conclusively deflating—the first of many withering figurative references to the contents of Falstaff's mind and body. Falstaff's refusal to continue the contest at this point and complain instead about the unsavoriness of the Prince's similes suggests that he accepts the analogy between his mood and city drainage—not necessarily as accurate, but as a limit case of comparison.[7]

Even for Harry Berger, there *might* be nothing more to say about this exchange as part of the conspiratorial performances of Falstaff as self-dramatizing seducer and Hal as his victim. For my purposes, however, the phenomenological linkages in this series provide an unusual form of access to early modern self-experience. Casual though his reference may seem, Falstaff's comparison of his melancholy to that of cat or bear depends for its intelligibility upon three interrelated presuppositions of Renaissance cosmology. The first is that the simple hydraulic model which governed early modern psychology was based, as Katharine Park puts it, "on a clear localisation of psychological function by organ or system of organs."[8] The second is that the four humors of bile, black bile, phlegm, and blood were not confined to the human body but were instead distributed differentially to all those creatures possessing a heart and blood.[9] And the third is that the emotions were also shared by humans and animals, thanks to their common possession of a sensitive soul. Falstaff's self-proclaimed affinity with cat and bear rests upon this hierarchy of the soul. In its highest form, soul was defined by Aristotelian philosophers as "the life principle of the individual body—that which differentiated living from non-living things" and divided hierarchically into three parts. The lowest, the vegetative soul common to plants and animals, was responsible for growth, nutrition, and generation; the highest, the intellective soul unique to human beings, governed intellect, will, and memory. In between came the sensitive soul which controlled perceptual, motive, and appetitive faculties.[10] As the English Jesuit Thomas Wright explained in 1604, "Those actions . . . which are common with vs, and beasts we call Passions, and Affections, or perturbations of the mind."[11]

Recognizing the logic—the cosmologic—embedded in Falstaff's comparison to cat and bear has, I want to argue, profound consequences for the history of the early modern subject. Recent scholarship has asked us to recognize psychological materialism as one basis for conceptualizing historically different self-experience. Michael Schoenfeldt praises humoral discourse for its "seductive coherence," "its experiential suppleness," and its "remarkable capacity to relate the body to its environment, and to explain the literal influences that flow into it from a universe composed of analogous elements."[12] Katharine Maus points out that in vernacular writing of the period "the whole interior of the body—heart, liver, womb, bowels, kidneys, gall, blood, lymph—quite often involves itself in the production of the mental interior, of the individual's private experience."[13] My own work has tried to enforce an "interpretive literalism" on locutions of bodily self-experience, since what is "bodily or emotional figuration for us, preserved metaphors of somatic consciousness, was the literal stuff of physiological theory for early modern scriptors of the body."[14] As these comments imply, scholarship has thus far confined itself to the body's humoral contribution to the construction of individual subjectivity. None of us has described how consciousness in the humoral body might actually function in relation to the analogously constructed universe or recognized how subjectivity in the humoral body is regularly breached and penetrated by its phenomenological environment. To the picture of the humoral body as a "semipermeable, irrigated container in which humors moved sluggishly," we need to add an epistemically nuanced picture of humoral subjectivity in similar terms—as a form of consciousness that is open, penetrable, fluid, and extended outwards to the higher animals with whom it shared affective workings.[15] The mental interior of the individual subject, so understood, begins to seem less bounded and contained than in prior accounts, less opposed to the world outside. If, as Shigehisa Kuriyama has written, "The history of the body is ultimately a history of ways of inhabiting the world," then what is true of the history of the body must also be true for consciousness.[16] Humoral subjectivity becomes recognizable as a form of consciousness inhabited by, even as it inhabits, a universe composed of analogous elements.

The similes exchanged between Falstaff and the Prince in the passage quoted above suggest, therefore, why it will not do to recognize the psychological materialism of the individual human subject unless we also interrogate the place that psychological materialism has in the analogical network of early modern ontology. In the hydraulic humoral model of psychology, a great many of the body's organ systems and hence the bodily fluids produced by them belonged not just to human beings but to animals as well. It follows that humans and animals must share in the psychological consequences—the self-experience—of possessing them. But as Prince Hal's caustic reference to Moorditch suggests, we will need also to understand what humans and animals share with the inanimate realm of objects. Rather than a proverbial set of loose associations, the simile contest constructs an epistemic set, a natural class, that places Falstaff's aging body in a particular analogical relation to its physical environment—one composed of animals, sounds, and elemental liquids, all of which would be accepted by an early modern audience as literally (if maybe laughably) describable in terms of melancholy. Clearly this exchange reveals difference in ways of knowing about and feeling oneself related to the physical world, a difference which Charles Taylor has explained as a key to the history of subject-object relations:

> Melancholia is black bile. That's what it means. Today we might think of the relationship expressed in this term as a psycho-physical causal one. An excess of the substance, black bile, in our system, tends to bring on melancholy. . .[But] there is an important difference between this account and the traditional theory of humours. On the earlier view, black bile doesn't just cause melancholy; melancholy somehow resides *in it*. The substance embodies the significance. . . . Black bile produces melancholy feelings, because these manifest what it is, its ontic-logical status.[17]

But Taylor's comment, while provisionally useful for thinking about early modern human melancholy, does not take us much closer to an understanding of the melancholy common to cats, bears, lions, lutes, bagpipes, and sewage ditches. For this, we need to remember the building blocks of the ancient macrocosm still durable in early modern Europe: the elements of earth, water, fire, and air and the qualities of cold, wet, hot, and dry with which they were linked. The elements and the qualities combined in various ways and degrees to constitute the particular, objectively real properties of all matter, animate and inanimate alike.[18] In these correspondences—as we have endlessly been told—lower forms of life were expressed and contained in the higher forms. As Bacon noted, "there is no nature which can be regarded as simple; every one seeming to participate and be compounded of two. Man has something of the brute; the brute has something of the vegetable; the vegetable something of the inanimate body; and so all things are in truth biformed and made up of a higher species and a lower."[19] The cosmic chain reached its highest earthly expression in man, the paragon of animals, "the Epitome or Abstract of the whole world, in whom something of every thing (to speak Platonically and yet truly) is placed and inserted."[20] But the lower levels were expressive too: the humor melancholy to be found in human and other living bodies was analogically linked to the earth through their shared properties of cold and dry.[21] Old men such as Falstaff, by losing radical heat and moisture and thus becoming subject to an increase of melancholy in their bodies, approached earth qualitatively even as they approached the deaths that would return them to it. As Hamlet explains to Horatio, "Alexander died, Alexander was buried, Alexander returneth to dust, the dust is earth, of earth we make loam, and why of that loam whereto he was converted might they not stop a beer-barrel?" (5.1.208–12). But melancholy, as well as signaling the cold, dry, retentive behavior of old age (retentiveness being perhaps another reason for Hal to imagine Falstaff coveting the clothing of the condemned), could also be a byproduct of the body's processes of internal combustion. "Melancholy adust" represented the cold, dry ashes—the soot—of a body's excessive heat, consumed by the expenditure of choleric humors and the agitation of the body's spirits.[22] Melancholy adust explains the aftereffects of spent rage, the melancholy of warriors or men younger and more active than sedentary Falstaff. Melancholy in this form especially was bodily waste, ominously darkening the color of the body's other fluids and spirits and clogging their flow. In *The Terrors of the Night*, Thomas Nashe likens "the thick steaming fenny vapours" of bodily melancholy to waste water: "even as slime and dirt in a standing puddle engender toads and frogs and many other unsightly creatures, so this slimie melancholy humour, still still [sic] thickening as it stands still, engendreth many misshapen objects in our imaginations."[23] This analogy explains the Prince's deflating comparison of Falstaff's mood—understood not in post-Enlightenment terms as a disembodied mental event but rather as the feelings "somehow" residing in congealed bodily liquid stored in heart and mind—to what Sugden calls the city's "depository of all kinds of filth and rubbish."[24]

The doctrine of natural correspondences also adds epistemic significance to the other references in this series, especially perhaps Falstaff's self-comparison to the melancholy of the gib cat. As editors suggest, cats' howling and nocturnal habits would have associated them with melancholy; but here, as elsewhere in this schema, the analogies multiply and deepen. In naturalist Edward Topsell's entry on the cat in his *Historie of the Four-Footed Beastes*, for example, feline melancholy explains the animal's coloration: "Cats are of diuers colours, but for the most part gryseld, like to congealed yse, which commeth from the condition of her meate."[25] Using inductive reasoning born of the thermal classifications of Aristotelian biology, Topsell describes melancholy as a physical attribute reciprocal with the extreme coldness of the cat's flesh.[26] This coldness, which constitutes, saturates, and explains feline being, expresses itself in what Topsell sees as the ice-like streaks and patterns of its parti-colored fur since fur, being an excrement, is necessarily characteristic of the flesh from which it grew. For Topsell, a cat's vocalizations, being its natural language, were also biologically based, but nonetheless affecting, its "voyce, hauing as many tunes as turnes." He writes of male cats' wildness "in the time of their lust" who "at that time (except they be gelded) will not keepe the house: at which time they haue a peculiar direfull voyce."[27] As with Falstaff, a cat's melancholy is a humor—hence a temperature, a temperament, a disposition, and a liquid of specific consistency organizing its relations to the world. Melancholy produces a cat's way of being no less than—and by virtue of—the temperature of its flesh.[28] The rutting cat's direful sounds and nocturnal habits link it to the nighttime sounds of the doleful lover playing his lute, while—in a self-deprecating move on Falstaff's part—comparison to the Lincolnshire bagpipe may link both cat and knight to the vanity and verbal flatulence which bagpipes shared, figuratively, with "an inflated and senseless talker, a windbag."[29]

The latter moralistic association, moreover, suggests how easily ostensibly neutral biological discourse inmixes with the overdeterminations of Aesopian moral discourse.[30] Thus in the poetic fable of Adamic creation in the Third Eclogues of Sidney's *Arcadia*, the cat joins in with the other animals who must donate an attribute toward God's shaping of the human ruler they all think they desire. These faculties seem variously physical, behavioral, and affective: the lion gives heart, the sparrow "lust to play"; the bear offers climbing, the elephant "a perfect memory; / And parrot, ready tongue." The stag "did give the harm-eschewing fear" and the cat "his melancholy."[31] Behaviorally, the cat's donation of a useful part of its character would seem more ethical than physical, on a par with the stag's contribution of fear rather than with the physical or mental capacities donated by bear, parrot, or elephant. But classification here is conceptually more elusive than that, and more telling of the analogical thought underlying Hal and Falstaff's similes. Cat melancholy—Sidney's fable suggests—is both originary and exemplary, part of the natural order, a property the cat in its splenetic abundance may decide to bequeath. Melancholy locates the cat metonymically, just as it locates Falstaff, in a determinate place in relation to a host of other things, animate and inanimate, natural and human. In *I Henry IV* these melancholic things are reposited in the retentive waters of Moorditch.

It is cosmological fixing, then, that gives the series of similes its epistemic weight in the construction of humoral subjectivity. Hal and Falstaff have begun their dialogue postulating a periphrastic ability to rename—and in so doing, to remake—the nature of reality: "Marry, then, sweet wag, when thou art king, let not us that are squires of the night's body be call'd thieves of the day's beauty" (1.2.23–25).[32] Their turn to the proverbs of melancholy, however, offers a limit to the world-making capacities of the motivated word, for simile fixes both participants in analogical relationships founded in a theoretically immutable, emblematic order. "To know the peacock," William Ashworth has said of this cosmology, "you must know its associations—its affinities, its similitudes, and sympathies with the rest of the created order."[33] The process was one of discovery of what was already there, as Thomas Wilson explained: "Therefore those that delite to prove thynges by similitudes, must learne to knowe the nature of diverse beastes, of metalles, of stones and al suche."[34] As with peacocks, so with cats; and so too with Falstaff and the bagpipe—which is precisely why the final move to Moorditch is felt to be so contaminating. For these associations are grounded in the pre-modern doctrine of sympathies and correspondences, what John Sutton has nicely described as "the nested system of spirits in the cosmos, the environment, the human body, and in inanimate objects."[35] Natural sympathy, that bond of likeness which drew like things together in forces of mutual attraction and pulled unlike things apart, explained, for example, the soul's receptivity to music and to sounds generally, as Thomas Moffett points out: "the very noise of bells, guns, Trumpets, breaketh the clouds, . . . Musick it self, cureth the brain of madness, and the heart of melancholy."[36] What I want to draw attention to, then, are the historical possibilities lodged in the analogy between the cat's melancholy and Falstaff's. Not only does the elemental nature of cat melancholy support the elemental embodiment of Falstaff's, but the playful spinning out of melancholy's forms into animals, musical instruments, and sewage ditches emphasizes how broadly the passions were thought to be distributed as a sensible feature of a natural world traversed by a host of sympathies and antipathies. In this sense, Falstaff's comparison of his mood to a cat's may be self-interested, but it is not sentimental. It serves less to project and objectify human melancholy outward through the familiar procedures of anthropomorphism than to introject the natural, God-given self-sameness of cat melancholy—expressed in flesh and fur and howling—into an emotionally justified, ethically naturalized, and humorally subjectified Falstaff.[37] Sidney's archetypal cat has donated its melancholy to that representative of fallen man, that offending Adam, Sir John Falstaff.

A similar movement of self-justification through reference to animal affect occurs in *Macbeth* when the beleaguered usurper, his castle surrounded by his enemies, likens himself to a baited bear: "They have tied me to a stake," Macbeth says to himself, "I cannot fly, / But bear-like I must fight the course" (*Macbeth*, 5.7.1–2). Earlier he had berated a fearful servant for his bird-like pallor—"The devil damn thee black, thou cream-fac'd loon! / Where got'st thou that goose-look?" (5.3.11–12)—in contrast to his own (increasingly desperate) claims to fearlessness born of the witches' prophecies: "The mind I sway by, and the heart I bear, / Shall never sag with doubt, nor shake with fear" (5.3.9–10). Here, Macbeth's reference to the bear begins with a likeness in physical circumstance—"they have tied me to a stake"— at the hands of persecuting humans and moves metatheatrically towards more complex trajectories of identification and fantasy.[38] Like the bear in the baiting arena met by waves of attacking mastiffs, Macbeth enters onstage alone to meet the first encounter with his human attackers—here Young Siward, whom he easily defeats before facing more ferocious onslaughts. One effect of his simile is oddly distancing: to make Macbeth's defeat, though predictable, not certain (bears customarily survived the dogs' attacks and were baited again).[39] But, because it is spoken by Macbeth about himself in relation to an environment made up of surrounding humans, the simile's larger effects draw us into his state of mind—serving not to bestialize him but rather, as phenomenological figuration, to convey the heightened texture of his self-experience, his determination to quell panic and "fight the course." In its expression of beleagerment and compulsion, its objectification of the human opponent as animal-Other to the bear as fantasy-Self, the simile insists upon Macbeth's identification with the bear as the subject of its own heroic drama—desiring flight but unable to attain it, constrained to conduct its battle for self-preservation within the limits of its chain and the spectatorial circuits of the arena. The bear's conscious experience of terror, moreover, would have been understood as entailing a transformation in its flesh. As Thomas Moffett notes, animals' flesh was thought to change with their experiences and the character of their affects:

Patrocles affirmed, that a Lion being shewed to a strong Bull three or four hours before he be killed; causeth his flesh to be as tender as the flesh of a Steer: fear dissolving his hardest parts and making his very heart to become pulpy. Perhaps upon the like reason we use to bait our Bulls before we kill them: for their blood is otherwise so hard, that none can digest it in the flesh, but afterwards . . . it becometh tender and nourishing food.[40]

Similar thinking, we should remember, underlies Lear's anguish about how the practices of cruelty might have transformed the flesh of his daughters: "Is there any cause in nature that make these hard hearts?" (3.6.77–78).

It is thus important to recognize the bear's experience, in seventeenth-century terms, as exemplary of the passions, human and animal, insofar as the passions were understood as a primary instrument of self-preservation comparable to what elsewhere in the natural order promoted the stability of inanimate objects. As Wright explains,

God, the author of nature, and imparter of all goodnesse, hath printed in euery creature, ...an inclination, faculty, or power to conserue it selfe, procure what it needeth, to resist and impugne whatsoeuer hindereth it of that appertaineth unto his good and conseruation. So we see fire continually ascendeth upward, because the coldnesse of the water, earth, and ayre much impeacheth the vertue of his heate; . . . the Hare flieth from the Hounds, the Partridge hideth her selfe from the talon of the Hawke.[41]

The bear's passion for self-preservation justifies and naturalizes Macbeth's; the bear's passion is subsumed into and equated with Macbeth's own: "bear-like I must fight the course."

Stephen Dickey has argued that Elizabethan spectators were amused by animal-baiting spectacles, citing contemporary testimony of "great amusement," "good contentment," and unspeakable "pleasure."[42] But recognition of the deep transformations wrought by fear on the flesh of bull, bear, or human in the passage from Moffett cited above works to complicate this too-simple picture of callousness. Insofar as Macbeth's simile works to draw us into identification with his terror and defiance, we are also drawn into a fantasy projection of animal selfhood—led imaginatively beyond the boundaries of isolate human subjectivity into the wilder territory of an animal's suffering and its desire for mere survival.[43] Together, the baited bear and

Macbeth represent something like what Deleuze and Guattari have denominated a "Body without Organs"—a "*field of immanence* of desire, the *plane of consistency* specific to desire."[44] In this conception of a Body without Organs, the body's desires are neither localized nor named. The human body organized by Western epistemologies into a sex, a morphology, a subjectivity, a surface and depth, and a central place in the natural order is replaced by a dynamic entity of intensities and flows, a body conceived simply as a unit of matter in time, a body desiring its own continuance and the satisfaction of its appetites.[45] For the early moderns, of course, desire was only possible in a Body *with* Organs, but their understanding resembles that of Deleuze and Guattari in that the fluids emanating from those organs to produce desire saturated animate flesh even as they flooded and changed a creature's heart and mind.

As Falstaff's and Macbeth's self-comparisons to animals suggest, identification across the species barrier was compelling because it seemed both to reinforce affective self-experience and offer an escape from it into the imagined self-sameness of animal passion. For my purposes, such similes have particular significance as evidence for the early modern conception of the sensitive soul as governing a subject's appetites and emotions. Joint possession of the sensitive soul, as I noted earlier, constituted the essential similarity between humans and animals.[46] In the emotions, human and animal beings had their earliest and most basic of survival skills, their fundamental orientations of aversion and desire, flight and attraction: "These passions then be certaine internall acts or operations of the soule, bordering vpon reason and sense, prosecuting some good thing, or flying some ill thing, causing therewithall some alteration in the body."[47] The passions, located between "reason and sense," were not identical to the bodily humors, but the two were closely allied in their workings, teleological function, and significance. As Wright explains,

> me thinkes the passions of our minde, are not vnlike the four humours of bodies, . . . for if blood, pflegme, choller, or melancholy exceed the due proportion required to the constitution and health of our bodies, presently we fall into some disease: euen so, if the passions of the Minde be not moderated according to reason (and that temperature vertue requireth) immediatly the soule is molested with some maladie.[48]

This similarity explains not only how passions could originate within the body and then express themselves externally but also how a body's reaction, whether to an external stimulus acting upon the senses or to an internal prompting of memory or imagination, necessarily entailed the humors:

First then, to our imagination commeth by sense or memorie, some obiect to be knowne, . . . the which being knowne . . . in the imagination which resideth in the former part of the braine, . . . presently the purer spirits, flocke from the brayne, by certaine secret channels to the heart, where they pitch at the dore, signifying what an obiect was presented, conuenient or disconuenient for it. The heart immediatly bendeth, either to prosecute it, or to eschew it: and the better to effect that affection, draweth other humours to helpe him, and so in pleasure concurre great store of pure spirits; in pain and sadnesse, much melancholy blood; in ire, blood and choller.[49]

Though Wright does not say so, this description of how human passions worked in relation to the recognition of external sense objects would also have applied, necessarily, to the workings of animal passion—and to the changes in animal fluids and flesh that such passions brought about. It was obvious to him that animals, like humans, recognized and remembered what was good or bad for them; both kinds were animate creatures endowed with a heart, the passions' seat: "all passions may be distinguished by the dilatation, enlargement, or diffusion of the heart: and the contraction, collection, or compression of the same."[50] Common possession of the heart guaranteed that "men and beasts with one appetite"—meaning with a delimited appetite (here, the concupiscible appetite) and a shared appetite—"prosecute the good they desire and with an other they flie the euill they abhor."[51]

But in the comparative workings of hearts and emotions, differences between human and animal become almost as meaningful as similarities. In Renaissance natural philosophy, animals played a key role heuristically in the early modern production of practical knowledge about the passions. In beings lacking the constraint of reason—it was thought—the passions were at their purest, most intense, and most visible. "Wee may best discouer [them] in children," says Wright,

because they lacke the vse of reason and are guided by an internall imagination, following nothing else but that pleaseth their senses, euen after the same maner as bruit beasts do: for as we see beasts hate, loue, feare and hope, so doe children.[52]

Thus, while Falstaff in a calculated bid for sympathy might report feeling melancholy without actually being so and even perform the bodily dejection associated with that self-report, his feline counterpart could not. Cat melancholy might be expressed by howling or the color of fur, but it could not be falsified or used promotionally to deceive. Cat melancholy—being incapable either of sincerity or insincerity—is for the same reason self-present, self-identical, a form of animal plenitude, a feature of the flesh. This is also why cat melancholy is more generic than individualizing: in the discourse of proverbs and natural history alike, animal traits such as humors and passions tend to belong to the species rather than being unique expressions of and by an individual member. Indeed, it is precisely this tendency away from the individual and toward the generic which marks a paradoxical tension in the conversation between Hal and Falstaff: even as they seek to particularize the facts or fictions about Falstaff's melancholy, they extend that melancholy outward to its likenesses in the world and move it closer to the fecal undifference of Moorditch.

Where Falstaff and Macbeth most closely approximate the early modern philosophical discussions of animal emotions is in their desire to understand their emotions as like animals' in being exemplary and thereby emblematically meaningful. Indeed early modern taxonomies of the passions are virtually unthinkable without the examples for both animal and human cognition provided by the physiology of animal emotion and its behavioral effects. (As Levi-Strauss famously remarked, animals are important to human classifications not so much because they are good to eat as because they are good to think with.)[53] In English moral philosophy, the *locus classicus* of animal exemplarity is probably to be found in Wright's discussion of the eleven primary emotions experienced by wolf and sheep as they recognize each other as objects of fear and desire:

First, the Wolfe loueth the flesh of the Sheep; then he desireth to haue it; thirdly, he reioyceth in his prey when he hath gotten it: Contrariwise, the Sheepe hateth the Wolfe as an euill thing in himselfe, and thereupon detesteth him, as hurtfull to herselfe; and finally, if the Wolfe seaze vpon her, she paineth and grieueth to become his prey: thus we haue loue, desire, delight, hatred, abhomination, griefe, or heauinesse, the six passions or our coueting appetite.[54]

But Wright is less interested in the uncomplicated emotions of the fearful sheep than in what he represents as the complex emotional texture of the wolf's experience as it confronts obstacles to the fulfillment of its desire in the shepherd and his dogs:

then the Wolfe, fearing the difficulty of purchasing his prey, yet thinking the euent, though doubtfull, not impossible, then he erecteth himselfe with the passion of Hope, perswading him the sheepe shall be his future spoyle after the conquest: and thereupon contemning the dogges, despising the shepheard, . . . with a bold and audacious courage, not regarding any daunger; hee setteth vpon the flocke; where, in the first assault, presently a mastife pincheth him by the legge; the iniurie he imagineth ought not to be tollerated: but immediatly inflamed with the passion of Ire, procureth by all meanes possible to reuenge it: the Shepheard protecteth his dog, and basteth the Wolfe . . . The Wolfe perceiuing himself weaker then he imagined, & his enemies stronger than he conceiued, falleth sodainly into the passion of Feare, (as braggers doe, who vaunt much at the beginning, but quaile commonly in the middle of the fray) yet not abandoned of all hope of the victory; therefore he stirreth vp himselfe, and proceedth forward; but in fine, receiuing more blowes of the shepheard, more woundes of the dogges, awearied with fighting, fearing his life, thinking the enterprise impossible, oppressed with the passion of Desperation, resolueth himselfe that his heeles are a surer defence, than his teeth . . . By this example we may collect the other fiue passions of the inuading appetite, hope, boldnesse or presumption, anger or ire, feare and Desperation.[55]

In this mock-heroic agon, Wright throws himself without a trace of anthropomorphic embarrassment in the wolf's drama. He underscores the animal's emotional progression from hope to defeat by infusing it with a full-blown stylistic apparatus—the extended syntactic parallelisms of the verb forms as the wolf circles his prey; the elevated heroic diction of spite, contempt, audaciousness, and revenge; the exaggerated trajectory of the rise to combat and fall into retreat. The result is to produce a dynamic subject position for the wolf and to make those of the shepherd and his dogs almost entirely inadmissible. Immersion in the wolf's point of view produces a set of clearly cognitive, even metacognitive activities activated by and activating changes in the wolf's emotions as he appraises, reappraises, and decides how he feels about developments in his *Umwelt*.[56] Even more important, this account of lupine emotions is less the result of anthropomorphic thinking than it is an example of early modern fluid physiology at work in the behavior of animals and humans alike. In physiological terms, what animate the wolf's recognition of its environment, dictate its assessment of opportunity and peril, and govern its responses to what it desires or fears are the spirits which move along the neural pathways from the wolf's brain out to its body and back; these are the "purer spirits" that, according to Wright, "flocke from the brayne, by certaine secret channels to the heart." What this account does not do (perhaps cannot do) is to separate the wolf's affective responses from his cognitive appraisals because, for Wright as for other early modern thinkers on the passions, affects are by definition bodily states—psychophysiological responses to perceived changes in the environment.[57] The wolf weighs the pros and cons of the attack, persuades himself to go forward, thinks the event not impossible, regards not his danger, imagines his injury intolerable, perceives "himself weaker than he imagined, &

his enemies stronger than he conceiued." In wolf consciousness (as in human, this account implies), affects produce cognitive changes and cognitive changes produce affective responses. Thus, as the event approaches its climax and denouement, the signifiers of emotional and cognitive experience—"aweared with fighting, fearing his life, thinking the enterprise impossible"—thicken and superpose themselves.

What is important to recognize, in terms of an early modern history of the passions, is that Wright's account of the emotional origins of the wolf's behaviors is necessarily little different from his accounts of the emotional behaviors of a human being caught up in similar conflict between pursuit of an object of desire and avoidance of the obstacles to it. Insofar as Wright endows the wolf with self-in-the-act-of-knowing, he attributes to him not only what Antonio Damasio has called a core self, a "transient protagonist of consciousness," continuously generated in pulses by interactions with objects in the environment, but also with elements of what Damasio calls an autobiographical self, insofar as that involves the activation of memory.[58] For Wright, what seems to make the wolf's emotions expressively animal rather than characteristically human is the nature and, in a sense, the ethical neutrality of the object of its desire—sheep on the hoof, meat raw rather than cooked.[59] Even the suddenness of the wolf's change from hope to rage to defeat is paralleled in Wright's account (quoted earlier) of the suddenness with which the human heart responds—"immediatly bendeth"—to a stimulus from the "purer spirits."[60] The static melancholy of the proverbial cat has been superseded by the dynamic experience of an emotionally conflicted wolf caught between the affective poles of desire and aversion, hope and fear. The cat as humoral object—or perhaps subject *manqué*—has been succeeded by the wolf as humoral subject full-fledged.

Indeed the overlap between animal and human affect is critical to at least two of Wright's larger arguments in *The Passions of the Mind in General*: one, that the Aquinian taxonomy of eleven basic emotions is rooted in the natural order and governs the workings of the sensitive soul in all those creatures endowed with one; and two, that the great overlap between human and animal in the possession of the sensitive soul proves how hard it is for the rational soul to control the unruly passions when they fix on an object of desire and—in the space of a moment—inflame or dilate or contract the heart with their contrariety, their insatiability, their importunity, their impossibility: "There is no man in this life, which followeth the streame of his passions, but expecteth, and verily beleeueth to get at last a firme rest, contentation & full satiety of all his appetites: the which is as possible, as to quench fire with fuell, extinguish a burning Ague with hot wines, drowne an Eele with water."[61] Wright's wolf is not, therefore, a surrogate human being of the kind familiar in Aesopian fable but a "real," if hypothetical animal, whose rhetorical function here is to show what following the stream of one's passions might be like in a life-critical event, even one lasting only a few minutes. This way of thinking about animal behavior as driven "as if continually in a passion" is not unusual in itself.[62] What distinguishes Wright's wolf is that the workings of his passions are exemplary of our own. Because he has passions and a body, because he has a complex physiological apparatus for successfully appraising and reappraising the challenges of his environment, because his interaction with shepherd and dogs is profoundly social in its communication of moves and countermoves, Wright's wolf is indeed a humoral subject. The workings of his passions, by means of the spirits animating his neural pathways, give proof from the other side of the species barrier of what John Sutton has proposed of mind-body relations of the early modern human subject: "the body theorised by early modern neurophilosphers was never just an inert house for a ghostly soul. The body's fluids and spirits, and the traces it conceals, were always active, always escaping notice, always exceeding the domain of the will, always giving shape and flavour to the soul's plans."[63] The commitment of Wright to his humoral wolf, no less than of Macbeth to his subjectified bear, shows us why.

Clearly Wright's overall investment in Aquinas's taxonomy of the eleven primary passions determines his hyperbolic portrayal of lupine affect. But it owes less to anthropomorphism per se than to the doctrine of correspondences and sympathies, itself of course a doctrine decidedly anthropocentric by design. This is why his account of the affects has much in common with the animal affects described elsewhere in early modern behavioral thought. In Topsell's *Historie of the Foor-Footed Beastes*, there is not only significant continuity between human and animal emotions but also, as in Wright, a descriptive vocabulary in which ethical, physical, and psychophysiological discourses intermix. The result is a taxonomy of animals thoroughly moralized not in terms of their relations to men but in terms of their relations to each other, thanks to their own position on the analogical chain of sympathies, antipathies, and correspondences, and the various qualities that their bodies and minds possess. For Topsell, as for other early modern thinkers, it was not just that the qualities of animals resembled those of human beings, but that those qualities were directly transferable from animal to human as humans applied and incorporated animal flesh into their own: "many beastes are vsed for meate, nourishment, and medicine, and for that cause are not only applied outwardly, but inwardly to the body of man ... for because of the similitude they carry with mankind in body and affections, they suffer many diseases in common with vs."[64]

In the communicability of affects and the similarity of diseases, we come full circle to the melancholy of gib cats and lugged bears but with a more eclectic appreciation of early modern psychological materialism. As I have tried to suggest, recognizing the humoral constitution of animals along with its affective entailments serves to widen the active scope of the passions well beyond the species barrier, extending the passions' salience out to the universe at large and underscoring the passions' ontological status in nature. Thus to embed humoral affectivity in the world is not to take it out of the body; rather, it is to deterritorialize it, to remap it, to extend it. How would it feel to experience one's own passions as part of the natural order and how would one speak that experience? While answering such questions would forever be beyond the scope of this or any other critical essay, traces of that phenomenological experience, I have been arguing, may be captured from time to time in Shakespearean and other contemporary texts. For such an enterprise, it is helpful to remember Linda Charnes's useful distinction between identity and subjectivity—identity being a relatively fixed and objective feature of social (and/or textual) being and subjectivity being the moment-to-moment experience of that identity.[65] In these terms, early modern identity contains a cosmological component that, as we have seen in Falstaff, fixes the individual through simile and makes him knowable in his affinities, his sympathies, his linkages. And in this model of humoral subjectivity, the early modern subject's passionate experience of self turns out to be a feelingly intimate transaction with world as well.

Chapter 6
English Mettle

Mary Floyd-Wilson

> Constable: . . . . Where have [the English] this mettle?
>   Is not their climate foggy, raw, and dull,
>   On whom as in despite the sun looks pale,
>   Killing their fruit with frowns? Can sodden water,
>   A drench for sur-reined jades—their barley-broth—
>   Decoct their cold blood to such valiant heat?
>   And shall our quick blood, spirited with wine,
>   Seem frosty? O, for honour of our land,
>   Let us not hang like roping icicles
>   Upon our houses' thatch, whiles a more frosty people
>   Sweat drops of gallant youth in our rich fields—
>   . . . .
> Dauphin: By faith and honour,
>   Our madams mock at us and plainly say
>   Our mettle is bred out, and they will give
>   Their bodies to the lust of English youth,
>   To new-store France with bastard warriors.
>
> —Henry V, 3.5.15–31

In *Henry V*, the French are stunned by the English soldiers' fortitude.[1] Having expected an easy victory, the French Constable exclaims, in astonishment, "Where have [the English] this mettle?" This is one of a series of questions I aim to answer in this essay. What can we learn about this "mettle" which will expand our capacity to interpret early modern passions—that is, to historicize emotion? Is there something particularly "early modern" about mettle in *Henry V*? And what does mettle have to do with the ethnological distinctions represented, and under construction, in the play and in English culture—distinctions implied by the Constable's assumption that the French should have more mettle than the English? The play gives us hints that its representation of emotion is inseparable from early modern conceptions of ethnicity.

Then and now, "mettle" means the quality of one's temperament and usually denotes a particularly spirited and courageous nature. Mettle is rarely the property of the elite or refined. Tamburlaine has mettle.[2] But Hamlet's

NEXT *Choller* ſtandes, reſembling moſt the fire,
Of ſwarthie yeallow, and a meager face;
With Sword a late, vnſheathed in his Ire:
Neere whome, there lies, within a little ſpace,
A ſterne ei'de Lion, and by him a ſheild,
Charg'd with a flame, vpon a crimſon ſeild.

We paint him young, to ſhew that paſſions raigne,
The moſt in heedles, and vnſtaied youth:
That Lion ſhowes, he ſeldome can refraine,
From cruell deede, devoide of gentle ruth:
Or hath perhaps, this beaſt to him aſſign'd,
As bearing moſt, the braue and bounteous mind.

T.2.   *Phlegma*

Figure 6.1. Emblem of choler from Henry Peacham, *Minerva Britanna* (1612), Folger Shakespeare Library. Reproduced by permission of the Folger Shakespeare Library. As the accompanying poem explains, the unsheathed sword signifies ire; the lion represents both unrestrained cruelty and a "brave and bounteous mind."

mettle is muddied.[3] In Philip Massinger's *A Very Woman* (performed 1634), a slave's estimable worth lies in the "activeness" and "fire" of his "mettle."[4] To situate this word in *Henry V*, we should recall its derivation from "metal"—of arms and armor—a derivation that gives it the substantive connotation of the durable "'stuff' of which a man is made."[5] In nonanthropomorphic terms, mettle is an earthy matter akin to resilient mineral deposits or metallic ore buried in the ground. We should keep this elemental sense of mettle in mind when we consider its emotional implications. Indeed, it will be one of my assertions that the mettle in early modern bodies has more than a metaphorical relationship to the elements of the natural world. Gail Kern Paster has reminded us that the Renaissance natural world was a "network of analogy" wherein the world inhabits the body, and "human passions . . . take on an elemental force and character contingent upon a . . . set of correspondences between inner and outer worlds."[6] Taking a cue from this statement, I propose we assess the materiality of human mettle. How is it akin to the durable substances that lie in the veins of the earth?

In *The Passions of the Minde in Generall* (1604), a handbook on rhetoric and the management of one's emotions, Thomas Wright explains that depending on the physical composition of a person, the texture of any passion will vary. This composition is characterized by non-animate elements:

> divers sorts of persons be subject to divers sorts of passions, and the same passion affecteth divers persons in divers manners: for, as we see fire applied to drie wood, to yron, to flaxe and gunpowder, worketh divers wayes; for in wood it kindleth with some difficultie, and with some difficultie is quenched; but in flaxe soone it kindleth, and quencheth; in yron with great difficultie it is kindled, & with as great exteinguished, but in gunpowder it is kindled in a moment, and never can be quenched till the powder be consumed.[7]

Just like iron, people with mettle are not easily kindled, and neither are they easily extinguished. They do not ignite with every little spark, but when they blaze with valor, they burn long and steadily, without the self-consumption of gunpowder.[8] While "courageous" might describe a person's disposition, "mettle" is not a tendency toward certain emotions.[9] Mettle pertains instead to the physiological property that determines the initiation, experience, and duration of an impassioned state.

It is in his preface that Wright makes clear he has ethnic interests in the study of emotion, for he presents his work as a kind of handbook for his own English countrymen, whom he characterizes as impressible, imprudent, and emotionally naïve. As northerners, affected by a cold climate and their distance from the continent, Wright's English are barbaric and easily moved. They are unlike the more southern Spaniards and Italians whom he grudgingly admires as wary, circumspect, and controlled.[10] Wright is not unique. Ethnicity in the early modern period is defined more by emotional differences than by appearance: distinctions rest on how easily one is stirred or calmed—on one's degree of emotional vulnerability or resistance—or one's capacity to move others.[11] As we shall see, *Henry V* is aimed at representing the English people's temperament in such a way that it challenges their unflattering status in this emotional discourse.

Wright's thesis that the environment determines temperament is a Renaissance commonplace with classical roots. Shakespeare's French Constable draws on this same knowledge when he wonders how England's "foggy," "raw," and "dull" climate can produce "valiant heat" in its people's blood. He had expected, instead, that the English would possess "cold blood" and prove a "frosty people." The Constable assumes that the natural elements of the north are mirrored in the internal elements of its natives. And he bases this assumption on the authoritative ethnological discourse in the period— regionally framed humoralism—or what I call "geohumoralism."

In the broadest sense, geohumoralism is a name for the ways in which the humoral body is shaped by the six Galenic "non-naturals," those components that one can regulate to help ensure good health or temperance: air, exercise and rest, sleep and waking, food and drink, repletion and excretion, and the passions.[12] In questioning from whence the English have "mettle," the Constable indicates that at least two of the non-naturals—air and diet—have the force to instill, quicken, (or make leaden), mettle in a people. He is not only puzzled as to how foggy England could generate valiant blood, but he also wonders why the French lack mettle, given that they drink blood-quickening wine (as opposed to English barley broth).

Thus, to expand our conception of early modern ethnic distinctions, the basis of difference is not only how passions are experienced, but also what air people breathe, how quickly they move, whether they sweat, etc. Clearly we are not talking about fixed racial categories here, for the non-naturals can be manipulated to alter a person's temperament and appearance. At the same time, there are certain basic tendencies that differentiate a northern man from a southern one. We might say that cold air, a diet of beef, excess ale, heated movement, heavy sleep, bodies replete with humors, and volatile passions all construct our typical early modern Englishman. But to put it another way, the six non-naturals can also be understood as the ways in which the self (the microcosm) transacts with the world (the macrocosm). Whether we classify the non-naturals as environmental, physical, or psychological conditions, they are interactive. They move elements in and out of the relatively contained person (air, food and drink, repletion and excretion); they characterize one's movement *through* the world (exercise and rest), or one's *consciousness* of the world (sleep and waking). They can blur or harden the boundaries between inner and outer, body and world. And ethnic distinctions, I am suggesting, rest on measurements of *how* the self interacts with the world: the degree to which one is open or detached, leaky or replete, languid or alert.

But to view the *passions* as ecological may be most difficult for us to grasp as post-Cartesian readers. Air and diet are recognizably environmental, as are repletion and excretion. Exercise, rest, sleep, and waking all emphasize the physiological—bodies in motion, bodies breathing, bodies being nourished, etc. But the passions seem to be the odd men out, for we understand emotion as internal, or part of our self, and not as an ecological or physiological force that moves in and out of the body. And yet early modern passions do cross the self's shifting and fluid boundaries. The heart dilates or constricts in response to certain stimuli. When the emotions are stirred, people are moved to act or withdraw. Indeed, some early moderns construed the passions as residual environmental impressions, originally induced by an ecology that undermines any conception a solid, static, or contained self.[13]

As my brief discussion of Wright indicates, the English, as northerners, are at an emotional disadvantage due to the nature of their environment. But geohumoralism is a contradictory discourse, easily subject to ideological manipulation and discursive rearrangement. We are, for example, to take away from *Henry V* that the French are wrong about their assessment of the English temperament. The Constable's ethnological knowledge (though he may not know the source) is derived from Hippocrates' *Airs, Waters, Places*, an ancient medical text that establishes an analogous relationship between bodies and weather through its discussion of Scythian tribes in the frigid north:

The people differ little in physique as they always eat similar food, wear the same clothes winter and summer, breath moist thick air, drink water from snow and ice and do no hard work. The body cannot become hardened where there are such small variations in climate; the mind, too, becomes sluggish. . . . The cavities of their bodies are extremely moist, especially the belly, since, in a country of such nature and under such climatic conditions, the bowels cannot be dry.[14]

Hippocrates' Scythians do not simply resemble their environment, they are the loose and baggy embodiments of that environment. If constituted in these terms, then, the English should be porous, dull, lethargic, cold, and wet.

Early modern writers prove well-versed in Hippocrates' theories and, though they had particular quarrels with his conclusions, they tended to apply his descriptions generally to northern Europeans, including the English. The Spanish physician, Juan Huarte writes in *The Examination of Mens Wits* (1594), for example, "True it is *Hippocrates* saith, . . . [those] who live under the North, as are the English, Flemmish, and Almains springeth, . . . their whitnesse is parched up with much cold."[15] It is by way of Hippocrates' influence on early modern ethnography that "Scythian" came to denote the archetypal northerner. As embodiments of their environment, Hippocrates' Scythians may remind us of Mikhail Bakhtin's description of the Rabelaisian grotesque body, which is "not separated from the world by clearly defined boundaries."[16] We have learned from the work of Peter Stallybrass and Gail Kern Paster how Bakhtin's class-inflected opposition between the open, leaky, grotesque and the closed, finished, classical body has explanatory power for Renaissance constructions of gender.[17] And Hippocrates' characterization of Scythian men and women corresponds with the early modern assumption that women are the natural grotesques. Among the Scythians both sexes, Hippocrates observes, are cold, wet, smooth and hairless: they are "the most effeminate race of all mankind."[18]

What Hippocrates helps us see is the significance of Bakhtin's paradigm for the conception of somatic and temperamental differences that generates the Constable's question—those of ethnicity. And Bakhtin himself gives us a hint that there may be a fundamental connection in the early modern period between Hippocrates' Scythian—as an ethnological type—and the Rabelaisian grotesque:

of all the ancient writers, Hippocrates . . . exercised the greatest influence on Rabelais . . . all the works in the [Hippocratic] anthology present a grotesque image of the body; the confines dividing it from the world are obscured, and it is most frequently shown open and with its interior exposed. Its exterior aspect is not distinct from the inside, and the exchange between the body and the world is constantly emphasized.[19]

It is this emphasis on an "exchange between the body and the world" that casts Hippocrates' northerner as the quintessential grotesque, making him more undetermined and subject to flux even, we may imagine, than the women and laborers of dryer or hotter environments.[20] In early modern

humoral discourse, such excessively cold and moist bodies—the phlegmatic—are typically denigrated for their effeminacy and cowardice.[21] Their
greatest distinction, however, is a complete lack of distinction. Unlike melancholics for example, who are haunted by fearful imaginings, the phlegmatic
simply lack the urge to fight.[22] Idle, dull, and lethargic (neither angry nor
pleased, as Wright observes), those afflicted with cold, moist complexions
are also understood to be incapable of sustaining an emotion or even an
appetite.[23] And in contrast to the cool and "imperturbable self-containment"
produced by neo-Stoic discipline, which Michael Schoenfeldt has argued
was an ideal for Shakespeare and his contemporaries, the phlegmatic northerner's passionless state is an effect of exceeding porousness.[24] The passionless are not only those "[u]nmooved," possessing exteriors as hard as stone,
but also those with no exterior at all, in a perpetual state of cold flux.[25]
Without a fixed exterior, and subject to a constant "exchange between the
body and the world," the phlegmatic English, whom the Constable expects
to encounter, would be incapable of sustaining an emotion, much less the
spirited endurance implied by "mettle."

Of course, the primary point of this scene in *Henry V* is to mock the
chauvinistic French. The English soldiers show themselves to be fiery in
their actions. This is not to suggest that the play refutes geohumoralism,
but to recognize that this discourse provided the early moderns with conflicting emotion scripts. Though Hippocrates had his advocates, as we saw
in Huarte's statement, many Europeans of the period cite the ancient theorist only to refute him. Jean Bodin in *Method for the Easy Comprehension of
History* writes, "I do not know why Hippocrates thought the Scythians were
cold ventrally. Nature itself demonstrates that this is false."[26] Writers tended
to reason, instead, that bodies have a counteractive, rather than analogous,
relationship to the environment—a theory of temperatures articulated by
Aristotle, Pliny, and Vitruvius, among others, that maintains that cold climates seal in the body's humors, making northerners excessively hot, moist,
and replete with thick, gross matter.[27] But before we jump to the conclusion that this saved the English from the unruly excesses we identify as
grotesque, it is crucial to understand that in geohumoral discourse northerners, whether they are hot or cold, leaky or full-up, are always intemperate.

In his description in *The Optick Glasse of Humors* (1631) of the northerner's body, Thomas Walkington makes plain that impermeability is just as
alarming as excessive porousness: cold, moist air, Walkington contends, causes
the "passages of the humors [to be] dammed up, the braine stuffed with
smoakie fumes, or any phlegmaticke matter, the blood too hote and too

thicke, as is usuall in the *Scythians* & those in the septentrionall parts, who are of all men endowed with the least portion of witt and pollicie."[28] It is by reason of their "grosse bloud and thick Spirites," explains the Belgian writer Levinus Lemnius in *The Touchstone of Complexions* (1581), that the barbarous northerners "are seene to be bolde and full of venturous courage, rude, unmannerly, terrible, cruell, fierce."[29] Indeed, early modern characterizations of northern blood as exceedingly hot and viscous not only work in concert with the classical stereotype of the bellicose Scythians and Goths but also with truisms regarding the barbarian invasions. It is a historical pattern, Renaissance writers maintain, that intemperate northerners will make war on their southern neighbors.[30] Combining the tenets of Aristotelian geohumoralism with historical precedents, King Henry V himself recognizes that war with France necessarily means that the Scots will invade England, "pouring like the tide into a breach, / With ample and brim fullness of his force, / Galling the gleaned land with hot assays" (1.2.149–51). Certainly France and Scotland had diplomatic ties that strengthened Henry's prediction, but his emphasis on their swarming numbers and their heat attributes the Scots' actions to their regionally determined temperament— a temperament that many writers ascribed to the English themselves.[31] Lemnius, for example, observes that the English resemble the Scots in being ruled by the heated appetites of "theyr high and hauty stomachs."[32] In the same way that the Scots' "hot assays" force England into an effeminately submissive position, extended in the metaphor of the Scot as a weasel sucking England's "princely eggs" (1.2.170–71), the Dauphin imagines that the French women will happily yield to the heat of English lust, thus cuckolding and effeminizing his entire (masculine) nation.

While Hippocrates' Scythians blur any distinction between the environment and the person, thus precluding self-government because the "self" lacks the boundaries necessary for desires, the Aristotelian northerners also resemble the Bakhtinian grotesque in that they are driven entirely by dammed-up fleshly urges. Within the symbolic social structure of the humoral body, where thin and subtle spirits were often deemed more refined and "civilized," the northern body is hampered by its "grosse" and "thick" spirits.[33] In this paradigm, the northerners' sensual heat is retained as dense, unexpended moisture, and it is excessive moisture that unites the Aristotelian and Hippocratic portraits of the northerner. The northerners' barbarous nature can be explained, Bodin contends, by their great "abundance of blood and humor," which makes it more difficult for them to "separate themselves from earthly dregs."[34] Unlike those drier and more civilized wits in the south, the northerners' thick humors cloud their minds; they are, Pierre Charron asserts in *Of Wisdom*, like beasts in their inability "to contein and governe themselves."[35]

While it is true, as Schoenfeldt argues, that in a pre-Cartesian world "bodily condition, subjective state, and psychological character are . . . fully imbricated," it is also true that in early modern geohumoral discourse, the "body and mind are swayed in opposite directions," so that "southerners excell in intellect, the scythians in body."[36] Whatever their internal temperature, northerners are marginalized in geohumoral texts as the most bodily determined, often compared to commoners, and best fitted for physical labor and the "manuall artes."[37] Temperamentally, they resemble adolescents "who suddenly desire new things and then quickly loathe them." According to Bodin and Botero, they are easily provoked "into fury by heat of courage," but just as "easily passified."[38] Though initially valiant, they are exceedingly volatile; everything sets them off, and once in-flamed, they burn out entirely. Quite simply, northerners lack mettle.

Whatever strain of geohumoralism we invoke here, it fails to explain from whence the English in *Henry V* have their mettle. But it is the seeming illogic of English mettle that helps disembed Shakespeare's English soldiers from the determinism of their own northern environment. To put it bluntly, it is mettle that distinguishes these English from their fellow northerners— the hot-blooded Irish, Scots, and Welsh, and it is mettle that divides them (as Norman bastards) from the hyper-civilized French.

Rather than reading the tenuously unified front of Jamy the Scotsman, MacMorris the Irishman, and Fluellen the Welshman as an anticipatory representation of a future British community, I propose we consider how it matters that these "British" characters are already conflated with the English as humorally "northern" in the period's ethnological discourse.[39] These ethnological types, or "humorous grotesques," as Stephen Greenblatt has called them, occupy a complex symbolic place in the play. But (*pace* Greenblatt) it is not to symbolize King Henry's exemplary power to subdue "the last wild areas in the British Isles."[40] Quite the contrary. They embody instead the intractably wild and untamed temperament of England's past. As opposed to the English commoners, the Irish, Welsh, and Scots in *Henry V* function as the repositories, and even regenerative sources, of England's ancient valorous heat. Yet that heat—for the very reason that it is untamed—is also shown to be inferior to a more tempered English "mettle," and thus requires English leadership.

This does not mean that MacMorris, Jamy, and Fluellen share a temperament; indeed, the differences among them are primarily temperamental. The notorious scene in which MacMorris repeats the cryptic question, "What ish my nation?"(3.3.61) can be read as demonstrating, somewhat schematically and incrementally, the length of each man's emotional fuse. It matters that the argument at hand is: "who is truly valorous?" The issue that Fluellen presses to dispute is whether, and to what degree, Jamy the Scot ("a marvellous falorous gentlemen"[21]) and MacMorris follow the "disciplines" or rules of war that Fluellen so prizes. Though Gower has identified MacMorris as a "very valiant gentleman" (11–12), Fluellen believes him to be an "ass" and completely lacking in direction and order. And it is hardly surprising when we discover that MacMorris is fearlessly rebellious, easily provoked, and undisciplined. He is so eager for battle that he finds it a "shame to stand still" and "discourse" when there are "throats to be cut"(50–52).[41] And when Fluellen artlessly aims to "correct" him, MacMorris threatens to "cut off [his] head"(71). Proving only slightly more subdued is Jamy the Scot. Though he swears along with MacMorris that he will pay his life "as valorously as [he] may," he also has some interest in hearing the "twae" debate the disciplines of war (56–58).

Of the three "grotesques," Fluellen's temperamental relationship to English valor is by far the most complicated. Fluellen's subscription to the "disciplines of war," however comic, distinguishes him as more tempered than the Scots or the Irish, akin to Wales's status as an incorporated border country. As the "most intimate of the foreigners," the Welsh, historically, were also intertwined with the English through the Tudor mythography, which the play invokes as a point of mockery when Pistol calls Fluellen a "Trajan," implying perhaps that the Welsh character of the Trojan lineage troubled some English citizens.[42] And yet, while the Trojan ancestry has an equivocal status in the play, Fluellen, I believe, is intended to represent the English people's temperamental or emotional past.

Acknowledging his "passion for 'history,'" critics have identified Fluellen as a kind of historian, but he is, more accurately, a living anachronism.[43] Not only does he seem to live among the ancients (able to call up, as Phyllis Rackin notes, Alexander the "Pig's" friend "Cleitus" more easily than King Henry's own "Falstaff"), but he is also there on the battlefield, when the English have beaten France, to equate Henry with Edward the "Plack Prince of Wales."[44] Fluellen's assertion brings the play full circle, for it was Edward's warlike spirit that the King was counseled to resurrect in Act I. It is, moreover, Fluellen's quirky historical distance that gives him a clown's license to speak bluntly to the King, which he does most pointedly in his declaration that the victory has shown that Henry cannot wash "the Welsh plood out of his body." Obviously, the dominant sense of Fluellen's statement is that the King's "Welsh plood" is tenacious—and even racially indissoluble—but his phrasing also indicates that England's Welsh blood has been subjected to diluting forces. What Fluellen celebrates are the untamed and ancient roots of the King's show of valor. Similarly, it is Fluellen's embodiment of uncorrupted northern qualities that ensures his capacity to teach Pistol "a good English condition" with a "Welsh correction" (5.1.69–70). And while the scene with Pistol positions ancient Welsh valor as superior to English degeneracy, it also reminds us that "Englishness" and "Welshness" are not equivalent.[45] Significantly, it is King Henry's assessment of Fluellen's temperament that indicates how we should distinguish the two: he describes Fluellen as "touched with choler, hot as gunpowder" (4.7.164–65). That is to say, from an English perspective, the Welsh are still too easily stirred and too vulnerable to self-consumption. As we shall see, what contrasts English mettle to these other British constitutions is that it must be deliberately *roused*, and once roused, it has staying power.

Though I have acknowledged in passing that the early modern English temperament can be both disciplined and corrupted, I have primarily emphasized the deterministic interaction between the non-naturals and ethnicity: how a conspiracy of influences produced ethnological types. But the non-naturals could, of course, be manipulated—through changes in air, diet, or emotional behavior—and such manipulation generated further changes in what we deem ethnic traits. Notably, the French suspect that their own mettle has been bred out, and this loss is attributed to their willful subscription to studied practices, such as dancing. What I propose is that the French soldiers' fear of national degeneration echoes what was an English, and ethnologically invested, backlash against the supposed temperamental consequences of the civilizing process.

Though scholars have long been aware that nationhood played a role in early modern conceptions of civility, I want to suggest that at the very origins of what Norbert Elias has called "the civilizing process" were the ethnological anxieties that I have been outlining. What is the civilizing process but a systematic manipulation of the non-naturals? Certainly, Thomas Wright helped us see that the control of emotions was inextricably tied to regional identity. Erasmus, the author of *On Good Manners for Boys* (1530) (identified by Elias as the seminal text in the transformation of Europe's "mental and emotional structure") stated in a private letter that one of his life missions was "to civilize the Dutch."[46] Significantly, Erasmus characterized his fellow Dutch in stereotypically northern, geohumoral terms: they were fierce, gluttonous, dull-witted, "mean and uncultivated" barbarians: a "hungry race of people, born for the belly alone."[47] It is no accident, then, that Erasmus opens his courtesy manual with the statement: "No one can choose his own . . . *nationality*, but each can mould . . . himself."[48] I am suggesting that Erasmus's recognized capacity to criticize the vulgar without accepting the behavior of great lords speaks to the double vision his northern ethnicity affords—a double vision that all northern nations possessed. In Elias's narrative, the whole of European society underwent a kind of emotional maturation process, moving away from a warrior culture in which the "instincts, the emotions were vented more freely, more directly, more openly than later."[49] But in the north, where the native environment, it was presumed, engendered aggressive emotions and barbarous behavior, the evolution of civility had a more complicated narrative.

For the English, as northerners, the acquisition of civility—as a transformation of their native "mental and emotional structures"—was a process fraught with tension and ambivalence.[50] As Richard Helgerson's work has shown, "to be English was to be other," whether it was the otherness of their barbaric culture that they sought to reform or the otherness of the civility they embraced.[51] Courtesy manuals were imported, to a large degree, for nationalistic reasons. Justifying his translation of *The Courtier* (1561), Thomas Hoby concedes that the English have been "counted barbarous . . . time out of minde" in their "maners."[52] Fashioning a gentleman in England meant, of course, cultivating qualities that would distinguish him from the middling sort. Yet it also meant refining away a disposition that, for some, constituted "Englishness" itself. This conflict between class and ethnicity comes into focus in *The Touchstone of Complexions* (1581) when Lemnius supports his assertion that to eradicate their native barbarism, the northerners' humoral complexion should be tempered:

Not withstanding education, institution, and discipline, altereth the usuall nature, and ordinary conditions of every Region: for we see the common sort and multitude, in behaviour and manners grosse and unnurtured, whereas the Nobles and Gentlemen (altering their order and dyet, and digressing from the common fashion of their pezantly Country-men) frame themselves and theirs to a very commendable order, and civill behaviour.[53]

All men born in the north possess "behavior and manners grosse and unnurtured," or a "pezantly" nature, and it is only by vigilant discipline in deportment and diet that the upper classes are able to "digress" from the "ordinary" influences of their home country. Like Erasmus, Lemnius not only imagines that civil behavior should be cosmopolitan, erasing national boundaries, but he also defines civility in opposition to what northern conditions produce.

Lemnius's sentiments are echoed in that most famous of northern plays, *Hamlet*, in the Prince's seemingly digressive speech on the festive, and typically regional, behavior of the Danes. Although *born* to the Danish *manner* of drinking, a characteristically northern flaw which leads all other nations to "clepe [the Danes] drunkards," Hamlet prides himself on his disciplined resistance to this native inclination (1.4.18.3). His concern for his countrymen's failures suggests deep frustrations with the threatened determinism of one's nativity, "for nature cannot choose his origin" (18.10) and more particularly with the distinct disadvantages of a northern birth. In Hamlet's judgment, Denmark sits on the margins of the civilized world, "traduced and taxed of other nations" for its "heavy-headed" and barbarous customs (18.1–2). The Dane adopts here a foreign voice, ventriloquising what more sober nations say and founding his own singularity on an alliance with those who view his nation as base and uncivil.

Engaged, as it is, in the complexities of early modern geohumoralism, Hamlet's speech makes plain the problematic nature of northern identity. With temperance as an ideal most accessible in median climates, the native characteristics of cold Denmark are necessarily immoderate. Whether that immoderation stems from humoral excess ("the o'ergrowth of some complexion") or manifests itself in the customs that feed those humors ("some habit that too much o'erleavens / the form of plausive manners"), it is excess itself that marks the Danes as Danes (18.11–14).[54] Hamlet's disdain for his nation's swinish and common manners expresses the social hierarchy that structures early modern ethnography. In a sense, he implies that to behave like a Dane reduces all men and women—elite and base—to the level of corporeal appetite.[55] Yet part of Hamlet's struggle—to act, or to reconcile his desired actions with his conscience—is played out through the mournful awareness that he has forfeited his Danish disposition. The Dane finds that his "native hue of resolution" (the northern soldier's naturally heated complexion, which Fortinbras and Laertes still possess) is now "sicklied o'er with the pale cast of thought" (3.1.86–87).[56]

While Hamlet fears that he, individually, may have lost the resolution to act, the Dauphin in *Henry V* articulates a broader cultural fear that the civilized pursuits of an entire nation can lead to a people's degeneration. The Duke of Bretagne, in his response to the Dauphin, makes it clear that the "breeding out" of "mettle" is associated with the cultivation of class-inflected bodily habits—in this case, dancing: "They bid us to the English dancing schools / And teach lavoltas high, and swift corantos" (3.5.32–33). Though he speaks for France, the Dauphin's concern echoes a hostile English response to the civilizing process that stems from the nation's growing positive identification with their barbaric past. It is a recurring theme in the anti-theatrical writings of the period, for example, that idle pursuits, often those identified with the court, have led to the decay of England's native martial prowess. Stephen Gosson, in fact, asserts that in his nation's former days of glory, before they were infected with the vices of other nations, Englishmen were as valorous as the ancient Scythians.[57] Yet in expressing his anxieties about the French national temperament, the Dauphin also indicates that "mettle" can be bred back in. Alarmed by France's indolent effeminacy, he seems almost sympathetic to the possibility that French "madams . . . will give / Their bodies to the lust of English youth, / To new-store France with bastard warriors." What the Dauphin articulates here is a northern challenge to the Mediterranean-centered argument that the barbarian invasions destroyed classical civilization; the implication is, instead, that they regenerated declining populations with the infusion of heated blood.[58]

It makes sense that a play so profoundly concerned with the relationship between the non-naturals and ethnicity would represent the negative effects of the civilizing process by drawing parallels between a cultivated landscape and cultivated (or overcultivated) persons.[59] The French have lost their mettle, it seems, because they have overcultivated themselves and their environment. For them military defeat means yielding their "vineyards to a barbarous people" (3.5.4), and they lament most of all that their French gardens and the "vineyards, fallows, meads, and hedges, . . . [will] grow to wildness" (5.25.54–55). While such interventions in nature are often celebrated as the height of human art and science, there is an implicit critique here of overcultivation, which translates to disproportionate care of the self as well. That England is a "slobb'ry . . . dirty farm" may be less an insult than grudging admiration for the untamed qualities of the English temperament.

That *English* mettle cannot be "bred out" is demonstrated, I believe, by the play's strange reversal of the microcosmic / macrocosmic relationship of geohumoralism. Rather than suggesting that the French environment or French practices will corrupt or civilize the English soldiers, Shakespeare indicates that English valor—as a substantive and physiological property—has the capacity to alter the French landscape. Though the play is full of such examples, the most fantastic one is Henry's threat that the rotting bodies of the English dead will abound with enough valor to transfigure France itself:

> And those that leave their valiant bones in France,
> Dying like men, though buried in your dunghills
> They shall be famed. For there the sun shall greet them
> And draw their honours reeking up to heaven,
> Leaving their earthly parts to choke your clime,
> The smell whereof shall breed a plague in France.
> Mark then abounding valour in our English.
> That, being dead, like to the bullets grazing,
> Break out into a second course of mischief,
> Killing in relapse of mortality. (4.3.99–108)

Valor, as Henry portrays it, is grounded in the material body—its bones and earthly parts. But it is not, significantly, confined to the living microcosm. As the English corpses decay, it is the putrefying smell of valor's "earthly parts"—what we might identify as mettle—that will choke the French clime. Henry endorses here an emotional effect that cannot be produced by individual self-discipline: it is an aggregate, teeming, and excessive passion that breaches the boundaries not just between self and world, but also between life and death. English mettle is the spirited experience of emotion, and English mettle is, simultaneously, a non-animate elemental property.

But for the play to represent English mettle simply as an unrefined element runs the risk of rendering it common, rather than resistantly and uniquely *English*. Indeed, the challenge of the play is to mark the English temperament as more barbaric than the French, yet more civilized than the Irish, the Scots, and the Welsh; as more refined than the commoner, yet more robust than the decadent noble. As a whole, the *Henriad* resists the ethnographic equation made between traits associated with the lower orders and Englishness. Rather than functioning as repositories of the country's work-a-day virtues, the laboring classes are as dissolute and corrupt as fallen and decaying nobles. And in *Henry V* in particular, scenes with Pistol, Bardolph, and Nym are devoted almost entirely to proving them "white livered," however much they may boast. Civility may threaten "mettle," but we are not to assume that base commoners will outbrave their social superiors.

Though rooted in the English body and nourished by the English air, valorous heat, these scenes suggest, is not to be confused with mere appetite.

At the same time, valor among the English aristocracy is also a diminished thing. If we trust Falstaff's assessment, Prince John and Henry IV are both cold-blooded, despite the puissance, or "blood and courage," of their forefathers, Edward III and Edward the Black Prince. Just before they marvel at the English army's "mettle," the French aristocracy reminds us that the English can be construed as "Norman bastards"; we are prompted to grapple with the cultural and ethnological significance of the Norman invasion. For Edmund Spenser in *A View of the State of Ireland*, it was the Norman conquest that established a clear and positive difference between the civilized English and the barbaric Irish. However, in *Henry IV, Part II*, we are presented with the possibility that the English court has already declined into a state of cold effeminacy, not unlike the French, as suggested by Falstaff's claim that such "sober-blooded" (4.2.79) and "demure boys" (81–82) as Prince John necessarily "fall into a kind of male green-sickness, and then when they marry, they get wenches" (83–85).[60] Anticipating the Constable's conjecture, Falstaff attributes Prince Hal's heat to diet: "for the cold blood he did naturally inherit of his father he hath, like lean, sterile, and bare land, manured, husbanded, and tilled, with excellent endeavour of drinking good, and good store of fertile sherry, that he is become very hot and valiant" (105–9). It was in the tavern, of course, where Hal learned to "*drink* with any tinker in his own language," a skill which earned him the tapsters' praise as "a lad of mettle" (I.1.2.5.10–17).

In *Henry V*, we are given to understand that the English are distinct from, and superior to, the "civilized" and the "barbaric" because their natural heat must be awakened with great labor. Thus, the King's war council speaks the language of resurrection: "Awake remembrance" (1.2.115); "The blood and courage that renowned them / Runs in your veins" (118–19); "[R]ouse yourself / As did the former Lions of your blood" (123–24). And in the same way, Henry's stirring speeches to his soldiers are intended, of course, to incite their courage. The qualification I am making here is that English valor is deemed unique, powerful, and sturdy because it *requires* the effort of such rhetoric, as well as the physical and emotional restructuring (or uncivilizing) that Henry prescribes: "lend the eye a terrible aspect" (3.1.9), "hold hard the breath and bend up every spirit." Henry's explicit instructions on how to restructure one's constitution and deportment—"[S]tiffen the sinews, conjure up the blood"; "set the teeth, and stretch the nostril wide" (3.1.7–15)—are an aggressive undoing of a civilized temperament.

Consider the intentional ambiguity of the line "Be copy now to men of grosser blood," for it suggests not only that the elite are the disciplined soldiers to be imitated, but that the English nobility must reproduce themselves in grosser terms and rediscover their yeoman-like "mettle of the pasture." Similarly, Henry's promise that joining the fight shall "gentle" the soldier's "condition" speaks as much to the nobleman as to the commoner. For it is not the lower orders who will regret their absence from the field, but the gentlemen in England, now abed, who will hold their manhoods cheap. The "gentling" experience of war, and the stirring effects of Henry's rhetoric, are aimed at what the true English soldier, no matter his degree, should possess: mettle. Targeting his speech at resistant soldiers such as Michael Williams (whom Fluellen declares "has mettle enough in his belly"), the King strives to ignite what merely smolders in his countrymen. Moreover, it is the insistent representation of *exertion*, by Henry and by the play itself, which constructs the English as even having mettle. Clearly Henry's words are not intended for those British barbarians who are, with little provocation, hot as "gunpowder."

In beseeching its audience to "suppose," "work," "piece out," "make," "imagine," and "grapple," *Henry V* establishes that the rekindling of England's valorous heat is a painstaking process. Most apt for my point is the Chorus's charge that the spectators "behold" the play in "the quick [i.e. hot] forge and working house of thought," likening their imaginative efforts to the burning fires needed to heat iron to malleability. Tautologically, whoever responds to the Choruses' exhortations is a true Englishman because only a true Englishman can so respond. As Thomas Heywood will exclaim some years later, challenging the claim that the theater has robbed the English of natural valor, "what English blood" and "hart" would not be "new mold[ed] by the likes of *Henry V*?"[61]

Chapter 7
Hearing Green

Bruce Smith

*Sentences (1) and (2) are equally nonsensical, but any speaker
of English will recognize that only the former is grammatical.
(1) Colorless green ideas sleep furiously.
(2) Furiously sleep ideas green colorless.*

—*Noam Chomsky,* Syntactic Structures (1957)

In Shakespeare and Fletcher's *The Two Noble Kinsmen* there is a
scene in which a character called The Doctor subjects a character called The
Jailer's Daughter to a seventeenth-century equivalent of the psychoanalysis
that Sigmund Freud performed on "Dora" and other hysterical women in
early twentieth-century Vienna. The Jailer's Daughter has fallen hopelessly
in love with her father's prisoner Palamon and has gone mad. Differences
between the two regimens of medical analysis are sharp. Freud's is based on
physics: the psyche is imagined to be an enclosed system in which energies
are repressed, transferred, and released. The Doctor's is grounded in body
chemistry. The Jailer's Daughter, so the Doctor tells her father, suffers from
a "distemper," an imbalance among the body's four basic fluids.[1] When The
Doctor describes the cause of her madness as "a most thicke, and profound
melancholy" (4.3.46-47), what he has in mind is not so much an emotion as
the viscous, heavy qualities of black bile. "The intemperat surfeit of her eye."
The Doctor surmises, "hath distemperd the / Other sences" (4.3.67-68). The
recommended cure is homeopathic. Since "it is a falsehood / She is in"
(4.3.90), The Doctor prescribes a series of new falsehoods that will engage
all the senses and "reduce what's / Now out of square in her, into their former law and / Regiment" (4.3.92-93). Put her in a dark place, he counsels the
father, surround her with sweet smells, come to her in disguise as Palamon,
invite her to eat and drink with you, "sing to her such greene/ Songs of Love,
as she says *Palamon* hath sung in / Prison" (4.3.78-79).

Green songs? Thomas Wright in *The Passions of the Minde in Generall*
(first printed 1601, revised 1604) can give puzzled modern readers some help
here. Writing a quarter century before Descartes convinced most European
intellectuals (and their successors down to our own day) that they could

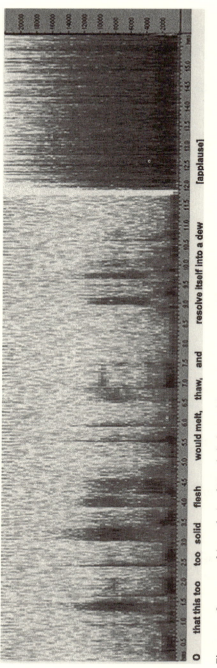

Figure 7.1. Spectographic analysis of Hamlet's first soliloquy (1.2.129–30), with applause.

think without their bodies, Wright assumes that thinking always has to start with sense experience. First the viewer's eyes are pierced by light rays that convey the shape and colors of another person's body. Then an aerated fluid called *spiritus* carries the sensation to the phantasy or imagination, which in turn sends the image to the heart. The heart, once it apprehends the object presented by the imagination, "immediately bendeth, either to prosecute it, or to eschew it: and the better to effect that affectation, draweth other humours to help him."[2] In Wright's scheme reason stands in an uneasy relationship to the passions. Reason ought to direct the passions, but the passions have a friendlier working relationship with the senses. Indeed, the passions can prevent reason from knowing the truth about objects that the body, through the senses, sees, hears, touches, tastes, and smells. Again Wright:

whatsoeuer we vnderstand, passeth by the gates of our imagination, the cosin germane to our sensitiue appetite, the gates of our imagination being preuented, yea, and welnie shut vp with the consideration of that obiect which feedeth the passion, and pleaseth the appetite; the vnderstanding looking into the imagination, findeth nothing almost but the mother & nurse of his passion for consideration; where you may well see how the imagination, putteth greene spectacles before the eyes of our wit, to make it see nothing but greene, that is, seruing for the consideration of the Passion. (51)

Why green? Why should passionate looking be green and not red or yellow or blue? At least three reasons suggest themselves. Green was, and is, a color associated with youth and hence with rashness. Popular proverbs— "Jogging while your boots are green" (cf. *The Taming of the Shrew* 3.2.213), "Green wood makes a hot fire"[3]—help explain the Nurse's recommendation of Paris to Juliet: "An Eagle Madam / Hath not so greene, so quicke, so fair an eye / As Paris hath."[4] In medical terms, greenness of complexion was taken to be a symptom of the cool, moist anemia to which young women like the Jailer's Daughter were prone. In the heat of his passion Romeo refuses to associate fiery-eyed Juliet with Diana, goddess of the moon, since "Her Vestal liuery is but sicke and greene" (2.1.49-40). Nonetheless, Juliet's father diagnoses his daughter's devotion to Romeo as the very illness that her lover has eschewed: "Out, you greene sicknesse carrion, out you baggage! / You tallow face!" (3.5.156-57). There were, finally, physical reasons why a passionate looker should desire to see green. Ficino in the second of his *De Vita Libri Tres* (1489) takes the occasion of addressing old people who linger too long in "the gardens and green fields" of Venus to consider just why the color green delights the eye above all other colors.[5] The answer lies in its perfect tempering of light and darkness. Ancient opinion that colors are made up of differing amounts of fire, air, water, and earth is confirmed by Helkiah Crooke in *Microcosmographia: A Description of the Body of Man* (1616, 1631), among many other early modern writers about vision.[6] Earth is the one element of the four that inhibits translucency and hence imparts color to objects. To Ficino's way of seeing, green neither dilates the eye with too much light nor dulls the eye with too much darkness: rather, "the color green tempering most of all black with white, furnishes the one effect and the other, equally delighting and conserving the sight" (205).

The Doctor's diagnosis and Wright's description of perception suggest that "green" has significance beyond its proverbial, medical, and physical senses. In Wright's account, green is not something that one sees; it is something one sees *with*. It is not an external object but an internal state of being. The Jailer's Daughter will take notice of "green songs" because that is what her greensickness predisposes her to hear. In modern epistemology green is regarded as a strictly optical phenomenon. It is the sensation produced on the retina by light waves centered on 540 millimicrons. Early modern epistemology, so Shakespeare, Fletcher, and Wright suggest, was different. Green could be heard as well as seen. The charades proposed by the Doctor imply that it could also be smelled, tasted, and touched. All told, these two texts call into question at least three premises of modern epistemology: (1) that the senses function as five separate faculties, (2) that reason is a faculty that exists above and beyond the senses, and (3) that the knowing subject exists apart from the objects he or she perceives. The third challenge is the most fundamental of all. In the Doctor's analysis of the Jailer's Daughter's madness and in Wright's explanation of perception, external objects do not exist apart from the bodily ways in which the subject comes to know them. The thinking subject can try to subordinate sense perceptions to understanding, but Galenic medicine made thinking absolutely dependent on seeing, hearing, touching, tasting, and smelling. Before Descartes located the nexus between soul and body in the pineal gland, it was no overstatement to declare "Sentio ergo sum."

What would it mean to *hear* green? Pursuing that question with respect to a range of early modern texts will bring us, via phonetic linguistics, to questioning the Cartesian premises on which deconstruction is based.

To hear green would, for a start, mean to hear passionately, to hear longingly. In early modern Scots *green* was recognized as a verb. *To green* was "to desire earnestly, to yearn, to long *after, for*" (*OED*, "green," v2). James I favors the word in several of his poems. His short treatise on Scots verse includes a poem about a man who cannot sleep: "That nicht he ceist, and went to bed, bot greind / Zit fast for day, and thocht the nicht to lang."[7] In another poem James himself confesses, "Scarce was I yet in springtyme of my years, / When greening great for fame aboue my pears / Did make me lose my wonted chere and rest" (19). With respect to sound, the verb *to green* reverses the usual direction of sensation. Ordinarily sound comes to the listener from the outside. It penetrates the listener's body through the ears. Especially if one accepts the extramission theory of vision, in which light rays are projected outward from the crystalline sphere of the viewer's eyes to objects in the world around, hearing casts the subject in a more vulnerable position than seeing does. Take, for example, the visceral response to unpleasant sounds. Bacon in *Silva Silvarum* explains why squeaking and shrieking, the sharpening of saws, and the grinding of stones set a listener's teeth on edge: "The *Cause* is, for that the *Obiects* of the *Eare*, doe affect the *Spirits* (immediately) most with *Pleasure* and Offence."[8] The emphasis here falls on "immediately." Colors in and of themselves do not, Bacon claims, much offend the eye. A painted representation of a horrible sight hardly carries the force of the thing itself. Smells, tastes, and touches involve bodily participation with the thing being experienced. "So it is *Sound* alone, that doth immediately, and incorporeally, affect most" (177). Elsewhere in *Silva Silvarum* Bacon catalogues "the passions of the mind"—fear, grief and pain, joy, anger, light displeasure or dislike, shame, wonder, laughing, and lust—and notes that "evermore the spirits, in all passions, resort most to the parts that labour most, or are most affected." Hence lust causes "a flagrancy in the eyes" (571).

A direct physiological connection between hearing and genital desire is anatomized by John Donne in an undated Whitsuntide sermon on Acts 10:44, "While Peter yet spake these words, the Holy Ghost fell on all them which heard the word." "They say," Donne reports, "there is a way of castration, in cutting off the eares: There are certain veines behinde the eares, which, if they be cut, disable a man from generation."[9] For this curious intelligence Donne is ultimately indebted to Hippocrates' medical treatise on "Airs, Waters, Places."[10] In Galen's anatomy of the human body it would be *spiritus*—what Wright calls "purer spirits" (45)—that would carry sensation from the ears directly to the penis, just as, in the more conventional explanation, it is *spiritus* that carries sensation from the ears to the imagination and thence to the heart. According to Crooke, the coursing of *spiritus* in the veins can be compared to the moving of the wind: "it passeth and repasseth at his pleasure, vnseene, but not unfelt; for the force and incursion thereof is not without a kind of violence: so the seede although it be thicke and viscid, yet passeth thorough vessels which haue no manifest cauities; the reason is because it is full and as it were houen with spirits" (174). To green for a particular sound would, in effect, change the direction of the energy: it would mean to listen from the inside out, from the penis to the ear.

In Book Two of *The Faerie Queene* the hapless swain who lies sleeping "in secret shade"[11] at the heart of Acrasia's Bower of Bliss is, the reader discovers, named Verdant, or "Green" (1.12.82.8). As usual in *The Faerie Queene*, the reader learns the personage's name only *after* he has been seen in action—or, in this case, in inaction, as Acrasia's victim has been situated among the bower's "shady Laurell trees" (2.12.43.2), "couert groues, and thickets close" (2.12.76.6) and its strangely *illegible* sounds. It is through sound, in fact, that Sir Guyon and the Palmer first come to know the bower:

Eftsoones they heard a most melodious sound,
 Of all that mote delight a daintie eare,
 Such as attonce might not on liuing ground,
 Saue in this Paradise, be heard elsewhere:
 Right hard it was, for wight, which did it heare,
 To read, what manner musicke that mote bee:
 For all that pleasing is to liuing eare,
 Was there consorted in one harmonee,
Birds, voyces, instruments, windes, waters, all agree. (2.12.70.1–9)

The passions that these sights and sounds engender in Verdant become Acrasia's physical possessions, as she bedews his lips with kisses, "And though his humid eyes did sucke his spright, / Quite molten into lust and pleasure lewd" (2.12.73.7–8). Greenness, in all its erotic appeal, is something that Andrew Marvell's garden shares with Spenser's Bower of Bliss. One wonders whether Marvell's "green thought in a green shade" is quite the metaphysical affair that some critics have made it out to be.[12] Frank Kermode and Keith Walker paraphrase the line in such a way that the emphasis falls on the *meta*, not the *physical*: "making the created world seem as nothing compared with what can be imagined by the rational contemplative."[13] Such a reading sorts oddly with the line's analogue in *The Reign of King Edward III*, cited in H. M. Margoliouth's edition of Marvell. When King Edward chances to encounter the Countess of Salisbury in the course of his Scottish wars, he conceives a passion for her that all his lords see clearly. "I might perceive his eye in her eye lost," Lodovick tells another courtier, "His eare to drinke her sweet tongues vtterance."[14] When the king asks Lodovick to write a letter to the countess on his behalf, he suggests they retreat to a "sommer arber": "Since greene our thoughts, greene be the conuenticle" (2.1.61, 63).

As the consorted sounds of the Bower of Bliss suggest, to hear green would likewise mean to hear music (and this is crucial) *without regard to its legibility.* "*Tunes* and *Aires,* euen in their owne Nature, haue in themselues some Affinity with the *Affections,*" Bacon observes in *Silva Silvarum.*

> As there be *Merry Tunes, Dolefull Tunes, Solemne Tunes; Tunes inclining Mens mindes to Pitty; Warlike Tunes; &c.* So as it is no Maruell, if they alter the *Spirits;* considering that *Tunes* haue a Predisposition to the *Motion* of the *Spirits* in themselues. But yet it hath been noted, that though this variety of *Tunes,* doth dispose the *Spirits* to variety of Passions, conforme vnto them; yet generally, *Musick* feedeth that disposition of the *Spirits* which it findeth. (38)

That is to say, to hear *green* one must first *hear* green. In the culture of early modern England there is surely no more striking instance of hearing green, with emphasis both ways, than the phenomenal popularity of the ballad "Greensleeves" and its progeny. An entry in the Stationers' Register on September 3, 1580, for "A newe northern Dittye of ye Ladye Greene Sleves" probably refers to a broadside that was handled, folded, pasted up, wadded, and worn to oblivion. The earliest surviving text dates from four years later, in the ballad anthology *A Handful of Pleasant Delights* (1584). Transcriptions of the tune began to appear in manuscripts of music for the lute about the same time. Within nine months of the first licensing, no fewer than seven spin-offs had been entered in the register or appeared in print.[15] In *Hero and Leander* (datable to the mid 1580s) Marlowe's blazon of the clothing that Leander so admires on Hero includes

> wide sleeves greene, and bordered with a grove,
> Where *Venus* in her naked glory strove,
> To please the carelesse and disdainfull eies,
> Of proud *Adonis* that before her lies.[16]

The focus on sleeves can be explained in part by the relative expensiveness and ostentatiousness of these detachable garments. The focus on green may stem in part from the northern origins specified on the original broadside. In early modern English imagination the north is the preeminent land of balladry, of fierce fights like the Battle of Chevy Chase, of dense oak forests that shelter Robin Hood as the lord of midsummer pageants, and of the trickster lover Jocky, who figures in the repertory of the mid-sixteenth-century minstrel Richard Sheale as well as in numerous seventeenth-century broadside ballads.[17]

The ballad of "Greensleeves" is more about green than it is about sleeves, as singing the ballad or hearing it sung so readily reveals. The tune falls into four phrases, labeled A, B, C, and D in Musical Example 1. (Figure 7.2) In the first stanza phrases A and B are focused on the singer: they situate him as a spurned suitor. Virtually identical until the final cadence, both phrases reach climaxes of pitch, volume, and passion on the words "loue" and "loued" before descending to the lowest pitches in the entire tune. Abruptly, phrases C and D turn the focus from the singer to the object of his love and sound out the highest pitches of the entire tune on the words "Greensleeues." The second stanza sets in place the same structure of singer (phrases A and B) versus the object of the singer's love (phrases C and D). Succeeding stanzas then catalogue in phrases A and B all the articles of clothing and other gifts that the singer has given the lady—kerchers, petticoats, jewels, gold-embroidered smock, red-gold girdle, purse, gay gilt knives, pincase, crimson stockings, white pumps, gown "of grossie green" (grassy green? grosgrain green?), satin sleeves, gold garters, silver aglets, a gelding to ride, green-clad men to serve as attendants, dainties to eat, "musicke still to play and sing"—before turning in each case to the same passionate climax

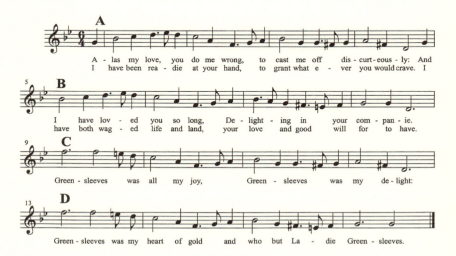

Figure 7.2. Musical Example 1, "Greensleeves." Adapted by permission from Claude M. Simspon, *The British Broadside Ballad and Its Music* (1966).

on "Greensleeues" in phrases C and D. The effect of repetition after repetition of phrases C and D (eighteen in all according to the *Pleasant Delights* text) is to turn the words "Greensleeues" into a kind of mantra. By the end of the ballad, the high pitch on which those words are sung and the passion that the high pitch invites, becomes something far more compelling than the article of clothing to which the words refer, far more compelling even than the lady whose pet name is derived from that article of clothing. One is struck by the name of one of the imitations licensed in 1580: "Countenaunce in Countenaunce is Greene Sleves."[18] "Greensleeues" becomes, in effect, the singer's passion. And the name of that passion is green-sickness. In Bacon's terms, the tune of "Greensleeves" has, in itself, an affinity with melancholy that "feeds the disposition" of the spirits that the tune finds. To judge from the ballad's popularity, such spirits were rife in the 1580s.

Given its transformation of the singer's body, and the listener's, from hot and moist (the passion of lust) to cold and dry (the passion of melancholy), "Greensleeves" seems to offer a perfect example of the kind of music Phillip Stubbes singles out for attack in *The Anatomy of Abuses*, first published three years after the original broadside of "Greensleeves" appeared. Music is a gift of God, Stubbes's spokesman Philoponus will concede, and is capable of delighting man and beast, reviving the spirits, comforting the heart, and making it readier to serve God, as David did in the Psalms, "but being vsed in publique assemblies and priuate conuenticles as directories to filthie dauncing, thorow the sweet harmonie & smoothe melodie therof, it estraungeth yᵉ mind[,] stireth vp filthie lust, womannisheth yᵉ minde[,] rauisheth the hart, enflameth concupisence, and bringeth in vncleannes."[19] Stubbes thinks first and foremost here of dance music not only because it sets bodies in lascivious motion but because it is wordless. Later in the same chapter Stubbes contrasts the plenitude of pipers in every town, city, and country region with the deficit of divines. The written licenses granted to pipers, minstrels, and musicians will do them no good at the last judgment, Stubbes warns, "for the Worde of GOD is against your vngodly exercyses, and condemneth them to Hell" (sig. O5v). Pipers provide the sharpest possible contrast to expositors of the word of God because their music is wordless: they cannot pipe and sing at the same time. It was the passionate abandon of piped music, associated with Asia, that prompted Greek intellectuals to favor the lyre of Apollo, as Plutarch reports in his life of Alcibiades.[20]

Trying to describe to Mistress Page the patent discrepancy between Sir John Falstaff's flattering words and his true intents, Mistress Ford declares, "But they doe no more adhere and keep together, then the hundred Psalms to the tune of Greensleeues."'[21] By the time *Merry Wives* was first performed in 1597–98, "Greensleeves" had provided the tune for at least four moraliz-ing ballads, but Mistress Ford's point still stands: the psalms, of all texts, demand music imbued with the power of *logos*. The Protestant right wing, with its dependence on the literal word of God recorded in the Bible had good reason to be suspicious of Gregorian chant. For intoning the psalms the Latin rite used eight formulas, or "tones," that allowed singers to follow the rhythms and the rhetorical heft of the parallel lines in the original Hebrew texts, but during the offices these syllable-by-syllable formulas were framed by antiphons, or responses, that allowed the voice to float free of the text in sequences of abstract tones called melismas.[22] Take for example the psalm numbered 22 in the Vulgate Bible ("Dominus regit me") and 23 in English Bibles since the sixteenth century ("The Lord is my shepherd"). According to the Use of Sarum, "Dominus regit me" was to be chanted daily as part of the Office of Prime, as well as at the Second Hour of Night dur-ing the Feast of Corpus Christi.[23] In the Corpus Christi service, it was to be preceded by an antiphon, "Paratur nobis mensa Domini adversus omnes qui tribulant nos," anticipating one of the succeeding psalm's most famous lines ("Thou preparest a table before me in the presence of mine enemies") and was to be followed by another antiphon, "In voce exultationis resonent epulantes in mensa Domini," amplifying the psalm's image of feasting and specifying the exultation or joy that inspires the antiphon's melismas. The transcription of the entire sequence of Antiphon-Psalm-Antiphon in Musi-cal Example 2 (Figure 7.3) has been adapted from the most complete man-uscript of music surviving from the pre-reformation church in England.[24] The psalm itself is cast in the fifth tone. In the antiphons the melismas, the sequences during which the singing voice soars free of the text, are marked with asterisks. For congregants at services, such moments represent prime instances of hearing green.

The sharpest possible contrast to the antiphons in the Latin rite would seem to be offered by the plodding, four-square setting of Psalm 23 in the collected settings of the psalms begun by Thomas Sternhold in 1547, aug-mented by John Hopkins in 1549, and brought to completion with additions by other translators in 1562.[25] William Whittington is the translator of this version of the 23rd Psalm (see Figure 7.4).

Here, seemingly, is logocentricism with a vengeance. The ubiquity of Sternhold and Hopkins's settings in early modern England (they were printed with many editions of the Book of Common Prayer) suggests that it is William Whittington's literal simplicity that Mistress Ford has in mind as a foil to Falstaff's duplicity. The second part of the title page to the 1561 edition and most subsequent editions declares that the word-by-word gravity of the Sternhold and Hopkins psalter is intended as antidote not just to antiphony but to balladry:

PSALMES OF DAVID IN ENG- / lish Metre . . . / VERI METE TO BE VSED OF / all sortes of people priuatly for their godly/ solace and confort: laiying aparte all / vngodlye Songes and Balledes, / which tende only to the nouri- / shing of vice, and corrup- / ting of youth.[26]

Whittington's setting of the 23rd Psalm in fact appropriates the 4/3/4/3 rhythm of many ballads. In that fact might there be residues of green? That would depend, ultimately, on who was doing the singing and who the listening and what they were remembering. Mistress Ford, for one, would be a sceptical listener in church.

Figure 7.3. Musical Example 2, Psalm 23 ("The Lord is my shepherd"), with antiphons before and after. Adapted from Walter Howard Frere, *The Use of Sarum* (1898–1901).

To hear green would mean to hear the totality of sound in an act of speaking, to hear not just the words or the syllables but all the sounds in between. When a person speaks, the vocal chords, the jaw, the tongue, and the palate are in constant motion. The result is a continuous stream of sound, not a chain of discrete sounds. Phonetic linguists recognize this situation even as they proceed to impose units of analysis on the stream of sound. The smallest units are phonetic *features*, momentary configurations of sound frequencies produced when air is expelled while larynx, jaw, tongue, and palate are held in certain positions. One or more features can make up a phonetic *segment*, a sequence of frequencies that remains relatively unchanging long enough for speakers of a given language to hear it as a *phoneme*. A sequence of phonemes in turn can be heard as an *utterance*; a sequence of utterances, as a *speaking turn*. In this sequence of sound formations complete breaks are few, occuring mainly between utterances and at the end of a speaking turn.[27] Note that *syllable* and *word* are absent from the sequence of sound formations. Strictly speaking, syllable and word are units of analysis appropriate to phonology (the study of sound structures), not phonetics (the study of sounds).[28] Precise measurements of how long it takes to make one alternating movement in the larynx or the mouth indicate an interval of 150 to 300 milliseconds. Normal conversation moves along at the pace of 10 to 20 segments per second, implying only 100

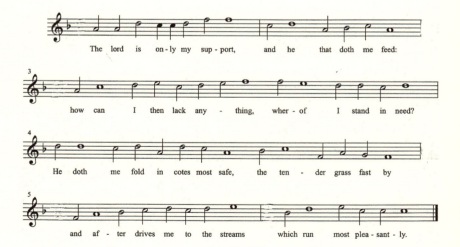

Figure 7.4. Musical Example 3, Psalm 23 as set by Thomas Sternhold and John Hopkins. Adapted from *Psalms of David in English Meter* (1562).

milliseconds in which to make the required adjustments in the vocal apparatus. The speaker has no choice, then, but to blend one segment into another by a process that phonetic linguists know as *coarticulation*.[29] Contractions stand as obvious orthographical signs of a phenomenon that is going on all the time, within words as well as between words, when a person speaks.

A visual representation of the whole process is made available by spectrographic analysis. Take, for example, Hamlet's first soliloquy (Shakespeare 1968: 7681,11.2.129–30 in Shakespeare 1989). In Figure 7.1 the horizontal axis measures time; the vertical axis measures frequencies of sound, heard as pitch. The minds of English-speaking listeners may consciously register ten separate words, but their ears take in a continuous stream of sound. A closer approximation of Hamlet's speech in letters would look like this:

Othatthistootoosolidfleshwouldmeltthaworresolveitselfintoadew.

That, indeed, is how each of the utterances would have been written down if Hamlet had been speaking in Latin and his words had been recorded in the first century B.C.E.[30] Really, though, there ought to be no letters at all. As Roy Harris observes in *Rethinking Writing*,

the only kind of representation which is "faithful" to the phonetic facts would be one which did not divide the continuum into segments at all—as we see in a sound spectrogram. Alphabetic transcription inevitably misrepresents speech to the extent that it is obliged by its own conventions to mark a series of subdivisions that do not exist. For the semiologist, any belief that an optimally accurate alphabetic transcription mirrors the structure of the utterance is rather like supposing that the best kind of drawing of a jet of water must be one in which each droplet is separately shown.[31]

In the spectrograph of Hamlet's speech many more sounds are present than the phonetic segments [oː] [θ] [a] [t] [θ] [ɨ] [s] etc. D. B. Fry estimates that modern subjects *listen to* only about half of the speech sounds they *hear*.[32] Why do subjects attend only to those particular sounds and not the others? Linguists have suggested several explanations, ranging from hardwiring in the brain to passive filtering to dependence on acoustic cues in the listening environment to the listener's own bodily knowledge of how meaningful sounds are produced by the vocal tract.[33] What happens to the other half of the sounds? As nonsignifying sounds they belong to the spectrum of green. In terms of early modern epistemology, their appeal is to the passions, not to reason.

In his attempt to establish scientific principles for the study of sound in *Silva Silvarum*, Bacon clearly wishes that all sounds were musical tones, definite in pitch, definite in duration. Speech sounds belong to the much larger category of "immusical sounds," a category that also includes "all *Whisperings*, all *voices of Beasts, and Birds*, (except they bee *Singing Birds*;), all *Percussions*, of *Stones*, *Wood*, *Parchment*, *Skins* (as in *Drummes*;) and infinite others" (35). It is the incommensurability of speech sounds that presents Bacon his greatest challenge: "It seemeth that Aire, (which is the Subiect of *Sounds*) in *Sounds* that are not *Tones*, (which are all *vnequall*, as hath beene said) admitteth much Varietie; As wee see in the *Voices* of *Liuing Creatures*; And likewise in the *Voices* of seuerall *Men*; (for we are capable to discerne seuerall *Men* by their *Voices*;) And in the *Coniugation of Letters*, whence *Articulate Sounds* proceed; Which of all others are most various." If musical tones are circles, squares, and triangles, speech sounds are "*Figures* . . . made of lines, Crooked and Straight, in infinite Varietie" (36). Circles, squares, and triangles are susceptible to measurement and precise description; crooked and straight lines are not. Bacon is like most early modern writers in confidently referring to speech sounds as "letters." Other writers, like John Hart in his spelling-reform polemic *An Orthography* (1569), follow Aristotle in referring to individual speech sounds as "voices." Even so, Hart believes that voices and letters ought to coincide: "euen as euery body is to be resolued into those Elements whereof it is composed, so euery word is to be undone into those voices only whereof it is made. Seeing then that letters are figures and colours wherewith the image of mans voice is painted, you are forced to graunt the writing should haue so many letters as the speach hath voyces, and no more nor lesse."[34] Hart and Bacon clearly want to be modern semantic linguists, but neither of them can ignore the embodiedness of spoken sound.

However much early modern writers wanted to describe speech as a sequence of discrete letters or voices, they nonetheless recognized that what gets *articulated* in articulate speech is continuous, undifferentiated sound. Spenser hears it as the buzzing of bees. The House of Alma in Book Two of *The Faerie Queene* comprises three chambers, each presided over by a different counselor. The first chamber is devoted to things future, the second to things present, the third to things past. The first chamber, assigned to Phantastes, is painted in sundry colors with thinly dispersed images of things "such as in the world were neuer yit," as well as things "daily seene, and knowen by their names, / Such as in idle fantasies doe flit" (2.9.50.4, 6–7). The room is no less replete with sounds:

And all the chamber filled was with flyes,
>Which buzzed all about, and made such sound,
>That they encombred all mens eares and eyes,
>Like many swarmes of Bees assembled round,
>After their hiues with honny do abound. (2.9.51.1–5)

The buzzings are irrational sounds, provocations to hearing green:

All those were idle thoughts and fantasies,
Deuices, dreames, opinions vnsound,
Shewes, visions, sooth-sayes, and prophesies;
And all that fained is, as leasings, tales, and lies. (2.9.51.6–9)

The venue in which Thomas Dekker hears similarly confused sounds is the theater. He describes the phenomenon, not as green but as black. Like Spenser's buzzing, Dekker's "black" is seething with passions, passions that are incited by the very sort of dance music that Stubbes excoriates, passions that are expressed as speech giving way to noise:

I haue often seene, after the finishing of some worthy Tragedy or Catastrophe in the open Theaters, that the Sceane after the Epilogue hath beene more blacke (about a nasty bawdy Iigge) then the most horrid Sceane in the Play was: The Stinkards speaking all things, yet no man vnderstanding any thing; a mutiny being among them, yet none in danger: no tumult, yet no quietnesse: no mischife begotten, and yet mischiefe borne: the swiftnesse of such a torrent, the more it ouerwhelmes, breeding the more pleasure.[35]

The meaning of "black" here seems to extend beyond the color of tragedy to a sense of "black" as "foul, iniquitous, atrocious, horribly wicked" (*OED*). In more scientific terms, the first English phonetician, Robert Robinson, recognizes that the articulation and projection of vowels and consonants require a third kind of sound, produced from the throat, which Robinson calls "vital sound." Out of it "all the sounds of different quantitie doe arise."[36] Modern commentators on Robinson have interpreted this "vital sound" as the equivalent of what we would call voiced sounds (as opposed to whispering), but there may be an indication here of the neutral [ə], the schwa, that the vocal tract produces when no part of the apparatus is in motion.[37] The first, unstressed syllable of the English word *canoe* [kənu] is one instance of this neutral sound; so is the "uh . . . " made by many English speakers today as they try to gather their thoughts between utterances and hold onto their speaking turn.

In their own distinctive ways, then, early modern writers recognized a matrix out of which articulate speech emerges. George Puttenham speaks for most of these writers in identifying this matrix with the irrational and hence with the passions. "There is no greater difference betwixt a ciuill and brutish vtteraunce," Puttenham observes in *The Art of English Poesie*, "then cleare distinction of voices: and the most laudable languages are alwaies most plaine and distinct, and the barbarous most confuse [*sic*] and indistinct."[38] Hart brings the same criterion to his spelling reform scheme. "The letter ought to keepe the voyce, and not to be ydle, vsurped in sound or to be misplaced" (C2v). Superfluous letters function, in Hart's hearing, like "vicious humors" that need to be purged (C3v).

What constitutes the "plaine and distinct" speech that Puttenham uses as a criterion for distinguishing laudable languages from barbarous? For Hart it would be an exact correspondence of letters to voices. For Thomas Campion it would be verse that is free from rhyme. To Campion's ear excessive rhyming is a kind of buzzing: "The facilitie and popularitie of Rime," Campion decares in *Observations in the Art of English Poesie*, "creates as many Poets as a hot sommer [creates] flies."[39] The Roman rhetoricians advised only sparing use of rhyme, Campion notes, "least it should offend the ear with tedious affectation" (36). The term "affectation" is precisely chosen. Rhyme is a species of irrationality: "The eare is a rational sence and a chiefe iudge of proportion; but in our kind of riming what proportion is there kept when there remaines such a confusd inequalitie of sillables?" (36). Campion recognizes that repetition is basic to poetry's appeal. What he champions over the repetition of certain phonemes is the repetition of certain time values, as if English were like Latin in measuring how long vowels are held rather than how much stress they receive. One of the songs Campion contributed to Philip Rosseter's *A Book of Airs* (1601) illustrates the principle by exactly matching the time values of the musical notes with the time values of the sapphic metre that he has imposed on the conspicuously unrhymed English words (Figure 7.5). In this precise alignment of note values and vowel values Campion provides a musical equivalent of Hart's orthography—and a radical example of logocentricism in music. The "childish titillation of riming" is to be abjured in large part because it works against rational clarity: "it inforceth a man oftentimes to abiure his matter and extend a short conceit beyond all bounds of arte" (37).

In *A Defence of Ryme* Samuel Daniel turns Campion's rationalist criteria against him. Rhythm and rhyme, Daniel feels, endow poetry with "the effect of motion."[40] Amid this motion, rhythmic patterns provide points of distinction, "being such as the Eare of it selfe doth marshal in their proper roomes, and they of themselues will not willingly be put out of their ranke" (131–32). Rhyme, for its part, provides "due staies for the minde, those incounters of touch as makes the motion certaine, though the varietie be infinite" (134). To Daniel's ear both rhythm and rhyme thus serve to separate and to order sounds that would otherwise be experienced as continuous motion. By imposing form on this continuous motion, rhythm and rhyme recapitulate Genesis and, in so doing, shore up reason against engulfment by the passions:

For the body of our imagination, being as an vnformed *Chaos* without fashion, without day, if by the diuine power of the spirit it be wrought into an Orbe of order and forme, is it not more pleasing to Nature, that desires a certaintie, and comports not with that which is infinite, to haue these clozes, rather than, not to know where to end, or how farre to goe, especially seeing our passions are often without measure. (138)

The quantitative verse that Campion proposes would, according to Daniel, work against right judgement, since it would divert the mind from the "matter" of the poem and call attention instead to sound *as sound*:

For seeing it is matter that satisfies the iudiciall, appeare it in what habite it will, all these pretended proportions of words, howsoeuer placed, can be but words, and peraduenture serue but to embroyle our vnderstanding, whilst seeking to please our

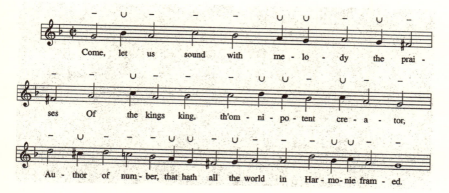

Figure 7.5. Musical Example 4, Thomas Campion, "Come let us sound with melody." Adapted from Philip Rosseter, *A Book of Airs* (1601).

eare, we inthrall our iudgement: to delight an exterior sense, wee smoothe vp a weake confused sense, affecting sound to be vnsound. (136)

All told, rhyme in Daniel's analysis serves as an antidote to endless motion, to confusion, to mere sensation, to the sway of the passions.

Ben Jonson, for one, would not be so sure. Jonson's poem "A Fit of Rhyme Against Rhyme" enacts, stanza by stanza, a tension between mindless sound and sound mind:

Rime, the rack of finest wits,
That expresseth but by fits,
                    True Conceipt,
Spoyling Senses of their Treasure,
Cosening Judgement with a measure,
                    But false weight.[41]

To give the reader's eye the same sharp contrast that the reader's ear can hear, Jonson not only offsets the lapidary *thereness* of "True Conceipt" but capitalizes it as if it were a Platonic Idea. What exactly is the "Treasure" of which rhyme "spoils" the senses? The succeeding lines suggest that it is the true conceit, or right conception, that the understanding should be able to find in the imagination's transcript of sense experience. In the case of sound, that means an exact coincidence between sound and meaning:

Wresting words, from their true calling;
Propping Verse, for feare of falling
                    To the ground.
Joynting Syllabes, drowning Letters,
Fastning Vowells, as with fetters
                    They were bound! (29.7–12)

Three particular disruptions of the sound / meaning bond are catalogued in the latter three lines: contractions ("Joynting Syllabes"demonstrates the phenomenon by reducing the three syllables of *syl-la-ble* to two), obliterating distinctions between phonemes ("Letters" indicates Jonson's predisposition to see what he hears), and arranging vowels according to sound alone (the "fetters" privilege sound over sense). All three involve "drowning" discrete syllables and words in the stream of sound. Jonson's own *metier* as a verse maker is to be found in the chiseled, waterproof solidity of the short lines: "True Conceipt," "But false weight," "To the ground," "They were bound."

Better examples could not be found of Jonson's adherence to what he

and his contemporaries understood as "the plain style." Traditionally associated with dialectic (the goal of which was simply to teach, not to move or
delight), the plain style favored as close as possible an alignment between
denotation and connotation.[42] In Jonson's case the centripetal drive toward
denotation is heightened by a preference not only for monosyllabic words
but for monosyllabic words that begin and end with strong consonants:
"*weight*," "*ground*," "*bound*." In such words there is little possibility of
"drowning Letters." In the stream of speech there are three types of land-
marks that serve to divide the stream into discrete units: (1) vowels at syllable peaks, (2) abrupt consonants, and (3) low-frequency glides (the [j] in
your, the [w] in *wore*) produced as the vocal apparatus moves from one
position to another.[43] Generally speaking, vowels and glides enhance the
stream effect of sound; consonants, especially the stops [p], [b], [t], [d], [k],
and [g], contribute to an effect of distinctness.

The ratio of vowels to consonantal stops, particularly in how words
begin and end, gives us one way of comparing how early modern verse writers variously negotiate the stream of sound. Shakespeare's contemporary
reputation for mellifluousness was something for which Jonson himself was
partly responsible. In the catalogue of Shakespeare's virtues that Jonson
includes in *Timber, or Discoveries,* "true conceit" is conspicuously absent:
Shakespeare, says Jonson, "had an excellent *Phantasie*; brave notions, and
gentle expressions: wherein hee flow'd with that facility, that sometime it
was necessary he should be stop'd."[44] Shakespeare's own complaint against
an insubstantial rhymer in sonnet 85 ("My toung-tide muse in manners
holds her still") can provide an example:

I thinke good thoughts, whilst other write good wordes,
And like vnlettered clarke still crie Amen,
To euery Himne that able spirit affords,
In polisht form of well refined pen.[45]

In the first line, made up entirely of monosyllabic words, the sharp distinction between "good thoughts" and "good words" is accentuated with termi-
nal [d] sounds and [t] + [s] sounds. That measured restraint quickly gives
way, however, to an outpouring of resentment that gathers force in iambs
that are almost anapests ("And like un*let*tered," "To every *hymn*") and in
waves of initial vowels ("*A*nd," "*u*nlettered," "*A*men," "*e*very," "*a*ble," "*a*ffords")
that spill over from line two to three and from line three to four before
returning to a modicum of composure in the plosives of "*p*olished . . . *p*en."
Need one point out that this twenty-one-word, thrice-enjambed effusion is

an indulgence in passion, in jealousy, in green-sickness? Greenness here is something that can be heard as well as seen. Not for nothing did Jonson persistently associate Shakespeare with nature ("Sweet Swan of Avon!"), even as he acknowledged the durability of the "well torned, and true filed lines" that he himself aspired to write.[46]

To hear green would mean, then, allowing rhyme, alliteration, and assonance to divert the sense of hearing from its rational work. To hear green would mean attending to sounds that spiral away from denotative meaning toward wordless sensation. Iago's warning enkindles Othello's jealousy precisely because of these green sound effects: "Oh, beware my Lord, of iealousie, / It is the greene-ey'd Monster which doth mocke / The meate it feeds on" (3.3.169–71). The opening exclamation immediately wrests the imagination away from the regimen of words. As it happens, [o:] is the most intense vowel sound in English: it strikes the ear more forcefully than other vowel sounds.[47] Joel Fineman has called attention to the pervasiveness of [o:] in *Othello* and has interpreted its effect as an opening into the Lacanian Real and hence as a challenge to the fixity of language in the Symbolic Order.[48] The suggestiveness of Iago's [o:] in Act Three, scene three, is at once audible. "But oh," Iago concludes the speech, "what damned minutes tells he ore, / Who dotes, yet doubts: Suspects, yet foundly loues?" Othello responds in kind, like the singer of an antiphon: "O miserie" (3.3.174–75). The power of Iago's speech over Othello's passions is very much an effect of assonance and alliteration. Sounds of [o] insinuate surprise or moaning in "l*o*rd," "jeal*o*usy," "m*o*nster," "d*o*th," "m*o*ck," and "*o*n." Quick panting is invited by the [i] sounds in "*i*t," "*i*s," "wh*i*ch," and again "*i*t." Stronger still is the keening intimated by the [i:] sounds in "jealous*y*," "gr*ee*n," "m*ea*t," and "f*ee*ds." The ruminative [m] in "*m*onster," "*m*ock," and "*m*eat" completes the job of aural seduction. The stops in "mo*ck*," "mea*t*," "i*t*," and "fee*ds*" give the completed utterance a deadly inevitability. The passionate power of "willow" later in the play is unmistakable, especially as those sounds are sung again and again as a refrain in between the lines of a narrative: "*Sing Willough, Willough, Willough,*" "*Sing Willough, &c.,*" "*Sing Willough &c., / Willough Willough,*" "*Sing all a greene Willough must be my Garland*" (4.3.41, 43, 45–46, 49). The effect of these repeated utterances has less to do with a type of tree than with the passion of melancholy. In [w] [l] [o:] Desdemona's passion devolves from words into deep green, just as the Jailer's Daughter's passion does when, in her first utterance, she tries to remember the refrain of a song she once knew: "I have forgot it quite; The burden on't was *downe / A downe a*'" (4.3.10–11). The daughter's song, the ballad of "Greensleeves," Desdemona singing "Willow, willow, willow": all these siren-songs beckon listeners to hear green.

The threat of words and syllables to devolve into nonsemantic sound is always present in early modern verse, especially in the pastoral mode. On occasion we can see that devolution happen before our very eyes on the printed page, just as it happens within our very ears when we vocalize the text to ourselves. Take, for example, Nashe's spirited celebration of spring in *Summer's Last Will and Testament*. The [s] sounds and anapestic rhythms of the first stanza, ringing out in sharp contrast to the stops of "*cold*" and "*sting*," fly free of words entirely in the stanza's final line. By the third stanza, bird songs have become pandemic throughout the human scene:

Spring, the sweete spring, is the yeres pleasant King,
Then bloomes eche thing, then maydes daunce in a ring,
Cold doeth not sting, the pretty birds doe sing:
Cuckow, iugge, iugge, pu we, to witta woo.
The Palme and May make countrey houses gay,
Lambs friske and play, the Shepherds pype all day,
And we heare aye, birds tune this merry lay:
Cuckow, iugge, iugge, pu we, to witta woo.
The fields breathe sweete, the dayzies kisse our feete,
Young louers meete, old wiues a sunning sit,
In euery streete, these tunes our eares do greete,
Cuckow, iugge, iugge, pu we, to witta woo.
　　Spring the sweete spring.[49]

When the song's opening phrase, "Spring, the sweet spring," is repeated as a coda, the sound of [s] has become far more suasive than the meanings denoted by "spring" and "sweet" the first time around. Especially in the original performance in 1592, when the lines were sung by Ver and his train, "*ouer-layd with suites of greene mosse, representing short grasse*" (sig. B3), Nashe's verses were calculated to appeal to the passions, not to the understanding alone. For readers with open ears, now as in 1592, Nashe's verses work a radical deconstruction on the English language.

Garrett Stewart has argued that an element of deconstruction is present in all written texts when they are vocalized, aloud or silently, in the act of reading:

Reading is the displacing without forgetting of one word by the next in the syntactic chain. When this displacement operates a shade too quickly or too slowly—one word shadowed in passing by its neighbor partly assimilated to it by recurring in it—the "will" to morphophonemic structure is thus found exerting its full, indeed overflowing, pressure on the written sign. At such moments, within the economy of grammar and the duration of reading, what we might call the two-fold "rate" of exchange between words is upset; pace becomes unreliable, the toll on syntax increased. . . . Laterally entailed, that is, words do not speak, or get spoken, just for themselves.[50]

For Stewart, the "blurring at the borders" between phonemes creates "the possibility of more paradigmatic choices than can simultaneously be made" (26). He proceeds to attend to the blurs in a range of English poets, as well as in prose writers like Sterne, Dickens, Lawrence, Joyce, and Woolf. Stephen Booth delights in a similar plenitude of possibilities generated by the "physics" of metrical pairings, rhyme, alliteration, anaphora, and chiasmus: "All those literary phenomena are enabling acts, acts that enable their audiences to perceive two or more distinct identities at once and as one."[51] Booth's test case is Act Three, scenes nine and ten, of *Antony and Cleopatra.* What Stewart and Booth both listen for are new words, instances of "transegmental drift" (25) in Stewart's case and a "fusion and confusion of entities" (77) in Booth's. The green potential in early modern verse is more radical than that. It dissolves words, not into other words, but into nonsemantic sound. It does not just break words down into phonemes that can be recombined with other phonemes in new and interesting ways; it *liquefies* words. That potential is enabled by a physiology of knowing in which the passions "hear" sensations before reason does. The sensations circulate throughout the body as an aerated fluid on which reason's imprint is always insubstantial The green potential is just as present for critics who are willing to go deconstruction one better and listen to the totality of speech sounds beyond the 50 percent that are heard as words. The binaries of deconstruction are marks made on water.

Chapter 8
Humoral Knowledge and Liberal Cognition in Davenant's Macbeth

Katherine Rowe

Lady Macduff:	*What had he done, to make him fly the land?*
Rosse:	*You must have patience, madam.*
Lady Macduff:	*He had none.*
	His flight was madness. When our actions do not,
	Our fears do make us traitors.
Rosse:	*You know not*
	Whether it was his wisdom or his fear. (4.2.1–7)

This debate between Rosse and Lady Macduff about Macduff's departure[1] touches on a persistent concern of seventeenth-century English passions theory: the natural turbulence of undirected passions. That turbulence is both the subject and source of Lady Macduff's anxious fury. First she charges that her husband (fled to England) has turned traitor. Then she charges a parallel disloyalty within the small kingdom of the family: affections that turn against natural reason "make us traitors." Rosse cautions her not to let her fears overwhelm her own judgment:

> My dearest coz,
> I pray you school yourself. But for your husband,
> He is noble, wise, judicious, and best knows
> The fits o'th' season. I dare not speak much further,
> But cruel are the times when we are traitors
> And do not know ourselves; when we hold rumour
> From what we fear, yet know not what we fear,
> But float upon a wild and violent sea
> Each way and none. I take my leave of you; (4.2.15–22)

The injunction to "school yourself" should be a corrective, delivered with self-control from a position of superior knowledge. Yet Rosse seems infected by Lady Macduff's mistrust. His "wild and violent sea" invokes an ubiquitous topos of early modern psychology, the tempest of ungoverned passions. Unsure of himself, he describes such passions as traitorous, then flies

A M I D the waues, a mightie Rock doth ſtand,
 Whoſe ruggie brow, had bidden many a ſhower,
And bitter ſtorme; which neither ſea, nor land,
Nor *IOVES* ſharpe-lightening euer could deuoure :
 This ſame is *MANLIE CONSTANCIE* of mind,
 Not eaſly moou'd, with euery blaſt of wind.

Neere which you ſee, a goodly ſhip to drowne,
Herewith bright flaming in a pitteous fire :
This is *OPINION*, toſſed vp and downe,
Whoſe Pilot's *PRIDE*, & Steereſman *VAINE DESIRE*,
 Thoſe flames *HOT PASSIONS*, & the *WORLD* the ſea,
 God bleſſe the man, that's carried thus away.

Vide Lipſium de
Conſtantia.

Z 1.   *Præcocia*

Figure 8.1. "Nec igne, nec unda." An emblem of inconstant and constant minds, in the neo-Stoic mode, from Henry Peacham, *Minerva Britanna* (1612), 158. Reproduced by permission of the Folger Shakespeare Library.

the scene with unnerving dispatch. This anxiety exposes instabilities in a parallel set of polities: the state of Scotland, Macduff's family, the commonwealth of the mind. Of course, these instabilities are overdetermined by the presence of a tyrant, the absence of a spouse (for whom Ross makes a poor substitute), and the force of an emotion—fear—that by definition suspends the higher cognitive faculties. Overdetermined as they may be, however, the emotions expressed in this scene are labile—turbulent and changeable—because they are also contagious. Though he hushes her, Rosse seems to catch his self-description from Lady Macduff's conclusion, echoing it in a way that confirms "our fears do make us traitors."

Almost fifty years later, Sir William Davenant (a careful reader of Shakespeare and of this play in particular) offered to correct such contagious uncertainties on a national scale. In "A Proposition for Advancement of Moralitie by a New Way of Entertainment of the People" (1653), a bid for state support of a public stage, Davenant proposed a theatrical "Academy" of moral entertainments. His theater would provide an arena for the professional instruction and management of the passions roiling Cromwell's uneasy populace. Popular ignorance of the passions breeds "dispair of knowledg" and eventual rebellion, for "the people will ever be unquiet whilst they are ignorant of themselves, and unacquainted with those Engines that scrue them up, which are their passions, in true characters of the beauties and deformities of vertue and vice."[2] As in Shakespeare's play, the chief means for governing turbulent passions in Davenant's moral theater are social and rhetorical. On both Shakespeare's and Davenant's stage, passions are properly explained and schooled—self-governance is achieved or lost—through face-to-face exchange. While the playwrights share common strategies for schooling the passions, however, Davenant's mechanical metaphor points towards a shifting perception of these face to face scenes, from affective contagion to a more self-possessed, calibrated give and take. Ross's admonition invokes strategies of gentlemanly self-discipline that Lady Macduff's contagious affects challenge. The wider, mixed audience in which Davenant proposes to circulate such affective disciplines requires ever more careful techniques for managing such contagion.

Davenant's concern with the civic instruction of the passions is a local instance of a general problem of knowledge in seventeenth-century England. Thomas Browne described this problem as the "Erroneous Disposition of the People" whose "uncultivated understandings, scarce holding any theory, . . . are but bad discerners of verity."[3] As Steven Shapin observes, even the staunchest empirical scientists of the period acknowledged that the senses and affections bias judgment, not just in the common sort but also in Englishmen of discretion.[4] Although the problem is socially widespread, however, the commons (like women) are especially easily screwed up, "being naturally passionate and turbulent" ("Proposition," 244). Yet their passions are also naturally "reducible," Davenant finds, and this offers unique opportunities for cultivation (244). Other state institutions fall short of the concrete persuasions required to cultivate popular understanding, he continues. Because the military works by compulsion and the Church speaks in abstractions, both institutions leave "the clouds of common mindes" to "continue undisperst, and breed dispair of knowledg, which begets aversion, and aversion begets open defection" (244). Davenant describes in brief here an internal economy widely accepted in early modern psychological theory. The affections and the higher cognitive processes—judgement, memory, imagination—mutually inform one another. Together they prompt the will to action. The passage suggests that the common sort are prone to especially labile passions that overrule judgment. Lacking direction and uninstructed in their own inner workings, they sway like Lady Macduff on turbulent seas of emotion. For Davenant, Thomas Hobbes, and other political thinkers of the 1650s and 1660s, such turbulence challenges a stable polity. Not knowing their own passions and swayed by sense, the commons cannot know themselves as civil subjects. Most troubling for early modern political theory, such physiological wavering means their allegiance can never be secured.[5]

One solution to the problem of swayable senses was to rely upon specific vocations for expertise in the one sense their practitioners mastered. Robert Boyle concludes, for example, that one may trust the eye of a jeweler to judge the luster of a diamond, or the palate of a skillful taster to choose one's wine.[6] This does not, however, answer the larger problem of unruly passions stirred up by the rest of the unguided senses. Davenant presents the theater as a vocation in one way comparable to Boyle's jeweler. His design for a moral "Academy" recasts the public stage as privileged space for the cultivation of understanding; its proper expertise and its object are the arousal and governance of the passions. The stage offers superior access to the senses, he argues, which theater professionals (men of experience and discretion like himself) can use to guide an audience to moral understanding (or at least acquiescence). Properly managed entertainments thus "divert the people from disorder, [and] by degrees enamour them with consideration of the conveniences and protections of Government" (245). Davenant makes notably larger claims for the professional theater than Boyle does for his jeweler: the theater engages multiple senses, martialling a broad band of stimulae to direct affective responses. His operatic dramaturgy during and after the Interregnum was designed to put such principles into practice. And though he failed to gain support for the specific proposals in "A Proposition," Davenant remained a successful producer of moral entertainments under Cromwell and after the Restoration—most familiarly, with his operatic adaptations of Shakespeare. As Jacob and Raylor observe, Davenant's opera simplified the mysteries of the Jacobean and Caroline court masque to Theophrastian "beauties and deformities of vertue and vice" (244), vivid and popularly accessible.[7] Boosting the appeal of theatrical devices to multiple senses in this way, he expanded their political and social claims.

With its scenes of fearful prophecy, emotional uncertainty, and unpredictable politics, Shakespeare's *Macbeth* (1606) provided an especially rich ground for experiments in theatrical education. The encounter between Rosse and Lady Macduff is one of many scenes of sympathetic instruction in the play. Davenant's revisions to these scenes offer a palimpsest of the changing terms under which knowledge about the passions circulated, in increasingly level venues of public assembly and urban community—the venues imagined and negotiated in his pamphlets. These experiments with theatrical affect addressed the emerging class of civil gentleman as well as the court.[8] Bodily disciplines of self-mastery and restraint were a key feature of gentlemanly self-fashioning in Stuart England, as Michael Schoenfeldt has shown.[9] Such disciplines required systematic translation for a mixed Restoration audience, aspiring to know themselves as civil subjects but in many cases untrained in the classical models of Stoic philosophy. The popularization of Neostoic practices was already a vexed issue by the time Davenant took it up. English Neostoicism had early on served both oppositional and absolutist political discourses; as Reid Barbour has shown, they were not inevitably received as a medium for civil order.[10] This legacy seems to have troubled later political theorists as they explored strategies for instilling obedience and worried about the potential for faction in an educated populace.[11] Thus, for post-Restoration English audiences, the subjects of several changes of regime, Rosse's fears arguably straddle two estates. Swaying "each way and none" they epitomize the wayward loyalties Davenant sought to redress in the commons. But they also evoke the potential for disaffection among the commons's superiors. His fearful discontent makes him an oppositional figure, as Rosse uneasily acknowledges. Though this is the result of political tyranny, he is hardly one to reassure an audience of the "conveniences and protections of Government." These concerns help explain why Davenant cut Rosse's part when he revived *Macbeth* after the Restoration. More is involved in that cut, however. The contagious nature of Shakespearean fears models a kind of affective exchange no longer suited to the internal disciplines Davenant promotes. In the passage quoted above, for example, Rosse seems to catch Lady Macduff's fearful anxiety and to translate it into an elliptical rationale for changing sides.

A careful reading of such exchanges in Davenant's adaptation of *Macbeth* (1674) illuminates a shift in the phenomenology of emotion during the seventeenth century—a shift that speaks to some of our central challenges as twenty-first-century readers of early modern affects. The two *Macbeths* straddle the gradual and uneven transition from early modern humoralism (with its environmentally permeable body and labile animal spirits) to the proprietary body theorized by Descartes and Locke. Late seventeenth-century natural philosophy re-imagined the body, John Sutton reminds us, as a "solid container, only rarely breached, in principle autonomous from culture and environment, tampered with only by diseases and experts."[12] Proprietary models of consciousness require, Sutton observes, not only a body sealed off from its physical environment but cognitive processes sealed off from their physical environment of senses, passions and humors. Consequently, operations such as memory, judgement, and will, were reimagined in this period as the autonomous, executive faculties of a self-possessed individual, rather than the fluid action of animal spirits (Sutton, 117–18). Thus, for example, John Locke elaborates the topos of internal "assent," familiar from humoral models of cognition, into a theory of liberal consciousness. Locke revises a humoral theory of material influence (the administrative faculty of judgment "assents" to what is reported by the senses, persuaded by the material force as well as the content of those reports) into a rational consciousness that (in theory, at least) freely agrees to or dismisses the testimony of the senses.[13] Charles Taylor describes a similar shift in late seventeenth-century European philosophy—consciousness that knows itself primarily from the inside—as a distinctively modern feature of a cognitive life sealed off from informing senses and passions in this way.[14] Taylor's modern exceptionalism has been fruitfully challenged on the grounds that it overstates the singlemindedness of early modern neurophilosophy and that "radical reflexivity" is not a historically new phenomenon.[15] Yet his story of proprietary inwardness remains powerful as an account of one of several conflicting models of affective life, converging in diverse disciplines. The interplay and competition between these models in seventeenth-century English passions discourse can provide critical insights into the methodological challenges modern scholars face in the study of emotion more generally.

The principle of proprietary, internal controls voluntarily applied—what Sutton terms "voluntary cognitive proprieties" (118) and Shapin calls cognitive "decorum" (101)—is one legacy of this period of experiment. That decorum was important to a range of contractarian theories emerging in the seventeenth century, both economic and political, and remains a cornerstone of liberal thought.[16] By simultaneously insisting on the critical importance of emotion to such larger social systems yet situating emotions inaccessibly inside the self, this principle of decorum also conditions the paradoxical sense of license and reserve modern scholars confront whenever we set out to analyze emotions. As Catherine Lutz observes, it is a modern commonplace that everyone has feelings; yet the phenomena are individual and internal, they rise and fall within the boundaries of our bodies proper.[17] Modern emotions are understood as immediate, transitory, and natural—separate from discipline and convention, but a necessary warrant to (and challenge to) both. In this context, emotions are known idiopathically. True knowledge of emotions falters at the limits of private, proprietary experience. Such normative notions about the proprietary nature of emotion might be called, following Anna Wierzbicka's lead, a dominant set of cultural "scripts." "Emotion scripts" are the shared (but not always internally consistent) "attitudes towards feelings, different communications strategies associated with feelings, and different norms governing the handling of feelings (one's own and other people's)" that characterize different cultures. [18]

When modern critics discuss the passions of early modern subjects, we are instructed in part by our own scripts regarding the individual, proprietary, and transitory nature of the phenomena we aim to study. On the one hand, we may be suspicious of arguments that extrapolate across the gulf of individual, time-delimited experience. Beyond the problem of accuracy in translation, such arguments lack the authenticity of immediate, unreconstructed access—mediated as they are by the material record and by the processes of reconstruction and interpretation that changing context and social conventions require.[19] (We weren't there.) On the other hand, we may tend to self-select for emotion scripts we recognize, in ways that are hard to see. Recent critical histories of the subject suggest that the early modern texts which most strongly evoke for us the possibility of knowing from the inside are those that meet the demands of a proprietary inner life.[20] Hamlet's soliloquies or Pepys's euphemisms are familiar examples: rhetorical structures that signal affective immediacy because they withhold the heart of their mystery. (Something is there that we can't know.) Yet these scripts only partly match those of the cultures whose textual traces we analyze. In this context, Rosse's speech offers an illuminating corrective. It does conform to the emotion scripts of a proprietary consciousness in several ways: it conjures the felt immediacy of his fears, his exquisite self-awareness, and he certainly withholds information (the "fits o' th' season" that he intimates). Yet Rosse's emotions are also leaky and labile in ways that register less clearly to modern ears. Instead of countering Lady Macduff's anxiety he picks it up and internalizes it, to the point that his own fears seem at once the source of and response to treasonous rumor—less internal mysteries than intersubjective fits themselves. Such affective contagion has its own place in modern psychology: often pathologized (mass hysteria, borderline personalities), or restricted to popular entertainment venues (professional sports, blockbuster movies), and marketing (buzz, word of mouth). In early seventeenth-century England it was an ordinary and pervasive feature of humorally conceived passions.

The aim of this essay is to trace the changing phenomenology of early modern affect in scenes of emotional exchange like the one between Rosse and Lady Macduff, as they are explored on the seventeenth-century English stage. Early modern performance practices conditioned affective experience, shaping the way consumers came to name their emotions, interpret them, and understand them as social and political currency.[21] The contagious affects of a humoral body were a vexed but fundamental feature of theatrical performance in early Stuart England, as contemporary passions theorists and anti-theatrical polemics variously attest. Joseph Roach observes that the transport of emotions between actors and audience was recognized as a species of rhetorical *enargeia*: "an inspired image in the mind of the speaker so striking that it transforms his actions as if the actual object were present to his senses and thereby communicates its vivid impression to the bodies and minds of the spectators."[22] The nature of such affective exchange, its discipline, and uses, changed with the increasingly proprietary construction of emotional life during and after the civil war. Restoration play-texts offered ever more detailed accounts of the passions, promoting a wider circulation of knowledge about emotion among an increasingly level class of consumers. At the same time, the demonstrations of the passions available in the theater flourished in prose media associated with the stage: consumer's guides to English plays, illustrations of the passions and humors in theatrical "characters," etc. This expanding technical knowledge recharged concerns about the humoral hierarchies of different kinds of person. Is emotional exchange destabilizing or instructive? Is more or less knowledge of the passions conducive to public order? Who should have access to such knowledge and under what conditions? The modern alignment of contagious emotions with physical disorder, popular appetite, and economic leverage is in part a legacy of late seventeenth-century revisions of such humoral concerns.

In exploring these revisions I want to stress that Restoration phenomenology did not so much replace humoral models as reorient their intersubjective structures from ecological disciplines (conceived broadly in terms of air, climate, diet, etc.) to disciplines of social display and emulation. Late seventeenth-century phenomenology internalized affective controls in a civil subject, as scholars such as Norbert Elias and Charles Taylor have shown. But such controls remain in important ways intersubjective: dependent on the social circulation of knowledge about the emotions and the public division of affective labor between different kinds of person. Moreover, the emotion scripts redescribed in terms of internal discipline in this period never were (nor become) internally consistent or unified. Michel Serres reminds us of the significant "lag between philosophical debate and scientific information" in any paradigm shift.[23] Such lags are particularly evident in the way Davenant's entertainments deploy theater technologies, exploring the rationalist psychology emerging in the work of close associates such as Hobbes. Davenant's dramaturgy approaches contractarian models of cognition, promoting individual knowledge and management of affective life. Yet he accommodates this process to the humorally based capacities of different estates. In practical terms, Davenant conceives of theatrical passions as lasting as well as immediate phenomena; particular affects may be transitory, but structures of emotion endure. To manage them effectively one works within available scripts and conventions. This partly explains Davenant's pursuit of a new civic regime of emotional education through theatrical adaptation, instead of simply writing a new play. Playtexts, he recognizes, dramatize and make legible widespread social scripts for emotion.

To conceive of cultural change in terms of temporal lags—what Serres calls "counter-currents" and "turbulences"—is to see any complex cultural structure (such as emotion) as a "disparate aggregate" of technical ideas from different periods (45).[24] Historical aggregation may in part explain why, as Barbara H. Rosenwein observes, "not only does every society call forth, shape, constrain, and express emotions differently, but even within the same society contradictory values and models ... find their place."[25] Our

current, popular vocabulary of emotion displays its own polychronic principles in the persistence of purportedly dated concepts such as a Freudian
unconscious or a dualist inner life.[26] Americans may still feel pathologically
"screwed up," in Davenant's mechanistic sense, despite the move in modern
neurological, psychological, and anthropological theory to new notions of
embodied mind.[27] Similarly, in the late seventeenth century, humoral kinds
and concerns persist and are incorporated in contractarian models of inner
life, as expertise in the passions diffuses from elite skill to something all subjects are expected to understand in themselves. To frame the genealogy of
Western emotion concepts to allow for Serres's idea of temporal lag and
polychronicity is to see gulfs of time and cultural context not as permanent
obstacles to understanding early modern affects, but as features of emotion
as such. Emotions, understood this way, are historically composite phenomena, anchored in the biology and social practices of different periods.

Looked at one way, Rosse's feelings are easy to sympathize with. Scholars
have emphasized his shiftiness in general and the guile of this speech in particular. Reading along these lines, we might gloss the speech above along the
following lines: Rosse cautions Lady Macduff to hold her tongue, refers cryp-
tically (like Hamlet) to things he knows but won't divulge, and keeps his
own counsel. We might acknowledge a certain realpolitik in Rosse, not unlike
Davenant's own ability to survive changing regimes. In a state of civil war,
anyone would wish to ride the tides of fortune so well and follow the right
political wake. Significantly, this speech is spoken in a cognitively reflective
mode. Unlike Davenant's commons, Rosse *can* give a nuanced account of
the internal processes that sway him. Thus his reflection offers hortatory or
didactic exposition of how a courtier might respond to overwhelming
anxiety. In this respect it would seem to fulfill Davenant's objectives for theatrical instruction. Yet Rosse's fears also confuse him, in a radically intersubjective way that Davenant cannot support. Macbeth's oppressive tyranny
produces both mental disorder and social displacement in the early modern
sense of the word *confuse* ("to rout," "disorder," and "overthrow").[28] Rosse
knows himself in unaccustomed terms, as a traitor, and this self-knowledge
comes from internal and external events he does not control.

When we read Rosse's emotions in self-possessed terms, in other words,
we risk over-emphasizing his political and emotional autonomy. We are
likely to miss the vertiginous experience troped by the image of a self tossed
on "wild and violent seas" that are at once emotional and political. Rosse's
metaphor—the topos of a stormy ocean—dominates early modern passions

theory. Thomas Wright explains in *The Passions of the Minde in Generall* (1604), for example, how an army of unruly passions "toss and turmoile our miserable souls, as tempests and waves the Ocean sea, the which never standeth quiet, but either in ebbing or flowing, either winds doe buz about it, or raines alter it, or earthquake shake, or stormes tyrannize over it."[29] This topos resonates in multiple ways. It evokes the storm-tossed ship of State, familiar from popular emblems of Fortune, the perilous journey of the soul (Alciati offers several examples), and the Petrarchan ship of the self, as in Sir Thomas Wyatt's "My Galley Chargéd with Forgetfulness" (1557). Henry Peacham draws ambiguously on all of these traditions in his Neo-stoic emblem of inconstant and constant minds (Figure 8.1). Like Peacham's nearly wracked ship, Rosse's directionless passions seem to lack any pilot except fear: the passion negatively associated with subjection to Fortune, and also with inconstancy, error, and ignorance.[30] The watery imagery in his speech implies the sway of turbulent humors, here doing the disruptive work of Fortune. Notably for Rosse, as for Petrarchan complainers, humoral self-knowledge does not always entail self-mastery. Humoral passions are movements in and between the environment and a permeable body.[31] This intersubjective, hydraulic economy explains the odd causality of fears that—as Rosse describes them—both respond to rumors and generate them. If we read his complaint with an eye to its humoral logic, in other words, he seems less like a self-directed insider than one who knows that he doesn't know—and fears the consequences of his uncertainty.

Rosse's fears exemplify the radical potential of the passions in general to sway even those who know themselves well, in spite of self-knowledge. In this respect, his speech elaborates a humoral model of emotion similar to the one outlined by Wright. Passions are secondary responses to sense perceptions, communicated through the movements of animal spirits. By "sensitive apprehension" Wright explains, the senses inform the wit and imagination. When the system works properly, these faculties direct the passions or affections (in several sorts), and they in turn move the will to act (31). Passions become internal messengers in their turn, informing the higher cognitive processes—memory, will, and reason—but also properly governed by them. The process can founder on the inordinate influence of the senses, as suggested above. But Wright insists that when carefully regulated, it is an inherently moral one. "As our wit understandeth whatsoever our senses perceive, even so our will may affect whatsoever our passions doe follow: for as the object of the wit is all truth, reall, or apparant, so the object of our will is all goodnesse indeed" (31–32). Rosse's fears typify an ordinary miscarriage within this psychological polis. Both a source of rumor and response to it, his fears appear as internal informants, floating hints to change sides. Subsequent actions suggest that Rosse was right to fly Macbeth's service. But the transfer of loyalty remains a vexed issue in the play and a liberal theory of self would be troubled by its origin in humoral seas of fear. As Edward Reynolds reminds his readers in 1640, on the eve of civil war, "those things which wee doe in Feare, are void and invalide to binde."[32]

A humoral inner life poses serious challenges to proprietary models of cognition, since awareness of the labile nature of one's passions does not necessarily translate into executive control. Contractarian thinkers in the period addressed this problem by separating cognitive processes such as memory, judgment, and will from the passions and the senses that sway them.[33] Davenant's description of the passions as mechanical "Engines," set apart and against the civilizing attention that can be brought to bear on them, depends on such a separation. The theatrical entertainments he proposes are designed to elicit something like Cartesian disengaged reason, constructing affections as internal objects (bodily states) potentially separate from cognitive processing. At least this is how it works for those capable of elite curiosity. For those incapable, the theater offers vivid illustrations of virtue and vice which teach through direct access to the senses:

the generality of mankinde are solely instructed by their senses, and by immediate impressions of particular objects, never vexing their heads with reviews and subtle examinations; and are so much the sooner gain'd, by how much the first representations are either more illustrious or charming; whether this be by the Eye or Eare, wants not its severall effects; it being in the most refin'd and Æthereal Spirits a curiosity and desire of knowledge; in common soules, an abject admiration: For as great *Buildings*, fair *Pictures, Statues*, and *Medals*, intice the *Virtuosi*, so *Triumphs, Pageants, Cavalcades*, or any thing new, brings the common people about them. (244)

For the "generality" of the commonwealth, that is, "immediate impressions of particular objects" still operate in the humoral mode, raising passions (aversion or pleasure) directly.[34] "Triumphs, Pageants, Cavalcades" appeal to the common ear: heard by the throng in the street before they come into view. Architecture, sculpture, pictures, and stamped metal are static art forms with limited access; these evoke the superior link between vision and reason in contemporary medical anatomy, and open up a cognitive space very different from the presumed immediacy of moving art forms like a pageant.[35] For the more refined sort, Davenant argues, such elite forms offer an opportunity for salutary Cartesian disengagement ("reviews and subtle examinations") attended by a second order of passion—a passion for understanding itself ("curiosity and a desire of knowledge").[36]

The presence of a mixed audience in this social scene is both a difficulty and an asset for Davenant. He spends some attention in the "Proposition" on ways to guarantee a pacified assembly and counter Puritan suspicions of "too great a diversion of pleasure" (246). By 1656, as Jacob and Raylor show, Davenant shifted tactics on both questions. His later writings on the stage organize this mixed audience into hierarchies of consumption. Theatrical entertainments will promote public competition between members of the gentry, drawn together at the London theater to outshine and outspend each other, thus benefiting local merchants (Jacob and Raylor, 231). This new strategy, based on Hobbesian principles of emulation, treats the passions themselves (at least those of the gentry) not as the objects of discipline but as vehicles of urban economy.[37] Even as he abandons his arguments about the moral force of sensory instruction in the theater, however, Davenant continues to press his point that the theater provides a unique environment for authenticating virtuous character and promoting social good. "Those who are not misgovern'd by passion, have an instinct to communication, that by vertuous emulations each may endeavour to become the best example to the rest; for men meet not to see themselves, but to be seen by others, and probably he who doth expose himself to be a publique object, will strive to excel before he appears."[38] The face-to-face arena of the theater, in other words, promotes a stable economy and polity through competitive public scrutiny; playgoing ratifies the standing and virtue of each civil gentleman who puts his capacity to govern his passions on display.[39]

What is disturbing about Rosse's fear in this context is that it cannot complete its proper cognitive or social circuit. His fears inform judgement so poorly that they paralyze Rosse, their movements pushing "each way and none." The fact that he understands this process so clearly does not allow him to disengage from his passions and pilot them—or anyone else's, for that matter. Far from schooling Lady Macduff's feelings they offer hollow comfort. Two dynamics specific to fear in contemporary accounts of the passions are important here. First, fear (like hope) is in its earliest forms a cognitive stance as well as a physiological response, a "passion of uncertainty" directed at the unknowable future.[40] "Fear may be defined as a pain or disturbance due to imagining some destructive or painful evil in the future," according to Aristotle. [41] Humoral medicine elaborated such disturbances in terms of the movement of animal spirits. Cognitive uncertainty springs from the precipitous flight of the spirits into the heart, away from the extremities, leaving a body incapable of action. "In a sudden daunt and onset of an unexpected evill," Reynolds explains, "the spirits which were before orderly carried by their severall due motions unto their naturall works, are upon this strange appearance and instant Oppression of danger so disordered, mixed, and stifled, that there is no power left either in the Soule for Counsell, or in the Body for Execution" (279).[42] In extremity of fear, one oscillates between possible outcomes in a state of terrible irresolution, or internal civil war. "Weakness, Forreign Incursions, Intestine Tumults, and an Emptying of the Parts" (296). This is why agreements made in fear are legally void.

A second, more salutary quality of fear remediates uncertainty by clarifying moral consequences. These effects may be especially vivid and their intersubjective reach correspondingly strong. When Macduff famously calls for an audience to witness Duncan's dead body, for example, he begins with the prospect of horrified paralysis: "Confusion now hath made his masterpiece" (2.3.62), "Approach the chamber and destroy your sight / With a new Gorgon" (2.3.68–69). From destroyed sight Macduff proceeds to alarums, waking Malcolm and Banquo to "see the great doom's image" and "countenance this horror" (2.3.74–77). His call to "countenance this horror" delivers a triple imperative to auditors onstage and off: look at the cause of this horror, reflect it in your own faces, weigh in morally on its consequences. The Latin derivation of "horror"—visible roughness of surface—emphasizes the vivid symptoms of fear. The affects the thanes might catch from Macduff are all "horrors" because they register internal disorders transparently on the surface of the body, ridged like a rugged landscape or shivered like windblown waves.[43]

English theorists such as Wright and Reynolds see such affective contagions as both a virtue and a practical challenge. Far from stoic in their approach, they advise direct use of the passions. Deployed correctly, Wright asserts, "feare expelleth sinne" (10).[44] In secular contexts the applications are more specific but equally powerful. In one extraordinary digression for example, in Book V, Wright prints a full oration aimed at using fear of Turkish invasion to unify the nations of Europe in sympathy. Discussing the predominance of the body over the soul, Reynolds argues that "Education, Custome, and Occasion" may equalize the balance between emotion and understanding, bringing "intellectual maturity" (10). The first two are familiar neo-Stoic forms for controlling the passions, but *occasion* (Reynolds writes on the eve of civil war) works differently. It "alters the naturall Inclination of the Will and Affections" abruptly, by reason of some sudden emergent Occurrences, contrary to the standing temper and complexion of the Body. Thus we reade sometimes of men in Warre, who notwithstanding of themselves timorous and sluggish, yet being deprived of possibilitie of flight, and hope of mercy if they should be conquered, have strangely gained by their despaires and gotten great and prosperous Victories by a forc'd and unnaturall Fortitude. (11–12)

Fearful prospects thus open a channel for external as well as internal redirection of the passions, a process often figured as receptiveness to counsel. Reynolds writes that "men in a fright and amazement, looke one another in the face; one mans countenance, as it were asking counsell of one another" (283). Cognitive uncertainty entails a social occasion, where the face-to-face exchange of counsels counters perturbed humors and cognitive paralysis. Macduff seems to have something like this exchange in mind in the "New Gorgon" scene. Banquo acts on similar principles when he breaks into Macbeth's fearful speculations about the witches. "Look how our partner's rapt," Banquo observes, and then moves in to offer advice.

One symptom of Scotland's disordered polity in Shakespeare's play is the progressive failure of such affective exchanges. Macbeth's impassiveness to the counsel of subordinates, his incapacity to register the natural symptoms of fear (paleness, starting, bristling hair), his state of fixed reprobation—all follow on the deliberate sealing up of his passions and those of Lady Macbeth. Such deliberate sealing up is what steels them both to the murder, estranging them from a natural disposition to passion (the "taste of fears" [5.5.9], "th'access and passage to remorse" [1.5.42]) and making them incapable of counsel. In exploring the relationship between fear and counsel, Shakespeare's play reflects an emerging lexical division between horror and fear in contemporary debates about the nature of despair. Michael MacDonald's work on recusant literature, for example, suggests that horror and fear are opposed spiritual states: the former a condition of reprobation and perseveration, the latter a condition that admits counsel, illustrative example, recantation, and the possibility of salvation.[45] Like despair, horror is a state in which no change for the good can be imagined or effected: the certainty of unredeemable sin holds the sufferer in a permanent state of shock. Fear, by contrast, knows a future that may be changed—however terrible the prospect—to expel sin. Radical blocking of intersubjective exchange appears a worse perversion in other words—and leads to more fixed despair—than Rosse's confusion.

It is easy in this context to see why *Macbeth* suits Davenant's project of civic entertainment. Anatomizing affects such as horror and fear, the play provides an ongoing analysis of the uses and perversions of the passions. The action repeatedly focuses attention on the emotions of on-stage spectators rather than on the spectacles themselves (such as Duncan's murder off-stage). Key scenes are filled with auditors, ranked by degrees of passionate capacity and knowledge: the bemused courtiers at the banquet in which Banquo's ghost appears (3.4); the doctor and waiting woman who comment on Lady Macbeth's sleepwalking (5.1); Macduff, Malcolm, and Rosse in the scene at the English court (4.3). The dialogue is punctuated by repeated theatrical glosses, calling attention to the play of emotion on the actors' faces as they start, blanch, and freeze in horror. Lennox scrutinizes Rosse as he arrives from battle: "What haste looks through his eyes! So should he look / That seems to speak things strange" (1.2.46–47). The witches gloss Macbeth's astonishment at the parade of kings and Macbeth himself glosses his changing countenance continuously: "You make me strange / Even to the disposition that I owe, / When now I think you can behold such sights / And keep the natural ruby of your cheeks / When mine is blanched with fear" (3.4.111–14). Even before the Scottish doctor diagnoses Lady Macbeth's "perturbations," the play has catalogued its central passions in forensic detail.

Shakespeare frames the passionate exchange of knowledge in courtly terms. Moments such as the "New Gorgon" speech work as instructional systems, teaching readings of the passions attentive to social relation and degree. As in Wright, these scenes negotiate ongoing concerns about the social management of emotion: how far should knowledge of the passions travel; who should model emotional governance and learn to move it in others. Wright, for example, addresses his treatise on the nature and uses of the passions to "Courts, Fields, and Senates" (iv), only to narrow his audience to those "prudent civill Gentlemen" who aim to win "gracious carriage" of themselves (2). These gentlemen negotiate courtly circles in which even "Noblemen by birth" are so "appassionate in affections, that their company [is] to most men intolerable" (6). Wright is sensitive to the courtier's challenge here: how to interpret the monarch's countenance and public affections correctly and thus "reap some commodity touching [ones] professions" (2). But he is more anxious that the knowledge he imparts flow according to degree and condition, limiting access to those (children, young men, women, servants, barbarians) whose passions are by nature inordinate.

Superiors may learn to conjecture the affections of their subjects mindes, by a silent speech pronounced in their very countenances . . . by this we may know the cause, why children, and especially women, cannot abide to looke in their fathers, masters, or betters faces, because, even nature it self seemeth to teach them, that thorow their eyes they see their hearts; neither doe we hold it for good manners that the inferiour should fixe his eyes upon his superiours countenance, and the reason is, because it were presumption for him to attempt the entrance or privie passage into his superiors minde, as contrariwise it is lawfull for the superior to attempt to knowledge of his inferior. (29)

What subordinates know of the passions of their superiors, and how they act on that knowledge are simultaneously cognitive and political problems in *Macbeth*. Responding to the Scottish inheritance of the new monarch and court, Shakespeare explores the proper boundaries of emotional exchange: who has access to the monarch's mind and under what pressures a circle of loyal counsellors will shrink or grow. Courtiers fly Macbeth's court in increasing numbers, most notably Malcolm, Donaldbain, Rosse, and Macduff. For everyone but the Macbeths, for some time, their flight signifies at best inconstancy, at worst, treason. For the audience, however, our privileged access to Macbeth's tyrannical passions confirms the honor and good sense of those who flee. In other words, our intimacy with Macbeth's bloody passions has the effect of glossing positively what otherwise looks like disloyalty and inconstancy. The degree to which this is a counterintuitive move—translating inconstancy into a salutary kind of impressibility—is clear in the scene between Lady Macduff and Rosse.[46] Macduff's flight to England looks uncomfortably like cowardice or treason, as his lady complains. Rosse's hollow comfort fails to settle the question, and it remains notoriously unresolved, even under Malcolm's rigorous quizzing of Macduff in 4.3.

In this courtly context, the monarch's challenge is to be impressible to counsel but not oversweyed by it, to reliably govern his own emotions and those of others, and to control how widely privy knowledge of his mind circulates. Macbeth handles these challenges badly—letting his disorders show at the banquet, losing more and more of his counsellors, finally being reduced to explicating numbed passions to a nameless servant. Duncan's problem, in turn, might be said to be too ready access—he's too open to barbaric northerners such as Macdonwald ("a gentleman on whom I built / An absolute trust"). By contrast, Malcolm's handling of Macduff in 4.3 shows skillful governance of his own emotions and those of others; in the process it dramatizes a civil, Anglicized form of emotional sovereignty. Macduff finds Malcolm in England at the beginning of this scene, and begs him to unseat the tyrant; suspicious of his loyalties, Malcolm tests him by claiming to be more vicious even than Macbeth. As scholars have long recognized, this exchange innovates on stock topoi of courtly counsel, incorporating a series of exempla from the advice to princes genre. The familiar moral is that anyone tyrannized by his own passions cannot govern well, while the direction of loyal counsellors provides an important corrective.[47] Sally Mapstone observes that early historiographic versions of this scene inflect Malcolm's vices differently, according to the politics of successive historians.[48] As Mary Floyd-Wilson has argued, such strategic revisions of source often involve significant shifts in the ethnographic claims advanced by the different historiographers.[49] The degree to which Shakespeare shares Wright's anxieties about the affective capacities of the English is clear in his suppression of a key phrase from Holinshed's version of this scene. When Holinshed's Macduff finally despairs of Malcolm, for example, he lays the blame on the "inconstant behaviour and manifest vices of Englishmen" (*Historie of Scotland*, 276). Shakespeare's 4.3 plays down the role of constancy, translating it once in the conversation as "stableness" and leaving out the matter of English vice entirely. Instead, the play recasts Malcolm's cautious dissembling as a judicious ability to sway and be swayed by others. When he finally comforts Macduff, revealing his ploy, Malcolm promises, ". . . even now / I put myself to thy direction . . .What I am truly / Is thine, and my poor country's, to command" (4.3.122–23; 132–33).[50] Shakespeare's version of this scene, in other words, revalorizes inconstancy as the judicious ruler's receptiveness to good counsel. At the same time, the play systematically displaces the spectre of English inconstancy northwards, in the person of corrigible turncoats such as Rosse and Macduff—whom Malcolm goes on to correct as the scene closes, directing him gradually through the stages of manly grief. Such scenes of top-down, masculine instruction partly explain why gurus of management are so quick to take up Shakespeare as an authority.[51]

Davenant's interest in *Macbeth* and the changes he makes in the play have to do with the way it dramatizes the government of affect in the context of shifting loyalties. Scholars have long recognized the conservative bias of this version: adapted in the late 1660s, it offers a royalist allegory of the failures of the government under Cromwell and the restoration of Charles II.[52] Davenant's revisions follow the civic bent of the 1653 "Proposition" as well, however, demonstrating the role of the theater in disseminating knowledge of the passions. Teaching civic virtue to a wide audience, he charts a course between the socially level passions imagined in Hobbes and the consistently top-down scenes of instruction in Shakespeare's play.[53] The two plays dramatize fundamentally different epistemologies of emotion, in both language and dramatic structure. Where Shakespeare's language and plot tend to obscure the causal relations between passions and action, Richard Kroll observes, Davenant streamlines the play into legible causes and effects.[54] These stylistic differences reflect wider shifts in the decorum of socio-emotional exchange after the Restoration. In Shakespeare's play the differences that concerned Wright (differences between men and women, adults and children, nobles and commons, English and Scots) aggravate Scotland's emotional disorder. In Davenant's revision, these differences are noticeably leveled, though not erased.

For Davenant, the challenge of spreading expertise in the passions to a mixed audience entails reallocating the emotional labors in Shakespeare's play. In the exchange between Lady Macduff and Rosse, for example, Davenant recasts their fear in ways that restrict its infectious reach. In place of Rosse, Lennox discourses more mildly with Lady Macduff on the effects of fear in general. Notably, Davenant leaves out the question of emotional direction between the two (there's no injunction that Lady Macduff "school" herself). But he reintroduces the issue in a new scene with Lady Macduff that lays out the proper way to use the passions of others to guide ones own. Davenant adds several scenes for the Macduffs, all showpieces of sensible, royalist counsel.[55] But he dramatizes the problem of fearful contagion most clearly in 2.5, when they encounter the witches. The witches sing a gruesome chorus ("We should rejoyce when good Kings bleed" [2.5.40]) at which Macduff starts in obvious fear. Explaining this reaction to his wife he asserts, "It was a hellish Song: I cannot dread / Ought that is mortal; but this is something more" (2.5.47–8).[56] After a second creepy song he turns to her in surprise, observing "I'm glad you are not afraid." She explains. "I would not willingly to fear submit: / None can fear ill, but those that merit it" (2.5.69–71). This demonstration of self-possession in the face of the portents bucks him up:

Am I made bold by her? how strong a guard
Is innocence? if any one would be
Reputed valiant, let him learn of you;
Vertue both courage is, and safety too (2.5.72–75)

In this exchange, Davenant rewrites two Shakespearean scenes: the encounter between Lady Macduff and Rosse and Malcolm's emotional management of Macduff. As Rosse's were, Macduff's emotions are labile, distracted, fearful, and fully warranted. As in the scene with Malcolm, Macduff needs direction. But Davenant's 2.5 displaces the uncertain condition of Rosse's fear upward to his superiors—to a context that is both socially and dramatically contained (there's no Lady Rosse readily available to supply emotional counsel). At the same time, Davenant displaces emotional governance downward from the prince to the family (the wife, for that matter). These displacements allow for the expression of uncertain passions but without the affective contagions endemic to the Shakespearean scene. Lady Macduff's reasoned dismissal of the witches depends on a Lockean refusal to assent to the passions they naturally arouse. Macduff takes courage not by absorbing her resolution but by considering her example.

Lest we miss this distinction, the scene offers one more temptation: Macduff speaks to the witches and they weave him a prophecy as nastily equivocal as Macbeth's. So Lady Macduff steps in a third time to pull him out of fearful speculation, calling his attention to his affect and its suspicious cause: "Why are you alter'd, Sir? be not so thoughtful: / The Messengers of Darkness never spake / To men, but to deceive them . . . Their words are like / Their shape; nothing but fiction" (2.5.84–86, 89–90). Returning from his thoughts, Macduff agrees—both to her analysis and its underlying premise of self-governance and responsibility. "I'll take your counsel; for to permit / Such thoughts upon our memories to dwell, / Will make our minds the Registers of Hell" (2.5.92–4). Similar corrections revise other key scenes of affective contagion towards a more proprietary phenomenology. Thus when Macduff calls the thanes to view Duncan's body, the horror is no longer a "New Gorgon," but "a sight enough to turn spectators into stone" (2.3.38–9). No material transformation takes place in the onlooker imagined here; rather, the audience understands the experience of horror by analogy. "True" affective experience remains sealed off from public exchange, a fact that Davenant emphasizes in Macduff's new exit line: "I find this place too publick for true sorrow: / Let us retire, and mourn" (2.3.92–93).

The addition of singing witches has complex dramaturgic motives, also grounded in proprietary notions of theatrical cognition. As Richard Kroll has shown, Davenant systematically flattens Shakespearean ambiguities according to principles of sceptical, linguistic reform shared by contemporaries such as Hobbes, Walter Charleton and Sir Kenelm Digby. Like these theorists, Davenant prefers clear explications of cause and effect and emphasizes the superior cognitive force of audio-visual examples over abstractions and precepts (Kroll, 840–41). Accordingly, his operatic additions tend to demystify the occult causes of Shakespeare's play. The lyrics for the singing witches, for example, repeatedly assert that one bad choice leads to another, bad passions darken, and the interests that drive this are political, not supernatural: "He will—He shall—He must spill much more bloud; / And become worse, to make his Title good" (2.5.37–38). The choreography seems to have followed suit. In an early theater copy of the score, marginal annotations to Davenant's new 2.5 suggest the dances included personifications whose actions gloss Macduff's lines, explicitly connecting his emotional transformations to stage business. When Macduff concludes that "Vertue both courage is, and safety too," a prompter's cue directs "both Courrage and Safety too Dance" (f. 17).[57] Here the dancing witches serve as auditory and visual glosses on Macduff's internal condition rather than potential sources of dramatic action in their own right, as they are in Shakespeare's play. Positive affects (courage) and their political consequences (safety) both follow on reasoned counsel. The true and legible causes of disorder in the state are clearly inward and proprietary in this added scene, the results of vicious choices rather than occult influence.

In 4.3 Davenant takes a surprisingly different tack, abbreviating the Shakespearean matter of Malcolm's excessive sins and Macduff's hesitant grief. Malcom's vices must have been embarrassingly vivid in the light of Charles's wanderings on the continent, as Kroll notes (853). Macduff's grief would seem to overemphasize the cost of changed allegiance. Yet in other adaptations (*The Law Against Lovers*, for example) Davenant does not shy from exploring the costs of changing loyalty in an unstable regime. In fact, his cuts in 4.3 reinforce the additions in Macduff's earlier scenes of counsel. They effectively deemphasize Macduff's exchange with Malcolm and the *demonstratio* of externally governed passions. In the process, they reduce the role of the sovereign as restorer of emotional order and expand the roles of those faced with the decision to betray a king. Indeed, Davenant reassigns the closing lines of 4.3 from Malcolm to Macduff, who sets off to war invoking Heaven's aid in a just cause. At the same time, Davenant drags out the steady attrition of counselors from Macbeth's camp. The return of Malcolm comes to depend on a collection of subordinates who choose to shift loyalties under great pressure, not on the heir's canny management or moral title.[58]

This shift of attention to the knowledge, choices, and loyalties of gentlemen retainers depends again on recycling Rosse. Rosse's departure may be too quick and his reasons too confused to suit Davenant's anatomy of shifting loyalties. But cutting Rosse also allows the strategic divisions of emotional labor described above: displacing his labile passions to Macduff, and allocating more stage time to the strained allegiance of lesser courtiers.

Lennox gets some of Rosse's lines but the more interesting ones go to Seyton, who stays with the usurper to the last. Seyton's character consolidates a remarkable range of functions: he takes over the lines of the messenger reporting Macbeth's early success in battle, those of the Old Man who catalogues the natural omens that attend Duncan's murder, and finally the Scottish Doctor's lines in the sleepwalking scene. In his person, in other words, Seyton consolidates knowledge about the passions that Shakespeare's play distributed across a wide range of estates and character functions: nuncio, allegorical commoner, forensic expert, and historical nobleman. As Seyton becomes our primary interpreter of Macbeth's disordered passions, he also acquires a breadth of knowledge about the monarch's interior life that only the audience and monarch in Shakespeare's play possess. Confident in his forensic skills, Davenant's Seyton uses them reasonably, making political choices on the basis of principle (royalist principle, to be sure). In expanding Seyton's role in this way, Davenant provides a character that a mixed audience can see, hear, and interpret in familiar humoral terms, but who models a very different mode of cognitive self-possession. The consolidation of forensic expertise in the passions, in a gentleman like Seyton, fulfils Davenant's assertion in the "Proposition" that only those of "such singular understandings as have been experienc'd in variety of men and affairs" should "direct our behaviour in publick" (244). Experience in affairs counts, significantly, more than courtly estate (12–13). To be sure, the most labile of subordinate passions in the play are laundered through Macduff's aristocratic marriage. Yet Davenant's Seyton incorporates a range of expertise and experience, levelling the hierarchies of instruction imagined in Shakespeare and Wright. Davenant's scenes of public passion address problems of competency more than they do anxieties about access.

The newly assimilated expertise of a character like Seyton illuminates changes that cross a variety of genres and media in this period. Davenant's expanded emotional glosses typify the tendency of Restoration dramatists to specify affects with elaborate, LeBrun-like descriptions embedded in their dialogue. Such glossing reinforced existing prose-based techniques for depicting the passions on the page, instead of through face-to-face audition.[59] As early as 1649, for example, John Bulwer pitched his anatomy of the muscles of the head to a general audience of "intelligent readers." *Pathomyotomia: or a Dissection of the Significative Muscles of the Affections of the Minde* (1649), a guide to the mind's construction in the face, cultivates both laymen and physicians. Bulwer's efforts to justify the general relevance of technical descriptions of "every Muscle of our head and Face" imply this was a

relatively new and difficult audience to address in prose.[60] But such technical knowledge quickly became a popular commodity. Compendia such as
Francis Kirkman's *The Wits: or Sport Upon Sport* (1662), frequently reprinted,
spoofed the humors of different nations in dialogues illustrated from the
Restoration stage.[61] By 1724 Thomas Butler captured similar scenes in his
Thesaurus Dramaticus. Offered as a consumer's guide to the theater, the
work anthologizes "all the celebrated passages . . . and other poetical beauties in the English plays, ancient and modern: continued down to the
present year." Here the curious reader can survey exemplary instances of
theatrical passion and in the process acquaint himself with ways to master
what will otherwise screw him up. Understanding and managing the passions, in this context, is the individual labor of a civilized consumer. As
Reynolds cautions, "True desires as they are right in regard of their object,
so are they laborious in respect of their motion" (196). Davenant's published
text of *Macbeth* (1674) seems designed to serve this labor. Indeed, unlike the
text of the folio *Macbeth* (1623), Davenant's is a reading text, incorporating
prefatory matter (Heylyn's Argument) that itself circulated in prose.[62]

To the extent that we still speak of the "work" of emotion, in a post-
Lockean and post-Freudian world, we subscribe to a concept of internal
experience that expanded with the emergence of political economy in late
seventeenth-century England.[63] To the extent that we know emotions as
intersubjective movements—essentially more immediate, pressing and genuine, say, in children (labile) than adults (settled), or women (labile) than
men (stoic)—we invoke categories anchored as deeply in earlier Renaissance passions theory as in Enlightenment, Romantic or Freudian models of
feeling.

Chapter 9
Five Pictures of Pathos

Gary Tomlinson

*The voice of antiquity, which the Renaissance knew well, chimes
with the image.*
—*Warburg,* The Renewal of Pagan Antiquity, *555*

Aby Warburg may seem a strange figure to begin a paper that
will eventually circle toward the composer Claudio Monteverdi. The great
historian of Renaissance visual culture had little to say about the Italian
seventeenth century, less than about many other things. Yet attending to one
fundamental aspect of his work on images will launch us along a path leading to the song, unexpectedly clear, of the seventeenth century—a path
along which we may also hear, as in fantastic modulations, the eighteenth
and fifteenth centuries unfolding a musical logic that spirals in on the era
of Monteverdi. The path winds from Warburg's modern scholarship, in
some features presciently postmodern, back through an early modern
historico-ethnographic apprehension of the distant past, to a premodern,
lived psychology. All these—Warburg's or our own methodological pre-
dilections, early modern historical distanciation, and premodern psychology—meet in the seventeenth century and its upheavals.

Beginning with a historian of images such as Warburg in order to lead,
finally, to Monteverdi also makes a cautionary point: Attempts to gain some
overview of the nature of early modern passions and of their revelation in
expressive culture dare not stop at the borders of any one medium or sense.
At least through the Renaissance, visual and aural stimuli in particular were
understood to have their impact on the soul through the same set of corporeal, spiritual, and psychological mechanisms. To speak of an image
impressed upon the soul in this period is not to exclude musical stimuli, but
rather, as we will see, to conceive of image itself in a more encompassing
way than we tend to do. The quotation I have taken from Warburg as my
epigraph—a rare synaesthetic moment in an art historian not notably sensitive to music—captures well this ecumenical *imago*.

Over the seven decades since Warburg's death, there has been no shortage of commentary on his notion of the *Pathosformel*. This idea, usually translated as "emotional formula" or "emotive formula" or, more literally, "formula of pathos," was basic to Warburg's method. It elicited important comment already from his acolyte Gertrud Bing, and it still sits front and center in analyses of his work by Ernst Gombrich, Konrad Hoffmann, Carlo Ginzburg, and others.[1]

At first view the idea seems almost naively simple. Starting already in his dissertation on Botticelli (1893), Warburg endeavored to trace the influence of pagan antiquity on Renaissance artists in their adoption of specific gestures of movement from ancient sculpture. These gestures—the play of the breeze over garments or hair, the torsion of a body in supreme effort or fear—created "an intensification of outward movement" that irrupted in the midst of the less expressive rhetoric of medieval painting. The gestures could be used with restraint and a knowing empathy toward the ancients, as in the case of Botticelli abetted by Poliziano; they could harden into a stylized "muscular rhetoric," to which Warburg applied the term *baroque*, in Antonio Pollaiuolo; and they could be transmitted across the Alps in works of Dürer, there to have their extreme forms tamed and balanced with other, calmer gestures from antiquity.[2]

Wherever they occurred, these emotive formulas tapped a wellspring of inner feeling. The ancient gestures of *motion*, Warburg quickly came to assert, constituted a pagan, bodily revelation of *emotion*. In them we witness the outward, somatic expression of an inner, psychic impulse. We see the tracing of an apprehension of the world and hence a sketch of subjectivity. Their revival and reuse in the Italian Renaissance signaled for Warburg the empathetic recognition, on the part of the artists of the time, of "the supremacy of the antique in all gestural rendering of emotion."[3]

Warburg's linking of these pictorial gestures to emotions and his assertion of the supremacy of the ancients in rendering them were tied to the most sweeping of his intuitions concerning the origins and progress of culture. They reached back at least to the formative years of his university training, took on new significance during his sojourn of 1895-96 among the Pueblo Indians of New Mexico and Arizona—an extraordinary episode in an extraordinary life—and accompanied, with deepening consequences, all his later cultural-historical studies. In the years after Warburg's death, Bing could even assert that Renaissance astrology, that central topic of Warburg's mature years, had posed itself altogether to him, finally, as something like an immense *Pathosformel*.[4]

But how did the ancients attain their supremacy in rendering emotion as gesture? For Warburg the emotive, irrational, Dionysiac impulse behind Greek ritual and myth—the Nietzschean impulse captured in the *Pathos-formel*—marked the ancients' proximity to the origins of religion in word and image. From his teacher Hermann Usener Warburg had learned a theory of these origins. Primitive humans reacted, especially with fear, to all strong impressions from the world around them. They expressed these reactions in exclamations which, repeatedly associated with the same impressions, came to indicate them. These first words were neither conventional marks of concepts nor namings of the internal essences of things. Instead they captured things in prerational gesture, as if pointing a finger at them. They were, as linguists today might say, the first deictics. But the impressions these gestural words indicated called, in the primitive imagination, for agents bringing them about. This process of personification of the external world created the gods of polytheistic religions. They took their names, then, by association with the words pointing to the phenomena they were thought to cause.[5]

To this linkage of the beginning of language with the origin of gods Usener connected another topic that must have been especially intriguing to young Warburg: the origin of the symbol. In addition to the personification of external impressions that resulted in gods, myths sprang from a metaphorical process of image making. The personified impression, that is, united in myth with an icon of the impression. "Thus originated," Usener wrote, "the mythic picture or motif, thus a symbol, thus the concrete, pictorial god-idea." (Thus also, Usener added, originated the use of poetic tropes and hence poetry.) Through this combination of animistic personification and metaphorical image making, thing and picture were conflated in mythic thought, undifferentiated, while later, rational thought came to compare and separate them.[6]

The influence of Usener's thinking on Warburg was strong and lasting. We feel it in notes Warburg jotted in 1891 outlining a history of epistemology. In this scheme knowledge evolved from a stage of interjection to a stage of comparison to, finally, a stage of categorical judgment: "Pine! This here!" Warburg wrote to exemplify the stage of interjection; "The pine is like a man," for the second, comparative stage; and "The pine is a tree," for the stage of judgment.[7] We see Usener's influence also in Warburg's explanation of the ritual culture of the Pueblo Indians, and thus in his likening of a distant past to an ethnographic present. When, many years later, in his lecture on the Indians, Warburg wrote that they "think in images," or when he generalized that "Between a culture of touch and a culture of thought is the culture of symbolic connection," he looked back on Usener's theories about imagistic mythic thought, the origin of the symbol, and the deictic character of the first language. Witnessing in the dances of the Indians an example of his middle culture, the culture of mythic symbolism, Warburg felt he had come across a living, functioning, *moving* instance of the *Pathosformel*.[8]

Warburg's emotive formulas, then, whatever other sources they also reflect, represent a deep influence on him of Usener. Merely as gestural echoes in the Renaissance of earlier icons they would not carry any great significance; but Warburg conceived of them as much more than this. He saw revealed in them the Renaissance fascination with a kind of bodily, iconic thought that conflates inner psychic states with outer gesture. He saw a token of the recognition in the Renaissance of ancient patterns of thought near the beginnings of human awareness of the divine and near also the invention of language and symbol. Hence he found in them a sign of the renewal of the pre-rational (Warburg said "irrational") modes of such thought. Not for nothing did astrology come to seem to Warburg a culture-wide *Pathosformel*.

Not for nothing, also, do we still relish the heuristic charge of Warburg's emotive formulas. Our affinity to them has been marked across many decades of interpretations of Renaissance epistemology, from the likes of Panofsky through Foucault and beyond. Our first picture of pathos, then, is Warburg's. It speaks to us still not so much because of the particulars of its cultural history or the theoretical fancies of Usener in its background. It compels, instead, because in its concerns it inaugurated a century in which an irrational that the West had once been pleased to imagine itself beyond came to seem doggedly persistent; because, taking off from Nietzsche along a road followed also by Freud, Adorno, and others, it showed that modernity was no shield against terrors of non-reason both personal and societal. Warburg's balancing of rationality and its opposite explains why we are still drawn to his conception of Luther and the astrologers, to his reading of the sweep of the hair of Botticelli's Venus, to his bemused, fascinated reaction to Hopi dances.

Usener was, then, the crucial proximate source of Warburg's *Pathosformel*; but Giambattista Vico was its truest ancestor. The connection of Vico's *Scienza nuova* of 1744 to Warburg's theories has occasionally been noted in passing.[9] But its full measure has never been taken, and Vico remains a presence in Warburg's intellectual formation shadowy enough that he can entirely escape the notice of so thorough an exegete as Gombrich.

This even though the Vichian heritage behind Warburg's ideas is easy enough to trace. It requires only a quick perusal of Usener's writings, in the first place, to locate his avowal of fidelity to some of Vico's basic doctrines. This comes, in fact, at the beginning of Usener's analysis of the common origin of myth, symbol, and poetry, so redolent of Warburg. Vico, Usener writes, was the first to recognize the significance of this shared origin, "without however finding a follower who understood him for almost two centuries"—without, that is, finding a follower until Usener himself.[10] From Vico Usener developed his method of tracing the names of gods to primitive humans' reactions to the world; he also borrowed Vico's discovery of the sources of religion in these fearful reactions. From Vico Usener adopted much more as well: the linking of personification and metaphor in the process that built concrete images of the gods; the idea that poetry arose together with symbol in this metaphorical process; the nonconceptual character of the first words and their deictic quality; the attempt to understand all this as a prerational mode of conceiving the world; and even, most generally, the universalizing, "key to all mythologies" approach that saw all polytheistic religions as an inevitable evolutionary reflex of the aboriginal mind.[11]

We may easily picture Usener firing Warburg's imagination in lectures on such topics. But with or without *Quellengeschichte* the importance of this Vichian heritage in Warburg's conceptions is transparent. Warburg's emphasis on the irrational, Dionysiac impulse of ancient Greek ritual, however Nietzschean it might also be, found ready affirmation in Vico's prerational origins of religion and its imagery. The compelling strength and truth of the emotions captured in Warburg's formulas of pathos—a truth that could speak loud to Italian Renaissance artists across 1500 years—reflected the Vichian derivation of religion from the most violent primitive emotions, coupled with the ancient Greeks' proximity to them. The gestural nature of these emotive formulas of Warburg captured the importance of bodily motion in Vico's conception of the earliest languages. These were, according to Vico, formed both from gesture (the origin of hieroglyphs) and exclamations; later they led to the metaphorical, comparative imagery of poetry, and later still to rational, categorical speech.[12] These three stages in turn reflected the three ages that Vico thought all societies traversed, the divine, heroic, and human ages. In Vico's arrangement we recognize the evolution that Warburg outlined in 1891, the epistemological progress from interjection through comparison to judgment; we recognize likewise the sequence of cultures of touch, symbolic connection, and thought he outlined in the Pueblo Indian lecture. Warburg's idea of the intertwined evolutions of language, symbol, and epistemology, the foundation of his idea of the *Pathosformel,* starts, in short, from Vico's *New Science.*

But Vico probed deeper than either Usener or Warburg in trying to understand the operation of primitive, imagistic, emotional, bodily thought. Its elucidation involved him in a mighty effort—twenty years' effort, he himself claimed—of scholarly defamiliarization. He had, he writes, "to descend from these human and refined natures of ours to those utterly wild and savage natures, which we cannot at all imagine and can comprehend only with great effort" (338). What Vico found at the bottom of his descent, the mode in which humans at the origins of society apprehended the world, he called poetic wisdom—*sapienza poetica.* This alternative, prerational order of knowledge forms the linchpin of Vico's distinctive historiography, philology, and philosophy. It also forms my second picture of pathos.

Poetic wisdom was not a product of the mind and its abstract reason, but originated instead in a lower power of the soul, closely allied to body: the *fantasia* or imagination. We can think of poetic wisdom as a historicized theory of knowledge that, like most other epistemologies in the western tradition, attempted to describe the relation between sensory impressions and soul but that, unlike them, availed itself only of the lowest, densest, most congealed and body-like part of the soul. A forceful, violent imagination, which atrophied with the later advent of reason and is hence almost impossible for us to grasp, enabled primitive humans to create corporeal images of the world. Vico wrote, in words anticipating Usener, "At the same time as they imagined the causes of the things they felt and wondered at to be gods, they gave the things they wondered at substantial being after their own ideas." Through "the power of a wholly corporeal imagination"—*in forza d'una corpolentissima fantasia* –they used the brute emotions stimulated by impressions of the world around them to conceive that world in a kind of sensate, somatic thought. They constructed palpable phantasms from their passions, and from these a metaphysics not at all "reasoned and abstract" but "felt and imagined" (375–76).

This metaphysics took the form of the heroic poetry of the first nations—but poetry in a more embracing sense than we might conceive it. Vico's heroic poetry, like his poetic wisdom all told, derived its name from the general creative import of the Greek *poiein.* It included all the plastic forms in which the primitive mind sculpted the world: images, emblems, hieroglyphs, gestures, and poetic tropes.

And it included among these plastic images, by no means least, songs.

Singing sits at the heart of Vico's poetic wisdom, and hence at the heart of the *New Science* altogether. In Vico's reasoning it does so as the consequence of a straightforward syllogism: Singing is the natural language of passion, as we can observe all around us; poetic wisdom was the mode of conceiving the world resulting from passionate emotions; therefore singing was the natural vocal medium of poetic wisdom. Or, in Vico's own words: "Humans vent great passions by giving themselves over to song. . . . The founders of the gentile nations . . . were expressive only under the impulse of the most violent passions, and they had to form their first languages singing" (229–30).

In their stimulation by violent, passionate emotions, the images created in Vico's poetic wisdom resemble Warburg's emotive formulas. The resemblance solidifies to near-identity when we consider the Vichian evolutionary schemes that supported Warburg's thinking. For both men, aboriginal humans created from emotion plastic icons of the world, and from these understanding. But Vico's picture of pathos is a decidedly broader canvas than Warburg's. Vico's *poiesis* features the mobile forms of song alongside gesture, picture, and specific poetic tropes; heroic songs were in his view so many more *imagines* of the *imaginatio*. They were the plastic, deictic form of aboriginal utterance.

Warburg's idea of images is, instead, mute.[13] He is far from Vico's tendency to merge all the expressions of the procreative *fantasia* under the rubric of image-of-the-imagination, phantasm-of-the-fantasy. More specifically, song rarely appears to Warburg as a kind of plastic, mobile image, and so he does not think of it as an emotive formula. Indeed in the only one of his published writings to engage at length with music, his study of the 1589 Florentine *intermedi*, Warburg viewed the song of the first operas as the opposite of the *Pathosformel*, as an immaterial refutation of its gestural materiality. By the time of the intermedi, he wrote, "The material stimulus had lost all its potency, and so a new form had to be found" in the *stile rappresentativo* of early opera.[14] Warburg's deafness to Vico's songs is, finally, the mark of a modernity that hampers us still, disabling our appreciation of the modes of musical epistemology Vico discerned at the origin of society.

Vico's discovery was equivocal, however, as ever since all anthropological discoveries of foreignness have been. Vico's alien poetic knowledge revealed itself through the most familiar of perceptions: his everyday experience of singing as the foremost language of passion. In this dependency its distance folded over on itself, landing close to home. The song that Vico understood as the uttered medium of ancient wisdom was supplementary in a Derridean sense: at once brutally, incomprehensibly aboriginal and savored night after night in the exalted passions of the opera house.

Moreover, the plastic creative powers of song mooted by Vico were no far-off, primitive mechanism. In them he remembered something nearer at hand, a lived experience of his recent forebears. The *corpolentissima fantasia* through which these powers operated was the mainstay of theories of perception throughout the sixteenth century and into the seventeenth. (Indeed, its position was only strengthened across this period by the decline of an earlier faculty psychology, as Katherine Park has shown.[15]) And the song that deployed these phantasmic powers harkened back, with a self-consciousness students of Vico have recently begun to sense, to the resonant singing of Marsilio Ficino.

Ficino's influential psychology of song relied on two contiguous faculties of the human organism, the airy spirit, intermediate between body and soul, and the fantasy or imagination at the base of the soul.[16] In explaining musical effects, Ficino advanced the idea of song as a quasi-material phantasm or image—literally, a creation of the fantasy or imagination—which takes on the features of a living spirit. In its "airy and rational" motions it is "a most powerful imitator of all things": intentions and passions of the soul, moral characters, words, gestures, motions, and actions. The singer, maker of this potent phantasm, projects it out into the world, where its powers are such "that it immediately provokes both the singer and the audience to imitate and act out" the things it presents.[17] We meet here a Renaissance description of a Warburgian *Pathosformel*—in, however, the medium of song.

Behind this sung sympathetic magic stood the Arabic philosopher al-Kindi, who described how the magus "conceives of some corporeal thing in his imagination," which then "acquires a material existence according to the species of the imaginative spirit. So that this spirit emits rays which move external things just as does the thing whose image it is."[18] More broadly, behind this song lay an experience of the cosmos and the human organism as connected, bound in a web of operative contiguities and affinities. Phantasmic song worked along these lines of affinity, affecting body and soul. It connected material and immaterial realms in unbroken continuity, and hence in its deployment of passions was not so much a technology, we might say, as a *metatechnology*.

This phantasmic metatechnology was widely dispersed through premodern psychologies, with differing emphases and not only as an explanation of song's power. Al-Kindi's rays are familiar to anyone who has lingered over sixteenth-century love lyrics or the *trattati d'amore* that stood behind them and traced their heritage back to Ficino. The arch-Aristotelian Pietro Pomponazzi, meanwhile, explained apparitions and other prodigies, including forceful songs, as just such a projection of corporeal phantasms. "When it happens," he wrote, "That the imaginative and cogitative forces are strongly fixed on something, . . . to the point that they have in their power the spirit and blood, the imagined and desired thing can be produced in real form by the forces of imagination and desire." Ficino's follower Francesco Cattani da Diacceto described astrological rites involving "a strongly emotional disposition of the imagination, by which the spirit is stamped with a . . . kind of imprint and, flying out through the orifices of the body, especially through the eyes, ferments and solidifies . . . the kindred power of the heavens."[19] Here we come full circle, veering back toward Warburg's intuition of Renaissance astrology as *Pathosformel*. The closing of the circle to include Vichian singing needs only the astrological songs of Ficino himself, which he performed, Orphic style, to enhance benign planetary influxes and ward off malign ones.

Ficino's songs, then, dominate our third picture of pathos. It was a picture current in a manner the first two were not, neither buried in humanity's distant memory (as Vico's) nor recognized as the unsettling, intermittent upwelling of that past (as Warburg's). Instead, reflecting the fact that the cosmos of operative affinities that underlay it remained a lived reality, it was an experience of the powers of song widely dispersed through the late Renaissance, articulated frequently by those who sought to analyze these powers—and felt even more frequently, no doubt, by those who came under their sway.

So the epistemology that Vico had struggled twenty years to comprehend and had located in society's primitive past resounded, only a century or two before him, in his own backyard. Vico remained in touch with the imagistic psychology of Ficinian song even while he ascribed it to humanity's prerational ages. Or, put differently, Vico culminated the history of Ficinian sung magic precisely by asserting, in the form of historical distance, its vast difference from modern rationality. The distance, however, did not loose Vico entirely from the powers of passionate song. Instead Vico's achievement was to *represent* as history a psychology of song that had been *experienced* in full and vivid immediacy a few generations before him. The effect of this representation—the supplementary effect, as I have said—was to distance, as the object of rational analysis, a prerational passion of the far-off past—recognized, however, only because of its irrational irruption into the present. In Vico's songs, for the first time, pathos grew uncanny.

The historical moment when this magical psychology of song receded into the distance, the moment when Ficinian firsthand experience gave way to the Vichian struggle to remember, is the early seventeenth century. It falls within the long musical career of Claudio Monteverdi. He stands at a crossroads of the passional history of the west, and he alone among the figures I have singled out paints for us not one picture of pathos but two.

The difference between the expressive means of Monteverdi's early maturity and those of his late works measures out a good part of the distance between Ficino and Vico. We may put it just so schematically, to start. In the earlier works the integrated metatechnology of Ficino's song persists. In the later ones a certain objectivizing space or gap obtrudes, posing an epistemological, historical distance and separating the passions and their musical expression from the soul. A *technology* of the passions emerges from the earlier metatechnology, and with it a modernity that speaks to us still.

It is more than the playfulness of a provocative heuristic to hear echoes of Ficino's magical song in Monteverdi's madrigals and music dramas of the period 1595-1620. In these works the composer constructed an integrated, sung rhetoric founded on correspondences among its constituent elements of word, tone, and musical gesture. In doing this Monteverdi extended and, we might say, fulfilled an attempt widespread through late-Renaissance song repertories to reveal systems of correspondence among different levels of sonic, verbal, bodily, and psychic significance. In the most profound instances of this Monteverdian rhetoric—many madrigals of the fourth, fifth, and sixth books (1603, 1605, and 1615) and some of the third and seventh (1592 and 1621); the recitative of *Orfeo* (1607); the surviving lament from *L'Arianna* (1608)—music matches words through shifts in rhythmic, melodic, and harmonic motion (abetted, in the polyphonic works, by subtle textural manipulation). The correspondences tend to be gestural more than iconic, attuned to psychic states more than to external objects. The gestural connection of word and tone is immediate, unselfconscious.

The kinetic correspondences of word and tone in this rhetoric are easily appreciated, in modern terms, as simulacra of both bodily motions and psychic movements or emotions—as representations, in other words, distinct from both. However, sixteenth-century psychologies of music, pervaded by the Ficinian spirit and imagination connecting body and soul, call for an adjusted interpretation. The correspondences are not so much images of emotions in a language distinct from the psyche as they are *parts or aspects* of those emotions, their gestural emission in voice and body. They are phantasmic forms projected outward from the soul. In contact with the psyche, they form a node in the web of larger micro- and macrocosmic harmonies that tie it to the world as a whole. Monteverdi's musical rhetoric, like the rhetorics of his predecessors and contemporaries, was a medium of this broader harmony. It amounted to a discovery in song of the hidden concords that underpinned word, tone, and psyche alike. In Monteverdi's first picture of pathos we see Orpheus, Ariadne, Amarilli, and Armida moving through a world that is everywhere in contact with their passions.

By the end of Monteverdi's career this seamless ontology no longer carried the same conviction. It could not quite sustain, now, the earlier rhetoric. Emotions came to seem discrete, bounded, objectified—separable, even, from the psyche experiencing them. This is the period when Monteverdi could demand from one librettist "vivid gestures and separate passions," and when another librettist could cite the composer's love of marvelous "changes of affection." It is the period when Monteverdi could attempt, in the preface to the *Madrigali guerrieri et amorosi* of 1638, to catalogue, Descartes-style, the "principal passions or affections of our mind" and to list their musical analogues.[20]

I do not speak here of any wholesale move away from rhetorical expression itself—elements of the language of Ariadne, for example, persist clearly enough through the late works, as does the overarching project of capturing word in tone—but instead of a ruffling of the smooth surface of the earlier rhetoric. What this disruption reveals is the decline of the Ficinian psychology of emotion, with its unbroken continuum from material body to immaterial soul. What emerges from it is a novel concern to identify, isolate, manipulate, and even at times analyze individual passions. It is as if the voices of Monteverdi's music came to talk passionately a little less and talk *about* passions a whole lot more.

The detachable nature of the emotions—one from another, all from the soul—can be seen in many features of Monteverdi's late music. There is in this period, first, a resurgence of pictorial madrigalisms that had grown rare in the music from around 1600. However much we may consider these to be psychic motions in music—like the gestures that had predominated earlier—they tend to be pointed outward, toward the objects in the external world they depict. Because of this objectification they tend also to call attention to themselves as discrete, bounded icons.

More interesting than these is the use of the instrumental accompaniment to construct an emblematic representation of a single passion. The
musical analogue Monteverdi invented for anger, his *stile concitato* of quick-
repeating continuo chords, provides a famous example. In its various
manifestations—it also features triadic, fanfare-like melodies—this style
can be more compelling or less. It is shown to best advantage, perhaps, in
the balletic *Combattimento di Tancredi et Clorinda*, where it is coordinated
with choreographed bodily motion; I continue to think, as I did years ago
in *Monteverdi and the End of the Renaissance*, that it shows to positive disadvantage in certain late, bellicose madrigals, where it amounts to an
impoverished musical iconism. In all its uses, in any case, it reflects a psychic motion; but, because of its distinctively tautological musical techniques, it does so in a manner that tends to cut off its own gestures from the
psycho-musical flow around it.

Ellen Rosand long ago described the descending tetrachord ostinato in
the *Lament of the Nymph* as an instrumental emblem of passion.[21] And
something similar could be said about the *ciaccona* bassline that recurs
frequently in Monteverdi's late works as an emblem of joy, contentment,
or even songfulness itself. These ostinatos, along with all the other repeating bass techniques that Monteverdi explored through his later years, carry
structural implications, of course. Indeed, they can be heard as precisely
anti-emotional, posing themselves as the neutral, rigid foundation over
which the voices may deploy a freer emotive rhetoric. (This is one obvious
glory of the *Lament of the Nymph*.) But to hear these ostinatos only this
way is probably to miss the general expressive import involved in all of
them. Each of these basslines, exactly in its structural predominance, casts a
single, monochromatic emotional light across the whole of the song it governs. In this context, when ostinato basslines like that of the *Lament* come
to function explicitly as emotional emblems, they pose the limit-case of
the externalized, objectified passion in Monteverdi's late style. They instance
a passion, indeed, that is now divorced even from the voice that once had
formed its spiritual, airy, unmediated contact with soul.

The discrete, objectified nature of emotion in Monteverdi's late style
shows itself also in the recitative of *Il ritorno d'Ulisse in patria* (1640) and
especially of *Poppea* (1642)—and this notwithstanding the persistent connections of this style to the recitative styles of Orpheus or Ariadne. In place
of the integrated fluidity, redolent of unbroken, impassioned speech of the
earlier styles, the late recitative presents itself as a quiltwork of individual
gestures distinguished from one another by shifts of meter, tempo, and

expressive tone. These gestures include pictorial melismas, canzonetta techniques like walking basslines, short arioso passages, outbursts of *stile concitato*, and stylized hesitations and stammering repetitions. They infiltrate and transform a language still at other moments echoing the earlier period.

With consummate virtuosity Monteverdi fashioned this varied style, even to the point of capturing within its expressive arc many of the miniature arias that otherwise might merely punctuate it. But the patchwork quality itself and the insistent marking of gestural discreteness it entails display the passions of the singer as so many bounded, gem-like, autonomous psychic symbols. The result, apparent again and again in the late recitative, is a displacement of tone from word; a space opens between the two in order that the one might represent the other. When Ariadne had called down the wrath of the heavens on Theseus, she veered toward unquenchable rage—but maintained the speech-like integration of the rest of her lament. (Figure 9.1). When, in a parallel gesture, Ottavia questioned heaven's vengeance against Nero, she shifted gears to accommodate a melismatic icon of Jove's thunderbolts, complete with walking bass in canzonetta style (Figure 9.2). We might put the difference this way, in a manner generalizable across much larger spans than this example alone: Ariadne delivers gestures of musical speech, while Ottavia offers musical gestures about words.

And, finally, what about the characters represented in *Poppea*? The objectified emotions of Monteverdi's late career find no clearer expression than in the fact that Poppea, Nero, Ottavia, Ottone, and the rest spend so much time self-consciously working with their passions. The drama as a whole takes for its project the demonstration of musical processes of emotional manipulation. All the novelties of Monteverdi's late recitative form an apparatus wielded repeatedly by one character to alter, before our ears, the passions of another. The apparatus carries the symbolic representation of passions evident throughout the late recitative style to the very heart of this opera. In an extraordinary musical tour de force, the audience is no longer a participant so much as a voyeur. Orpheus had embraced his hearers in a cosmos-spanning network of song; Poppea treats hers to a spectacle of musico-mechanical manipulation.

Scene after scene stages this passional technology. In act 1, scene 9, the accelerating pace of stichomythic exchange constructed by Monteverdi and Busenello is a device by which Seneca directs Nero's passions, goading him finally into a fury. Similarly, in act 2, scene 9 Ottone's hesitations, equivocations, and asides, which Monteverdi enhanced by breaking apart Busenello's prosody and reforming it as a language of stammering repetition, enrage

Ottavia. In response she pushes more and more menacingly her demand that Ottone kill Poppea, while Ottone begs for time so that he might manipulate and refashion his own emotions:

Dammi tempo, ond'io possa
inferocire i sentimenti miei,
dishumanar il core,
imbarbarir la mano, etc.

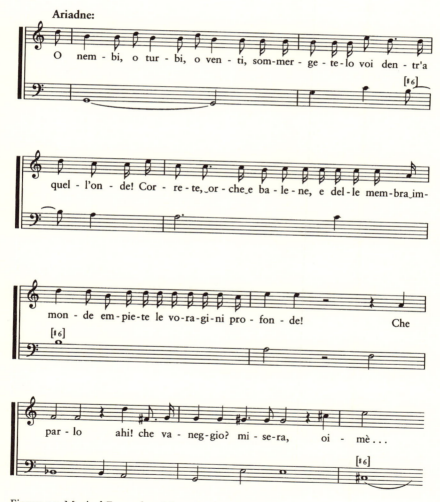

Figure 9.1. Musical Example 1, Monteverdi, *L'Arianna.*

Meanwhile, in act 1, scene 13 Ottone is the aggressor, laying claim to Drusilla's faith through a series of amorous affirmations. Again Monteverdi enhanced these by restructuring the more laconic exchanges Busenello had provided.

Figure 9.2. Musical Example 2, *L'incoronazione di Poppea* 1:5.

Sometimes the passional technology is distilled into a small congeries of musical techniques, which together comprise a sonic emblem of the mechanical revision worked on a protagonist's emotions. Here the assembling of a musical apparatus to manage and direct the passions is especially apparent. These moments, indeed, take over the emblematic instrumental expression of the late madrigals and scherzi. Arnalta's lullaby in act 2, scene 12 is one such case, operating on Poppea through its minor-mode descending tetrachord bassline and its calm, rocking harmonies against long-held notes in the voice.

Just the opposite of calming, instead, is the major-mode descending tetrachord over which Lucan dwells on the charms of Poppea's mouth in act 2, scene 6. Again in this scene Monteverdi radically reshaped Busenello's libretto, assigning most of one of Nero's speeches instead to Lucan and thus casting Nero as the yielding manipulatee of the poet, able to muster only the repeated exclamation "Ahi destin!" The insistent repetition in the bassline combines with Lucan's increasingly florid song to mime the tautological crescendo of a sex act—which leads, predictably, to climax: a final, prolonged "Ahi destin!" from Nero, after which Lucan recalls him from his sexual reverie:

Tu vai, Signor, tu vai
Nell'estasi d'amor deliziando . . . .

Finally, famously, there is Poppea, the great manipulator and manipulatee of passions in this opera. In her love scenes with Nero, her song is a miniature regimen of musical techniques operating to channel and enflame his passions—gestures, each of them, *about her words* more than *of her speech*. The techniques include languid, sensual hesitations, as when she relives with him a night of passion just past (Figure 9.3). The gestures include melting chromaticism, as when Poppea clings to Nero at their daybreak parting (Figure 9.4). And they include insistent repetitions, such as those by which she wrings from Nero his promise to return (Figure 9.5).

Moreover, at the same time as Poppea's song shapes Nero's passions, it also reveals how her own passions are directed by him. When in act 1, scene 3 Nero hints that Ottavia might be deposed, Poppea cannot contain herself; she interrupts him with repeated, insistent questions. And when he finally manages to complete his thought, she launches into one of those outbursts of irrepressible arioso—*orgoglioso*, Italians of Monteverdi's era might have called it—that mark her sense of triumph throughout the score (Figure 9.6).

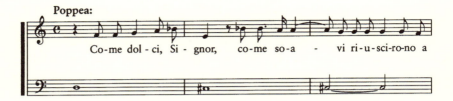

Poppea:

Co-me dol - ci, Si - gnor, co-me so-a - vi ri-u-sci-ro-no a

te la notte an - da-ta di que-sta boc - ca i ba - ci?

[♮]

Poppea:

Di ques-to, di ques-to se-no i i i po - mi?

Poppea:

Di ques-te di que-ste brac-cia di que - ste brac-cia

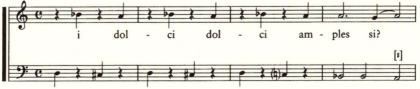

i dol - ci dol - ci am - ples si?

[♮]

Figure 9.3 Musical Example 3, *L'incoronazione di Poppea* 1:10.

The symbolic externalization of passions is not only the mark of the recitative medium in which *L'incoronazione di Poppea* moves; it is also the central concern of the plot itself of the opera. *Poppea's* peculiar fascination for us resides in this matching of its deepest dramatic agendas with the technical resources and fundamental expressive aims of Monteverdi's late style. One is reminded of *Parsifal.*

The broadest division of Monteverdi's changing expressive aims and techniques, then, is marked by a shift from one kind of emotive gesture to another; it is divided by allegiances to two distinct types of *Pathosformel.* In the first of these we hear resounding still the cosmos-spanning harmonies of Ficinian song and psychology. We participate, insofar as we moderns are not deafened to it, in a world integrated by concords that merge speech and song. We are seized by a plastic utterance of forceful phantasmic presence.

In the second, instead, we hear something more familiar to us—so familiar, indeed, that we have tended to extrapolate it back and hear in it the expressive mode of all Monteverdi's music. Here the listeners bear witness to the passions others display as so many crystalline symbolic forms. The auditors eavesdrop on this display from a space, novel in the mid-seventeenth century, between music and words; or, as in *Poppea*, they listen in on the mechanical alteration of the emotions of one character by the singing of another.

It is the problematic opening of new spaces in this Monteverdian representation of passions that leads me to ally it with Vico: spaces between tone and word, singer and listener, soul and bodily expression of emotion. Just as Monteverdi held emotions at arm's length in his late works—observing, analyzing, representing them—so Vico would cast out sung passion, along a historical axis that carried it far from him. Just as Vico would at once hear and not hear the passion of his heroic song, so in his last decades Monteverdi would strain to hear still a Ficinian cosmic harmony even as he dissolved—"analyzed," in the true etymology of the word—its continuities into separable component parts.

In these paradoxes Vico and Monteverdi frame the unsustainable aporia at the heart of the new objectification of passion. Vico can gauge the foreignness of passion only by its intimate proximity; he can countenance its crowding irrationality only by its distance. In a Ficinian cosmos of graded continuity, there is no *ir*rationality but only *sub*rationality: perceptions and feelings waiting to resound up the chain of being to higher realms. The non-rational furor of the poet is not bestial madness but the summons of the

Figure 9.4. Musical Example 4, *L'incoronazione di Poppea* 1:3.

Figure 9.5. Musical Example 5, *L'incoronazione di Poppea* 1:3.

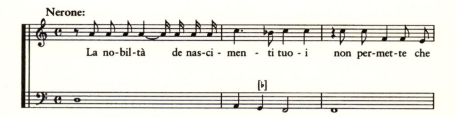

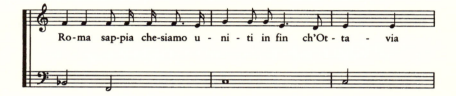

Figure 9.6. Musical Example 6, *L'incoronazione di Poppea* 1:3.

Poppea:

Van - ne van - ne ben

mane es-clu-sa col re - pu-dio da me.

[#3 4]   [4 #3]   [6]

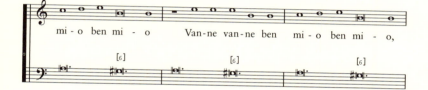

mi - o ben mi - o   Van-ne van-ne ben   mi - o ben mi - o,

[6]   [6]   [6]

van - - - ne ben mi - - - o.

[4   #3]

divine. In Vico's world, broken at the rift between material and immaterial realms, the irrational emerges as madness—the inspired poet, as Foucault once taught, turns into the delusional Don Quixote. Vico displaced this madness toward primitive locales, posing at one stroke the dilemmas of both modern historiography and anthropology. For his part, Monteverdi looked back on the old world and, prehensile as always, grasped at the new.

It is Warburg, finally, whose picture of pathos reminds us that Vico's strategy must fail, that the casting out of demons of irrationality leaves behind a void where they might reappear. Warburg speaks to us because he confronts the enigma of modernity that Vico was still able to avoid. This is the irremediable lodging of mysterious, unsettling spaces exactly in the deepest recesses of the psyche—noumenal recesses of a post-Kantian psyche, interpreted not as a place beyond, invisibly conditioning our thought, but as a frightening locus of irrationality within, resistant to it. Warburg demonstrates, in his writings and in his life, the modern conversion of the Renaissance's renewed Dionysiac passion into recurring neurosis or worse. Nietzsche before him had demonstrated something similar.

In his reliance on Vico and his recognition of the central importance of the Renaissance in passional history, Warburg traces a genealogy behind this modernity. The heritage reaches back through Vico's distanced analysis of primitive passion to Ficino's lived experience of emotive phantasms. Along the way it ushers to center stage a premodern power of song largely unimaginable and inaudible to Warburg, perhaps a little more imaginable, if still inaudible, to us. By virtue of the contrast between Vico and Ficino, the genealogy points to the seventeenth century as the watershed dividing an emergence of a modern problematics of passion from an earlier impassioned magic. It points to the age of Monteverdi as the place where singing lost its contact with the world and its grasp on the soul but, by the same turn, assumed a new power to represent both world and soul. Our sense of Monteverdi's wrestling with this change is what makes him sing for us still.

PART III

Disciplinary Boundaries

Chapter 10

The Passions and the Interests in Early Modern Europe: The Case of Guarini's Il Pastor fido

Victoria Kahn

O Powerfull Law! which Heaven or Nature,
Writ in the Heart of every Creature.
Whose amiable violence,
And pleasing rapture of the sense
Doth byas all things to that good
Which we desire . . .

—Guarini, Il Pastor fido, *trans. Richard Fanshawe*

What is at stake here is nothing less than the production of an entirely new kind of human subject—one which, like the work of art itself, discovers the law in the depths of its own free identity, rather than in some oppressive external power.

—Terry Eagleton, The Ideology of the Aesthetic

In his influential book, *The Passions and the Interests: Political Arguments for Capitalism Before Its Triumph*, Albert Hirschman traced the development of a positive view of the acquisitive passions and of self-interest not to Calvinism, as Weber had done, but to developments in early modern political theory. In response to Weber's question, "How did commercial, banking and similar money-making pursuits become honorable at some point in the modern age after having stood condemned or despised as greed, love of lucre, and avarice for centuries?" Hirschman argued that the language of interest emerged first and foremost from a new conception of politics, one based on an "objective" analysis of the passions and of the interest—or reason—of state.[1] This so-called objective analysis of the passions, which Hirschman attributed first and foremost to Machiavelli, eventually allowed for the perception that one passion might be used to counteract the harmful effects of another. Thus, by the mid-seventeenth century, Hobbes had come to believe that the fear of violent death might serve to dampen the aristocratic passion for self-aggrandizement that was so dangerous to the stability of the commonwealth. Later theorists, according to Hirschman, built on this idea of the countervailing passion to argue that the desire for material gain would serve as the best counterweight to the aristocratic preoccupation with honor and glory. In this way, the political debate about the passions and interests provided arguments for acquisitiveness before the triumph of capitalism.

In this essay I argue that Hirschman's account is fundamentally skewed by his neglect of the most important source of arguments about passion

Figure 10.1. Mirtillo and Amarilli playing blind man's buff. From Guarini, *Il Pastor fido* (Venice, 1602). Reproduced by permission of the Folger Shakespeare Library.

and interest in the early modern period: the classical tradition of rhetoric and poetics. Every Renaissance schoolboy was familiar with Cicero's remarks in *De officiis* and *De oratore* about the strategic appeal to the passions for the purposes of persuasion, including the use of one passion to combat another. Every schoolboy knew Cicero's analysis of the compatibility of the *honestum* and the *utile*, the good and the useful, in the realm of politics. These arguments, and others like them from Seneca, Quintilian, Aristotle's *Rhetoric* and *Poetics*, and their sixteenth-century imitators, colored all early modern discussions of the role of the passions in furthering the public interest.[2]

Once we attend to this tradition, we are in a position to revise Hirschman's thesis. If the idea of the countervailing passion is available in the early modern period before the mid-seventeenth century and in contexts other than that of political debate, then the political arguments traced by Hirschman are not unique in anticipating and helping to shape the early modern political subject of passion and interest. Equally important are the revival in this period of Ciceronian rhetoric and of Aristotelian arguments about the formal or aesthetic autonomy of art. Along with the rhetorical treatment of the passions, early modern critics began to consider representation—or what Plato and Aristotle called mimesis—as a means not only of soliciting but also of counteracting the passions. And this in turn means that sixteenth-century debates about literary representation and aesthetic autonomy have an important role to play in the political history of the passions and the interests, as well as in the transition to modernity.

For heuristic purposes, we might describe the two critical camps as an ethical Aristotelianism on the one hand and a formal or aesthetic Aristotelianism on the other. Critics in the first camp read Aristotle's *Poetics* through Horace's *Ars poetica* and Plato's strictures on poetry, according to which literature delights in order to instruct and representation is in the service of the rhetorical promotion of public interest (the dominant view of literature in this period). Against this moralizing of literature, a number of critics advanced counterarguments that isolated the artist's technical interest in his craft and the reader's aesthetic pleasure in the text. These critics liberated Aristotle's *Poetics* from Plato, Horace, and Aristotle's own *Ethics*—as, for example, Castelvetro did in his commentary on the *Poetics*, where he stressed the purely aesthetic pleasure of poetry.[3] For the majority of critics, however, artistic craft was the source of considerable anxiety about the subversive potential of amoral, rhetorical technique. An equally powerful ambivalence attached to the pleasure the reader derived from the poet's artful imitation, since aesthetic pleasure or aesthetic interest unconstrained by ethical imperatives was very often seen as undermining traditional morality. A revised history of the passions and interests in the early modern period needs to take account of rhetorical and aesthetic interest, as well as political and economic interest.

Any number of literary genres might serve as a point of departure for this revised history, but a central role must be allotted to the related genres of pastoral romance and tragicomedy, and in particular to Battista Guarini's *Il Pastor fido*, a hugely popular and important work that went through some twenty Italian editions between its first publication in 1590 and the edition of 1602, which included Guarini's critical notes and his accompanying treatise on tragicomedy. In his account of *Il Pastor fido*'s critical fortunes, Nicholas Perella observes that "throughout the seventeenth century, the *Pastor fido* was the most widely read book of secular literature in all of Europe." Guarini's prose defense of his work was equally important in the early modern world of literary criticism.[4]

As an example of a new genre—that is, a genre not discussed by Aristotle—Guarini's romance gave rise to a fast and furious pamphlet war in Italy. Beginning with the exchange in the late 1580s between Guarini and his Counter-Reformation critic Giason Denores, the debate concerned the representation of the passions and their relation to both the private interests of the reader and the public interest of the state.[5] Modern critics have construed the exchange between Denores and Guarini as an exemplary setpiece, one which pits Denores's Counter-Reformation didacticism against Guarini's defense of the aesthetic autonomy of art.[6] But the debate about *Il Pastor fido* is more complicated than this might suggest, for Guarini's defense of aesthetic autonomy is also an analysis of aesthetic ideology. In showing us how the artist constructs the aesthetic object, he directs our attention not to ethics in Denores's sense but rather to the strategic uses of representation, including the representation of the passions, in the realm of politics.

In late sixteenth-century Italy, romance was a vexed topic to say the least. Particularly vexing, in the mind of Denores and other critics, was that Aristotle had nothing to say about it. For the majority of critics who read the *Poetics* as normative rather than descriptive, Aristotle's silence was taken to signify that romance did not conform to the best classical rules for the construction of poetry. The multiple plot of romance (here the critics were thinking of Ariosto) violated the norms set down by epic. Similarly, the mixture of the marvelous with the historical threatened the epistemological distinction between the icastic and the phantastic, between faithful imitation and fanciful invention. Romance was thus from the outset associated with innovation, specifically innovation in genre. Like tragicomedy, with which it was often allied or even identified—as in the case of *Il Pastor fido*—romance indecorously mixed high and low characters, historical truths and obvious impossibilities, near tragedies with happy endings.[7] And since aesthetic decorum, for Counter-Reformation critics, was inseparable from political decorum (the hierarchy of genre mirroring social and political hierarchy) and since both were in turn subordinated to the ethical standard of the good, the aesthetic disproportion of romance could never be a merely aesthetic issue. Romance's deviation from the law of genre was construed as a form of epistemological and moral deviance. The "simulacra" of romance, Tasso complained, are "false according to Plato's discussion of imitation in *The Sophist*, and sinful, according to . . . the Christian poet's duty to imitate the workings of God's providence rather than to create 'phantasms' through the workings of his own imagination."[8] In a well known verbal and structural pun, the erring of the multiple plot represented a form of moral error; the aesthetic pleasure that readers took in the variety of characters and subplots was a form of moral weakness. In the worst case, disobedience to Aristotle's rules threatened to slide into spiritual and political disbobedience as well.

In elevating tragedy along with Aristotle and in criticizing romance and tragicomedy, Denores adopted the dominant Counter-Reformation position on the didactic and rhetorical function of art. For Denores, poetry was rhetorical because it was capable of moving the reader or listener to moral action; it was political because the goal of poetry was "to inspire virtue in the souls of the spectators and auditors, to the common benefit of a well ordered republic."[9] This common benefit or public interest ideally constrained all private interest, including the interest readers take in their own pleasure. Thus, while Denores noted the role of pleasure in the experience of tragic catharsis, he represented it as an instrument—what he called a "leggiadro inganno" or lovely deception—in the service of moral persuasion. And he argued that poets who refuse to subordinate pleasure to instruction are like false orators who, in order to deceive their judges, use arguments that are not "fair but sophistical and merely apparent."[10] Poetry in which the experience of aesthetic pleasure is merely instrumental, such as tragedy, is judged to be conducive to the public interest, whereas poetry which is enjoyed for its own sake, such as romance and tragicomedy, is associated with the sophistic orator's self-interested, calculated—we might even say Machiavellian—deception of his audience.

Although Denores represented this deception as something that was perpetrated on the audience, others critics feared that the readers of Guarini's poetry would themselves become crafty. For these critics, the poet's ability to stir up the passions by representing amorous intrigue (Denores' "gl'inamoramenti") was just one of the many dangers of pastoral romance.[11] They also feared that the deviant aesthetic pleasures of reading would in turn create interested readers, readers motivated by the pursuit of self-interest, whether in the form of political rebellion, theological heresy, or economic transactions. Thus one Daniello Bartoli described "two unfortunate sisters, the first to read that famous tragicomedy . . . [*Il Pastor fido*], who at the first reading became such good mistresses of impurity that they immediately opened a school, transforming their house into a brothel and advertising themselves as whores."[12] The fear that reading—in particular, the reading of romance—was itself a form of seduction had of course a long and august history: sixteenth-century Italian readers would have remembered in particular the episode of Paolo and Francesca from Dante's *Inferno*, in which the vehicle of Francesca's seduction is the medieval French romance, the "Galeotto."[13] In Bartoli's exemplary anecdote, however, erotic pleasure is quickly translated into the coin of economic exchange, as though to suggest that the representation of the passions does not simply conduce to unmediated imitation, but to a rather more mediated, calculated, interested pursuit of economic advantage. Other critics implied that the representation of the erotic passions could have dangerous political and theological consequences as well. Thus Cardinal Bellarmine is supposed to have remarked that *Il Pastor fido* "was responsible for the depravity of countless women, and that it had done more harm to the Catholic Church than Luther and the Protestant revolt."[14]

In response to these charges, Guarini confirmed his critics worst fears about the pleasures of poetry, the formal innovations of romance, and the sophistical techniques of aesthetic representation. First, he asserted that the chief aim of all poetry, according to Aristotle, was not to teach moral principles but to produce pleasure through imitation. Such pleasure was not a vehicle of ethical instruction but an end in itself. He then confirmed that romance was a new genre, but insisted that such innovation was licensed by the "changing times, changing mores, [and] the changing minds of audiences."[15] This emphasis on the historicity of genre, and the poet's license to invent, was profoundly disturbing to those who felt that the poetry was governed by timeless moral precepts, for it suggested that not only poetry but morality itself might be subject to change.[16] Finally, Guarini devoted by far the largest part of his polemical efforts to defending the art of poetic imitation, specifically the numerous technical decisions regarding plot, character, affect, and figuration, that had gone into the construction of *Il Pastor fido.*

In his focus on poetic technique, Guarini confirmed that romance was troubling as much because of its manner of representation as because of its subject matter. Thus, in response to Denores's insistence on the didactic and moral function of art, Guarini remarked:

How can you hold that poetics, which is an art and thus a habit of the speculative intellect, should take its principles from ethics, which is a habit of the active intellect? You will tell me that [poetics] takes its mores from the moralist; and I say to you that it takes them rather from the rhetorician, who is much different from the moralist on the definition of the virtues. But even if we admit that [poetry] takes [its definition of morals] from the moralist, I say to you that it does so not in order to teach them, but only to imitate them. . . . You will add, again, that [poetics] serves the politician insofar as the legislator allows the people to have [poetry] or not according as it presents good or bad morals. This is true; but it does not follow from this that [poetry] takes its principles from the politician. . . . As for its own intrinsic and formal principles, it has nothing to do with [the politician], but is a member of sophistic and rhetoric.[17]

The politician here is a Platonic politician who allows poetry into the city if it supports conventional morals. But the poet, Guarini asserted, is not bound by any such moralistic or pedagogical considerations. He is concerned only to imitate, not to instruct. Thus, to assert that poetry is a part of rhetoric and sophistic rather than ethics or politics is to say something particular about the nature of poetic representation. We might describe this difference by saying that what ethics or politics asserts, poetry or rhetoric only quotes. In Guarini's reading of Aristotle's *Rhetoric,* which he taught in his capacity as Professor of Poetics and Rhetoric at Ferrara, the rhetorician differs from the moralist on the definition of the virtues, precisely because he defines the virtues for the pragmatic purposes of persuasion and does not make any cognitive or ethical claims for his definitions. Like rhetoric in this view, poetry is a matter of art—of *technē*—rather than ethics. The goal of the poet is, in Guarini's words, "not to imitate . . . the good . . . but to imitate well."[18] Such imitation will yield pleasure—the primary end of poetry—and will also momentarily purge and temper the passions. It will not, however, offer moral instruction.[19]

It is precisely passages such as these which have led some modern critics to argue that Guarini is defending the aesthetic autonomy of literature.

But it is at just this point that Guarini reintroduces the connection between poetry and politics that he had earlier seemed to deny. Specifically, he suggests that artistic representation contains a key to negotiating the imperfect world of human passions and interests, a world vividly depicted in Guarini's own *Trattato della politica libertà*. There we learn that in ancient Rome—and, it is implied, modern republics as well—both the people and the nobility act according to "interesse privato" rather than "bene publico." This is a world in which private interest is "signor del mondo," a world, in some respects like the Rome of Machiavelli's *Discourses*, in which the conflicts that result from ambition, greed, and the desire for glory eventually result in the destruction of the republic.[20] In his defense of *Pastor fido*, Guarini tells us that authoritative texts such as Aristotle's *Ethics* and *Politics* can't help us negotiate this world of passion and interest since the picture of virtue they offer is too ideal and abstract, a criticism which recalls Machiavelli's censure of ideal republics in *The Prince*. In contrast, Aristotle's *Rhetoric* gives us a virtue which is "less idealistic and less perfect," and which men might therefore be persuaded to imitate.[21]

In his self-conscious reflection on rhetorical technique—on imitating well rather than imitating the good—and in his insistence on the practical advantage of such a rhetorical approach to virtue, Guarini recalls chapter 8 of *The Prince*. There Machiavelli addresses the question of whether a prince's acts of treachery and cruelty make him less or more vulnerable to violent overthrow. "I believe," Machiavelli answers, "this depends on whether the cruelty is used well or badly."[22] Well or badly, rather than good or evil, is the standard for artistic as well as political decorum; and it is precisely this homology between rhetorical craft and Machiavellian craftiness that makes a rhetoric of the virtues politically useful. Specifically, Guarini suggests, Aristotle's *Rhetoric* and the poetry it inspires teach us how to represent the virtues sophistically or formally, and to use those representations in our own interest. Such a sophistic approach to virtue turns out to be far more pragmatic than Aristotle's substantive, philosophical approach to virtue in the *Ethics*.[23] As we will see, in *Il Pastor fido* this concern with the uses of representation bears on the passions as well.

Guarini's interest in technique is also apparent in his remarks on sophistic reasoning and plot structure. In reading Aristotle's *Poetics* through his *Rhetoric* rather than his *Ethics*, Guarini directs us not only to the amoral technique of literature, but also to the related scandal (to use Terence Cave's word) of probabilistic reasoning.[24] As Cave and others have argued, the Aristotelian poet and orator share a concern with devising plausible fictions,

fictions designed both to move the passions and to engage the listener or spectator in an activity of probable reasoning. Yet, the *Poetics* also makes it clear that literary verisimilitude does not perfectly conform to the logical criteria of probable judgment, since literature traffics in deception and disguise, plausible impossibilities rather than implausible possibilities. Furthermore, the moment of "recognition" which Aristotle requires of tragedy and which later critics extended to other genres as well may result not from the cause and effect sequence of the plot but from paralogism or faulty reasoning. Recognition may turn on what in the *Rhetoric* Aristotle calls atechnical or inartistic proofs: vows, oaths, contracts, and marks such as Orestes' footprint in the *Oresteia* or Odysseus's scar in the *Odyssey*. In this way, poetics is inflected by rhetoric and specifically by the threat of fraud.[25] It was this trafficking in deception, including the author's manipulation of the plot, that particularly irritated some early readers of *Il Pastor fido*.[26]

Although Guarini boasted that his plot was free of what Aristotle called "inartistic signs," and that the dénouement developed logically from the drama itself, he also insisted on calling attention to the contrivance of his art. In *Il Verrato*, as we have seen, Guarini argued that the technique of art *is* sophistic logic, plot is always a matter of the author's plotting and this is what links the craft of the artist with the craftiness of his characters. In the later *Compendio* Guarini defended the "ordine comico" or "artifizio" ("comic design" or "artifice") of *Il Pastor fido*, in which "l'astuzia, la menzogna, lo 'nganno, l'accortezza, le gherminelle sono i mezzi che intrigano" ("cunning, lies, deception, shrewdness, and tricks are the means which go to make up the plot").[27] Here Guarini drew an even closer parallel between the poet and the romance schemer by suggesting that the artifizio or technique of art—art as representation—underwrites both aesthetic pleasure and worldly pragmatism or Machiavellian self-interest. As we will see, these are the two aspects of *Il Pastor fido* that were important to English readers of Italian romance in general and of Guarini in particular.

I now want to suggest that the polemic between Guarini and Denores about the relationship of aesthetic autonomy and pleasure to Machiavellian technique is also the explicit subject of *Il Pastor fido*. In both plot and rhetoric, *Il Pastor fido* raises the question of the relation of natural impulses to human art, and of unmediated passion to craft or self-interest.[28] This question is figured first and foremost in the plot as a question of law or vows: the motive of the romance plot of *Il Pasto· fido* is that a marriage vow between Diana's priest Aminta and the nymph Lucrina has been betrayed by the latter's errant passion. This infidelity is the origin of the curse on Arcadia, the law which decrees that a virgin must be sacrificed every year until two noble descendants of the gods are married. At the opening of the play, the descendants Silvio and Amarilli are betrothed—but Amarilli is in love with the shepherd Mirtillo, and Silvio is in love with hunting. Thus the anticipated marriage vow of Silvio and Amarilli appears to be in as much jeopardy as the vow that caused the curse, and the question the play poses at first implicitly and then explicitly is whether the laws of heaven and earth can be reconciled: the one decreeing "Ama, se lice" (love lawfully), the other decreeing "Ama, se piace" (Love if you like; 4.5.621, 623). In the end these laws are reconciled, as we might expect from the title of the work and its generic affiliations: the faithful shepherd remains faithful; in a recognition scene based on *Oedipus Rex* (or so Guarini claimed), Mirtillo is revealed to be the long-lost noble son of the priest Montanus and the elder brother of Silvio; in fact, he was originally named Silvio so if Amarilli marries him she won't be unfaithful to her original marriage vow. (This is the sort of improbability that critics objected to.) And Silvio, who at first experienced the nymph Dorinda's love as a form of coercion, in the end falls in love and consents to marry her. Pleasure, that is, is reconciled to virtue and passion is aligned with the public interest. The significance of this alignment, however, has been the subject of considerable debate on the part of Guarini's readers.[29]

I would like to suggest that its significance is at least two-fold. If the plot of *Il Pastor fido* dramatizes the ultimate harmony of divine providence and human desire (sanctioning individual passion to the extent that it conforms to the public interest), it also instructs us in a strategic rhetoric of the passions—a rhetoric that allows the illusion of this harmony to be created in the first place. In the first case, *Il Pastor fido* exemplifies what Terry Eagleton has called aesthetic ideology or the law of the heart: morality is aestheticized to the extent that we are shown a society in which the characters "live . . . neither [according to the law of] duty nor utility, but [according to] the delightful fulfillment of [their] nature."[30] In the second case, *Il Pastor fido* offers a critique of this early modern version of aesthetic ideology: the reassuring moral order of the dénouement is revealed to be the consequence of the characters' own amoral technique—of imitating well rather than imitating the good.[31] Thus, while the plot explicitly reconciles pleasure and virtue, free will and fate, natural and divine law, it also suggests that this reconciliation is less the result of divine providence and the providential ratification of simple human constancy than of human plotting in the form of a rhetoric of the passions, a rhetoric that turns every passion into a sign to be artfully manipulated. This is the case not only for the scheming nymph Corisca, but also for the good characters who find themselves resorting to disguise and deception: in a wonderful gloss on the Machiavellian effects of desire in Arcadia, the shepherdess Dorinda dresses up as a wolf and describes her unrequited love for Silvio as "a living wolf [who] upon [her] heart doth prey / As on a harmlesse lamb." In every case passion becomes a sign to be manifest or concealed, but always interpreted and manipulated on the basis of self-interest.[32]

We can begin to get a better understanding of the way in which *Il Pastor fido* foregrounds the problem of representation in relation to the passions if we compare it to Hirschman's paradigm. In *Pastor fido*, instead of the use of one passion to tame another, we find the use of the representation of passion to incite or further passion. Three examples may serve to illustrate this point. In all three cases, the emphasis is on the link between representation and strategic interest rather than disinterestedness. The first example is that of Mirtillo dressing up as a nymph in order to draw near to Amarilli, who is playing a game of blind man's buff. The scene (3.1) begins with Mirtillo reflecting on the fact that he himself may be deceived by love:

Ma se le mie speranze oggi non sono,
com'è l'usato lor, di fragil vetro,
o se maggior del vero
non fa la speme il desiar soverchio,
qui pur vedrò colei
ch'è 'l sol degli occhi miei;
e s'altri non m'inganna . . .

Though if my hopes (as mine are wont to be)
Are not of glasse, or my love make me see
Them through a multiplying glasse; If I
Be not deceiv'd both by my self, and by
Another: Here I shall that Sun behold
Which I adore . . . [33]

The variation of vetro/vero/vedrò is characteristic of the way in which Guarini's style calls attention to its own rhetoric, at the same time that it comments thematically on the distorting effects of desire, its link to misrepresentation or deception ("l'inganno"). First, Mirtillo worries that desire might make him see "maggior del vero." He then remarks that he can find in this clearing "non . . . altra cieca / che la mia cieca voglia." Finally, from such metaphorical blind passion, he proceeds to the literal game of blind man's buff. Looking on Amarilli blindfolded, Mirtillo comments, "Or sì che si può dire / ch'Amor è cieco e ha bendati gli occhi" ("I finde / Now it is true indeed, that Love is blinde").[34] But it is the chorus that drives home the point about the inseparability of passion and representation, the use of representation to augment the passions:

Cieco, Amor, non ti cred'io,
Ma fai cieco il desio
di chi ti crede;
ché s'hai pur poca vista, hai minor fede.

Love, thou art not blind, I know,
But dost onely appear so
To blinde us: if thy sight's small,
Thou hast, I'm sure no faith at all.[35]

In a short space, and with an extremely light touch, Guarini moves from the rhetorical play on vetro/vero/vedro, to the literally blind Amarilli, to the personification of Love only pretending to be blind in order to entrap lovers more easily. This shift between rhetorical and dramatic registers mirrors (or dramatizes) the rhetorical slippage between vero/vetro/vedro: we come to see the deception that was only figured in Mirtillo's musings. Then, in an ironic comment on the way that such a pyrotechnic display of art and what the characters call "lusinghe" (Fanshawe's "sweet language" [ll. 2289, 2301]) might distract the reader from the (moralizing) plot, Guarini has Corisca signal Mirtillo from the bushes to remind him of his goal. But (unlike Guarini's critics), Corisca is focused not on the ethical dimension of the plot—the restoration of "fede"—but on the uses of "lusinghe" (flattery) and disguise to achieve practical success. When Mirtillo fails to understand her signs, she emerges from the bushes to instruct the "gaping" lover: "prendila," seize Amarilli and kiss her. Clearly Guarini is enjoying the license of art to represent both virtue and vice, erotic passion and moral sentiment.[36] We might even say he uses the figure of the blindfold not only to justify the passionate kisses of his protagonists but also to allegorize and justify his own representation of lust—of passion as interest. As a poet rather than a moralist, he is by definition blindfolded: he is not obliged to recognize the objections of his moralizing critics.

My second example of the way in which representation is foregrounded and linked to the theme of countervailing passion comes from Act 3, scene 3. Once Amarilli takes off her blindfold and realizes she has been tricked, Mirtillo launches into a full-scale Petrarchan complaint about his cruel beloved. But Amarilli calls his rhetorical bluff: "Tu mi chiami crudele, immaginando / che da la ferità rimproverata / agevole ti sia forse il ritrarmi / al suo contrario affetto" ("Thou call'st me cruell, hoping, that to shun / That vice, into the contrary I'le run").[37] In Amarilli's view, Petrarchan rhetoric is itself a strategy of countervailing passion in the service of self-interested lovers. The following sticomythia of aphorisms about love illustrates this countervailing strategy both formally and thematically: to Mirtillo 's "Quel che nel cor si porta invan si fugge" ("We fly in vain what we about us carry"), Amarilli responds, "Scaccerà vecchio amor novo desio" ("A new desire an old will quite replace").[38] At the same time, as with Petrarchan lyric, such self-reflexive countervailing rhetoric calls attention to the aesthetic achievement of Guarini the poet.

In my third example, Silvio, the recalcitrant hunter who resists the love of the nymph Dorinda, berates Venus, "nemica di ragione, / macchinatrice sol d'opre furtive" ("foe to Reason, plotter of misdeedes") and challenges "vaine fantastive Love" to armed combat.[39] He is answered by Echo, that is, by the principle of repetition, quotation, or imitation. When Silvio asks, "With what dost thou still punish those that strive, / And obstinately do contend with love?" Echo answers "with love," thereby foreshadowing Silvio's eventual love for Dorinda.[40] There could be no clearer example of the way in which imitation or—to use the language of Guarini's prose defense—sophistic rhetoric is itself the principle of countervailing passion, which serves in the end to harmonize passion and interest both for the individual lover and for Arcadia as a whole. This reconciliation of passion and interest then turns out to be a figure for the reconciliation of divine providence and human plotting. Thus, in the conclusion to *Il Pastor fido*, the old shepherd Carino refers to heaven's "diverse ways" which recapitulate and redeem human nature's "crook't deceitful paths."[41] Like the echo scene, this recapitulation suggests that repetition or representation is itself a "providentially sanctioned" technique for dealing with the passions—for making them synonomous with the public interest.

Yet, it is precisely Guarini's defense of art as sophistic rhetoric that opens up *Il Pastor fido* to less orthodox readings than Guarini might have intended. If echo or imitation is a structural metaphor for the technique of countervailing passions, it also necessarily suggests technique as dangerous manipulation—for the imitation of faithfulness might just as well be called feigning. While the plot and the characters of *Il Pastor fido* reconcile pleasure and ethics, the law of nature and the moral law (the usual reading of *Il Pastor fido*), they also direct us to the technique of romance, and thus to the inflection of passion by self-interest. And they suggest that if there is an ethics to be derived from *Il Pastor Fido* it is the pragmatic ethics of Aristotle's *Rhetoric* rather than the high-minded standards of the *Nicomachean Ethics*. This rhetorical ethics—or *technē*—allows for persuasion to the good but only because first and foremost it is a matter of persuading well.

Like Guarini's prose defense of his pastoral romance, *Il Pastor fido* thus points up a different sort of connection between representation and politics from the moralizing one that Guarini criticized in *Il Verrato*. In hollowing out the passions—in making them signs to be interpreted and manipulated rather than expressions to be perceived—Guarini necessarily recalls not only Aristotle but also Cicero and Quintilian on the political uses of the passions by the orator in the lawcourt and forum. As Cicero wrote in *De officiis* (2.7.23), "But, of all motives, none is better adapted to secure influence and hold it fast than love; nothing is more foreign to that end than fear." Similarly, Quintilian taught that an audience is more easily moved by an appeal to the emotions than by reasoning (2.42.178) and that "love is won if you are thought to be upholding the interests of your audience" (2.51.206). In contrast to Aristotle's claim that rhetoric should focus on rational argument, Quintilian argued that oratory shows its highest calling in moving the passions: precisely because the logical arguments arise out of the case itself, "the peculiar task of the orator arises when the minds of the judges require force to move them, and their thoughts have actually to be led away from the contemplation of the truth" (6.2.4–5). Thus the judge who is moved by his passions and begins to take an interest in the case is compared to the lover who is "incapable of forming a reasoned judgment on the beauty of the object of [his] affections, because passion forestalls the sense of sight" (6.2.6). Like Cicero and Quintilian, Guarini does not simply represent the passions; he also provides a rhetorical analysis of them—what we might call a semiology or economy. He makes us understand that a passion which is construed as a sign has already become subject to calculation and manipulation (one might even say circulation): it has already become, in short, an interest. *Il Pastor fido* is political not because it dramatizes the *subordination* of the passions to the political virtues of constancy and obedience—something that Denores, for example, would have approved. Rather *Il Pastor fido* is political both because it places the *satisfaction* of the passions (both the characters' and the reader's) at the center of a newly aestheticized social order and because it makes this aesthetic ideology itself an object of rhetorical analysis and thus, potentially, of political interest.

Together, *Il Pastor fido* and the surrounding polemical debate offer a powerful corrective to Hirschman's thesis. It is not so much the passions as the *representation* of the passions that preoccupies those writers of the late sixteenth and early seventeenth century who are reflecting on problems of political obligation and the preservation of the state. Accordingly, Machiavelli is an important figure in a revised history of the passions and interests less because of what Hirschman calls his realistic analysis of the passions than because of his attention to the problems of representation and persuasion. And the same is true of later figures as well. For Guarini, the interest we take in literary representation is crucially linked to the interest of state, and this is the case not chiefly because literature has the power to persuade us to imitate its examples of virtue or obedience, but rather because—to the extent that representation is divorced from the traditional constraints of ethics—it teaches both the uses of simulation and dissimulation and the subversive potential of aesthetic pleasure. These lessons were important not only for later Italian readers of *Il Pastor fido* but for English readers of Italian pastoral romance as well.

Before turning to England, I want to pause to consider one of these later Italian readers of Guarini. Specifically, I want to suggest that we can see the link between Machiavellian technique and aesthetic ideology adumbrated in satirical form in Traiano Boccalini's *Ragguagli di Parnasso* (News from Parnassus) of 1612—a text that was partially translated into English in 1626 and 1656. Boccalini was the political antithesis of Guarini: an admirer of the Venetian republic rather than of the dukes of Ferrara, a scathing satirist of court life as well as of reason of state. A deft rhetorician, Boccalini managed to represent *Il Pastor fido* as both a negligible aesthetic trifle and a potentially subversive rhetorical performance. It is difficult to know whether the judgment of subversiveness is itself an ironic comment on Guarini's Counter-Reformation quietism, his political and religious orthodoxy; what is important for my purposes is that Boccalini himself clearly recognized the Machiavellian potential of pastoral romance.[42]

Boccalini prefaces his satirical account of *Il Pastor fido* by a pastoral fable of his own. He describes the flight of fidelity from the governments of the earth, the people's hatred of their princes, and the princes' "ill usage" of their subjects; and he tells that this conflict has been resolved by "the Illustrious Muses, assisted by the Heroick Virtues" who teach the sheep to obey their shepherds, and the shepherds not to mistreat their sheep (1.30.51–52). This parable of the uses of poetry to create "fedeltà" between rulers and subjects then sets the stage for the arrival of a "handsom Peasant of *Ferrara*, called *Pastor Fido*" at the court of Parnassus, along with his gift of a tasty

"Pastoral Tart." Apollo (the god of poetry, particularly pastoral) and the assembled courtiers proceed to devour it, until one of courtiers offends them by objecting that the tart is disgustingly sweet. Apollo's anger at this interruption is turned to laughter, however, by

> *Signeor Giovan della Casa,* [who] took the Plate [which had held the tart], and licking it with equal greediness and unmannerliness, told his Majesty and the Muses, that in things that do ravish with delight, men were not Masters of themselves, nor could they remember *Gallateo*'s rules, and that in time of *Carneval,* it was lawfull to commit exorbitances. (no. 31, 54)

As though echoing Guarini's Counter-Reformation critics, Boccalini suggests that aesthetic sweetness—the aesthetic pleasure of reading—can itself persuade to potentially unlawful behavior. Unlike Guarini's critics, however, Boccalini seems to view this potential for unlawful exorbitance at court in positive terms.

At the end of the *Ragguagli,* Boccalini devises a Machiavellian fable about the uses of pastoral.[43] Brought before the court of Apollo, Machiavelli is charged with teaching the princes of Europe the art of reason of state. When he protests that he has not invented or recommended anything new, but simply "copied" or imitated the "original" actions of princes, the Attorney General charges Machiavelli with teaching the principle of imitation itself. In other words, the very fact of imitation is Machiavellian: capable of revealing the arcana imperii simply by representing or copying them. Predictably, the Attorney General goes on to link such imitation not simply with aesthetic pleasure but with the calculated pursuit of self-interest: specifically, he argues that Machiavelli still deserves to be punished because "he was found by night amongst a flock of sheep, whom he taught to put . . . dogs teeth in their mouthes, thereby indangering the utter ruine of all shepherds," who would now have to be "more aware of their sheep, then of wolves" (1.89.176). Even worse, the increased concern with self-protection will cause the price of wool and cheese to rise and will thus be detrimental to the economic interest of shepherds and consumers. In this delightfully Nietzschean parable, Boccalini tells us that he reads the author of *The Prince* as a potentially subversive critic of tyrants, one who in describing the secrets of princely rule also teaches the people how to pursue their own interests by rebelling against their rulers. Pastoral in this reading is always already Machiavellian. Ironically, it was precisely this fear that seems to have intensified both the anxiety about and interest in Italian prose romance and pastoral in late sixteenth- and early seventeenth-century England.

The critical debate about *Il Pastor fido* as art or craft, morally neutral aesthetic pleasure or dangerous, Machiavellian self-interest, foreshadowed the reception of Italian romance in England. In late-sixteenth-century England, Italian prose romance was associated both with the dangers of aesthetic and erotic pleasure on the one hand and with Machiavellian craft or self-interest on the other. Roger Ascham's warning against "bawdie books . . . translated out of the Italian tongue" is probably the most famous complaint about Italian prose romance in this period.

Suffer these books to be read, and they will soon displace all books of godly learning. . . . And thus you will see, how will enticed to wantonness, doth easily allure the mind to false opinions; and how corrupt manners in living, breed false judgment in doctrine; and therefore suffer not vain books to breed vanity in men's wills, if you would have God's truth take root in men's minds.[44]

Ascham then went on to associate such wantonness and atheism with a similar lack of faith in the erotic sphere: Italianate Englishmen

commonly . . . come home common contemners of marriage, and ready persuaders of all others to the same; . . . [having been] free in Italy to go whithersoever lust will carry them, they do not like [it] that law and honesty should be such a bar to their liberty at home in England. And yet they be the greatest makers of love, the daily dalliers with such pleasant words, with such smiling and secret countenances, with such signs, tokens, wagers, purposed to be lost before they were purposed to be made.[45]

For Ascham, the emphasis on the manipulation of signs and tokens in the erotic sphere was characteristic of a general ambiguity in the realm of courtly manners, where the pursuit of "present pleasure" was associated with that of "private profit," and where the rhetorical manipulation of the passions "in Circes court" was closely linked to the pursuit of Machiavellian self-interest and faction at the royal court.[46]

In the last twenty years, students of sixteenth-century English literature have taken Ascham's criticism to heart, at least to the extent of emphasizing the political and economic interests that were interwoven with the aesthetic illusions of Elizabethan prose romance, pastoral poetry, and other formal professions of love. Quoting Sir John Harington's definition of love rivals as "those that be suters to one woman, as are competitors to one office," Arthur Marotti comments, "poems and speeches at royal tilts and entertainments as well as complimentary letters and verse all expressed social, political, and economic suits in the language of love."[47] More recently, Lorna

Hutson has argued that Elizabethan critics of prose romance, like critics of the theater, were anxious about the new humanist rhetorical skills of emplotment and persuasive argument. In the judgment of early modern readers, these skills were complicit with the newly impersonal market economy and undermined traditional forms of allegiance and social interaction.[48] In Hutson's important account, sixteenth-century romance and drama did not simply reflect contemporary social, political, and economic changes. Rather, the new literary culture—both the rhetorical skills that produced works of literature and the skills these works fostered in others—helped to create a new prudent and calculating subject, as well as a new sense of affect and "communicative action."[49] In response to Hirschman, then, we can say that literary culture was as important as political argument in shaping the protocapitalist subject. Moreover, this subject, unlike Hirschman, had a keen sense of the contributions of rhetorical and aesthetic interest to his political and economic interests.

Although Ascham was critical of Italian prose romance, both Elizabeth and her courtiers seem to have viewed the Neoplatonic conventions of pastoral romance as a more complicated vehicle of aesthetic ideology. Like Petrarchan poetry, pastoral romance promoted the fiction that the relation between sovereign and subject was not one of power but of affection, not coercion but consent. If the rhetoric of Italian prose romance represented a crisis of faithfulness for some late sixteenth-century readers, pastoral romance—not only in the reign of Elizabeth but increasingly in the reigns of James and Charles—urged fidelity to a monarch who governed (at least in theory) less by an appeal to calculated self-interest than by an appeal to aesthetic pleasure and to the passions.

This was certainly true of the pastoral romances and masques of the 1630s, whose celebration of Charles' peaceful foreign policy and of the domestic bliss of the royal marriage figured the relation of sovereign and subject as one of love and affection rather than coercion. It was also true of the royalist prose romances of the 1650s—although in response to contemporary events, royalist authors now argued for the aptness of the genre to allegorize the political upheavals of the civil war. This was in part because, as Lois Potter has suggested, Charles I and his son were themselves romance or tragicomic heroes to their supporters. In fact, "the two Charleses acted out virtually every role available to a ruler in romance or drama: the disguised lover, the husband parted from his wife/kingdom, the loving father of his country, the sacrificial victim, the wandering prince."[50]

Charles's parliamentary critics also used the language of romance to describe his misfortunes, although the intention here was clearly ironic. In the republican newsbook, *Mercurius Britanicus*, John Hall described the 1648 escape of Charles I from his parliamentary captors as "that late fine *Romance* of the Isle of Wight, a business that carries as much probability as anything that we read of *King Arthur* or the *Knights* of the *round* table."[51] Romance here does not conjure up a world of miraculous constancy in the face of tribulation but rather—as it did for Guarini's critics—a world of fiction and improbability, of imitation as a form of deception. This at least was the argument of Hobbes, who criticized the improbable fictions of romance in his "Answer to Davenant," and who in *Leviathan* associated romance with the self-aggrandizing passions and interests which had contributed to the civil war. The relationship of subject to sovereign should not be one of romance, Hobbes argued, but rather contractual obligation. Although such a contract presupposed reasoning about the passions, for Hobbes "the passion to be reckoned upon was fear." Fear of violent death in the state of nature convinces individuals that it is in their interest to contract to obey the sovereign, and fear of the sovereign's sword convinces them to keep the contract, once made.

Richard Fanshawe's 1647 translation of *Il Pastor fido* is clearly part of this cultural debate about the role of passion and interest in forging political obligation.[52] Specifically, Fanshawe saw that *Il Pastor fido* had something to offer to the Prince of Wales and his followers: not fear but love, and yet not only a virtuous image of constancy but a Machiavellian rhetoric of the passions that was particularly relevant to the crisis of allegiance—the crisis of faithfulness—of the English civil war. Thus, in the opening letter to Charles, Prince of Wales, Fanshawe called attention to the allegorical plot of *Il Pastor fido*: in particular he read the final marriage of Amarilli and Mirtillo as an allegory of the Duke of Savoy's own marriage to the Infanta of Spain, "from which fortunate Conjunction [Guarini] prophesies a finall period to the troubles that had formerly distracted that State: *So much depends upon the Marriages of Princes.*" Charles, Fanshawe hinted, might "by some happy Royall Marriage" similarly "[unite] a miserably divided people in a publick joy."

These prefatory remarks show that *Il Pastor fido* interested Fanshawe not only because it tells a story of a faithfulness which endures in the face of deception and misfortune, but also because this story begins with a coerced vow or contract which is broken off only to be reestablished as a "happy Royall Marriage." In one sense the plot serves both to represent the trials and tribulations of the suffering prince and to deny that they could have any possible effect on his constancy; in another sense, the plot drama- tizes the royalists' fantasy that the relation between sovereign and subject could never be one of coercion, but will always be one of affection and con- sent. If the relation between sovereign and subject must be conceived of as contractual, it should not be imagined as the Hobbesian or parliamentary contract of equal parties, but rather the marriage contract of husband and wife.[53]

In the poems and prose appended to his translation of *Il Pastor fido*, Fanshawe was even more explicit about the relevance of the nicer passions of pastoral romance to the events of the civil war. Like the Roman civil wars, in which faction and division prevailed, and in which "Might overcame Right, and the most powerfull was held the best man," the English civil war has seen the triumph of self-interest over personal virtue: as in Rome, "no man [now] thinke[s] that dishonest in him, which hath been profitable to another." It is in this context that we need to read Fanshawe's advice about the passions. Writing "To His Highnesse [The Prince of Wales] in the West, Ann. Dom. 1646," Fanshawe urged,

That which the murdring *Cannon* cannot force,
Nor plumed Squadrons of steel-glittering *Horse*,
Love can. In this *the People* strive t' out-doe
The King, and when they find they're lov'd, love too.
They serve, because they need not serve: and if
A good *Prince* slack the reins, they make them stiffe;
And of their own accords invite that yoke,
Which, if inforc't on them, they would have broke.[54]

Fanshawe's solution to the crisis of civil war, in which everyone acts according to self-interest, was to replace the language of interest with that of passion or affection—and thus to make a rhetoric of the passions serve the interest of the king. It is in the interest of the king to love rather than coerce his subjects because, freed from the legal burdens of political oblig- ation, they will then begin to love him in return. And consent predicated on the affections—on what Rousseau called the law of the heart—is more bind- ing than coercion, or than even the Hobbesian perception of self-interest, could ever be. In this way, the affection of the people is transmuted to ob- ligation in the form of their self-imposed, internalized discipline: "if A good *Prince* slack the reins, they make them stiffe." Thus Charles is invited to construct a romance plot along the lines of *Il Pastor fido* in which "ama, se piace" (love if you like) is reconciled with "ama, se lice" (love lawfully).

Fanshawe's translation of *Il Pastor fido*, like Guarini's text itself, thus functions on two levels: for both Guarini and his translator, the *technē* of art represents in formal terms the technique of politics in a world governed by passion and interest. The sophistic rhetoric of poetry teaches the prince how to represent his own passions in a way that will engage the affections of his subjects. If the future Charles II is the faithful shepherd of the romance plot, he is also invited to be—like Guarini—a maker of fictions, a Machiavellian manipulator of aesthetic ideology.

Where does this leave Hirschman? Hirschman's great contribution to the early modern history of passion and interest was to argue that the concept of interest was as much political as it was economic in this period: that Machiavelli's dispassionate analysis of the passions was itself in the service of the interest—or reason—of state. This recognition of the political uses of the passions eventually gave rise to the argument that greed—or the accumulation of wealth—could itself be of interest to the state by counteracting the self-aggrandizing passions of honor and glory. I have argued that in both political and literary texts of the early modern period, the concept of interest is inextricable from that of imitation—or, to rephrase this in the language of the time, imitation is always already rhetorical—because to represent the passions is to make them available for manipulation: an insight that is particularly associated with the genre of romance in the Renaissance. Furthermore, Renaissance romance not only exemplifies the political dimension of aesthetic interest; it also helps us to see something precluded by Hirschman's chronology: for, at the same time that literary representation is conceived as a mode of countervailing passion and thus of political interest, the achievement of *Il Pastor fido* and of royalist romance in England is to refigure the public interest as a matter of aesthetic pleasure or literary interest, simultaneously exemplifying and exposing the workings of what modern critics have termed aesthetic ideology.

In *The Political Unconscious*, Fredric Jameson described romance as a kind of magical narrative, one that involves a simplified, polarized world of good and evil. For Jameson, Nietzsche is the philosopher who helps us see that this ethical opposition is itself ideologically motivated, a romantic veiling of more fundamental relationships of power. By contrast, tragedy is the genre that troubles or exceeds the romance habit of moral dichotomizing, the genre which "rebuke[s] the ideological core of the romance paradigm."[55] In contrast to Jameson, the theory wars of the late sixteenth century in Italy suggest that tragedy is the genre most easily assimilated to the moralizing injunctions of Counter-Reformation critics; while romance in Guarini and Fanshawe's hands is not so much the mystified genre represented by Jameson as it is the Machiavellian genre par excellence. This is not simply because the romance plot involves errant passion and interest (although it clearly does), for the romance plot, typically, also involves idealized extremes of good and evil ascribed to it by critics such as Jameson and Frye.[56] Rather, the lesson that romance teaches is analogous to the lesson of Machiavelli's *Prince.* In contrast to those readers who have asserted that for Machiavelli there is no connection between virtue and virtù, between the world of ethical values on the one hand and the world of Machiavellian manipulation of passion and interest on the other, *The Prince* tells us that there is a connection—just not the one we want. Something of the same is true of pastoral romance, the rogue genre of Renaissance poetics.

Although often Neoplatonic in rhetoric, pastoral romance simultaneously presents a Machiavellian world of contingency, of fortuna and virtù, passion and interest, and anatomizes the rhetorical resources we have for dealing with such a world. In so doing, it provides a Machiavellian critique of its own idealizing fictions. As Boccalini clearly knew, the critique of romance values which Jameson ascribes to Nietzsche is a part of romance itself: this is why Ascham attacked Italian romance so vociferously and why Fanshawe could cast the faithful shepherd of *Il Pastor fido* as a manipulator of aesthetic ideology, substituting the discipline of pastoral romance for the coercion of civil war. Fanshawe's faithful shepherd is not a Machiavellian prince if by that we understand someone who believes it's better to be feared than loved; what makes him Machiavellian is the recognition that the representation of the passions is itself an instrument of sophistic rhetoric, designed to create the effect not only of obedience but also of consent.

In conclusion, a few additional words about aesthetic ideology are in order. In Eagleton's account, the ideology of the aesthetic artifact emerges in the eighteenth century along with "the construction of the dominant ideological forms of modern class society, and . . . a whole new form of human subjectivity appropriate to that order." In this period, the autonomous work of art and the autonomous subject are mirror images of each other:

The aesthetic is at once . . . the very secret prototype of human subjectivity in early capitalist society, and a vision of human energies as radical ends in themselves which is the implacable enemy of all dominative or instrumental thought.

The self-regulating subject who is created in the image and likeness of the autonomous aesthetic artifact is both an ideological fiction which upholds the status quo and a potentially dangerous source of resistance: "Free consent may thus be the antithesis of oppressive power, or a seductive form of collusion with it."[57] In the preceding pages I have tried to suggest that the prehistory of this ideology and of its ambiguous politics is to be found in Renaissance debates about the autonomy of art, particularly in relation to the "new" genre of pastoral romance.

Chapter 11
Sadness in The Faerie Queene

Douglas Trevor

If we attempt to map the emotional terrain of the first book of Edmund Spenser's *The Faerie Queene* (1590), we quickly find that sadness saturates the allegorical romance. In that it is in everyone who is estimable and in no one who is not, sadness functions as the psychological corollary to Gloriana's political power, used to quell antagonists whose vices are reified by their craven emotional states. When, on the contrary, emotions such as rage, lethargy, despair, confusion, and so flare up on the part of exemplary characters—particularly Redcrosse—sadness remains the quiet passion against which these other states of being are calibrated. Spenser's high estimation of sadness renders it as a badge of sorts for the spiritually elect. Thus is Redcrosse largely silent throughout the first book, and described again and again as "solemne sad."[1] Una is also pictured as "sad," even named "Sad Una" at one point, and given—lest we have any doubts—a "count'-nance sad" in Canto 6 (1.1.4.6; 1.3.15.3; 1.6.11.4). If we take Spenser at his word in his "Letter of the Author's" and see the poem as aiming "to fashion a gentleman or noble person in vertuous and gentle discipline,"[2] we might well conclude that such a "gentle discipline" should be marked with a sense of overriding sadness, not the kind of jolliness that Redcrosse "seemd" to possess when we first encounter him "pricking on the plaine" (1.1.1.8, 1). This endorsement of sadness in the poem not only creates a certain mood that is inflected with moral and religious righteousness; it also designates Spenser as a Protestant poet whose doctrinal beliefs are neither orthodoxly Lutheran nor Calvinist but rather shaped by concerns that evade the ideological and theological categories typically employed by scholars to assuage early modern, Christian denominational controversies.

According to OED, as early as the fourteenth century, the verb "sad" meant to "make solid, firm, or stiff," that is, to work on something so as to transform it to a harder, less malleable substance. The subsequent sense of "saddening," dated to 1600, as beating something (rather than someone) down "into a compact mass" reaffirms the sense whereby sadness happens *to* an entity rather than emerging from it. Related to this denotation is the way that "sadness" can indicate seriousness of purpose, as well as weariness or constancy, the primary adjectival and adverbial meanings of the word as early as the eleventh century.[3] None of these senses, I will argue here, are precisely what Spenser is after in *The Faerie Queene*; indeed, the frequent pairing of the words "sad" and "sober" (as when we see Archimago trying his best to fit the mood of the poem in 1.1.29.5) indicates that a certain sorrowfulness is being identified apart from mere solemnness, a sorrowfulness akin to the "depress[ion] in spirits" that the compilers of the *OED* date to 1628.[4] After all, Una typically expresses her sadness by lamenting and weeping (1.3.15.5), while the full irony of her praise of Redcrosse at the outset of the poem—"Faire knight, borne vnder happy starre"(1.1.27.3)—rests on a contradistinction to which Spenser returns again and again in the course of his work: those souls elected to the quintessence of happiness, eternal salvation, exhibit a non-mirthful relation to the world that indicates moral uprightness and Christian devotion.

At the same time that "sadness" is so esteemed in *The Faerie Queene*, "melancholy" quite clearly is not. The House of Pride, for example, is saturated in "dull melancholy" (1.5.3.5) and the melancholic figures we encounter are persistently malicious and fallen, none more so than Despair, who is first described not as was Redcrosse—"solemne sad" (1.1.2.8)—but rather "Musing full sadly in his sullein mind" (1.9.35.3). What is the difference between Redcrosse's estimable sadness and Despair's despicable one? Why, in other words, is one kind of sadness praised by Spenser while another is so disparaged?

The answer to this question lies, I think, in Spenser's attitude toward what he and other Christian writers in the late sixteenth century perceived as an alarming rise in materialist theories of the passions. These writers, including Timothy Bright—author of *A Treatise of Melancholie* (1586)—caution against hard-line Galenic readings of the body because these readings potentially support a "humoral" account of the soul.[5] Critics such as Bright and Spenser claim that such accounts threaten the divine omnipotence of an electing God by providing sinners with too convenient an opportunity to blame their failings on bodily fluids over which they have little control. Indeed, when Spenser characterizes Despair as "A drearie corse, whose life away did pas, / All wallowd in his owne yet luke-warme blood" (1.9.36.5–6) he not only impugns the tempter's self-centered sadness but also describes it in caloric terms ("luke-warme"). Phrases in the poem such as these that indicate a Galenic perspective on the passions invariably designate such emotions as morally questionable or dangerous, as when a "sad humour" loads the eyelids of Redcrosse and Una before Archimago bombards the knight of holiness with false dreams of sexual impropriety (1.1.36.2). If Spenser does not utterly rebuff all of the merits of Galenic analyses of the body, he certainly questions the motives that animate such investigations, suggesting in the process that the pursuit of materialist explanations of one's actions can lead one into a (spiritually) unhealthy quagmire in which personal conduct is ignored in favor of humoral scapegoating.

In his fine analysis of the early modern Protestant retellings of the death of Francesco Spira, Michael MacDonald points to some of the same distinctions between melancholy and sadness that I am making here. Spira, an Italian, publicly renounced his Protestant faith in 1548, only to fall into despair and die a short time thereafter of starvation. The way that Protestants interpreted his death subsequently, MacDonald argues, sheds light on the relation posited between emotions and faith in the period. For those who followed Calvin's interpretation, Spira's encounter with religious despair was proof that he was a reprobate. Others, however, in line with William Perkins, maintained that any believer could fall into the same state that Spira did and still fully recover his or her faith.[6] Acknowledging Despair's allegorical status as a threat to Redcrosse's holiness, we see that Spenser fits into the latter camp, insofar as Redcrosse feels the temptation to kill himself when he imagines himself as having fallen outside of God's grace ("For death was due to him, that had prouokt Gods ire" [1.9.50.9]), and fully recovers from this temptation in the House of Holiness. At the same time, however, Spenser does not fully share the view that an elected Christian might fall into despondency at any particular juncture, as Perkins—and Luther before him—maintained, for after his treatment in the House of Holiness, Redcrosse is no longer vulnerable to the kind of melancholy embodied by Despair. At the same time, he remains as he was before, predominantly sad.

Of course, Christian Galenists in the sixteenth century were well aware of the potential heresies entwined with materialist readings of the passions, and many of them responded to the dilemma in a way altogether typical in the period: that is, contradictorily. On the one hand, English writers such as Bright, Thomas Wright, Thomas Walkington, and others insist on reading the body through the rich lexicon of Galenic theory, with its panoply of views on character types, bodily permeability, the relevance of different bodily fluids to different emotions, the influence of astrology on a person's complexion, and so on.[7] On the other hand, these same medical writers try to make it clear that God's dominion over the human soul is in no way abrogated by the influence of bodily fluids. Part of this give and take exhibited by the authors of medical tracts in the period owes itself to their backgrounds; as Paul Slack has argued, the overwhelming majority of these writers were "men of diverse accomplishments and interests, not professional scientists working within the conventions of an established discipline." As a result, the work they produced typically "blurred boundaries between 'medical' and other types of publication in the sixteenth century," most notably devotional writings.[8] Syncretic tendencies would presumably belie any interest in advocating what I obliquely referred to above as "hardline" Galenism, by which I mean an account of the passions, and subsequently the soul, that would read the humoral as, if not transcendent over the spiritual, then one and the same. Clearly, no self-interested writer in early modern Europe would openly advocate such a position, although that did not prevent some skeptical readers from attributing heretical intentions to Galenists at large. As Noel Brann argues, "the very intensity of this campaign [against reading religious melancholy through humoral theory] by some of the age's leading theologians betrays a popular trend on the other side of the question to explain the phenomenon of religious despondency in terms of bodily disorder."[9] MacDonald concurs, insisting that "[e]vangelical Protestants distinguished clearly between that emotion [religious despair] and the unhappiness that comes from bodily disorders or from social and psychological situations."[10] In spite of the fact, then, that Galenic tenets remained the bedrock for European medical faculties in Catholic and Protestant countries throughout most of the seventeenth century, the delineation of what was meant by Galenism in spiritual terms continued to be made, in Owsei Temkin's words, "through accusations."[11]

Timothy Bright's *A Treatise of Melancholie* is one text whose reaction against the putative implications of Galenic materialism might have helped Spenser to arrive at his eventual position regarding not only the incorporeality of the soul but also the unacceptability of any theory of the emotions that accounted for the passions in wholly hydraulic terms.[12] Bright does not reject Galenism outright; in fact Robert Burton will cite him in opposition to Platonists in his *Anatomy of Melancholy*.[13] He does, however, want very much to limit the consequences of materialist readings of disposition, and in effect repurify a soul that has been, by this point, saturated with humors, blood and bile. Referring to Galenism, he writes:

The notable fruit & successe of which art in that kinde, hath caused some to iudge more basely of the soule, then agreeth with pietie or nature, & haue accompted all maner affection thereof, to be subiect to the phisicians ha[n]d, not considering herein any thing diuine, and aboue the ordinarie euents, and naturall course of thinges: but haue esteemed the vertues the[m]selues, yea religion, no other thing but as the body hath ben tempered, and on the other side, vice, prophanenesse, & neglect of religion and honestie, to haue bene nought else but a fault of humour.[14]

In response to Galenists such as Juan Huarte, whose 1575 *Examen de ingenios* (translated into English in 1594)[15] proposed humoral theory as a theory of nearly everything, Bright argues for the reestablishment of a religious discourse that is freed from the encroachment of materialist explanations, one in which the divine is held "aboue the ordinarie euents." As Bright goes on to explain, "[t]his affecting of the minde [by the body], I vnderstand not to be any empairing of the nature thereof; or decay of any facultie therein; or shortning of immortality; or any such infirmitie inflicted vpon the soule from the bodie" (38). Physical effects on the soul, in other words, are short lived. Moreover, the "affliction of conscience" does not, according to Bright, manifest itself in humoral terms at all, but rather "sezeth vpon the seate of wisedome it selfe" (184). In contrast and in opposition to those who would claim that a person is wholly formed by his or her complexion, Bright suggests that the spiritual essence of a person remains untouched by, even unrelated to, his or her humoral makeup.

Walter Ralegh's *A Treatise of the Soul* supports Bright's position that the human soul rests "entirely in the hands of God."[16] According to Ralegh, unlike animals, whose souls are "exercised by bodily instruments" human souls "are immortal, and have an heavenly beginning."[17] Ralegh dismisses Galenic claims of a corporeal soul on account of their founder's contradictory statements, for in the end "Galen confesseth, that he cannot tell what or where the substance of the soul is" (574). While Ralegh disallows any consideration of the location of the soul in the body, since spatial placement implies extension and hence mass, he weighs in on the soul's essence through the use of a triadic, Neoplatonic formula: "The soul, and this spirit which we are endued with, is a certain mean between the body and God" (577). Souls cannot be of the essence of God because God's perfection prohibits divisibility, but they can emanate from God—created by him, thus "simple," that is, indivisible, "in respect of the elements and of the bodies that are made of them" (574), but compound in comparison to God and thus in between ("a certain mean between") the physical and the divine.

Spenser's relation to Ralegh in the pages of *The Faerie Queene* has often been understood within the terms of the former poet's presumed strategy of public self-presentation; here, however, I would like to emphasize the intellectual relevance to *The Faerie Queene* of the theory of the passions put forward in Ralegh's *Treatise*. The ramifications of this theory are spelled out—in part—when Ralegh refutes the argument that "If the whole man be flesh, then the soul." On the contrary, he states, Augustine makes it clear that "If a body be that which hath length, breadth, and thickness; the soul is neither body, nor proceedeth from a body. And, to be short, the matter of the soul can be no bodily thing" (576). The end result, for Ralegh, is the belief that the soul "hath a peculiar and spiritual being, proper to itself" (577).

The argument offered by Ralegh for an immaterial soul is perhaps less interesting than is the fact that he felt a need to defend the doctrine in the first place. Indicative of the "peculiar" being of the soul, sadness in *The Faerie Queene* is neither communicable nor a disease. In fact, it has nothing to do with the body at all, unless it is sinful and melancholic, in which case—as Ralegh makes clear—the soul "may become fleshly by the properties of the flesh" (577). For Spenser, sadness—not joy—is the exact opposite of melancholy. None of the sad characters in *The Faerie Queene* would ever wish to lose their somberness; to do so would be to compromise their spiritual worth and implicate them immediately in the kind of moral bankruptcy represented in the House of Pride (1.4), or allegorized in figures such as Duessa, Archimago, and the Sans brothers. Spenser's resistance to Galenism, emblematized by his sympathetic portrait of "truly" sad characters who do not seek happiness because it is indistinguishable from sin, rehabilitates the Medieval notion of tristitia—that is, a moderate but enduring exhibition of restraint and contemplation. According to Stanley Jackson, the characterization of sadness not as a sign of holiness but rather as a sin postdates Galen and develops principally in the fourth century C.E., when desert monks in Egypt strove for spiritual purity and yet found themselves battling the unhappiness that accompanies extended periods of isolation and self-deprivation. Over the ensuing centuries, however, sadness was slowly rehabilitated: "as tristitia faded from the list of sins," writes Jackson,

so too did the positive sorrow that arose from remorse for one's sins and that led to penance and salvation. But the negative sorrow, or dejection about worldly matters, continued to be viewed as a sin and to evolve within the notion of acedia. Tristitia, as this positive sorrow, became more identified with the Christian tradition of the sufferer as an object of care, concern, and cure; the negative sorrow was associated with the idea of the afflicted person as an object to be moralized against.[18]

We have already seen such objectification of "negative sorrow" in a figure like Despair. An account more sympathetic than Spenser's might have depicted the tempter as Shakespeare will Hamlet, not loathsome but rather pitiably incapable of controlling his humors.[19] Spenser rejects such an option, in part because—as we will see shortly—allegory requires the passions to function in representational, rather than symptomatic, terms. This does not mean, as Jonathan Goldberg has argued, that the characters in *The Faerie Queene* "exist to disappear,"[20] but rather that their bodies function so as to be read as barometers of their spiritual worth.

If we consider the House of Holiness episode in *The Faerie Queene* in light of Spenser's desire to use the human body, and its healthy restoration, as metaphoric instruments for the description of spiritual purification, we realize that Canto 10 represents the poet's most deliberate jab at Galenic medicine. Cures that had become associated in the sixteenth century principally with the treatment of a diseased body are now resituated as allegorical indices in the service of a higher calling. "Inward corruption and infected sin," we are told,

> Not purg'd nor heald, behind remained still,
> And festring sore did rankle yet within,
> Close creeping twixt the marrow and the skin.
> Which to extirpe, he [Patience] laid down priuily
> Downe in a darkesome lowly place farre in,
> Whereas he meant to corrosiues to apply
> And with streight diet tame his stubborn malady. (1.10.25.3–9)

Rather than a foregrounding of the human body, the allegorization of what it means to be "cured" results in an intentionally transparent rendering of the Redcrosse Knight in the scene in which he is restored most fully to himself (or, perhaps more accurately, restored to his vocation as a knight of holiness).[21] Each successive stage of repentance is tied with a particular salve; thus Patience becomes the "Leach" that can cure "that disease of grieued conscience," while corrosives and a change in diet are used to attend to what Spenser calls his "soule-diseased knight" (1.10.23.7, 8; 1.10.24.1). The "proud humors," as Spenser calls them, can thus be read chiastically in the context of the poem's historical moment, first privileging the vice which the allegory treats (pride as the antithesis to holiness) but also designating the material resonance of humors, in the context of religious verse, as itself hubristic. When Redcrosse enters the "holy Hospitall" (1.10.36.1), the condition of his body is unimportant, or important only insofar as it indicates greater—that is, in Neoplatonic terms, higher—concerns. The knight's "fee-ble soule" is promptly treated by "seuen Bead-men," who now reenact Canto 4's procession of the Seven Deadly Sins in a more contrite manner, reclaim-ing corrupt ceremony as a process of spiritual cleansing (1.10.36.1, 3). Even the emphasis placed on charity in the Canto—earthly acts of devotion and selflessness that presumably need a body in order to be performed—is sub-sidiary to the "idea" of active virtue, which the poet praises Redcrosse for having "learned" (1.10.45.8), not for having enacted.

The transcendence of corporeality occurs emblematically in the figure of Contemplation, a man whose "earthly eyen [are] both blunt and bad" (1.10.47.3) and who has effectively discarded his body ("For nought he car'd his carcas long vnfed; / His mind was full of spirituall repast, / And pyn'd his flesh, to keepe his body low and chast" [1.10.48.7–9]).[22] The reader has been prepared for Contemplation's sorry physical state by the dejection that marks so many figures in the Canto: not only Una and Redcrosse, but also Reverence, with his "sad attire" (1.10.7.3), and Speranza, described by the poet as "Not all so chearefull" (1.10.14.3). Still, the figure is oddly reminiscent of Despair—self-occupied, if with heavenly matters rather than sinful—and as a result indicative of how perilously close Spenser's conception of praise-worthy meditation borders on his depiction of damned self-indulgence. Initially "agrieued sore" at having to "lay his heauenly thoughts aside" (1.10.49.3), Contemplation eventually indulges Redcrosse in a visionary expe-rience that is not *studied*, that is, not mediated or qualified by any mention of Redcrosse's physically inherent—a Galenist might say *dispositional*—capacity to understand what passes before him; instead, the rapture Red-crosse experiences transcends the senses, taking him out of his body and depositing him in an ecstatic *voluptas* from which he does not wish to return: "O let me not (quoth he) then turne againe, / Backe to the world, whose ioyes so fruitlesse are; / But let me here for aye in peace remaine" (1.10.63.1–3).

The antithesis of this spiritual ascent—an ascent akin to what Edgar Wind, in his landmark study of Neoplatonism, described as "the Platonic conversion or rapture" which consists of "turning away from the world in which we are, so as to rejoin the spirit beckoning from beyond"[23]—occurs in Canto 5, when we follow the grieving Duessa and her fallen Sansjoy down to Pluto's House. Regarding what we saw earlier, that sadness is the oppo-site of melancholy, we find joylessness—as embodied by Sansjoy—identifi-able not with the kind of sadness experienced by Redcrosse and Una but rather with the melancholic temperament of Despair. But why is it different for Redcrosse only to seem "iolly" (1.1.1.8) and Sansjoy to lack joy in his very name? What makes one character the embodiment of holiness and the other—along with his brothers—representative of a triad of fallenness? In John Maier's reading, Sansjoy's descent to the underworld is meant to repudiate the "fashionable form of *furor melancholicus*," espoused by Marsilio Ficino and other Neoplatonists, whereby a strictly Galenic account of melancholy as a diseased-ridden state is anaesthetized by the purported insight granted by such a condition.[24] As Redcrosse's experience with Contemplation makes clear, Spenser does not reject *furor* in-and-of-itself; rather, he explicitly rejects the kind of *furor* that can be understood via Galenic terms. To make this point clear, Sansjoy finds himself subject to a Galenic "cure" while in Hell. Æsculapius, a doctor imprisoned by Jove for utilizing "wondrous science" in the cure of the hunter Hippolytus, is another figure who, like Despair, sits in a "Deepe, darke, vneasie, dolefull, comfortlesse" cave, a spatial embodiment of the melancholic's diseased mind (1.5.40.1; 1.5.36.6). Duessa appeals to the doctor to employ "either salues, or oyles, or herbes, or charmes" (1.5.41.7) to revive Sansjoy and after some hesitation he complies: "And then the learned leach / His cunning hand gan to his wounds to lay, / And all things else, the which his art did teach" (1.5.44.1–3).

Unlike in the House of Holiness, medical practice in Pluto's House carries with it no allegorical significance. Thus does Æsculapius's success at saving Sansjoy's body highlight the stark differences Spenser draws between Galenic and spiritual cures, for it is not merely that Æsculapius treats physical suffering and loss of life but that to do so in *The Faerie Queene* means to invoke hellish powers that defy the Gods and reanimate that which would be better off left dead. To save Sansjoy is to save only a body, not a body and a soul; like his brothers, all offspring of blindness (Aveugle), Sansjoy is characterized first and foremost by what he lacks. Readers predisposed to believe in Galenism are encouraged by Spenser instead to question even a putatively successful medical intervention, in that this intervention occurs in Hell on the body of reprobate. To be without joy in *The Faerie Queene* is to be the emotive opposite of Redcrosse and Una, who are redeemed because of the sadness they feel in their (saved) souls. Emblematic of his profligacy, Sansjoy's passions remain rooted in his sinful flesh and "bitter mind" (1.4.38.9). Unlike Redcrosse and Guyon in Book 2—the latter termed, like Redcrosse, a "solemne sad" knight (2.6.37.5)—he has no recourse to righteous rage; when he becomes "Enflam'd with fury" (1.4.38.7) at the sight of his slain brother Sansfoy's shield, his anger wins him no points in the mind of his ultimate creator, either Spenser or the poet's God. As a fallen figure, all that is left to him are restoratives than can only go skin deep.

As was suggested by his decision to relegate Sansjoy to the hands of a doctor for whom a leach is just a leach, Spenser's animosity toward Galenism manifests itself not merely in the associations he draws between humoral dispositions and fallenness, but in his very use of allegory itself.[25] While accounts of Spenser's allegory continue to gain nuance, particularly in those readings that embed *The Faerie Queene* in the historical nexus of Elizabethan politics and colonial activities,[26] readers still see as the central component to the poet's allegorical method what Gordon Teskey has called "the Neoplatonic illusion of incorporeal intelligences."[27] This illusion, according to Teskey, is predicated on a hierarchical, ideological order that maintains the construct of allegory by reducing everything else "to the status of a substance imprinted by form."[28] In the allegorical world presented by Spenser, the microcosm inevitably and inexorably opens up to, and reaches fulfillment in, the macrocosm, a hierarchical perspective clearly not served by Galenic theory, in which different seats in the body exert different forces for different—often wholly unrelated—reasons.

For English Protestants such as Bright, Ralegh, and Spenser, core Neoplatonic tenets like the immateriality of forms and a universal hierarchy of spiritual transcendence were far more accommodating to the religious doctrines of predestination and election than were those Galenic intimations of a material soul that were spread by an increasing number of vernacular publications of medical texts, a number that Paul Slack estimates reached a record level in 1603.[29] I say *intimations* because, as I have already indicated, no medical writer in Spenser's day teased out the full implications of Galen's theories and pronounced, unequivocally, that the human soul was corporeal. Neither is it clear that Galen himself unambiguously endorsed a materialist soul. As J.-P. Pittion explains,

While Galen rejects the monist view of one soul with three faculties . . . he is not clear on the nature of the soul itself. His conception appears to have changed from the earlier treatises, where the soul is deemed to be a separate substance in the body, to later ones (e.g. *De temperamentis*) where it is considered a property of the body engendered by the *krasis* of the four elements.[30]

In spite of Galen's own shifting attitude toward the composition of the soul, clear differences between corporeal and incorporeal conceptions of the human *anima* were held at the end of the sixteenth century, with corporeal theories linked to Galen and incorporeal models aligned with Plato. Hardin

Craig summarized these positions in the following manner: "The Platonic position was that the soul is untouchable by physical causes and, if it does its duty through the will as the agent of an enlightened reason, may and should protect the body from suffering . . . The Galenic position is the more familiar one. According to it the ills of the body affect the well-being of the soul, drive it into misery and madness, so that it may be said that the body injures the soul."[31] Furthermore, some sixteenth-century physicians and medical writers, either unmindful of the contradictions in Galen's writings or indifferent to them, seized on the connections drawn by the ancient physician between the body and soul to enhance their own position as not merely identifiers of bodily ills but also commentators on the status and function of the human spirit.[32]

As evidenced by Book 1 of *The Faerie Queene*, Spenser clearly believed in a starker divide than many of his contemporaries between the ameliorative possibilities of Galenic cures and devotional practices that could aid an ailing soul. At the same time, however, Spenser's allegory makes it extraordinarily difficult to place him squarely in any single Christian line of thought. Critical silence on the question of redemptive sadness attests to the difficulty of reconciling Spenser's renunciation of melancholy with his support of non-humoral sorrow. Readings of the Despair episode in particular make clear that accounts of the "sad" passions in Book 1 are unduly slanted toward Spenser's take on the negative sorrow of acedia rather than the positive sorrow of tristitia.[33] In part this emanates from Redcrosse's clear encounters with the sin of acedia—lethargic behavior that indicates idleness and spiritual torpor—in the poem: his lounging with Duessa under Fradubio's tree (1.2.28–45), for instance, or his encounter with Idlenesse in Lucifera's castle, where Spenser tells us that such a figure perpetuates his slothfulness by claiming to eschew work "For contemplation sake" (1.4.20.4). So too do templates in the sixteenth century abound for assessing melancholy in skeptical terms: both Galenic, with the increased emphasis on the part of medical writers in the period on the physical perils of the disorder, religious, and—as in the case of Bright—combinations of both.

In his study of the demise of a viable concept of genial melancholy in the early modern period, Winfried Schleiner emphasizes that Martin Luther was an outspoken critic of melancholy, denigrating the emotional state because it was often intentionally sought by self-pitying types, especially scholars who saw in the "melancholic" label as described by Ficino an opportunity to promote themselves as intellectually gifted.[34] For Luther, spiritual temptations, including despair, were unavoidable, but were to be met with optimism and mirth, not depression: "No one realizes how much harm it does a young man to avoid pleasure and cultivate solitude and sadness," he wrote in a letter to Prince Joachim of Anhalt in 1534.[35] Spenser shares both Luther's hostility toward melancholic moods, and—as we have already seen—his sense whereby even the righteous are tempted by despair, but the English poet also reclaims as viable the Medieval concept of tristitia, what in his hands resembles righteous sadness.[36]

Reading Spenserian sadness through Protestant frames risks occluding, however, the degree to which Spenser's rehabilitation of sorrow shares an affinity with the devotional perspective held by many Renaissance Catholic writers. It is, after all, the English Catholic Thomas Wright who, in *The Passions of the Minde in Generall*, opines that "sadnesse bringeth repentance,"[37] while—before him—Thomas More devotes an entire work, the *De Tristitia Christi* (1535), to celebrating Christ's exemplary display of sadness, weariness, and fear *(tristitia tedio paurore)* leading up to and during his crucifixion. In contrast to Luther's enjoinment to avoid introspection if it leads one to sorrow, More argues instead that our time on earth should be one of sadness: "if we get so weary of pain and grief that we perversely attempt to change the world, this place of labor and penance, into a joyful haven of rest, if we seek heaven on earth, we cut ourselves off forever from true happiness."[38] As we might expect, More makes much of Christ's comment to Peter and the two sons of Zebedee ("My soul is sad unto death;" *Matthew* 26: 38), arguing that the Son of God "[h]ad the ordinary feelings of mankind" *("quod uulgatos humani generis affectus")* and displayed these feelings in the hope that his followers would imitate them, irrespective of their natural inclinations: "Therefore, since He foresaw that there would be many people of such a delicate constitution that they would be convulsed with terror at any danger of being tortured, He chose to enhearten them by the example of His own sorrow, His own sadness."[39]

My point in bringing in More's *De Tristitia* is not to argue that Spenser was a crypto-Catholic, but that interpretive matrices that attempt to read a "Protestant versus Catholic" dichotomy in Spenser's depiction of religious passions in *The Faerie Queene* fail for a number of reasons.[40] In the first place, the use of allegory itself, with its variously "darke conceit[s]" ("A Letter of the Author's," 737) mystifies narrative intent in some of the same ways that Protestant reformers described Catholic liturgical practices as effacing the Word of God behind ornate spectacle and idolatrous exercises.[41] While Spenser addresses such concerns in the opening of his "Letter of the Author's" by acknowledging "how doubtfully all Allegories may be construed" (737), the apology he forwards on behalf of his choice of method is quite brief, and the "Letter" itself is removed altogether from the 1596 edition. Rather than attempt to read *The Faerie Queene* as wholly emblematic of Protestant doctrine and poetics—the kind of reading Barbara Lewalski proposes for seventeenth-century lyric[42]—it seems more credible to regard Spenser as deploying a number of different strategies in the service of discrediting any construct of faith as materially driven. The evidence put forth by Spenser's depictions of the passions in Book 1 suggests, in other words, that the author was more troubled by the effects of humoralism on Christian conduct than by any putatively Catholic elements of spirituality, insofar as these elements—for example, in the House of Holiness, Dame Caelia's performance of "good and godly deedes" (1.10.3.9) and her use of rosary beads (1.10.8.3)—reify somber and sad conduct that is becoming to the righteous Christian.[43]

In the service of an immaterial soul, and in opposition to the specter of an all-consuming corporeality that he believes threatens the sanctity of any conception of Christian faith, Spenser composes Book 1 of *The Faerie Queene* not only as a paean to Queen Elizabeth and England, but also as verse that reaffirms the transcendence and incorruptibility of a spiritual dominion demarcated by sadness, which confirms the soul's status as either saved or damned. That no subsequent English epic uses allegory to make similar claims attests to the growth of other intellectual movements such as philosophical skepticism and the beginnings of scientific empiricism. Spenser was far from oblivious of such trends. Rather, as I have suggested here, he glimpsed some of their possible repercussions for the holy life he imagined and then marshaled a litany of imagistic, lexical, and allegorical strategies to oppose them.[44]

Chapter 12
"Par Accident": The Public Work
of Early Modern Theater

Jane Tylus

At the heart of Bernard Weinberg's two-volume *History of Literary Criticism of the Italian Renaissance* is a thesis that largely vindicates the beliefs of new criticism, then in its heyday. Weinberg's narrative takes us from a world that cared deeply about literature's *effects*, to one that fought for the recognition that literature could, and should, be hermetically sealed from the realms to which it might only incidentally refer. For Weinberg's narrative, traced with admirable scholarship and precision, directs us to see the late Renaissance as a moment that finally rejected Horace's insistence on the utilitarian aspects of literature for Aristotle's more enlightened—because more aesthetically inclined—*Poetics*. By the time that Weinberg arrives at the year 1600 and the virulent debates over a single, now much-neglected play, Giambattista Guarini's *Pastor fido*, he is able to state that the Renaissance ends with a theory of literature's ethical uselessness: "in this modern conception of poetry, the moralizing end gives way to an end of pleasure."[1] Any rhetorical utility that a work such as Guarini's might have for a general audience would be purely accidental. Or, in the words of Michel de Montaigne, defending himself from those who protested the publication of his oneiric essays, "Et ne me doibt on sçavoir mauvais gré pourtant, si je la comunique. Ce qui me sert, peut aussi par accident servir à un autre" ("And yet it should not be held against me if I publish what I write. What is useful to me may also by accident be useful to another").[2]

To be sure, Weinberg's project is far more than simply a new critical one designed only to fit new critical ends. Annabel Patterson's more recent work on censorship, for example, corroborates Weinberg's study insofar as it argues that a clear strategy lay behind increasing attempts to justify literature's autonomy from politics and religion in the late sixteenth century.[3] At the same time, however, my purpose in this essay is to begin to map out a slightly different story, one that will attend to drama's only "accidental" utility in the late sixteenth century as a crisis against which some of theater's advocates felt the need to defend themselves. As will become clear, a number of late Renaissance dramatists chose to vindicate the still disreputable medium of theater by appealing to its utility, Pierre Corneille and Guarini among them. Their belief that theater could be useful by eliciting hidden passions both offered a significant departure from earlier theories of drama's potential efficacy and provides a link with the present volume. Moreover, the extent to which the eliciting of concealed sentiments tended increasingly to be focused on women—in part a testimony to the female spectators in theatrical audiences and, on the continent, to the startling new phenomenon of the female actress—suggests a further departure from, and indeed, a complication of, previous claims for theater's usefulness.[4] What possible "utility" could a female character, let alone an actress, actually provide?

I want to approach this undeniably schematic mapping by way of one of the most famous speeches in dramatic literature, Hamlet's advice to the players. While *Hamlet* differs strikingly from the academic settings in which much Italian theater was defended and performed, it nonetheless provides us with a useful starting point (and, as will be seen, ending point) to a broader discussion about the continental theater of the period. As the actors assemble at the beginning of Act 3 to prepare the evening's entertainment for the king, Hamlet harangues them at length about their trade in a passage that a well-read contemporary audience would not have found terribly original. The "end," he informs the players, of "the purpose of playing . . . both at the first and now, was and is, to hold as 'twere the mirror up to nature: to show virtue her feature, scorn her own image, and the very age and body of the time his form and pressure" (3.2.21–23).[5] Such lines attesting to theater's mimetic virtues had their earliest source in Donatus's preface to the comedies of Terence, said in this oft-quoted passage to furnish an "imitatio vitae, speculum consuetudinis, imago veritatis." A tradition of Italian humanism would extend Donatus to include tragedy as well. For Leon Battista Alberti, plays laid open the excesses of private and public men alike; in the pseudo-Machiavelli's "Dialogo della Lingua," comedy is a "specchio d'una vita privata" ("a mirror of a private life") that could have "effetti gravi e utili alla vita nostra" ("serious and useful effects on our lives"); and the playwright Leone de'Sommi, writing in Mantova in the 1560's, argued that plays provided "una imitazione overo essemplar ritratto de la vita umana, dove si hanno a tassar i vizii per fuggirli, et ad approvar le virtù per imitarle" ("an imitation or rather exemplary portrait of human life, through which one is led to tax the vices by fleeing them, and to approve virtue by imitating it").[6]

But while these passages from Shakespeare and his august predecessors argue for a long, arguably banal tradition of seeing plays as useful mirrors, Hamlet's speech finds an uneasy echo in a moment from the play itself several scenes later—a moment rarely considered in light of the earlier passage. This is, moreover, a scene in which Hamlet becomes player rather than commentator, and the mirror acquires a status that is not simply metaphorical. Shortly after the "mousetrap" play is interrupted by Claudius's exit, Hamlet approaches his mother in her closet. As he brusquely enters, he orders her to "Come, come, and sit you down, you shall not boudge; / You go not till I set you up a glass / Where you may see the [inmost] part of you" (3.4.18–20). Given Hamlet's recent speech to the players, Gertrude's response comes as a surprise: "What wilt thou do? Thou wilt not murther me? / Help ho!"—a cry that in turn provokes the shout of that other, concealed, spectator, Polonius, who finds himself mistaken for "a rat" and "dead for a ducat." Prescient of Polonius's dying gasp to come, Gertrude's cry suggests a direct connection between mirroring and murder, although such mirroring is aimed at revealing more than "scorn." In Hamlet's line, it becomes a process aimed at exposing Gertrude's "inmost part," an exposure which she interprets as prelude to a violent death. As such, the scene comments on the humanist legacy in which Hamlet, fresh from Wittenberg and familiar with his Donatus and Alberti, has been trained.

As this essay will suggest, one way of reading Shakespeare's tragedy is to see Prince Hamlet not so much as a paradigm for the psychologized modern subject but as the residual force of a humanist theater that sought to reveal "the virtues we should display and the spots or deformities in ourselves which we should confess and reform" as Roland Mushat Frye has characterized it.[7] Yet Hamlet—and *Hamlet*—attempt to do more than "imitate . . . a life." As the prince himself suggests, he wishes to "cleave the general ear with horrid speech" and "make mad the guilty" (2.2.355). Rather, like Giovan Battista Guarini's *Pastor fido* and Pierre Corneille's classic *Le Cid*, two contemporary continental plays that had an enormous impact on European theater of the late Renaissance, *Hamlet* employs real and theatrical mirrors to try to expose and utilize interior passions, particularly female passions, in a manner that is unsettlingly violent for characters and spectators alike. In linking the expression of hidden female passion to a discourse of violence, the plays under discussion both comment on, and to some extent respond to, the crisis faced by a theater attempting to justify its usefulness.

In Europe, this crisis is both exacerbated and, as the following pages will show, to a certain extent resolved with the advent of the actress on the stage. England, of course, had to wait some sixty years after *Hamlet* for a similar resolution. But in the meantime, Shakespeare interrogates both the "crisis" itself and the manner in which other playwrights have addressed it. And he does so in a manner that Weinberg's scholarly study can only preclude us from grasping.

One of the principal legacies of fifteenth-century Italian humanism was its emphasis on visibility as a mode of knowing—or as one critic has neatly summarized the philosophy of the architect, artist, playwright, and poet Leon Battista Alberti, "Nothing is truly known until it is seen."[8] Alberti spent much of his career designing spaces, such as the loggia, for a viewing public. One of the first to write a Renaissance play based on Latin comedy, he had a fundamentally dynamic conception of urban space as a place in which public action might be framed and observed.[9] The dominant metaphor of Alberti's architectural treatise, *De re aedificatoria*, is, in fact a theatrical one: the piazza is nothing more than a quidrivium, a place where roads and passersby meet, and a theater is nothing more than a piazza surrounded by steps.[10]

Sucn an interest in creating spaces of visibility defines one of the more influential moments of Florentine and fifteenth-century humanism.[11] It would have a lasting impact on the visual arts, insofar as Alberti propagates the belief that there is little that cannot be captured in space by the architect and represented on a canvas by the painter: "These movements of the soul are made known by movements of the body."[12] Yet the supposedly natural manner in which things are brought *into* the realm of the visible, and the uses that are made of them, were thrown into question by the very medium whose name accentuates the primacy of the visible: the theater.[13] And this is a medium that was founded, as Alberti knew, in violence. Or so his reference in the *De re aedificatoria* to the theater invented by Romulus as an occasion for the rape of the Sabine women would suggest.[14] Yet while Alberti glosses over the event, marvelling instead over the crudity of Romulus's stage, others explicitly link Romulus's invention to affairs of state, and hence to the urban and political contexts which lay behind Alberti's incipient humanism. Shakespeare's own contemporary Thomas Heywood, writing 150 years after Alberti, used Romulus to respond to anti-theatrical attacks launched by Puritans at a moment when England was beginning to consider the possibilities of an overseas empire:

[Romulus] built a Theater, plaine, according to the time; yet large, fit for the enter-
tainement of so great an Assembly, and these were they whose famous issue peopled
the Cittie of *Rome*, which in after ages grew to such height, that not *Troy* . . . [nor
Carthage, Memphis, Thebes, or Babylon] were any way equall to this situation
grounded by *Romulus*: to which all the discovered kingdomes of the earth after
became tributaries.[15]

Heywood does not go into detail about the abduction that took place on
Romulus's stage, but readers of Ovid would have easily recognized this as an
allusion to the luring of the Sabine women to a "spectacle" by a band of
lusty youths eager to generate "famous issue" that might some day people
the "Cittie of Rome."

   In the period between Alberti and Heywood, between the mid-
fifteenth century and the early seventeenth, theater was transformed from
an unrealized idea, a ghostly victim of the ruined amphitheaters of Roman
empire studied by Alberti and others, to a tangible reality, institutionalized
in the courts and cities of Europe as rooms and buildings for spectacles were
constructed and acting guilds gained prominence. It was also in this period
that writers such as Heywood and Machiavelli felt compelled to stress the
importance of theater for a general common good, following in the foot-
steps of a dramaturge such as the Ferrarese Pellegrino Prisciano, who cited
theater's ability to socialize citizens.[16] But such socialization, as the allusions
to the Sabines and subsequent references to contemporary audiences suggest, depended on the identification of scapegoats who would bear the burden of communal cohesion. While one rarely finds references to actual
abductions, one does find an ongoing fascination with metaphorical abduction, or as George Puttenham puts it in *The Arte of English Poesy*, the "apprehension" of the spectator's conscience.

   In Puttenham's lively account, written in the late 1570s, apprehension is
performed by the actual dramatic spectacle itself, or more precisely, by all
"four sundry formes of Poesie Drammatick reprehensive." According to
Puttenham, who turned to another Roman, Horace, for the story of theater's
beginnings, drama originated in the lawless yet powerful figure of the Satyr.
This licentious creature provided a convenient disguise for those poets
and "recitours" who showed that they were "conversant with mans affaires,
and spiers out of all their secret faults."[17] Only gradually did drama evolve
into more modern and less savage forms. Thus old comedy "openly and by
expresse names reprehends commonly of marchants, souldiers, artificiers,
good honest householders, unthrifty youthes, and young damsels" (47) and
others theoretically in the audience; while tragedy "layd open to all the

world the lusts and licentiousness" of princes who have been guided by their "soveraignetie and dominion" into wicked paths (49). To physically lay hold of someone becomes, in the dramas spawned by Romulus's theater, a figurative laying hold. Such reprehension, by Hamlet's time, may even become explicit apprehension. Heywood goes on to note "two straugne accidents" that have appeared in his day. In one case, the ghostly apparition of a murdered husband onstage forces a woman in the audience to exclaim that she sees "the ghost of her husband fiercely threatening and menacing [her]"; in the other, the enactment of the murder itself forces a belated confession. Upon witnessing the dramatization of their crimes, both women find their "consciences" "extremely troubled," and cry out, "'Oh my husband, my husband!'" The two are ultimately arraigned, condemned, and burned, proving that theater can assist in the "discov[eries] of many notorious murders, long concealed from the eyes of the world" (G1–2).

Such citations may make it appear that Hamlet is working with a conception of dramatic utility that found straightforward expression in late Elizabethan England: the play was the "thing" to catch the conscience not only of "marchaunts" but of a king—or a queen. Shakespeare's own troubling treatment of these scenes, as we will see in more detail, suggests that he did not find the argument for theater's utility as straightforward as did Puttenham or Heywood, as they borrowed from earlier continental arguments to demonstrate theater's ethical and rhetorical role in the community. In the meantime, however, as Weinberg suggests, many of those writing on the continent tended to minimize both theater's potential invasiveness and its utility. The Florentine playwright G. B. Gelli suggested in a proto-deCerteaudian moment that comedy is about the "everyday"—"La comedia . . . non tratta d'altro che di cose che tutto'l giorno accaggiono al viver nostro" ("Comedy treats of nothing other than things that happen on a daily basis in our lives")—while in the prologue to *La Strega*, Grazzini notes that "these days one no longer goes to hear comedies in order to learn how to live, but for pleasure and delight, to while away the hours and to flee melancholy: whoever wants to learn how to be a good citizen or a good Christian doesn't go to comedies to figure this out, but reads a thousand good and holy books and listens to the preachers."[18] Tragedy, a genre that had never enjoyed great success in Renaissance Europe, was deemed too savage for a "civilized" world; hence Guarini seems to echo Grazzini when he defended his *Pastor fido* of 1587 from attack by the Aristotelian academic Giason Denores, asking why ethical drama was needed when everything necessary for man's salvation was contained within "la parola evangelica."[19]

If drama's defense in Italy earlier in the century had been its communal utility, its ability to expose, indirectly, the failings of its audience—thus Aretino says in the wicked 1528 prologue to the *Cortigiana*, "if I did not respect Lady Comedy I would announce (*publicherei*) all of your faults (tutti i defetti vostri)"—by the end of the sixteenth century Hamlet's protestations in his mother's chamber and his advice to the players seem outdated. At least they would seem to be outdated in a Catholic country such as Italy that needed to defend its cultural productions from a suspicious Counter-Reformation at the same time that it had to defend the public presence of women onstage.

Yet before making any of the obvious categorizations—Shakespeare's Protestant England against Guarini's Catholic Italy, or the tragedy which Thomas Heywood conceptualizes as rhetorically forceful as against the inconsequential comedy that preoccupied Grazzini and Gelli—one must ask to what extent Hamlet's intrusion into Gertrude's "closet" in the interest of holding a mirror up to her nature, and presumably, some of ours, is really an isolated, English event. I will argue in the following pages that in the late Renaissance drama of the Catholic continent, one finds the same residually humanist effect that Shakespeare interrogates in *Hamlet*, even as it extends beyond inveighing against readily obvious virtues and vices. As Gertrude's closet is invaded elsewhere, certain questions become particularly pressing with regard to the humanist legacy which Hamlet appears to uphold. How much does a community need to know about both its private subjects and its rulers in order to guarantee communal health? How much must be made visible to others and what function does that act of visualization serve, if any? How useful, that is, is theater, particularly in regard to the female passions which, as we shall see, will preoccupy the late Renaissance stage on the continent as in England? And in a world in which the relationship of public to private was becoming radically redefined—in which, as some historians have argued, the "private" as such is only beginning to exist—how private are, and should be, the passions, particularly the amorous ones?[20]

In the comments that follow, we shall have occasion to see *Hamlet* engaging a humanist agenda that suggested, *pace* Montaigne, that theater's utility was far from accidental. At the same time, other plays written in the wake of the decline of humanist ideology attempted to legitimize theater's necessary exposures by exploiting the figure who appeared on the European stage a century before she appeared in England: the actress. As we turn to a continental theater that is no longer the urbane comedy of Machiavelli or the imagined theater of Alberti, we find excessive attention given to what Puttenham calls "*secret* faults": faults that can only be revealed when a character is tricked into unveiling what she is laboring to hide, and in a manner that can only indirectly be applied to an audience also caught by surprise in the throes of its own secret imaginings.

At the same time, the deployment of those female passions onstage works very differently in these plays than it does either in *Hamlet* or in Heywood's account of murderous wives. The first work to consider is Guarini's own *Pastor fido*, the very play for which the playwright disavowed any utility except for the purging of melancholy, noted by Guarini as the "architectonic end" of tragicomedy.[21] The second, a drama that was no doubt influenced by Guarini's pastoral (not least because it is also a tragicomedy), and in turn no less influential, is Corneille's *Le Cid*. Roughly contemporaneous with Shakespeare's *Hamlet*—Guarini had finished the *Pastor fido* by 1587, and Corneille's *Cid* premiered to a stunned Paris in 1637—both works feature noblewomen whose supposed spaces of privacy are invaded. Both reveal, under circumstances which are as compromising as those to which Gertrude is subject, the "tainted" nature of their passions. Both Amarilli, the noble shepherdess, and Chimène, the daughter of a count, confess, that is, illicit passions on the stage—passions which made the *Pastor fido* and *Le Cid* alike the targets of considerable ecclesiastical and academic attack.[22] Unlike Gertrude, however, the female protagonists of Corneille's and Guarini's seminal plays make these admissions when they believe themselves to be alone or with only a trusted confidante. Yet not only does the public nature of the stage militate against the possibility that they might utter secrets in private, but so does the presence of a hidden, and manipulative, spectator.

Such doubleness argues that Guarini and Corneille were calling attention to the very artifices that Roland Barthes assumed early modern theater fought to conceal when he peevishly suggested that the function of the Italian stage is "to reveal what is reputed to be secret (feelings, conflicts, situations) while concealing the very artifice of the process of revelation."[23] The ploy of the hidden spectator in *Le Cid* and the *Pastor fido* —and, of course, in the scene between Gertrude and the prince in *Hamlet*—is hardly new with these three plays. Yet what is innovative is the use of that hidden spectator to invade what the female character imagines to be an intimate space: neither the piazza of comedy nor the court of tragedy, but the woodland clearing in the *Pastor fido*, the boudoir in *Le Cid*. Thus revealed in these compromised contexts is a secret "fault" ultimately rendered useful in the course of the plays themselves. Also utilized, in far more indirect fashion, is the actress's relatively recent presence, be it on the public stages of Paris where *Le Cid* had its debut, or the courtly stages of northern Italy for which Guarini long labored to have the *Pastor fido* performed.[24]

In the *Pastor fido*, Amarilli is for both modern and early modern audiences alike a paradoxical figure. She is a shepherdess who is at the same time a noblewoman, condemned to marry another shepherd of aristocratic lineage so that Arcadia's curse might be lifted. It is thus in her hands, more literally in her body, to provide for her country a "cure" from the plague that has attacked Arcadians ever since the notorious infidelity of another shepherdess and the subsequent curse of the chaste goddess Diana. But Amarilli is not in love with the reclusive hunter Silvio, nor is he with her. It is therefore not surprising that in Act 2 of the play we hear her confessing her reluctance to marry Silvio, and that an act later, in what she imagines to be the lonely and solitary woods of Petrarchan lyric, she unburdens herself of her secret passion for the shepherd Mirtillo. She can only hope that this strange shepherd who has only recently arrived in Arcadia is fully prepared to return her affections should she make hers known to him.

Perhaps predictably, however, Amarilli's confession of illicit love for the shepherd Mirtillo is overheard by the scheming Corisca, whose machinations throughout the play provide the driving force for the *Pastor fido*'s lively narrative. Most importantly, Corisca's efforts to have Amarilli executed for an adulterous passion will inadvertently lead to the very marriage that she has sought to prevent (in a comic twist on the story of Oedipus, Mirtillo is revealed as the missing son of the noble Montano, and thereby eligible for marriage to Amarilli). The union of the two "noble" shepherds will procure at last the health of a once-diseased Arcadia. Corneille's *Cid* will also end, in its original version, with the king mandating the marriage of Chimène to Rodrigue, the saviour of Castile who has killed her father, and yet the man whom she still passionately loves—something Rodrigue discovers when, bloody sword in hand, he enters unseen into her boudoir where she is revealing her tormenting secret to her servant. That Rodrigue has become, since the murder of Chimène's father, the chief support of the state—he alone emerged to protect Castille from the invasion of the Moors—means that Chimène will not be allowed to pursue the vendetta against his life that her filial duty exacts from her. As in the *Pastor fido*, the disclosure of a scandalous female passion provides a means through which the *bene comune* can be saved: if Chimène loves her father's murderer, then she must not be allowed to threaten his life. And in both plays, it is a patrarichal figure—the king in one instance, the high priest Montano in the other—who will publicly authorize the passion that has been unknowingly disclosed before a spying audience, and achieve for the characters and theatrical audience alike an ending characteristic of the newfangled genre of tragicomedy.

Such bald summaries can hardly do justice to the complexities of the two plays. Yet it is certainly the case that they both attempt to neutralize their exposure of private passions by harnessing them to a public good both women unknowingly support and, at least initially, resist. To this extent, Amarilli and Chimène alike resist their own theatricalization in the sense conceived in the humanist terminology of an Alberti or a Heywood: they protest their inclusion in a larger community and the open, public space in which that community is represented. It is therefore crucial that both protagonists be seduced into thinking that they are alone and therefore invulnerable, occupying a world untouched by theater when they reveal, supposedly only to themselves or a trusting servant, their authentic selves. Yet Corneille and Guarini have deliberately fashioned a theater that undoes these moments of false intimacy for a putatively public, and hence, theatrical good.

Thus in one instance from *Le Cid* which the play's original audience found scandalous, Rodrigue chooses to furtively enter Chimène's house and discover whether or not her feelings for him have changed since he murdered her father. As he conceals himself behind a curtain, Chimène pours out her grief to her servant Elvire, seeing the moment as one in which she can finally be free: "Enfin je me vois libre, et je puis sans contrainte / De mes vives douleurs te faire voir l'atteinte; / Je puis donner passage à mes tristes soupirs; / Je puis t'ouvrir mon âme et tous mes déplaisirs" (3.3.; "Finally I am freed, and without constraint, I can make you see the force of my lively grief; I can give way to my sad sighs; I can open my soul to you and all my unhappiness") (803–6).[25] These "soupirs" are not, however, only for a dead father; they are also for the man who slew her father. "Par où sera jamais ma douleur apaisée, / Si je ne puis haïr la main qui l'a causée?" ("But how can my grief ever be appeased, if I cannot loathe the hand that caused it?"), to which Elvire responds, horrified, "Il vous prive d'un père, et vous l'aimez encore!" (He kills your father, and still you love!). Chimène confirms her suspicion with "C'est peu de dire aimer, Elvire : je l'adore." ("It is not enough to say I love him, Elvire: I adore him") (819–20). Yet it is only when she unveils her plan to pursue Rodrigue's murder and then kill herself that Don Rodrigue emerges from his hiding spot, asking Chimène to kill him and provoking both her paralysis and her cry: "Rodrigue en ma maison!"

Rodrigue devant moi!" ("Rodrigue in my house! Rodrigue before me!")
(861–62). Armed not only with his sword, stained with Don Gomès's blood,
but with the knowledge that Chimène still worships him, Rodrigue plunges
into battle with the invading Moors and wins over a king who will be more
than eager to preserve his newest champion.

And this is a king who, like Rodrigue, will seek to place himself in a
privileged position vis-à-vis female passions, and by way of a theatrical
stratagem as underhanded as that employed by his champion. The penulti-
mate scene of *Le Cid* is one in which Chimène is forced to become the unknowing participant in a theatrical stratagem, as the king of Seville seeks to
"discover" for himself and his court the love she conceals for Rodrigue. Don
Fernand, King of Castile, is anxious to protect Rodrigue from the vendetta
which Chimène has continued to pursue, despite what we know to be her
own love for Rodrigue. However, before she bursts into the courtroom to
demand retribution, the king instructs his followers to "contrefaites le triste"
(pretend to be sad) and to be complicit in his plan to inform Chimène
falsely that the valiant Rodrigue died of wounds in the battle with the
Moors. Predictably, when she hears of her loved one's death, Chimène
faints, prompting one observer, Don Diègue, to remark, "Mais voyez qu'elle
pasme, et d'un amour parfait / Dans cette pasmoison, Sire, admirez l'effet"
(1353–54) ("But see how she faints; Sire, admire the effect of a perfect love in
her swoon"). Helpless in the theater of the court, Chimène has again unknowingly exposed before not one audience but two the "secrets of her soul"—
a revelation which procures Rodrigue's immunity and thus the future health
of Castile.[26]

Le Cid can be said to thematize what Heywood celebrated as the useful effects of theater on the audience, as we witness a female character dis-
armed by the forceful nature of the play before her into confessing her most
secret passion, at odds with what she conceives as her social and filial duty.
Throughout these suspenseful scenes, Chimène becomes the central object
of scrutiny ("Mais voyez qu'elle pasme"), but only and especially when she
is no longer aware that she is acting, when she has been tricked—through
theatrical stratagems as pointed as Hamlet's play before the king—into
yielding any consciousness of her own theatricality. This in itself can be
said to constitute a radically new accomplishment on a stage inhabited by
the figure of the actress, in regard to whom male spectators apparently sought
to discover their *true* emotions, their personalities *behind* their masks. As
Fernando Taviani has noted in a seminal essay focussing on the first generation of Italian actresses, the verses that were written to celebrate their

accomplishments often speak not of their *own* talents but the talents of the (male) spectators in catching them in their more compromising moments: namely, when they are suffused by an uncontrollable blush.[27] Corneille, as it were, seeks to inscribe such a moment into his play, by staging for us Chimène's swoon in the scene before the king. Yet despite the presence of such artifice in *Le Cid*, we are still faced with another attempt to render post-humanist theater useful, although in a way unimaginable to Alberti. *If* Chimène and, by extension, the actress who performed her role, can be forced to reveal who she "really" is, then the theater has been able to purify itself and its society alike of the spectre of the manipulative, public woman. We are made to believe that we see instead an essentialized femininity, subject to and dependent on the theatrical mechanisms that surround it. And once Chimène is reduced to expressing a femininity that hinges exclusively on her candid acknowledgment of her love for Rodrigue, we can be assured of the absolute necessity of her having exposed her passion, without which the safety of Castile would be jeopardized. The social, public role she has conceived for herself—the avenging of her father's death—is revealed as *only* a facade, as *only theater*, which the mechanisms of theater itself can easily penetrate.

Like the *Pastor fido*, Corneille's *Cid* met with a great deal of protest, most of it centering on Chimène and the suddenness with which she could be dissuaded from seeking her lover's punishment. The aspiring courtier and dramatist Georges de Scudéry, among others, found Rodrigue's furtive entrance into Chimène's rooms an affront to theatrical decorum, while Chimène, in her continuing affection for her lover despite all that he had done, was nothing less than a "monstre" who has forsaken filial duty for illicit love.[28] Yet Scudéry's criticism overlooks Corneille's defense of the stage, here and elsewhere in his writings, as an institution that can recognize private passion as a basis *for* the well-ordered and stable state. The fact, moreover, that Corneille calls attention to the processes through which theatrical machinations disarm the private space—Rodrigue intrudes into Chimène's private chambers not once, but twice, as though we might have missed the emphatic intrusion the first time—shows how anxious he is for an audience to be keenly aware of the way in which late Renaissance theatricality *works* as it links public necessity to the exposure of hidden passions.

Guarini likewise is careful to show us how an invasive theatricality must work in order to expose concealed and authentic passion. Yet at the same time, he expresses his distaste for such invasiveness, as though to distance himself from the machinations through which such passions are revealed.

Act 2, scene 5, where we see the shepherdess Amarilli onstage to lament her impending marriage to the hunter who disdains her, is our first glimpse of the play's female protagonist. She makes it clear that she is to be married to the hunter Silvio as a metaphorical sacrifice to the state: once the descendants of two gods join in marriage, the health of Arcadia can be assured and its harsh law punishing unfaithful young women lifted. In this soliloquy well into Act 2 and thus well into the play, Amarilli unburdens her hidden desire in the supposed solitude of the woods for a life untouched by law and public duty: she wishes that she were a "felice pastorella, / cui cinge a pena il fianco / povera, si, ma schietta, / e candida gonella, / ricca sol di se stessa" ("a happy shepherdess, whose poor but clean and humble skirt barely covers her thigh; she is rich only in herself").[29] Yet while Amarilli makes the "care selve beate" her privileged audience for her desires for a "vera vita, che non sa che sia / morire innanzi morte" ("true life, that knows not what it is to die before death") and to exchange her fate with another, someone else is onstage. Lurking in the wings is the scheming shepherdess, the erstwhile courtesan Corisca, who has already pledged to find some manner of stealing Amarilli's true love, Mirtillo, for herself. In becoming the "mistress of her secret" ("padrona del suo segreto"), in seeking to "penetrar" not only Amarilli's words but her very heart—"voglio penetrar ancora / fin ne'l 'interne viscere il suo core," Corisca placidly announces when the scene is over and Amarilli has disappeared (2.5.829–34)—the former courtesan acquires a measure of power in the world of Arcadia by exposing Amarilli's soliloquy as only a fiction of privacy.

This power is played out in the next few acts, as Amarilli is supposedly undone when she confesses, in yet another soliloquy (again overheard by Corisca) her passion for Mirtillo; and then arraigned by the priest for her infidelity to the shepherd she is supposed to marry. For a painful moment, it appears as though the schemes of the spy Corisca, anxious, like Iago, to compromise her social better, will be victorious. And yet the fiction of privacy in which Amarilli has believed, and through which she has been exploited, will ultimately result not in her death but in Arcadia's salvation, when (in Guarini's byzantine narrative) Mirtillo is mysteriously revealed to be the noble descendant whom Amarilli must, in fact, marry. It is thus not female passion per se that saves Arcadia, but the articulation *of* that passion and the uses to which it is put. While the crass Corisca is upbraided by the play's satyr himself as evil and possessed of a "canina ed importuna lingua" (2.6.947; "a brutish and impertinent tongue"), she is obviously central, as are the spying Rodrigue and lying King of Castile, to the resolution of the play: she is the character who allows for the "apprehension" of Amarilli's most secretive passions.

For both Guarini and Corneille, equally engaged in defending their plays before their scandalized audiences, theater's legitimation depends on its ability to stage an illicit passion on which a *bene comune* is in turn dependent.[30] That these passions are articulated unwittingly and unwillingly, that the private space in which the heroines believe they find themselves is powerfully constrained by social forces, suggests that late Renaissance theater continues to be informed by a humanistic theory of theater. The playspace is always and already public, and all that unfolds in that space must happen for the public good. Literally apprehended in their misguided desires to occupy a space outside of public theater, forced against their wills and yet at the same time, forced to follow their passions, Chimène and Amarilli are deployed by their respective playwrights to justify the existence of tragicomic theater. Far from introducing us to the spectre of a surveillant state, such a recognition constituted for Guarini an escape from the "maninconia" or melancholy that afflicts modern man and to which modern theater could address itself. Melancholy only ensues, in Guarini's theory of humorism, when man is disaffected with and isolated from the public sphere. As Guarini claimed in his lengthy responses to the pesky academician Denores, thanks to tragicomedy's public manipulations of private space, we all become part of a larger social and political network. In a striking metaphor, Guarini compares the melancholic to someone who has been overwhelmed by centrifugal forces and must be "costretto" or constrained to return to a center: the very "center" which his theater's tragicomic powers sustain.[31]

In such ways can Guarini and Corneille be said to have attempted to save late Renaissance theater—suffering from the brutalities of tragedy and the inconsequentialities of comedy—from its apparent uselessness. Continental theater's new lease on life, that is, emerges from its explicit engagement with women as both characters and as actresses, as it invades their falsely public lives to reveal their authentically private ones, and in a manner which is only apparently invasive. The paradox, however, of their efforts, attested to in their theoretical tomes and imitated by a myriad of French and Italian playwrights after them, is that their plays mark a turning point in the history of European theater. For the stage would increasingly take on the role of a primarily social, rather than a rhetorical or civic institution. The advent of the actress as a staple on the European stage, both in the public theaters and in the courts, would ultimately serve to relegate theater to a space of entertainment rather than of rhetorical efficacy—and perhaps in part because Corneille's and Guarini's own post-humanist fictions of justifying an audience's passionate attentiveness to beautiful, articulate women were doomed to fail.

Needless to say, very different categorisations must apply in Shakespeare's case, for he wrote in an England without actresses, and indeed, an England that had long been critical of their introduction onto the European stage. One might therefore expect a very different dynamic in England with respect to female characters. Yet if one turns to the Jacobean legacy that was to follow *Hamlet*—Webster, Fletcher, Ford, Cyril Tourneur—one finds an almost unnervingly merciless treatment of women whose private imaginings are forcibly turned outward and often against themselves, as in *Duchess of Malfi*. The absence of a redemptive moment sharply differentiates Jacobean tragedy from its continental counterparts.[32] Yet Shakespeare himself will flirt with tragicomic alternatives in the years shortly before macabre experiments with tragedy appeared onstage. *Measure for Measure* and *The Tempest*, for example, with varying degrees of success, both reconcile the invasion of newly constituted privacy with a "providential" plan that attempts to fulfill the desires of a female subject.

But before *Measure for Measure* and *The Tempest*, there was *Hamlet*, arguably Shakespeare's most profound engagement with the issue with which Corneille and Guarini wrestled, theater's *raison d'être*. Nowhere is the "purpose of playing" stated more baldly in Shakespeare's corpus than in Hamlet's speech to the players—or demonstrated more problematically than in the scene in Gertrude's closet. Intervening, however, between these two moments is the notorious "Mousetrap," the interrupted play-within-the-play. In preparation for the tragedy, Hamlet muses over the powers of theater to reveal truths spectators have labored to conceal. Like Heywood, he has "heard / That guilty creatures sitting at a play / Have by the very cunning of the scene / Been strook to the soul, that presently / They have proclaim'd their malefactions" (2.2.588–92). Hamlet's plan will be to have the players "Play something like the murther of my father" before the king so that he can "observe his looks" and "tent him to the quick." Through another's play, although one subtly infused with lines of Hamlet's own, the prince tests Puttenham's thesis as he strives to expose secret faults and lead a murderer to justice through the indirect means of reprehension. The "Mousetrap" and Claudius's flight from the stage immediately precede Hamlet's encounter with Gertrude, and it is a scene which should have us—and Hamlet—thinking only of the truncated tragedy's *success* in apprehending spectators. Like Heywood's guilt-ridden wives of ten years hence, Claudius disrupts the spectacle, but his confession is made not publicly but privately. Lke the spying Corisca of *Pastor fido*, Hamlet stands close to overhear the consequences of his elaborate plan, but unlike Corisca, he hears nothing. Even if Hamlet believes that he has already discovered what he wished to know—"I'll take the ghost's word for a thousand pound" (3.2.286)—he finds himself unable to *act* on his belief: were he to kill Claudius in the privacy of his room, he would run the danger of sending his confessing soul to heaven rather than hell. Perhaps the overwhelming need to act at this juncture leads him toward another private chamber: his mother's.

And it is in the closet scene, and perhaps only there where Hamlet fulfills his desired role as an effective *actor*, one who will "cleave the general ear with horrid speech."[33] The question, however, is why Hamlet chooses to become a player here, and what he seeks to gain from the encounter. To be sure, the scene is initiated by Polonius, who believes that it is up to the Queen to interrogate the nature of Hamlet's madness: she must "tax" the prince "home." At the same time, he is concerned that her maternal propensities will not permit her to be sufficiently strict ("Pray you be round [with him]," he instructs her [3.4.5]). Hence his fatal decision to hide behind the arras. Yet Hamlet has simultaneously announced in his soliloquy that he will set out in this "very witching time of night" to be "cruel" to his mother, if not "unnatural"; he does not wish for the "soul of Nero," matricide that he was, to "enter this firm bosom," and asks only that he "speak daggers" rather than employ them. On the one hand, of course, he will indeed use a dagger against the ineffectual Polonius, a thrust into the arras that suggests that Hamlet allows for no innocent spectators; all who have chosen to attend the play are in some way guilty, despite his (ironic) claim earlier to Claudius: "Your Majesty, and we that have free souls, it touches us not" (3.2.241). But Polonius's murder is merely a deflection of the violence fully intended for Gertrude. Hamlet has thrust a glass before her in the hope of surprising her into a confession for, presumably, two things: her complicity in her husband's murder, and her lust for Claudius and subsequent remarriage.

Scholars have frequently commented on the extent to which Elizabethans would have shared Hamlet's apparent revulsion at the widow's marriage to her brother-in-law, and they have on occasion seen Gertrude's words, "thou turn'st my eyes into my very soul, / And there I see such black and grained spots / As will not leave their tinct," as an admission of guilt. Yet an admission to what effect is the question, since the scene ends neither with the queen's promise to forego her marriage nor a confession of complicity in Hamlet senior's death. In this, the Folio differs sharply from the so-called "bad Quarto." In the latter text, Gertrude openly reveals her innocence in King Hamlet's murder ("But as I have a soul, I swear by heaven, / I never knew of this most horrid murder"; 11.83–84) and "vow[s] by that majesty / That knows our thoughts and looks into our hearts" to assist Hamlet in his act of vengeance, pledging to "conceal, consent, and do my best, / What stratagem soe'er thou shalt devise" (95–98).[34] The Folio and second quarto remain vague on the first point, and are unforthcoming on the second; we have neither a straightforward disclosure of the queen's guilt nor any such clear alliance between mother and son. Moreover, only in versions subsequent to Q1 does Hamlet dwell on the virtues of the "glass," whether it be the mirror of playing or the one used in Gertrude's closet. The meta-theatrical musings in what are presumably later versions of *Hamlet* elicit from Gertrude precisely the opposite of what one would expect. Neither does Gertrude explicitly confess her guilt, nor does she promise to avoid Claudius's bed or to enter into an alliance with Hamlet. It is as though the theatrical metaphors that are so pervasive in the second quarto and in the Folio militate *against* the very "work" theater is ideally supposed to per-form as a discoverer of hidden passions..

Just as importantly, with this scene we witness the arrival, for the last time in the play, of the Ghost. As Hamlet immediately recognizes, he comes to "chide" his "tardy son," "laps'd in time and passion." But he also instructs Hamlet to desist in his attack upon Gertrude, still dwelling on thoughts of her own impending murder: "Look, amazement on thy mother sits, / O, step between her and her fighting soul, / Conceit in weakest bodies strongest works" (3.4.112–14). In his first appearance to Hamlet on the battlements, the Ghost instructed him not to "let thy soul contrive / Against thy mother aught. Leave her to heaven, / and to those thorns that in her bosom lodge / To prick and sting her" (2.5.85–88). But Hamlet's desire to know exactly what "thorns" these are, his will to apprehend his mother and finally play the efficacious actor when he has been incapable of playing it anywhere else, drive him to the excesses in which the Ghost finds him. The Ghost has requested no such confession, no apprehension of his wife, no interrogation of her passions in the interest of healing a wounded state and putting a wan-derer from the afterlife to rest. In terms of the Ghost's instructions to him, Hamlet's most aggressive theatrical ministrations have been beside the point, little more than a displacement of the moral act of vengeance he has been instructed to carry out against his uncle. His desires to imagine his mother's carnal sins, "the rank sweat of an enseamèd bed," are reduced to nothing more than prurience itself. As such, they are similar to his "sexual explo-rations [of Ophelia] in scathing witticisms," in William Kerrigan's phrase (115), another woman whose closet he also chose to enter ("My lord, as I was sewing in my closet, / Lord Hamlet, with his doublet all unbrac'd. . . . [2.1.74–75]).[35] Such ministrations have earned Hamlet nothing, save to ex-pose the gratuity of the theatrical violence in which he will participate only when it regards the "weaker" and more vulnerable sex.

Indeed, in this late Renaissance play that announces the death knoll to humanism's optimistic theatrical agendas, Gertrude can be said to have the final word by virtue of her very silence.[36] In this light, she rather than Hamlet emerges as the figure most alien to the world of the play. While Hamlet has fruitlessly employed the devices of the stage for the purposes of exposing female passions, Gertrude becomes the precursor of a marginal-ized modernity that would escape and, in escaping, critique the mechanisms of a theater that insists on revealing secret passions as a function of its use-fulness. What Gertrude feels for Hamlet, we know: her sorrow as he dies. What she feels for Claudius or what she felt for Hamlet's father, we do not know; and the Ghost, catalyst to this particular tragedy, has instructed Hamlet not to find out. The theater will not aid us in this ontological exer-cise insofar as Hamlet's mother is concerned. She is apprehendable neither as an example to the audience's female spectators, nor as a character whose passions might be rehabilitated for reasons of state. The dying Hamlet seems finally to recognize the magnitude of his failure to "reveal all": "What a wounded name, / Things standing thus unknown, shall I leave behind me" (5.2.344).

Gertrude's unknown "she," of course, was also a "he," and therefore not apprehendable in the sense in which the actress playing the role of Chimène, caught in a timely swoon, would have been. And yet by invok-ing the mimetic strategies within which the continent's actresses had been trapped, Shakespeare critiques both the theater of the humanist past and that of the post-humanist present. What happens to this theater when its revelations are revealed as only gratuitous, prurient and invasive rather than efficacious, effecting no narrative resolution and procuring little more than Polonius's death, "par accident," as well as Ophelia's madness and Gertrude's silence? More importantly, what happens when the public business of ven-geance and punishment is sidestepped by an investigation into something that has no place on the public stage, the community of men's political affairs that represented the tragic sphere for Renaissance theater? *Hamlet* stages the difficulty of bringing together, on the one hand, humanism's faith in the necessity of rendering "visible," and on the other, the potentially violent and often grotesque manner in which the hidden is brought to light. Gertrude's recalcitrance and the Ghost's timely intervention enable us to see the extent to which Shakespeare's humanist prince, acting on behalf of a theater that wants to link its practices to the service of morality, is forced to confront the unnaturalness and, perhaps, the non-necessity of that process itself.

With this notion of unnaturalness and non-neccesity one comes full circle to Weinberg. For the possibility of theater's non-necessity may very well be what provoked late sixteenth-century playwrights to produce a very different literary history from the one to which we have been accustomed.

Chapter 13

Strange Alteration: Physiology and Psychology from Galen to Rabelais

Timothy Hampton

Fou a latere *altéré.*

—*Rabelais*

Cardenio's Passion

Midway through the first part of *Don Quixote* the Don and his friends find themselves in an inn, where they pass the evening listening to a series of tales of love and betrayal. Among these tales is the sad story of Dorotea, who has been betrayed by a certain Don Fernando—himself the betrayer and seducer of the beautiful but poor Lucinda, whose story was related a bit earlier, by her lover Cardenio. As Dorotea tells how she became the object of Don Fernando's attentions, the mere mention of Don Fernando's name produces a strong reaction in one of the listeners. This is his rival for the hand of Lucinda, the melancholy Cardenio himself: "As soon as she, who was telling the tale, spoke the name of Don Fernando Cardenio's face changed color, and he began to sweat, with such a great alteration that the Curate and the Barber, who were watching him, feared that there might come upon him one of the fits of madness which they had heard came over him from time to time."[1] What is interesting about this description is the detail with which Cervantes describes Cardenio's dismay. The passage tells us that Cardenio's face changes color, and that his body begins to perspire—two physical indices of discomfort or pleasure. Cervantes goes on to categorize these phenomena as an "alteration" or "alteración." The addition of the extra term suggests that the changes in Cardenio's body do not by themselves communicate the exact nature of his state. Pallor and perspiration, after all, are perfectly natural responses to a number of situations. Only when these reactions are linked under the technical category of an "alteration" do they become signs, physical manifestations of a psychological

state, and hints that a fit of madness ("un accidente de locura") is beginning. The word "alteration" connects the signals put out by the body to a
discourse, turning them into indices of the soul.

A similar moment occurs in a very different document of Renaissance
culture. In the opening passages of a neo-Platonic dialogue on love, the
"Solitaire Premier" (1541), by the French poet Pontus de Tyard, we see the
poet, known as "Solitaire," leave the forest where he passes his days to visit
his beloved, whose name is Pasithée. Upon seeing him she asks him why his
health has declined. He replies that she is as perceptive as ever, that his face
reveals "an interior alteration" ("vous jugez à ma face quelque altération
intérieure"), which is the result of the thoughts that are continually at war
within him ("qui me font tant rude et continuelle guerre") and that have
driven him to his current indisposition. However, he adds, that indisposition might better be called a "furor, which vexes and agitates my spirit, than
an illness" ("se doit plustost nommer fureur, qui vexe, et agite mon esprit,
que non pas maladie").[2] And he goes on to identify this furor as the furor
that inspires poetry itself. His alteration, in other words, is poetic frenzy.

Both Cervantes and Tyard use the term alteration to describe a crucial
moment of imbalance or change in the self. Alteration, in these texts, at
least, seems to be a kind of shorthand for the manifestation of the passions
on the body, for the way disease becomes legible. For Cervantes, physical
signs are indices of a psychological crisis, and the Barber and Curate (who
care, respectively, for the body and the soul) are alerted to Cardenio's incipient fit. For Tyard, the case is more ambiguous, as Pasithée mistakes inspiration for illness. Yet in both cases the term alteration refers to a shift in the
body that is also a shift in the soul or psyche. Moreover, and most striking,
the term seems to be used interchangeably to refer either to the "outside" of
the self (as in Cervantes's description of Cardenio's body) or the "inside" (as
in Solitaire's naming of his own psychic state). Indeed, alteration seems
to be a term which holds in tension the experiences of outside and inside,
the "physical" and the "psychological." In Cervantes, alteration is a hint that
the self is under strain. From Tyard we learn the difficulty of locating that
strain.

The Renaissance medical notion of alteration is thus both physiological and psychological. The term names the interrelationship of two forms of
experience that, since Descartes, European thinkers have tended to separate.
This is, of course, a cliché of intellectual history. But, cliché or not, it is the
case that the essential tie between the body and the temperament or psyche
is one of the features of early modern thinking about the self that is least

obvious and accessible to modern readers. Yet for Renaissance medical thinkers the alteration of the soul and the alteration of the body are mutually interactive and shape each other. Neither can be isolated. To the extent that modern readers have split these two phenomena they have done so often by making one of them (the body) a sign of the other (the psyche), and by treating that "other" as the source of a knowledge which the body helps disclose when it is properly interpreted. To some extent this strategy may involve the ways in which different discourses (say, medicine or literature) shape knowledge. Thus, for example, a medical man passing the night in Cervantes's fictional inn might read Cardenio's alteration as requiring, perhaps, a good meal more than the presence of Lucinda. In fact, it may well be the achievement of literature to make disorders of the body signs of disorders of the soul. Or, at the very least, we know we are in the world of the novel when we read Cardenio's physical discomfort as the indicator of his psychological disarray, and not vice versa.

In any event, these passages raise the question of how the post-Cartesian reader of the passions comes to distinguish between physiology and psychology, to split the restive regime of corporality from the fragile regime of the will. Yet what is also at issue is how different forms of discourse construe and represent those two regimes. In this context, we can understand Nietzsche's insistence—in his own attempt to rethink the relationship between power, language, and morality—on the preeminence of physiology in the shaping of psychology. "Man's 'sinfulness' is not a fact," he writes in the *Genealogy of Morals*, "but merely the interpretation of a fact, namely of physiological depression." "I consider even 'psychological' pain," he continues a moment later, "to be not a fact but only an interpretation— a causal interpretation—of facts that have hitherto defied exact formulation—too vague to be scientifically serious—a fat word replacing a very thin question mark."[3] In what follows, I will suggest some of the ways in which the concept of alteration provides just such a question mark—one whose history can help us understand the shifting regimes of physiology and psychology in the Renaissance.

This problem of linking the material and the intellectual or spiritual, of defining the powerful interplay between body and identity, has been a critical focus for much recent work on the European Renaissance. Thus, for example, in a fascinating discussion of the importance of the Galenic theory of the humors for English Renaissance literature, Michael C. Schoenfeldt takes issue with Stephen Greenblatt's well known claim that "the self is at its most visible, most expressive . . . at moments in which the moral will has ceded place to the desires that constitute the deepest stratum of psychic experience."[4] To the contrary, argues Schoenfeldt: Renaissance selves are defined, not through moments of crisis, when the moral gives way to the physiological or sexual, but through the very strategies of discipline through which the body and psyche are held in balance. For Schoenfeldt the Renaissance self is defined—pace Bakhtin—through careful control and monitoring of a self always in flux. "The Renaissance seems to have imagined selves as differentiated not by their desires, which all more or less share," he writes, "but by their capacity to control these desires."[5] My own discussion will try to suggest another dimension to these debates around body and self. I am, in fact, not particularly interested in "locating" the self at all—in either the controlling will (Schoenfeldt) or the rebellious desiring belly (Greenblatt).[6] Instead, I am interested in how an essentially neutral term of Galenic medicine becomes inflected in the Renaissance with various valences—both positive and negative—that lend it central importance in describing the passions (and make it an instance, perhaps, of Nietzsche's "fat word" replacing a "thin question mark"). Moreover, whereas much recent work on the relationship of body and selfhood in the Renaissance has tended to focus on literature as a series of thematic "instances" of other forms of control (education, medical discourse, popular ritual, etc.), I want to look at the ways in which the linguistic and formal complexities of literature make available certain resources for marshalling and responding to the crises of selfhood signaled by the shifting fortunes of Galenic alteration. This may help us approach one of the curious paradoxes of early modern literature—a paradox which, indeed, lies at the heart of the project of studying the passions. This is that modern readers tend to understand early modern psychic life in ways that are quite different from how they approach the life of the early modern body. That is, early modern poems, plays, and tales present themselves to us as accessible. They stage emotional and moral crises—"psychological" crises, if you will—that seem familiar and current. Yet these dramas constantly draw upon understandings of how the body works that are radically alien and barely comprehensible to modern readers.

In what follows, then, I will explore certain aspects of the history and use of the term alteration and its cognates in the Western European languages. At the most basic semantic level, of course (and this needs to be noted from the outset), an alteration is simply a change, temporary or permanent, in the nature or character of something. Yet the word is also a technical term in Galenic medicine, and a key element both in Renaissance discourses on the body and in the literary representation of passion. I will begin by tracing some of the history of the term in premodern medical thinking. Then I will look at the ways in which medical notions of alteration become intertwined with other types of "non-medical" discourse that are specific to the Renaissance. It is through the ways in which "alteration" binds physiology to other types of discourse, I will argue, that the term becomes central to how Renaissance subjects speak of passion, and that it becomes imbricated in discourses of the self. I will pay special attention to the deployment of the term in French, where it is involved in series of puns that help shape the discourses of the self in Renaissance French literature.

Alteration, Heat, Humor

The "alteración" that registers on the face of Cervantes's Cardenio may be linked to one of the central notions of Galenic medicine, the concept of *alloiousthai* or the changing of one kind of matter into another (from *allos*, or "other"). Renaissance translators of Galen render this term into Latin as "alteratio," from which it takes on different, fairly predictable forms in the various European vernaculars: alteration, altération, alteración, alterazione, alteração, and so on.[7] It is through and around these various vernacular cognates that my own argument will unfold. Galen asserts the importance of alteration in human physiology in his treatise "On the Natural Faculties. " Much of the treatise is an attack on the work of Erasistratus, who had developed a medical practice focusing uniquely on digestion. Erasistratus claims that substances that are beneficial or noxious to health are "contained" in the food that is digested. For example, he argues that if those who eat honey have an excess of yellow bile, the bile must be contained within the honey. This, says Galen, is absurd. Rather, the bile is produced by the body, through alteration (*alloiousthai*) of the honey: "the honey undergoes change, becoming altered and transmuted into bile"—or, in the Linacre translation widely used in the Renaissance, "inter corpus est mutantum, in hanc alterant ac vertunt."[8] In practical terms, the insight that matter is altered within the body leads to a rejection of Erasistratus's bedside manner of recommending fasting as the answer to illness (that is, if honey contains yellow bile and you have too much yellow bile, stop eating honey). And it makes possible Galen's emphasis on the generation of the humors in the maintenance of human health. For Galen, every organ has its own innate character, and the stomach is a producer of heat, which transforms substances by "cooking" or "concocting" them. This in turn leads to emphasis on the maintenance of heat, through which alteration occurs. Those parts of a given food which are not altered sufficiently are taken into the spleen as black bile and later circulated to help thicken the blood as needed. The parts which have been cooked adequately become yellow bile ("thin, moist, and fluid"), and are carried all over the body. Those which are overcooked ("having been roasted to an excessive degree") are considered "abnormal" and are often described as "corrosive" to the body.[9] The key to health thus becomes maintenance of the proper level of heat in the body. In this way alteration is not excessive and the movement of the humors does not get out of balance.

In premodern medicine, the generation and balance of humors binds the regimes of what we call physiology and psychology. Among writers of the Renaissance this relation finds one of its most succinct formulations in the work of the French royal surgeon, Ambroise Paré, who is often understood to be the inventor of modern surgery. Paré begins his *Introduction to Surgery* (1585) by noting that the movements of the soul are just like those of the body and that the surgeon can ignore neither. The perturbations of the soul find material manifestation in the perturbations of the body. Thus, for example, Paré writes of joyful feelings that they "cause the movement of spirits and of natural heat, which in turn dilate or compress the heart, thereby releasing or restricting the movement of spirits which change the color of the face."[10] Conversely, by controlling the heat of the body, the doctor can influence the movement of spirits and the emotional health of the soul.

Thus the movement of alteration, whereby matter is changed through natural heat to produce humors in the body, is also linked to the problem of how to balance the humors and the all important need to regulate corporeal heat. In this context the term "alteration" begins to take on a somewhat larger meaning than the technical significance it has in Galenic physiology. It comes to refer, through a kind of metonymic slippage, not merely to the process of changing digested matter through heat, but to the moment of change in bodily temperature—the moment at which phyisiological (and, hence, psychological) processes suffer a temporary imbalance. It is this disturbance of equilibrium that accounts for Cervantes's description of Cardenio's physiological alteration as presaging an "accident of madness" ("un accidente de locura"), a fit, a momentary contingency into which one falls. Indeed, when we recall the famous paradigmatic relationships between body, soul, and cosmos, so often illustrated in Renaissance medical manuals, we might posit that these virtual relations are only made actual—that is, legible on the body—at the moment of alteration or imbalance.

It is important to stress that the process of alteration in Galen seems to be essentially neutral, neither a good thing nor a bad thing. However, in later writers, because it signals a troubling of the equilibrium that is ideal in the body and soul it is understood to involve a negative movement, a process of corruption. The Latin term *alteratus* (again, with its later vernacular cognates) comes to imply being out of oneself, between two states (as distinguished from the more excessive term *alienatus*, which means to be out of oneself altogether). This sense of transformation or movement as a kind of corruption may be less than obvious to modern readers, schooled, as we are, in a kind of politics of self-transformation as growth. Yet it is precisely because of this fragility that the effect of external forces (beauty, weather, food) on the self is so dangerous. Thus, to take one example, Paré speaks in the twenty-second book of his *Introduction to Surgery* (in the section on plagues) of the power of the air to harm the body and corrupt the humors through excess heat: "If the air is excessively hot, cold, humid, or dry, it alters and changes [altère et change] the temperature of the body like itself."[11] Excessive rain, he goes on, is particularly dangerous, because it "alters and corrupts" the air and makes it susceptible to the plague. This link between the alterations of the body and the alterations of the atmosphere suggests the danger of extremes. For this reason, one frequently finds, in Renaissance vernacular literature, the verb "to alter" paired, in almost idiomatic or proverbial fashion, with verbs suggesting corruption or disintegration. And, indeed, it is as a verb connoting corruption that the word alteration will become part of the language of late-Renaissance political theory, where it will be used to describe the decline and fall of various states and forms of government.[12]

At the same time this nuance of "corruption" introduces a new dimension to the relationship of physiology and psychology—a dimension that links them to moral philosophy. Thus, for much of Renaissance humanism and certain forms of neo-Stoicism, the task of the man with the well balanced soul is to resist the contingent disorientations effected by alteration. So the Spanish humanist Juan Boscán reminds his friend Diego de Mendoza that, "The man who seeks virtue / will view things from on high, / and will allow nothing to alter him" ("Quien sabe y quiere a la virtud llegarse, / pues las cosas verá desde lo alto, / nunca terná de qué pueda alterarse"). Boscán makes a nice pun that opposes "lo alto" (the view from on high) with "alterarse."[13] To avoid being altered, says Boscán, stay "alto." Rabelais makes a similar point in the beginning of his *Third Book*, when he tells us that the profligate trickster Panurge has wasted the money and resources of his friend Pantagruel, but that Pantagruel paid no mind. "For he would have left behind the holy manor of reason if he had in any way been made sad or altered" ("si aultrement se feust contristé ou altéré").[14] For there is no thing beneath heaven, Rabelais reminds us, that is worth troubling our senses and spirits over. In this formulation it is the very mark of the reasonable man not to be altered. This link between psychic equilibrium and the resistance to alteration may be what powers one of Rabelais's most perplexing inter-lingual puns. Somewhat later in the *Third Book* he describes the fool Tribouillet, in the phrase I have taken for the epigraph to this essay, as a "fou *a latere*, altéré." The joke, if that is what it is, plays on the intersection of the Latin phrase "a latere" (literally, "from the side," but perhaps suggesting as well, "from the Lateran or papal seat") and the French form of "altered," which also suggests "thirsty."[15] As Boscán's poem suggests, there is a kind of spatial dimension to these formulations of selfhood. A steady self is one that doesn't move, or one that stays "above things," or, as Montaigne will later put it, "in its seat." By contrast, an unbalanced self is one that is shaken out of place. Triboullet's alteration seems to suggest a kind of movement sideways which has made him permanently mad.

The Thirsty French, the Lusty French, the French in Love

If the dynamics of alteration involved nothing but the processes of heat and corruption that I have sketched thus far, the importance of the concept and term for the history of the passions in the Renaissance would be quite limited. However, the conjunction of heat, alteration, and disequilibrium is implicated as well in yet another discourse which exerts a powerful shaping force on European Renaissance literature in virtually every language and genre. This is the discourse of Renaissance neoplatonism, which gained wide currency across early modern Europe through Marsilio Ficino's famous commentary on Plato's *Symposium* (written around 1475) and through the *Dialoghi d'Amore* (1535) of Leone Ebreo.

The conjunction of neoplatonism with Galenic theories of heat and alteration stems from the fact that thirst, produced, in the Galenic scheme, out of an excess of heat, is, in both Christian and classical contexts, a commonplace figure for desire. It depicts both sexual and spiritual desire, going back at least to the imagery of the "Song of Songs" ("Your love is better than wine"; "drink deeply, O lovers!" [1.2, 5.1]), and to Psalm 143, where the Psalmist speaks of his thirst for the Lord: "my soul thirsts for thee like a parched land" (v.6). For Ficino, the journey of the soul is a circular one, from God back to God. The motivating force behind this journey is love: "Love is a circle which turns endlessly, from the good back to the good" ("Amor circulus est bonus a bono in bonum perpetuo revolutus.")[16] And love is powered by desire, which is figured as thirst. The soul of the lover, as Plato notes in the *Symposium* (250d), is struck by the beauty of the beloved—both physical and spiritual—and is immediately drawn out of himself. Those who love, as Ficino puts it, are "inflamed with love and thirsting for beauty" ("qui amore accensi pulchritudinem sitiant").[17] Yet the lover can never be satisfied with the momentary embrace of a mere body, and must pursue beauty until it leads back to the presence of the Deity. In the process, the desiring soul is purified of its earthliness and transformed into a pure lover of the divine: "Love teaches the disciple who loves, and the disciple thirsts avidly after the lesson of love" ("disciplos diligat ac discipuli eam doctrinam avidissime sitiant").[18] It may be no accident in this context that the person most prey to powerful bouts of love is, Ficino tells us, the choleric person—exemplified by Socrates—because his fiery humor throws him into passion with undue violence.

The moment of transformation, at which the soul is shaken by the vision of beauty, is conventionally described in the Renaissance language of the passions as an alteration. A century after Ficino, Montaigne would marvel at the power of the erotic over the soul by noting that even Socrates, the greatest of philosophers, fell prey to passion at an age when his body was already chilled with age: "A touch, a chance touch, and on a shoulder, was able to heat up and alter a soul that was cold and enervated by age, and in the first of all men in questions of self-transformation. But why not, by God? Socrates was a man; and wanted neither to be nor seem anything else." ("Un attouchement, et fortuite, et par une espaule, aller eschauffer et altérer une ame refoidie et esnervée par l'aage, et la premiere de toutes les humaines en reformation! Pourquoy non, dea? Socrates estoit homme; et ne vouloit ny estre, ne sembler autre chose.")[19] With characteristic originality, Montaigne uses the language of passion, the violence of desire derived from discussions such as Ficino's, to counterbalance the kind of easy Stoicism seen in a writer like Boscán, cited above. Here it is Socrates's very alteration, the power of the body to disrupt moral training, that makes him human.[20]

The elaborate thermodynamics of Ficino's theory of desire take on yet another nuance when they are inserted into the linguistic context of Renaissance French. For if heat produces the alterations of the body, one may describe an overheated body as an altered body. Or at least this seems to be the thinking that underpins the appearance of a curious idiom in late medieval

French, "avoir une gorge altérée," literally "to have an altered throat." This idiom, in turn, is soon shortened to the phrase "être altéré," "to be altered," and comes to mean "to be thirsty."[21] This is a richly suggestive development for the language of the passions in Renaissance France. The Ficinian dynamics of desire I have just outlined depend on the twin concepts of thirst and transformation. Passion is an alteration or dislocation of the soul at the sight of beauty. That partial beauty provokes a thirst or "altération" for more beauty, which in turn leads to a purification of the soul. The spatial paradigm of self-transformation set up by Ficino's image of the soul traveling in a circle back to God opens up a set of movements which direct the self's response to the power of beauty. Whereas the simple movement between thirst and the satisfaction of thirst would be a movement between "altération" and "désaltération," (a return to stasis) the Ficinian model of desire turns thirst as altération into thirst as transformation. Both the state of imbalance and the process that seeks to redress that imbalance are expressed, in Renaissance French, with the same technical term. For writers seeking to describe the experience of passion, the same word describes what has happened to them and what they want to do about it. Alteration holds within it both passive suffering and active striving.[22]

These nuances are registered in Renaissance French writing about desire. For example, in a 1551 translation of Leone Ebreo's *Dialoghi* the translator, the poet Pontus de Tyard, has Leone Ebreo distinguishing between the unchangeability of God and the world of human experience, which is prey to "altération et corruption." He renders the Italian writer's discussions of the thirst or "sete" of desire by using the French terms "soif" and "altération." [23] Thus, just as we saw earlier that alteration seems to slip metonymically from denoting the concoction of food by heat to connoting a moment of imbalance, here it slips from evoking merely the status of the soul in the face of beauty to include the movement that the soul makes to satisfy and transform itself. The slippage provides literary descriptions of passion with a portmanteau term that simultaneously holds within itself the technical terminology of medical discourse, the psychic shock of amorous encounter, and the drive that transforms the self through love. Moreover this association of alteration with transformative desire contrasts with both the essentially neutral Galenic notion of alteration, and the negatively valenced link of alteration with corruption noted above. This means that to speak of the "altération" of the self in Renaissance French is simultaneously to speak of the physiological unbalance of the body (a corruption) and the desire of the soul for erotic transformation (a redemptive rebalancing in the movement toward God). This complicated node of meanings—and the problems of translation which it poses—informs many descriptions of passion in Renaissance French. For example, in the last passages of the "Dialogue de l'amour et de folie" (1555), by the poet Louise Labé, the author describes love. Love is desire, says Labé, and whoever loves cannot be without desire: "incontinent que cette passion vient saisir l'homme, elle l'altere et immue." That is, "as soon as desire seizes a man, it alters and moves him"—or, perhaps, "it makes him thirsty [for beauty] and [therefore?] moves him."[24]

In philosophical writings on the nature of love, the linguistic play suggested in Labé's treatise is often implicit, as writers struggle with the problems of defining different forms of desire and thirst. Philosophical writing on love often circumscribes or avoids the polyvalence of the term alteration. Tyard, whose translation of Leone Ebreo I mentioned above, generally seems to try to separate "soif" from "altération" in speaking about the thirst of the desiring subject. Yet even occasional mixing of the terms suggests that the network of meanings associated with alteration is already present in the translation of Neoplatonism to France. This fact is made abundantly clear, moreover, when we turn to Petrarchan love lyric, which exploits and plays with the same linguistic shadings I have been trying to distinguish and pin down. Thus in one of the sonnets of his *Erreurs Amoureuses* (1549) Tyard speaks of devouring the beauty of his lady: "buvant alterement, / d'une beauté l'amoureuse douceur" ("drinking the amorous sweetness of beauty thirstily"—or, perhaps, alteratively, "that is," "from" or "as alteration").[25] From this experience, we learn, his soul is driven mad and transported into error: "Un esprit, fol d'aveuglée fureur, / Qui transporté en devoyée erreur / Contre ma paix m'esmut mutinement" ("A spirit, mad with blind furor, / Which, in a transport of wayward error, / moves me mutinously /changingly.") The awkward, invented adverb "alterement" ("alteringly") suggests both the unbalancing of the soul at the sight of beauty (echoed by the equally unwieldly adverb "mutinement") and the thirst of the lover, who desires the very thing that has unbalanced him. It connotes both what disorients him and his response to that disorientation, both the initial drinking and the movement into "error" that will presumably lead him eventually to some kind of salvation.[26]

Thus the semantic richness of the verb "altérer" in Renaissance French mediates the relationship between bodily nourishment, psychic imbalance, and spiritual transformation. In the discourse of the lyric, this produces a kind of circularity whereby the power of the lyric self to take control over its own physiological imbalance—the very type of self-discipline noted by

Schoenfeldt in his discussion of Renaissance selfhood—threatens to slip away. This process, I am suggesting, is in part linguistic, stimulated by the language of passion which the poet inherits. For the more the subject is altered by passion, the more it is altered by thirst, and the more it is "altéré"— described along a metynomic line of transformations with the same term.

This process of dislocation and imbalance provides a context for looking at some of the ways in which poets respond to the dynamics of alteration. Consider, for example, the following poem by Joachim du Bellay, from his early collection entitled *L'Olive*, (1549), one of the first Petrarchan sonnet sequences in Renaissance France:

Sacrée, saincte et celeste figure,
Pour qui du ciel l'admirable, et hault temple
Semble courbé, afin qu'en toy contemple
Tout ce, que peult son industrie et cure:

Si de tes yeulx les beaux raiz d'avanture
Daignent mon coeur echaufer, il me semble
Qu'en moy soudain un feu divin s'assemble,
Qui mue, altere, et ravist ma nature.

Et si mon oeil ose se hazarder
A contempler une beauté si grande,
Un Ange adonq' me semble regarder.

Lors te faisant d'ame et de corps offrande
Ne puis le coeur idolatre garder,
Qu'il ne t'adore, et ses veux ne te rande.[27]

(Sacred, holy, and celestial face, / For whom the admirable and lofty temple / of the heavens seem to have bent down to contemplate / in you all that its industry and care can create: / If by chance the beautiful rays from your eyes deign to heat up my heart / It seems to me that, within me, a divine fire appears, / Which changes, alters, and ravages my nature. / And if my eye dares to dare / to contemplate such a great beauty, / I seem to see an Angel / Then, making an offering of soul and body to you, / I cannot stop my idolatrous heart / From adoring you, and giving you its devotion.)

Here the experience of erotic fascination takes on the shadings of religious conversion. The vision of the lady "changes, alters, and ravages" the poet's nature through a heat which is both divine and intensely physical. The response to that transformation is of course the desire for more of the lady's presence—a thirst or "alteration" which is implied in the notion of the heating up and alteration of the soul. Yet Du Bellay already seems to be taking a distance from the scene by asserting that he "seems" to be altered ("il me semble"). Indeed, Du Bellay displaces the sense of unbalance implied in alteration by shifting to a language of religion. The introduction of a religious lexicon in the context of a description of self-transformation makes the "alteration" of the soul in passion an "alteration" (in the simple sense of "a change") of the soul in *conversion*. In order to escape the power of alteration, the poet, in effect, retranslates or misreads the term itself. By activating a latent semantic nuance of the notion of "alteration" the poetic speaker moves out of the circularity of physiology and passion. This "rereading" of alteration by the second half of the poem makes possible, in the last lines, a kind of economic version of passion, in which the exchange of glances produces an increased offering on his part (soul and body), and finally the recognition that the conversion is a (happy) conversion to idolatry (accompanied by the disappearance, in the last strophe, of the verb "sembler" which had attenuated the claims of each of the preceding stanzas). The two tercets of the poem may be read as an attempt to control the power of the body by switching it into another register, away from the physiological knot signified by an alteration that dislocates nature itself.

The Du Bellay sonnet suggests that the drama of much of French lyric involves the consequences of alteration and the struggle of the poet to accommodate a transformation of the self while claiming his own autonomy. This struggle may be seen in powerfully programmatic terms in Maurice Scève's *Délie*, the greatest neo-Platonic lyric cycle of the French Renaissance. Scève describes the power of Délie's gaze on him and the birth of his desire as follows:

Je sens le noeud de plus en plus étreindre
Mon âme au bien de sa béatitude,
Tant qu'il n'est mal qui la puisse contraindre
A délaisser si douce servitude.
Et n'est fièvre en son inquiétude
Augmentant plus son altération
Qui fait en moi la variation
De cet espoir qui, jour et nuit, me tente.
Quelle sera la délectation,
Si ainsi douce est l'ombre de l'attente?[28]

(I feel the knot, tighter and tighter, constrain / my soul with the goodness of its beatitude, /such that there is no evil which can compel my soul / to give up such sweet servitude. / And yet there is no fever in its inquietude / Augmenting ever more its alteration / Which can bring about in me the variation / of this hope which, day and night, tempts me. / What will the pleasure be like / if the shadow of the expectation is so sweet?)

Like Du Bellay's sonnet, this ten-line "dizain" sets forth the terms of the poet's passion in language that is simultaneously spiritual and physical. Moreover, the twin themes of the poet's disarray and his desire for Délie are yoked together, yet again, by the term "alteration." On the one hand, it denotes the imbalance in the poet's soul brought about by the power of the lady over him. Indeed, as Scève wrote in a poem to Labé, love is a bending down of heaven which alters the soul ("c'est donq de l'ame une alteracion") and sends it into chaos.[29] So great is the lady's power, he notes in the passage above from *Délie*, that no fever could ever unsettle him more. Moreover, the fact that alteration suggests both thirst and desire prepares the way for the second half of the stanza (with the word alteration coming virtually at the midpoint), in which what is at issue is the poet's expectation of "delectation." The poet is altered, in that he is upset, but he is also altered, in that he desires delectation, and no fever can make him thirstier than he is. At the same time, however, the rhyming of "altération" with "variation," to which it stands in opposition, sets in motion the simplest, commonsense meaning of the word: no matter how much I may be altered, I'll never alter my love. This rhyming pair underscores the point of the poem—that a combination of fever and thirsty desire (that is, of alteration and alteration), which might distract a less steadfast lover, here produces one who will never err or alter his service to his beloved.

Thus, just as Du Bellay extracts a latent theological sense of "alteration," responding to his own physical and psychic alteration with a conversion to the religion of love, so here Scève retrospectively injects into the erotic alteration of the self what might be called a moral valence. Scève's very integrity as a lover lies in the fact that he will never give in to any alteration or variation from the object of his passion—no matter how much his body is altered. Both Du Bellay and Scève describe themselves as victims of the dynamics of alteration, before offering responses which affirm the agency of the self beyond the physiology of passion. Both poets move from a moment of imbalance denoted by the technical medical notion of alteration to a position from which that alteration can somehow be controlled. What is remarkable is that the shift from one moment to the other (paralleled, in both cases, by the unfolding of the poetic stanza as it moves from its first half to its second half) seems to involve a kind of retrospective misreading of the initially technical term "altération" as either "conversion" (for Du Bellay) or "inconstancy" (for Scève). In other words, both poets extract from the semantic well of the term "alteration" another sense which makes possible the righting of a subject thrown into the vortex of passion.

It may well be the intersection of a model of physiological change inherited from Galenic medicine with a theory of transformative desire derived from neo-Platonism that makes it possible for us find glimpses of a modern "psychology" in Renaissance lyric. Certainly, as the examples from Du Bellay and Scève suggest, the articulation of this psychology is in no small measure intertwined with the linguistic multivalence of the term "alteration" itself, which both poets manipulate in surprising ways. It would seem to be precisely the linguistic plenitude of the term—its imbrication in various positively or negatively inflected models of change—that makes possible the definition of a kind of moral stance on the part of the poet, a claiming of the authority to dominate one's own perturbations. Moreover, the claiming of the power to misread or retranslate one's own language of desire may suggest why Renaissance lyric is generally so obsessed with issues of literary authority. Far from a mere game of literary influence and history, the seizure of the language with which to write is also the conquest of the medium that might reorient the unbalanced, passionate self. These poets work within a linguistic tradition that limits and shapes the representation of the passionate self, and their manipulation of the tools of poetic diction and form may be one way in which they begin to turn against that tradition.

It is instructive, in this context, to consider the imbrication of physical malaise, psychic disarray, and moral constancy set forth in Scève and Du Bellay next to a similar moment in one of the most famous of all English Renaissance lyrics, the one hundred and sixteenth of Shakespeare's sonnets: "Let me not to the marriage of true minds / Admit impediments. Love is not love / Which alters when it alteration finds, / Or bends with the remover to remove. / O no, it is an ever fixèd mark / That looks on tempests and is never shaken; / It is the star to every wand'ring bark, / Whose worth's unknown although his height be taken."[30] The obvious differences between Shakespeare and Scève here stem precisely from the fact that, for Shakespeare, in this instance at least, the physiological implications of "alteration" are heavily muted. Yet Shakespeare's deployment of the language of change is not unrelated to what we have already seen. Shakespeare has set up the theme of alteration in this sonnet by focusing, in the preceding poem, on the problem of remaining constant through time. He notes there, in #115, that when he once said that he "could not love you dearer," he was unaware that his "most full flame should afterwards burn clearer." This ignorance of the fact that desire can increase is then revealed to be a kind of naive constancy. For it is undercut by the vicissitudes of time, which can "divert strong minds to th' course of alt'ring things." How, the sonnet seems to ask, can one remain constant to the object of desire, when desire itself is constantly changing? Sonnet 115 answers this question in a somewhat facile manner, with the emblematic assertion that "Love is a babe" (it can always grow). In #116, however, the negotiation between constancy and change is redefined in terms that suggest the larger consequences of Shakespeare's meditation on the alterations of the body under the pressure of desire. For if Scève and Du Bellay respond to the fluctuations of the passionate body by rereading the term "alteration," Shakespeare here makes constancy the very definition of love. By shifting focus onto the meaning of love (instead of the various meanings of alteration), Shakespeare shifts our attention from the regime of physiology and transmutes alteration into a moral and epistemological category. It now involves both the constitution of the self (which, throughout the *Sonnets*, seeks to control the fluxes of corporeal desire) and, more important, the relationship of subject and object.[31]

This same grafting of physiological alteration onto a discourse of moral constancy is recalled again in Act 1, scene 2, of *The Winter's Tale*. After Polixines allows himself to be persuaded by Hermione—herself urged by Leontes—to remain in Sicilia, he leaves the room, during which time Leontes confides to the courtier Camillo his suspicions about Hermione's fidelity. Polixines notes, upon returning, that the king "hath on him such a countenance / As he had lost some province and a region / Lov'd as he loves himself." And he upbraids Camillo for evading his various questions about Leontes: "Good Camillo, / Your chang'd complexions are to me a mirror / Which show me mine chang'd too; for I must be / A party in this alteration, finding / Myself thus alter'd with 't." To which Camillo replies ominously, "There is a sickness / Which puts some of us in distemper; but / I cannot name the disease, and it is caught / Of you that are yet well."[32] Leontes's own incapacity to remain within himself, the alteration which makes him appear to have lost something "lov'd as he loves himself," echoes the rhetoric of self-loss seen in the lyric poets discussed a moment ago. And Polixenes glosses, as it were, the meditation on the relationship of subject and object in sonnet #116 ("which alters when it alteration finds / Or bends with the remover to remove") when he remarks that he is altered because Camillo is altered. Polixenes gestures toward his alien status in the physiology of the distempered body of the state when—with yet another extrapolation of an ancillary sense of alteration—he states that his own position at court has been "alter'd," that is, shifted in space. Only when Leontes overcomes his own imbalance, can the court, and friendship, be restored to their proper locations.

From Physiology to History in Rabelais

Pierre de Ronsard wrote an epitaph of Rabelais in which he described him as "thirsty without a break" ("altéré, sans nul sejour"), adding that "the gay fellow drank night and day" ("le gallant boivoit nuit et jour").[33] Certainly, when we think of the overlapping themes of physiological need and thirst, Rabelais springs immediately to mind. And we should not be surprised to find that Rabelais explores resonances of alteration scarcely dreamed of by writers such as Scève, Tyard, and Du Bellay.

As we have seen, the essentially neutral notion of alteration inherited from Galen becomes connected, in the discourse of the lyric, to a moment of imbalance, when the physiological corruption of the body merges into the transformative dynamics of erotic desire. In Rabelais, by contrast, the term appears at moments of personal transformation which are also moments of narrative transformation, or, perhaps, one might even say, shifts in genre. Thus, for example, early on in *Gargantua*, we see the young giant in a state of primitive contentment. The list of his actions traces a circular figure suggesting a self-sufficiency or self-contained plenitude:

Gargantua, depuis les troys jusques a cinq ans, feut nourry et institue en toute discipline convenent, par le commandement de son pere, et celluy, temps passa comme les petits enfants du pays: c'est assavoir a boyre, manger et dormir; a manger, dormir et boyre; a dormir, boyre et manger.

(Gargantua, from the age of three to five years, was raised and instructed in all appropriate discipline, by the order of his father, and spent the time like the small children of his country: that is to say, in drinking, eating and sleeping; in eating, sleeping and drinking, in sleeping, drinking and eating.)[34]

This state of containment, which links Gargantua to every other child in the country, is broken, however, by the imposition of a series of tutors, whose job is to form him into the virtuous hero required by his princely status. Most of these tutors only succeed in corrupting and confusing the young hero with their antiquated and senseless programs of study, until he is put in the hands of the humanist Ponocrates, who sets him on the right path. Ponocrates's first action on taking over the boy's education is to administer a drug, "elebore de Anticyre." The power of the Hellebore will have the effect of cleaning away "the alteration and perverse habits of his brain" ("luy nettoya toute l'alteration et perverse habitude du cerveau")(88). This a curious formulation, since the "alteration" that needs to be cleared away here is, as it were, cultural; it is nothing more than the effect of bad schooling. Yet the cure for alteration is chemical, the administration of a drug. [35] At one level, Rabelais seems to be making a joke at the expense of the medical practice of his day. Yet at the same time he is extending, in good humanist fashion, the link between body and psyche advanced by Galenic medicine. If body and mind are interrelated, bad education is as bad for the body as it is for the mind; and the way to cleanse the mind and the soul is to cleanse the brain. Conversely, the proper development of the soul and mind involve the proper development of the body. Thus, we learn that the newly purged Gargantua is put on a rigorous exercise program, which involves, primarily, the lifting of weights: "And to strengthen his nerves, they made him two giant fish-shaped pieces of lead, each weighing eight thousand seven hundred quintalls, which he called 'alteres'" ("Et, pour gualentir les nerfz, on luy faict deux grosses saulmones de plomb, chascune du poys de huyt mille cept cens quintaulx, lesquelles il nommoit alteres") (95). The term for a weight which one lifts is, in modern French, "haltère" (linked to the word for high, "haut" or the Latin "altus"). In the Renaissance it was spelled with or without the initial h.[36] Yet by calling the weights "altères," and by setting "altères" in proximity to "altération" in his text, Rabelais implies that they are not only objects that one lifts, but that they are objects that alter or change one for the better. As such, they constitute the linguistic and gymnastic response to the "alteration" that has corrupted the boy. Here we see a good alteration, motivated by the puns on "altération," "haltères," and "altus."

The link between physiological alteration and the process of metamorphosis or transformation is strikingly demonstrated by the birth of Pantagruel, Gargantua's son. Pantagruel was born in a time of drought. And we are told that, shortly before he was born, the earth itself began to exhibit symptoms of overheating, as it exuded great drops of water "like when someone sweats copiously" ("comme quand quelque personne sue copieusement") (230). This simile is glossed by the explanation that the extreme dryness of the air had required the production of moisture to rebalance the humors governing the universe. This alterative setting is then brought into focus by the narrator's description of the origin of Pantagruel's name:

Car panta, en grec, vault a dire comme tout, et gruel en langue Hagarene, vault autant comme altéré, voulant inferer que à l'heure de sa nativité le monde estoit tout altéré, et voyant en esperit de prophetie, qu'il seroit quelque jour dominateur des altérés.

(For Panta, in Greek, means "completely," and gruel, in Hagarene, means "thirsty," suggesting thereby that at the hour of his birth the world was completely thirsty, and noting, by way of prophecy, that he would some day be a dominator of the thirsty.)
(231)

Alteration is linked to passage and transformation on both a geocosmic and personal level. Moreover, the prophecy pushes the same dynamic into a political context. For Pantagruel will indeed be a "dominator of the thirsty"; he will in fact defeat the army of the Dipsodes—the "thirsty ones"—who will invade his homeland of Utopia. Since the Dipsodes are ruled by a king named "Anarche," the prophecy points to the ways in which Pantagruel's moderate control of alteration offers a response to the excessive alteration suggested by unbridled appetite, which results in anarchy and civil disorder. Alteration here constitutes the link that connects political stability (restored after the defeat of the Dipsodes) to physiological stability. [37]

Thus the lexicon of alteration in Rabelais seems to appear at moments of powerful transition, of birth and personal transformation. Indeed, it pops up again a moment later in the description of Gargantua, whose wife has died in giving birth to his son. Caught between the happiness of the new father and the misery of the grieving widower, Gargantua asserts that he cannot attend the funeral, since he feels "strongly altered, and in danger of falling ill" ("je me sens bien fort altéré, et serois en danger de tomber malade") (234). Yet a moment later he has decided to turn to the future and look optimistically on the possibility of change. He orders some fresh wine (in order to cure his "alteration" or thirst), and vows to find another mate: "I need to think about finding another" ("Il me fault penser d'en trouver une aultre"). Here, as in the deployment of the word "altères" above, the peculiarities of Renaissance French orthography produce a link between the "alteration" felt by the sorrowing widower and the feminine Other or "aultre" (from the Latin "alter") who will ease his pain and satisfy his desire. And in both instances the notion of alteration, with its complicated valences, appears at a moment when the text is shifting generic registers. In the case of *Gargantua*, it comes when we move from the early sections parodying heroic or marvelous births to a narrative segment which presents itself as a kind of humanist treatise on education. In *Pantagruel*, the opening

chapters, which recall and mimic Biblical genealogies, give way to a narrative of heroic youth in the style of Xenophon's *Cyropaedia.*

The transformative dynamics of alteration in Rabelais reaches a kind
of climax, as it were, at the close of the *Third Book.* Pantagruel's friend
Panurge has spent the entire *Third Book* consulting various authorities as
to whether or not he should marry. His willfulness and self-deception prevent him from ever reaching the point at which he is able to act. Finally, he
and Pantagruel decide to embark on a sea journey, to consult the Oracle of
the Holy Bottle. As they prepare to set sail they provision their ships with a
cargo of Pantagruelion, a miraculous herb with myriad practical uses. Not
the least of its many useful properties is that it resists fire. In fact, we are
told, one may even wrap an egg in Pantagruelion, place both in a fire and
remove the egg "cooked hard, burnt, without alteration" ("cuyt dure, et
bruslé, sans altération") (616). It burns, without being altered. Nor is this
all; no matter what test we submit it to, Pantagruelion will never emerge
"corrupted and dissipated" ("corrompu et dissipé") (618), like other woods,
or like stones in a kiln; "Pantagruelion asbestos is renewed and cleansed,
instead of being corrupted or altered" ("Pantagruelion aspest plustost y est
renouvelé et nettoyé que corrompu ou altéré") (619). Now, this is a particularly strange description, in light of the discourses which overlap in the
Renaissance uses of alteration. For the property of resisting alteration precisely echoes the descriptions we saw earlier in Ficino and Leone Ebreo of
God, as that being which can never, in Tyard's translation of Leone, be
"altéré ou corrompu."[38] Yet it is precisely this herb, Rabelais goes on to
affirm, that most strikes fear into the hearts of the gods. For they realize that
Pantagruelion will permit peoples to sail across the oceans, pass the tro-
pics, and visit the poles. The Gods of Olympus, moreover, fear that one day
Pantagruel will marry, and that his children will inherit the herb named
for him. In fact, the many uses of Pantagruelion will make it possible for
men to visit the sources of the rains and invade the regions of the moon,
eventually reaching heaven itself, and mating with the goddesses.

What is striking about the myth of divine and human miscegenation
enabled by Pantagruelion is that it relies upon a model of human advancement that presumes progress and discovery, the accumulation of knowledge
and technical skill. In this regard it offers a quite different vision of desire
from what we saw in the lyric poets discussed earlier. Desire is now the
desire for technical advance which will lead to the improvement of humanity. In the lyric context, coupling with a goddess, be she divine or human,
is an immediate goal. Here it is a mere byproduct, the happy outcome of

human striving. In a somewhat larger context, as David Quint has noted, what is at issue in Rabelais's fantasy of technical triumph is the progress of humanity through time, the acceptance of history itself, which the self-involved Panurge resists by refusing to marry and procreate.[39] This same sense of historicity contrasts with the dramas of the self which we traced in our reading of Rabelais's poet contemporaries. Through the invention of Pantagruelion Rabelais projects his characters out of the paradoxes of alteration and into a model of progressive action in history. It takes giants and magic herbs, it would seem, to escape the quicklime of lyric desire.

Strange Alteration

Rabelais's deployment of the language of alteration marks a difference from what we saw in contemporaries of his such as Scève and Du Bellay. The poets I analysed earlier defined a model of transformation in which psychology and physiology were mutually imbricated, such that the psychic disturbance of erotic passion, an alteration, was countered by physical thirst which was, in turn, denoted as alteration. This circularity gives way in Rabelais to a model of transformation through action, either through self-transformation, through the domination of the thirsty Dipsodes, or (as in the case of Panurge) through eventual marriage.

At a kind of macro-level, we might understand this distinction as a distinction of genre. The prose narratives of Rabelais define a model of experience that projects the endless elaborations of lyric desire into the world of time and history, into a process of progressive transformation that involves, for Rabelais's heroes, political action. It redraws the multiple displacements of physiological passion and psychic disarray as a linear process of education and the exercise of virtue. This generic shift may account for Milton's description, in yet another narrative genre, of Satan's progress toward earth—itself a kind of trajectory of the bowels of the universe—as being difficult and laborious, "But hee once past, soon after when man fell, / Strange alteration!" This change from a struggle through the dark bowels of the universe to a track on which Heaven "Pav'd after him a broad and beat'n way" marks nothing less than the fall into history itself. And though the limitations of space prevent me from extending my analysis, we can look beyond Milton to note that "altération" will turn up again as a key term in Rousseau's discussions of the corruption and fall of natural man.[40]

Alteration, and the curious linguistic effects that surround it, may be seen as a point of juncture at which different discourses for representing the self intersect and confront each other. The Latin term "alteratio" and its vernacular cognates form a conceptual node or knot around which the construction of early modern psychology unfolds. As we have seen, alteration, with its origins as a descriptive term in Galenic medicine, becomes powerfully inflected with moral and even political valences in the Renaissance—turning, it would seem, from Nietzsche's neutral "small question mark" into his moralizing "fat word." Moreover, through their attempts to circumscribe and interpret those valences, Renaissance writers produce dramas of psychological mastery over language and body. Yet what is most surprising about the authors studied here is the linguistic dimension to their depictions of the passions. We have repeatedly seen them respond to the scene of emotional or physiological alteration by redefining the term itself, through a pun or a misreading. The response to alteration takes a markedly linguistic turn, as authors from Boscán to Rabelais play on the various senses of the word and its cognates, connecting it to "aultre" and "alto," nudging it into theological, moral, and topographical contexts. This suggests, quite surprisingly, I think, that it is through the very fabric of the language of the passions that early modern subjects begin to rewrite the traditional medical discourses that structure the relationship of body and soul. Alteration involves not merely the ways in which early modern writers understand the mutual imbrication of bodies and selves, but also the ways in which they begin to formulate new languages of change.[41]

Notes

Introduction

1. We are quoting Anna Wierzbicka, *Emotions Across Languages and Cultures* (Cambridge: Cambridge University Press, 1999), 32.

2. Steven Mullaney, "Emotion and Its Discontents," paper presented at MLA Division on English Renaissance Literature, Chicago, 1999.

3. Quotations from Shakespeare in this introduction follow *The Riverside Shakespeare*, 2nd ed., ed. G. Blakemore Evans (Boston: Houghton Mifflin, 1997).

4. Susan James, *Passion and Action: The Emotions in Seventeenth-Century Philosophy* (Oxford: Clarendon Press, 1997), 6.

5. For the most part, Thomas Wright uses "affections" and "passions" synonymously; see *The Passions of the Minde in Generall* (1604), ed. Thomas O. Sloan (Urbana: University of Illinois Press, 1971), 7–11. Edward Reynolds contends that the sensitive passions that humans share with animals are the "motions" of brute creatures, but cannot be called "affections"; see *A Treatise of the Passions and Faculties of the Soule of Man* (1640), intro. Margaret Lee Wiley (Gainesville, Fl.: Scholars Facsimiles and Reprints, 1971), 37–38. Early modern passions theorists were typically engaged in adjudicating such questions, as they worked through the competing models of emotion and cognition (often understood, in the Aristotelian mode, as integrated functions) they received from diverse classical authorities.

6. Amélie Oksenberg Rorty, "Introduction," in *Explaining Emotions*, ed. Rorty (Berkeley: University of California Press, 1980), 1.

7. Paul E. Griffiths, *What Emotions Really Are: The Problem of Psychological Categories* (Chicago: University of Chicago Press, 1997), 1.

8. Even Sylvan Tomkins, who analyzes differences in bodily tonus as a strong symptom of emotion in infants, privileges the infant's face and eyes as the key signifiers of emotional experience. See Sylvan Tomkins, *Affect, Imagery, and Consciousness*, vol. 1, *The Positive Affects* (New York: Springer, 1962). On cognitive science, see Antonio D'Amasio, *Descartes' Error: Emotion, Reason, and the Human Brain* (New York: Putnam, 1994). On behavioral psychology, see Paul Ekman, *Darwin and Facial Expression: A Century of Research in Review*, 3rd ed. (New York: Academic Press, 1973).

9. See Catherine A. Lutz, *Unnatural Emotions: Everyday Sentiments on a Micronesian Atoll and Their Challenge to Western Theory* (Chicago: University of Chicago Press, 1988), 98–101.

10. We owe these insights to Steven Mullaney, in a seminar on the early modern emotions, Folger Shakespeare Library, October 10, 1999,.

11. We are indebted for this perspective to Catherine A. Lutz, seminar at the Folger Shakespeare, Library, October 9, 1999.

12. Griffiths, *What Emotions Really Are*, 10–11.

13. Joseph LeDoux, *The Emotional Brain: The Mysterious Underpinnings of Emotional Life* (New York: Simon and Schuster, 1996), 40.

14. LeDoux, *Emotional Brain*, 17 (emphasis added).

15. Griffiths, *What Emotions Really Are*, 9.

16. Charles Birch, *Feelings* (Sydney: University of New South Wales Press, 1995), 2. We owe this reference to Anna Wierzbicka.

17. Rorty, *Explaining Emotions*, 4.

18. Jon Elster, *Alchemies of the Mind: Rationality and the Emotions* (Cambridge: Cambridge University Press, 1999), 48.

19. Elster, *Alchemies of the Mind*, 49.

20. For a rigorous account of this division of disciplinary labor, both as it informs imaginative writings from Milton onward and as it defines modern critical anxieties, see Kevis Goodman, "'Wasted Labor'? Milton's Eve, the Poet's Work, and the Challenge of Sympathy," *ELH* 64, 2 (Summer 1997): 415–46.

21. Rorty, *Explaining Emotions*, 4.

22. Charles Darwin, *The Expression of the Emotions in Man and Animals*, 3rd ed. (New York: Oxford University Press, 1998), 20, 24.

23. On this point, see Paul Ekman's introduction to *Darwin and Facial Expression*, xxvi.

24. Griffiths, *What Emotions Really Are*, 48.

25. We are heavily indebted to Steven Mullaney's account of Ekman's work here in a private communication.

26. Ekman, Afterword to *Darwin and Facial Expression*, 379.

27. See Figure 3 in Ekman, Afterword, 380.

28. For a powerful critique of the evidentiary value of posed faces, see James A. Russell, "Is There Universal Recognition of Emotion from Facial Expression? A review of the Cross-Cultural Studies," *Psychological Bulletin* 115 (1994): 102–41.

29. Russell, "Universal Recognition," 115.

30. James, *Passion and Action*, 1.

31. On this topic, see Lutz, *Unnatural Emotions*, 53–80.

32. Wierzbicka, *Emotions Across Languages and Cultures*, 46.

33. Wierzbicka, *Emotions Across Languages and Cultures*, 36.

34. What language identifies as primary emotions might then be compared to the generalized emotional responses that evolutionary psychologists have mapped in the brain and that developmental psychologists such as Sylvan Tomkins have identified as the six axes of emotional response expressed physically prior to language by the developing infant. See *Affect, Imagery, and Consciousness*.

35. In a summary of her comparatist methods, Wierzbicka suggests a relation between the semantic development of the Polish term *tesknota* and revolutionary events in nineteenth-century Poland. See "Human Emotions: Universal or Culture-Specific?" *American Anthropologist* 88 (1986): 588. For a collection of essays that begins to explore the interdisciplinary ground between literature and anthropology

in the study of emotion, see Jürgen Schlaeger and Gesa Stedman, eds., *Representa-tions of Emotions* (Tüningen: G. Narr, 1999).

36. Robert N. Bellah, Richard Madsen, William M. Sullivan, Ann Swidler, and Steven M. Tipton, *Habits of the Heart: Individualism and Commitment in American Life* (Berkeley: University of California Press, 1985), 117–18. Cited in Anna Wierz-bicka, "Emotion, Language, and Cultural Scripts," in *Emotion and Culture: Empiri-cal Studies of Mutual Influence*, ed. Shinobu Kitayama and Hazel Rose Markus (Washington D.C.: American Psychological Association, 1994), 186.

37. Wierzbicka, "Emotion, Language, and Cultural Scripts," 186.

38. S. Sommers, "Adults Evaluating Their Emotions: A Cross-Cultural Per-spective." In *Emotion in Adult Development*, ed. Carol Z. Malatesta and Carrol E. Izard (Beverly Hills, Calif.: Sage, 1984), 323. Wierzbicka, "Emotion, Language, and Cultural Scripts," 187.

39. Adele Pinch observes that "the many names for emotion travel as freely as emotions themselves"; see *Strange Fits of Passion: Epistemologies of Emotion, Hume to Austen* (Stanford, Calif.: Stanford University Press, 1996), 16. Wierzbicka's work cautions us to read apparently free play of emotions and emotion terms critically.

40. Hans Medick and David Warren Sabean make a similar observation in their introduction to *Interest and Emotion: Essays on the Study of Family and Kinship*, ed. Medick and Sabean (Cambridge: Cambridge University Press, 1984).

41. Strier, this volume.

42. Michael C. Schoenfeldt, *Bodies and Selves in Early Modern England: Physiol-ogy and Inwardness in Spenser, Shakespeare, Herbert, and Milton* (Cambridge: Cambridge University Press, 1999), 17. For related observations on the difficulties of historically comparatist study of emotional expression see Julie Ellison, *Cato's Tears and the Mak-ing of Anglo-American Emotion* (Chicago: University of Chicago Press, 1999).

43. Lawrence Stone, *The Family, Sex, and Marriage in England, 1500–1800* (New York: Harper and Row, 1977), 221.

44. We are quoting James, *Passion and Action*, 11.

45. See Maureen Flynn, "Taming Anger's Daughters: New Treatment for Emo-tional Problems in Renaissance Spain," *Renaissance Quarterly* 51 (Autumn 1998): 881.

46. Flynn, "Taming Anger's Daughters," 879.

47. Strier, this volume.

48. For versions of this caution as it arises in the study of affects in early eco-nomic discourse, see Craig Muldrew, *The Economy of Obligation: The Culture of Credit and Social Relations in Early Modern England* (New York: St. Martin's Press, 1998) and Theodore Leinwand, *Theatre, Finance, and Society in Early Modern Eng-land* (Cambridge: Cambridge University Press, 1999).

49. Juliana Schiesari, *The Gendering of Melancholia: Feminism, Psychoanalysis, and the Symbolics of Loss in Renaissance Literature* (Ithaca, N.Y.: Cornell University Press, 1992).

50. See Lynn Enterline *The Rhetoric of the Body from Ovid to Shakespeare* (Cambridge: Cambridge University Press, 2000). See also Schiesari's introduction for a summary of the critical challenge and the leverage early modern texts provide feminist psychoanalysis.

51. Along with recent work by Enterline and Cynthia Marshall (*The Shattering of the Self: Violence, Subjectivity, and Early Modern Texts* [Baltimore: Johns Hopkins University Press, 2002]), see also Harry Berger, Carolyn Dinshaw, Janet Adelman, Marjorie Garber, and Gail Kern Paster. Two recent collections of essays expand on the comparatist possibilities of psychoanalytic and historicist approaches in early modern studies. See Carla Mazzio and Douglas Trevor, eds., *Historicism, Psychoanalysis, and Early Modern Culture* (New York: Routledge, 2000) and Valeria Finucci and Regina Schwartz, eds., *Desire in the Renaissance: Psychoanalysis and Literature* (Princeton, N.J.: Princeton University Press, 1994).

52. Schiesari, *Gendering of Melancholia*, 26.

53. Debora Shuger, *The Renaissance Bible: Scholarship, Sacrifice, and Subjectivity* (Berkeley: University of California Press, 1994), 190.

54. David Hillman, "The Inside Story," in *Historicism, Psychoanalysis, and Early Modern Culture*, ed. Mazzio and Trevor, 298–99.

55. Sarah Winter, *Freud and the Institution of Psychoanalytic Knowledge* (Stanford, Calif.: Stanford University Press, 1999), 14.

56. Richard Mulcaster, *Positions wherin those primitive circumstances be examined, which are necessarie for the training vp of children* (London, 1581), 55–56.

57. Recent post-structuralist criticism has applied Lacanian psychology expansively in this way: to early modern reading practices (Marshall, *The Shattering of the Self*); to the social symptomatics of rhetoric (Enterline, *Rhetoric of the Body*); to popular culture (Slavoj Žižek, *The Metastases of Enjoyment: Six Essays on Woman and Causality* [London: Verso, 1994]). Philippa Berry sets out to use Julia Kristeva's feminist psychoanalytic theory of abjection in similar ways: *Shakespeare's Feminine Endings: Disfiguring Death in the Tragedies* (London: Routledge, 1999).

58. See Katharine Eisaman Maus, *Inwardness and Theater in the English Renaissance* (Chicago: University of Chicago Press, 1995); Debora Shuger, *Sacred Rhetoric: The Christian Grand Style in the English Renaissance* (Princeton, N.J.: Princeton University Press, 1988); Schoenfeldt, *Bodies and Selves*; Hillman, "The Inside Story."

59. Charles Taylor, *Sources of the Self: The Making of the Modern Identity* (Cambridge, Mass.: Harvard University Press, 1989), 159.

60. William Ian Miller, "Deep Inner Lives, Individualism, and People of Honour," *History of Political Thought* 16 (1995): 190–207. Miller shows that inner lives were powerful but negative components of self-experience in early masculine honor cultures: deeply associated with the alienation and shame of the outlaw. As a consequence, the rules for handling "deep inner lives" in Icelandic saga involved systematic, ironic deflection. Miller finds similar conventional irony persists in our own honor cultures (the playground, the committee meeting), serving the same defensive functions.

61. In her extensive survey of modern historiography of the emotions, Barbara H. Rosenwein outlines the conceptual limitations of Elias's "grand narrative." She describes recent challenges (by medieval historians in particular) and suggests some alternatives congruent with those explored in the present volume. See Rosenwein, "Worrying About the Emotions in History," *AHR* 107, 3 (June 2002) <http://www.historycooperative.org/journals/ahr/107.3/aho302000821.html> (7 Jan. 2003). See also Rosenwein's collection of essays, *Anger's Past: The Social Uses of an Emotion in the Middle Ages* (Ithaca, N.Y.: Cornell University Press, 1998).

62. Michael Macdonald's seminal study of despair in early modern reformist debates suggests how dynamically these different conceptual frameworks coexist and compete in the period. See "*The Fearefull Estate of Francis Spira*: Narrative, Identity, and Emotion in Early Modern England," *Journal of British Studies* 31 (1992): 32–61.

63. John Sutton, *Philosophy and Memory Traces: Descartes to Connectionism* (Cambridge: Cambridge University Press, 1998), 41. Sutton offers his own critique of Taylor's model, pointing out how humoral Descartes's own physiology remains. The fully disengaged physiology we attribute to Descartes, he shows, is a legacy of later reception; modern editorial practice tends to drop out those aspects of Descartes's writings that are most informed by humoral physiology.

64. Sutton, *Philosophy*, 166; Taylor, *Sources of the Self*, 159.

65. Elaine Scarry, *The Body in Pain: The Making and Unmaking of the World* (Oxford: Oxford University Press, 1985), 14.

66. Levinus Lemnius, *The Secret Miracles of Nature* (London, 1658), 73–74.

67. Tomlinson, this volume.

68. Gail Kern Paster, "The Body and Its Passions," *Shakespeare Studies* 29 (2001): 45. See also Paster, "Nervous Tension: Networks of Blood and Spirit in the Early Modern Body," in *The Body in Parts: Fantasies of Corporeality in Early Modern Europe*, ed. David Hillman and Carla Mazzio (London: Routledge, 1997), 110–11.

69. Maurice Pope, "Shakespeare's Medical Imagination," *Shakespeare Survey* 38 (1985): 179. We are indebted to Dick Geeraerts and Stefan Grondelaers for this citation. See also Peter N. Stearns, *American Cool: Constructing a Twentieth-Century Emotional Style* (New York: New York University Press, 1994), 66–67.

70. Zoltán Kövecses, *Metaphor and Emotion: Language, Culture, and Body in Human Feeling* (Cambridge: Cambridge University Press, 2000), 156–57, 165, and passim.

71. Kövecses, *Metaphor and Emotion*, 159.

72. Dirk Geeraerts and Stefan Grondelaers, "Looking Back at Anger: Cultural Traditions and Metaphorical Patterns," in *Language and the Cognitive Construal of the World*, ed. John R. Taylor and Robert E. MacLaury (Berlin: Mouton de Gruyter, 1995), 170.

73. Geeraerts and Grondelaers, "Looking Back at Anger," 171.

74. Geeraerts and Grondelaers, "Looking Back at Anger," 172. For an exploration of the resources cognitive science offers literary studies, in pursuing this line of analysis, see Mary Thomas Crane, *Shakespeare's Brain: Reading with Cognitive Theory* (Princeton, N.J.: Princeton University Press, 2001).

75. Paster, "The Body and Its Passions," 44.

76. Smith, this volume.

77. Paster, this volume.

78. William J. Mills, "Metaphorical Vision: Changes in Western Attitudes to the Environment," *Annals of the Association of American Geographers* 72 (1982): 243. See also Joseph Mazzeo, "Metaphysical Poetry and the Poetic of Correspondence," *Journal of the History of Ideas* 14 (1953): 221–34 and "Universal Analogy and the Culture of the Renaissance," *Journal of the History of Ideas* 15 (1954): 299–304.

79. Mills, "Metaphorical Vision," 245.

80. Rowe, this volume.

81. See Paster, "The Body and Its Passions," 44–50 and Floyd-Wilson, this volume for the distinctively material transactions of early modern affect. Pinch and Ellison pursue similar interests in the "transpersonal" and "transactional" domains of emotion in eighteenth and nineteenth century liberal culture, but they use these terms in a social rather than material register (see Pinch, quoted in Ellison, *Cato's Tears*, 4). Heather James, "Dido's Ear: Tragedy and the Politics of Response," *Shakespeare Quarterly* 52, 3 (2001): 360–82 and Victoria Kahn, "'The Duty to Love': Passion and Obligation in Early Modern Political Theory," *Representations* 68 (Fall 1999): 84–107 explore the intersubjective functions of early modern sympathy.

82. On the non-naturals, see Nancy G. Siraisi, *Medieval and Early Renaissance Medicine: An Introduction to Knowledge and Practice* (Chicago: University of Chicago Press, 1990), 101. Wright and Reynolds offer seventeenth century examples of the topos of passions as servants.

83. Tomlinson, this volume.

84. Hampton, this volume (emphasis added).

85. Trevor, this volume.

86. Tylus, this volume.

87. Kahn, this volume.

88. On the separation of aesthetics at the birth of the disciplines, see Goodman "'Wasted Labor'?" and "Passionate Work: Toward a Georgics of Feelings," Ph.D. dissertation, Yale University, 1994. See also John Guillory, *Cultural Capital: The Problem of Literary Canon Formation* (Chicago: University of Chicago Press, 1993); John Barrell, *The Birth of Pandora and the Division of Knowledge* (Houndsmills: Macmillan; Philadelphia: University of Pennsylvania Press, 1992); Mary Poovey, "Aesthetics and Political Economy," in *Aesthetics and Ideology*, ed. George Levine (New Brunswick, N.J.: Rutgers University Press, 1994), 79–105.

89. On emotion as historical perception see Ellison, *Cato's Tears*, 5. Stedman emphasizes the remarkable persistence of emotion concepts as they survive cultural change in *Stemming the Torrent: Expression and Control in the Victorian Discourses on Emotions, 1830–1872* (Aldershot: Ashgate, 2002).

Chapter 1. Against the Rule of Reason: Praise of Passion from Petrarch to Luther to Shakespeare to Herbert

1. On the mean, see J. O. Urmson, "Aristotle's Doctrine of the Mean," and David Pears, "Courage as a Mean"; on the emotions in Aristotle's moral theory, see L. A. Kosman, "Being Properly Affected: Virtues and Feelings in Aristotle's Ethics," in *Essays on Aristotle's Ethics*, ed. Amélie Oksenberg Rorty (Berkeley: University of California Press, 1980). On the opposition between the Aristotelian (Peripatetic) and the Stoic traditions with regard to the passions, see Martha C. Nussbaum, *The Therapy of Desire: Theory and Practice in Hellenistic Ethics* (Princeton, N.J.: Princeton University Press, 1994), esp. ch. 3.

2. For a useful overview, see William J. Bouwsma, "The Two Faces of Humanism: Stoicism and Augustinianism in Renaissance Thought," in *A Usable Past: Essays in*

European Cultural History (Berkeley: University of California Press, 1975, 1990), pp. 19–73.

3. On historical self-consciousness as a Renaissance marker, see Herbert J. Weisinger, "The Self-Awareness of the Renaissance as a Criterion of the Renaissance," *Papers of the Michigan Academy of Sciences, Arts, and Literature* 29 (1944): 561–67; on the centrality of emotionally moving an audience to the Renaissance conception of rhetoric, see Debora K. Shuger, *Sacred Rhetoric: The Christian Grand Style in the English Renaissance* (Princeton, N.J.: Princeton University Press, 1988).

4. Francesco Petrarca, *On His Own Ignorance, and That of Many Others,* trans. Hans Nachod, in *The Renaissance Philosophy of Man*, ed. Ernst Cassirer, Paul Oskar Kristeller, and John Herman Randall, Jr. (Chicago: University of Chicago Press, 1948), 103. I have used the Latin text in Francesco Petrarca, *De Ignorantia* (*De sui ipsius et multorum ignorantia*), ed. and trans. (into Italian), Enrico Fenzi (Milan, Mursia, 1999), 266.

5. Petrarca, *On His Own Ignorance*; translation slightly modified.

6. Petrarca, *On His Own Ignorance*, 104; *De sui ipsius*, 268.

7. On images of rhetoric as a form of violence in the period, see Wayne A. Rebhorn, *The Emperor of Men's Minds: Literature and the Renaissance Discourse of Rhetoric* (Ithaca, N.Y., Cornell University Press, 1995), esp. ch. 3. Shuger, *Sacred Rhetoric*, denies that these images are primarily to be read in terms of aggression (125).

8. Collucci Salutati, "Letter to Pellegrino Zambecari," trans. Ronald G. Witt in *The Earthly Republic: Italian Humanists on Government and Society*, ed. Benjamin G. Kohl and Ronald G. Witt (Philadelphia: University of Pennsylvania Press, 1978), 93–114, 111. Further page references in the text.

9. The statement is attributed to Anaxagoras in Cicero, *Tusculan Disputations,* trans. J. E. King, LCL (Cambridge, Mass.: Harvard University Press, 1945), III.xxiv.

10. *The Politics of Aristotle*, trans. Ernest Barker (1946; reprint New York: Oxford University Press, 1958), I.ii.9 (p. 5).

11. See Gregory Vlastos, "Introduction: The Paradox of Socrates," in *The Philosophy of Socrates*, ed. Gregory Vlastos (Garden City, N.Y.: Anchor Books, 1971), esp. 16; Pierre Hadot, *Exercices spirituels et philosophie antique* (1981), 3rd ed. rev. (Paris: Institut d'Etudes Augustiniennes, 1993).

12. Desiderius Erasmus, *The Praise of Folly*, trans. Clarence H. Miller (New Haven, Conn.: Yale University Press, 1979), p. 115. Further page references in the text.

13. Walter Kaiser's treatment of the text in *Praisers of Folly: Erasmus, Rabelais, Shakespeare* (Cambridge, Mass.: Harvard University Press, 1963) is perhaps overly inclined to de-ironize the praise, but is a useful guide to a positive view of many of Folly's positions.

14. *A Tale of a Tub*, section IX, in *Gulliver's Travels and Other Writings by Jonathan Swift*, ed. Ricardo Quintana (New York: Random House, 1958), 342.

15. See *The Yale Edition of the Complete Works of St. Thomas More*, vol. 4, *Utopia*, ed. Edward Surtz, S.J. and J. H. Hexter (New Haven, Conn.: Yale University Press, 1965), 98–103.

16. On the importance to the Stoics of this metaphor of emotions as diseases, see Nussbaum, *Therapy of Desire*, esp. chs. 1–4, 13.

17. On Stoic redefinition, see, inter alia, Malcolm Schofield, *The Stoic Idea of the City* (New York: Cambridge University Press, 1991).

18. For this polarity, see Bouwsma, "The Two Faces of Humanism." The importance of Augustine for the Renaissance defense of affectivity is one of the major theses of Shuger's *Sacred Rhetoric.*

19. See Charles Trinkaus, *Adversity's Noblemen: The Italian Humanists on Happiness*, Columbia Series in the Social Sciences (New York: Columbia University Press, 1940); George W. McClure, *Sorrow and Consolation in Italian Humanism* (Princeton, N.J.: Princeton University Press, 1991); and see Petrarch's *The Life of Solitude*, trans. Jacob Zeitlin (Urbana: University of Illinois Press, 1924).

20. More, *Utopia*, 226 (Latin), 227 (translation) for the two kinds of priests. On the Utopian gratitude for even pleasures recognized as lower, see 176, 177.

21. For a similar view, see William J. Bouwsma, "Renaissance and Reformation: An Essay on Their Affinities and Connections," in *A Usable Past*, 225–46.

22. Martin Luther, "Preface to Romans," in *Martin Luther: Selections from His Writings*, ed. John Dillenberger (Garden City, N.Y.: Doubleday, 1961), 25. On Paul's view, see John A. T. Robinson, *The Body: A Study in Pauline Theology* (Chicago: University of Chicago Press, 1952), esp. ch 1.

23. See *Luther: Lectures on Romans*, ed, and trans. Wilhelm Pauck, LCC (Philadelphia, 1961), 218–19. For the Latin, see *Luthers Werke* (Weimar: H. Böhlau, 1883–), vol. 56 (1938), 356. Hereafter cited as *WA* with a volume number.

24. "Preface to Romans," 25.

25. *The Freedom of a Christian, Selections*, 79. Further page references in text.

26. For Erasmus, see *The Collected Works*, vol. 6, *The Corrrespondence, 1518–1519*, trans R. A. B. Mynors and D. F. S. Thomson (Toronto: University of Toronto Press, 1982), 89.

27. *Commentary on St. Paul's Epistle to the Galatians* (1531), *Selections*, 160. Further page references in text. A complete translation (based on the Elizabethan one) was edited by Philip S. Watson (London: J. Clarke, 1953).

28. Luther constantly railed against those whose understanding of *concupiscentia* or temptation was only in terms of carnal lust. See, for instance, *WA, Tischreden* 4, No. 5097: "Illi inepti asini nullam sciverunt tentationem quam libidinem."

29. By "motion," Luther (and the Elizabethan translators) meant something like "an unwilled inner impulse." "Motions" could be (interpreted as) natural, Satanic, or divine, depending on their content.

30. The most famous version of this story, phrased in exegetical terms, occurs in the 1545 Preface to Luther's Latin writings. See *Selections*, 11.

31. This is the difference, Luther explained, between the "philosophical" and the religious understanding of "righteousness." See *Commentary on Galatians, Selections*, 100–101, 131–32; Preface to Latin Writings, *Selections*, 11–12.

32. *Commentary on Galatians, Selections*, 130; for the Latin, see *WA* XL¹, 368. The rest of the page references in this paragraph are to the 1531 Galatians commentary in *Selections* .

33. See his Preface to the Psalms, *Selections*, 37–41.

34. John Calvin, "The Author's Preface" to *The Commentary on the Book of*

Psalms, trans. Rev. James Anderson (Edinburgh, 1845), 1: xlviii; for Calvin's "sudden conversion," see 1: xl.

35. John Calvin, *Institutes of the Christian Religion*, ed. John T. McNeill, trans. Ford Lewis Battles, 2 vols. LCC (Philadelphia: Westminster Press, 1960), III.ii.21 (further references in text). See also *Commentary on the Book of Psalms*, 1: 182, 357.

36. Bertrand Evans, *Shakespeare's Comedies* (London: Oxford University Press, 1960), 4.

37. On the surprising correspondences between *The Comedy of Errors* and Descartes's *Meditations*, see Richard Strier, "Shakespeare and the Skeptics," *Religion and Literature* 32 (2000): 171–96. Unless otherwise specified, *Errors* is cited from the Arden edition by R. A. Foakes (London: Methuen, 1962).

38. The right of sanctuary in England after the Reformation and the sale of monastic lands was dubious; it was finally abolished in 1624. See Isobel Thornley, "The Destruction of Sanctuary," in *Tudor Studies Presented to A. F. Pollard*, ed. R. W. Seton-Watson (London: Longmans, 1924), 182–207.

39. For a literary work that fully articulates, with regard to a nunnery, the conceptions of holiness and sacrilege implied here, see Andrew Marvell, "Upon Appleton House, to my lord Fairfax," line 236 ("the unjust Divorce") and especially line 280: "'Twas no *Religious House* till now." See Gary D. Hamilton, "Marvell, Sacrilege, and Protestant Historiography: Contextualizing 'Upon Appleton House,'" in *Religion, Literature, and Politics in Post-Reformation England, 1540–1688*, ed. Donna B. Hamilton and Richard Strier (Cambridge: Cambridge University Press, 1996), 161–86.

40. Many editors print "festivity" for "Nativity," which seems to be a clumsy repetition from two lines above. Foakes prints "felicity." I have preferred to retain the Folio reading. Even if an emendation is accepted, however, the "gossip's feast" that the Abbess proclaims (line 405) includes the "nativity" idea.

41. Pinch's Catholicism is evident in his exorcizing Satan from the "mad" Antipholus of Ephesus in the name of "all the saints in heaven" (IV.iv.55).

42. My treatment of this topic contrasts with John F. Danby, "*King Lear* and Christian Patience: A Culmination," in Danby, *Poets on Fortune's Hill: Studies in Sidney, Shakespeare, Beaumont and Fletcher* (London: Chatto and Windus, 1952), 108–27.

43. For my text, I have used René Weis, *King Lear: A Parallel Text Edition* (London: Longman, 1993). Where the texts differ, my citations give Quarto followed by Folio references to this edition.

44. On the problematics of obedience in the play (parallel, in many ways, to that of patience), see Richard Strier, *Resistant Structures: Particularity, Radicalism, and Renaissance Texts* (Berkeley: University of California Press, 1995), ch. 7.

45. See William Empson, "Fool in *Lear*," in *The Structure of Complex Words* (London: Chatto and Windus, 1951), 125–57.

46. Luther, *The Freedom of a Christian, Selections*, 76; and Calvin, *Institutes* III.vii.6.

47. Gordon Braden's *Renaissance Tragedy and the Senecan Tradition: Anger's Privilege* (New Haven, Conn.: Yale University Press, 1985) uses Kent's defense of indecorum in anger as the subtitle for the book, and quotes the line (2), but Braden

is interested in more generalized questions of self-presentation in Renaissance drama. For his remarks on *Lear*, see pp. 209, 215–16.

48. The Quarto reading "To bear it lamely" is probably a misreading of "tamely" (see Weis's note, *Parallel Text*).

49. See, inter alia, Leonard C. Muellner, *The Anger of Achilles: Menis in Greek Epic* (Ithaca, N.Y.: Cornell University Press, 1996). Aristotle defines anger as a painful desire to punish [a person who has afflicted one with] undeserved belittlement. *The "Art" of Rhetoric*, II.2 (1378a), trans. J. H. Freese, LCL (Cambridge, Mass.: Harvard University Press, 1926), 172–73.

50. Seneca, *De Ira*, II,ix, in Seneca, *Moral Essays*, trans. John W. Basore, 2. vols., LCL (Cambridge, Mass.: Harvard University Press, 1928), 183.

51. On the instability of "noble anger" in the Greek (literary) context, see Ruth Padel, *Whom Gods Destroy: Elements of Greek and Tragic Madness* (Princeton, N.J.: Princeton University Press, 1995); in the political and public context, see Danielle S. Allen, *The World of Prometheus: The Politics of Punishing in Democratic Athens* (Princeton, N.J.: Princeton University Press, 2000).

52. On apocalypticism in Senecan tragedy, see Braden, *Renaissance Tragedy and the Senecan Tradition*, 5–8, 55–56.

53. The Duke of Albany can be seen as rising to "noble anger" in his denunciation of Goneril (especially in the much longer Quarto version), but even these speeches have an element of rant ("Humanity must perforce prey on itself" [Q IV.ii.47]) and madness (Albany's fantasy of allowing himself, Hercules-like, to "dislocate and tear / [Goneril's] flesh and blood" [Q IV.ii.61–64]).

54. Compare S. L. Goldberg, *An Essay on* King Lear (Cambridge: Cambridge University Press, 1974), 85.

55. For the view that Seneca lays unusual emphasis on a general right to suicide, see J. M. Rist, *Stoic Philosophy* (Cambridge: Cambridge University Press, 1969), 246–49, and Miriam Griffin, "Philosophy, Cato and Roman Suicide: I and II," *Greece and Rome* 33 (1986): 64–77, 192–202.

56. *De Ira*, II.vii (p. 181), II.ix (p. 183).

57. Danby sees this moment as ironic ("*King Lear* and Christian Patience," 122).

58. For "Ripeness of all" as Christian, see J. V. Cunningham, *Woe or Wonder: The Emotional Effect of Shakespearean Tragedy* (Chicago: University of Chicago Press, 1960), 7–13; for the phrase as indistinguishable between Stoic and Christian contexts, see William Elton, King Lear *and the Gods* (San Marino, Calif.: Huntington Library, 1968), 101–7.

59. The "great rage" is "cured" in the Quarto (IV.vii.75–6); whereas it is "killed" in the Folio (IV.vi.72–3). In the Folio, the Doctor is replaced by a Gentleman.

60. For a fuller development of this argument, see Richard Strier, *Love Known: Theology and Experience in George Herbert's Poetry* (Chicago: University of Chicago Press, 1983), ch. 7.

61. Quotations from *The Works of George Herbert*, ed. F. E. Hutchinson (Oxford: Oxford University Press, 1945).

62. On the importance of Herbert's poetry to women, as both readers and writers, in the seventeenth century, see Helen Wilcox, "Entering The Temple: Women,

Reading, and Devotion in Seventeenth-century England," in *Religion, Literature, and Politics*, ed. Hamilton and Strier. An Collins, discussed in Wilcox, may have been an invalid. For Herbert's importance to a later female writer with health problems, see Simone Weil, *Waiting for God*, trans. Emma Crawford (New York: Harper and Row, 1951), 68–69.

63. For the "sea of brasse," see 1 Kings 7: 23.

64. See, inter alia, Jared Wicks, *Man Yearning for Grace: Luther's Early Spiritual Teaching* (Weisbaden: Steiner, 1969); Heiko Oberman, "*Simul Gemitus et Raptus*: Luther and Mysticism," in *The Reformation in Medieval Perspective*, ed. Steven E. Ozment (Chicago: Quadrangle Books, 1971); Thomas F. Torrance, *Calvin's Doctrine of Man* (London: Lutterwordk, 1952). For a nice passage on groaning in Calvin, see *Institutes* II.i.3.

65. See *Twelfth Night*, ed. J. M. Lothian and T. W. Craik (London: Routledge, 1975), II.iv.43–48.

Chapter 2. *"Commotion Strange"*: Passion in Paradise Lost

1. *The Riverside Milton*, ed. Roy Flannagan (Boston: Houghton Mifflin, 1998), 577. All citations of Milton's poetry are from this edition.

2. *The Riverside Shakespeare*, ed. G. Blakemore Evans et al. (Boston: Houghton Mifflin, 1974; rev. ed. 1997), 647, 465. All citations of Shakespeare's plays are from this edition.

3. Flannagan, *Riverside Milton*, 577 n. 158.

4. See, for example, Ian Maclean, *The Renaissance Notion of Woman* (New York: Cambridge University Press, 1980), and Gail Kern Paster, *The Body Embarrassed: Drama and the Disciplines of Shame in Early Modern Europe* (Ithaca, N.Y.: Cornell University Press, 1993). In a popular book on humoral physiology and psychology, Juan Huarte explains that even Eve "was by God created cold and moist: which temperature, is necessarie to make a woman fruitfull, and apt for childbirth, but enemy to knowledge: and if he had made her temperat like Adam, she should have been very wise, but nothing fruitful." Juan Huarte, *Examen de ingenios: The Examination of Men's Wits (1594)*, ed. Carmen Rogers (Gainesville, Fl.: Scholars' Facsimiles and Reprints, 1959), 274.

5. *Apology for Smectymnuus* in *Complete Prose Works of John Milton*, ed. Don M. Wolfe et al., 8 vols. (New Haven, Conn.: Yale University Press, 1953–82), 4.250.

6. *Complete Prose Works*, 4. 667–68.

7. Kevis Goodman, "'Wasted Labor'? Milton's Eve, the Poet's Work, and the Challenge of Sympathy," *ELH* 64 (1997): 435.

8. I explore this material more fully in *Bodies and Selves in Early Modern England: Physiology and Inwardness in Spenser, Shakespeare, Herbert, and Milton* (Cambridge: Cambridge University Press, 1999). In that book, I emphasize the ethical and political importance of self-regulatory mechanisms, while here I attempt to account for a more positive account of passion.

9. Thomas Wright, *The Passions of the Minde in Generall* (1604), ed. Thomas Sloan (Urbana: University of Illinois Press, 1971), 64.

10. Thomas Venner, *Via Recta ad Vitam Longam. Or, A Treatise Wherein the Right Way and Best Manner of Living for Attaining a Long and Healthfull Life, is Clearly Demonstrated* (London, 1650), 330.

11. Seneca, *Epistle* 116.1, quoted in Martha Nussbaum, *The Therapy of Desire: Theory and Practice in Hellenistic Ethics* (Princeton, N.J.: Princeton University Press, 1994), 389.

12. Cicero, *Tusculan Disputations*, IV, xxix, 62; quoted in Katharine Eisaman Maus, *Ben Jonson and the Roman Frame of Mind* (Princeton, N.J.: Princeton University Press, 1984), 98.

13. See Nussbaum, *Therapy of Desire*, 359–401, and Nussbaum, *Upheavals of Thought: The Intelligence of Emotions* (Cambridge: Cambridge University Press, 2001), 90. In the latter book Nussbaum demonstrates the centrality of emotion to classical ethics.

14. Edward Reynolds, *A Treatise of the Passions and Faculties of the Soule of Man* (London, 1640), 47–48.

15. Flanagan, *Riverside Milton*, 1010.

16. Reynolds, *A Treatise of the Passions*, 45–46.

17. Reynolds, *A Treatise of the Passions*, 59–60.

18. William Bouwsma, "The Two Faces of Humanism: Stoicism and Augustinianism in Renaissance Thought," in *A Usable Past: Essays in European Cultural History* (Berkeley: University of California Press, 1990), 19–73.

19. John Milton, *Paradise Lost*, ed. Alastair Fowler (London: Longman, 1971), 428.

20. *Basic Writings of Saint Thomas Aquinas*, ed. Anton C. Pegis, 2 vols. (New York: Random House, 1945), 1: 924–25.

21. *Basic Writings of Aquinas*, 1: 925.

22. *Treatise of the Passions*, 61–64.

23. William B. Hunter rightly suggests that "Milton conceived of this dream in terms of contemporary dream and demon lore." "Eve's Demonic Dream," in *The Descent of Urania: Studies in Milton, 1946–1988* (Lewisburg, Pa.: Bucknell University Press, 1989), 46.

24. Levinus Lemnius, *The Touchstone of Complexions*, trans. T. Newton (London, 1581), 20.

25. Lemnius, *Touchstone of Complexions*, 22.

26. Stuart Clark, *Thinking with Demons* (New York: Oxford University Press, 1997), 187.

27. Timothy Bright, *A Treatise of Melancholy* (1586), 154, quoted in J. B. Bamborough, *Little World of Man* (London: Longman, 1952), 128.

28. Lodowick Bryskett, *A Discourse of Civill Life* (1606), ed. Thomas E. Wright (Northridge, Calif.: San Fernando Valley State College, 1970), 176–77.

29. Mary Ann O'Farrell, *Telling Complexions: The Nineteenth-Century English Novel and the Blush* (Durham, N.C.: Duke University Press, 1997), 5.

30. I have explored the complex relationship of autonomy to obedience more closely in "Obedience and Autonomy in *Paradise Lost*," in *A Companion to Milton*, ed. Thomas Corns (Oxford: Blackwell, 2001), 363–79.

31. Reynolds, *A Treatise of the Passions*, 64.

32. It is appropriate that Milton synchronizes this internal change with God's

deliberate alteration of the earth's climate (10.651–718), since, as Mary Floyd-Wilson demonstrates, climate and psychology were imagined to be intimately connected; see "*Othello*, Passion, and Race," in *Writing Race Across the Atlantic World, 1492–1763* (New York: Palgrave, 2003).

33. Wright, *Passions of the Minde*, 334. On this congenitally inconstant self and the premium it places on the maintenance of order, see my *Bodies and Selves in Early Modern England*.

34. See Kester Svendsen, *Milton and Science* (Cambridge, Mass.: Harvard University Press, 1956), 194: "The palace revolution in which passion snatches the rule of man from reason is an image combining biological, civil, and moral order."

35. Goodman, "'Wasted Labor,'" 431. In "Gender and Conduct in *Paradise Lost*," in *Sexuality and Gender in Early Modern Europe: Institutions, Texts, Images*, ed. James G. Turner (Cambridge: Cambridge University Press, 1993), 310–38, I explore how Eve's various courtly declarations of submission function as performative gestures that advertise her social and spiritual initiative.

36. I discuss Milton's attitude to the Passion, and his incomplete poem on the subject, in "'That spectacle of too much weight': The Poetics of Sacrifice in Donne, Herbert, and Milton," *Journal of Medieval and Early Modern Studies* 31, 3 (2001): 561–84.

37. The stark illustration that prefaces this chapter, from Carlotta Petrina's illustrations to *Paradise Lost* (San Francisco: Limited Editions Club, 1936), locates this emotional state in the abject posture of the disconsolate Eve. For an acute discussion of this and other illustrations by Petrina, see Wendy Furman and Virginia James Tufte, "'Metaphysical Tears': Carlotta Petrina's Re-Presentation of *Paradise Lost*, Book IX," *Milton Studies* 36 (1998): 86–108. In "Repairing Androgyny: Eve's Tears in Paradise Lost," in *Speaking Grief in English Literary Culture: Shakespeare to Milton*, ed. Margo Swiss and David A. Kent (Pittsburgh: Duquesne University Press, 2002), 261–83, Margo Swiss insightfully examines the figure of the grieving Eve.

38. *Complete Prose Works*, 2.403; 1.817–18.

39. *Complete Prose Works*, 1.819.

Chapter 3. Poses and Passions: Mona Lisa's "Closely Folded" Hands

1. George Boas, "The Mona Lisa in the History of Taste," *Journal of the History of Ideas* 1 (1940): 207–24.

2. Giorgio Vasari, *Le Vite de piu eccelenti pittori scultori e architettori* (Novara: Instituto Geografico, 1967), 3: 403. For the identity of the sitter and biographical information see Frank Zoellner, "Leonardo's Portrait of Mona Lisa del Giocondo," *Gazette des Beaux-Arts* 21 (1993), esp. 115–23.

3. Boas, "The Mona Lisa," esp. 215ff.

4. Walter Pater, *The Renaissance* (New York: Modern Library, 1873, 1963), 102; Sigmund Freud, *A Study in Psychosexuality* (New York: Random House, 1947), 88ff. Kurt Eissler, *Psychoanalytic Notes on the Enigma* (New York: International Universities Press, 1961), 26.

5. Paul Barolsky, *Why Mona Lisa Smiles and Other Tales by Vasari* (University Park: Pennsylvania State University Press, 1991), 62–64. See also Mary Garrard,

"Leonardo da Vinci. Female Portraits, Female Nature," in *The Expanding Discourse,* ed. Norma Broude and Mary Garrrard (New York: HarperCollins, 1992), 61.

6. For an overview of humoral beliefs, Zirka Filipczak, *Hot Dry Men, Cold Wet Women: The Theory of Humors in Western European Art.* exhibition catalog (New York: American Federation of Arts, 1997), 14–23. For portraits of melancholics, see Roy Strong, "The Elizabethan Malady: Melancholy in Elizabethan and Jacobean Portraiture," *Apollo* 79 (April 1964): 264–69.

7. *The Literary Works of Leonardo da Vinci,* ed. Irma Richter (London: Oxford University Press, 1939), 1: 341 no. 584, 344 no. 593, 347 no. 600.

8. Jacopo Barbaro, "On Wifely Duties" (1415), trans. Benjamin G. Kohl in *The Earthly Republic: Italian Humanists on Government and Society,* ed. Kohl and Ronald G. Witt (Philadelphia: University of Pennsylvania Press, 1978), 189–228, 202.

9. Quoted in John Pope-Hennesy, *The Portrait in the Renaissance* (New York: Pantheon, 1996), 198.

10. The extensive literature includes Jan Bremmer and Herman Roodenburg, eds., *A Cultural History of Gesture* (Ithaca, N.Y.: Cornell University Press, 1992) with several essays on the early modern period; Ann Adams, "The Three-Quarter Length Life-Sized Portrait in Seventeenth-Century Holland: The Cultural Functions of Tranquilitas," in *Looking at Seventeenth-Century Dutch Art,* ed. Wayne Franits (Cambridge: Cambridge University Press, 1997), 158–74; Mosche Barasch, "Character and Physiognomy: Bocchi on Donatello's St. George a Renaissance Text on Expression in Art," *Journal of the History of Ideas* 36 (July–September 1975): 413–30, and *Gestures of Despair in Medieval and Early Renaissance Art* (New York: New York Univ. Press, 1976; Michael Baxandall, *Painting and Experience in Fifteenth Century Italy* (Oxford: Oxford University Press, 1972), 56–70; Anna Bryson, "The Rhetoric of Status: Gesture, Demeanor and the Image of the Gentleman in Sixteenth and Seventeenth Century England," in *Renaissance Bodies: The Human Figure in English Culture c.1540–1600,* ed. Lucy Gent and Nigel Llewellyn (Melksham, Wiltshire: Reaktion Books, 1990), 136–53; Peter Burke, "The Presentation of Self in the Renaissance Portrait," in *The Historical Anthropology of Early modern Italy* (Cambridge: Cambridge University Press, 1987), 150–67; Norbert Elias, *The History of Manners,* trans. Edmund Jephcott (New York: Pantheon, 1978); Herman Roodenburg, "How to Sit, Stand, and Walk" in *Looking at Seventeenth-Century Dutch Art,* 175–86, and his forthcoming, *The Eloquence of the Body: Studies on gesture in the Dutch Republic* (Zwolle: Wanders); Jean-Claude Schmitt, "The Ethics of Gesture," in *Fragments for a History of the Human Body,* vol. 2; 129–47; Patricia Simons, "Women in Frames," in *The Expanding Discourse,* 39–58; Georges Vigarello, "The Upward Training of the Body from the Age of Chivalry to Courtly Civility," in *Fragments for a History of the Human Body,* ed. Ramona Naddaff and Nadia Tazi (New York: Urzone, 1989), 149–99. Ruth Kelso, *Doctrine of the English Gentleman in the Sixteenth Century* (Urbana: University of Illinois Press, 1964) and *Doctrine for the Lady of the Renaissance* (Urbana: University of Illinois Press, 1978) provide a useful overview since the major manuals of civility published elsewhere also proved influential in England.

11. Lorne Campbell, *Renaissance Portraits* (New Haven, Conn.: Yale University Press, 1990), 86. For early modern attitudes about neck positions, see Roodenburg, "How to Sit," Vigarello, "The Upward Training," 115 ff.

12. According to Gerard de Lairesse, for example, a painter should always portray his figures in accordance with their status, office, and dignity, and he can express such differences by their "posture, nature, color, and movement." Quoted in Roodenburg, "How to Sit," 181.

13. Baldassare Castiglione, *The Book of the Courtier* (Harmondsworth, Middlesex: Penguin, 1976), 211.

14. [M. Steeven Guazzo], *The Civile Conversation of M. Steeven Guazzo*, trans. George Pettie (1581) and Bartholemew Young (1586), ed. Edward Sullivan(London: Constable, 1925), 80.

15. The statement from *Décor puellarum* was quoted in a different context by Baxandall Baxandall, *Painting and Experience in Fifteenth Century Italy*, 70, and applied to Mona Lisa by Roy McMullen, *Mona Lisa. The Picture and the Myth* (Boston: Houghton Mifflin, 1975), 42 and Zoellner, "Leonardo's Portrait," 126.

16. Herman T. Colenbrander, "Hands in Leonardo Portraiture," *Achademia Leonardo Vinci* 5 (1992): 37–43 does not discuss their social connotations.

17. *Literary Works*, 1: 341, no. 583.

18. Juan Luis Vives, *"The Instruction of a Christian Woman": A Critical Edition of the Tudor Translation* (1523), ed. Ruth Kuschmierz (Ph.D. dissertation, University of Pittsburgh, 1961), Book I, chapter 11, 15–16.

19. Anonymous, *Haec Vir; or The Womanish Man* (London, 1620), pages unnumbered (p. 9 of text). For reprint and commentary see Katerine Usher Henderson and Barbara McManus, *Half Humankind* (Urbana: University of Illinois Press, 1985, 284 n. 25.

20. Leonardo showed women with the legs apart in narrative scenes, especially situations that referred to childbearing, such as *St. Anne, Virgin, and Child* (Paris, Louvre).

21. Carel van Mander, *Den grondt der edel vry schilder-const*, ed. Hessel Miedema (Utrecht: Haentjens Decker and Gumbert, 1973), 118.

22. Kenneth Keele, "The Genesis of the Mona Lisa," *Journal of the History of Medicine and Allied Sciences* 14 (1959): 135–39. For interpretations of landscape in relation to the figure, Martin Kemp, *Leonardo da Vinci: The Marvellous Works of Nature and Man* (London: Dent, 1981), 261–65, 275–77 and Garrard, "Leonardo da Vinci," 67–69.

23. Zoelner, "Leonardo's Portrait," 123.

24. Quoted in Simons, "Women in Frames," 44 n. 40. For the history of beliefs about the uterus, Laurinda Dixon, *Perilous Chastity: Women and Illness in Pre-Enlightenment Art and Medicine* (Ithaca, N.Y.: Cornell University Press).

25. Thanks to Charles Palermo for this observation.

26. Stefanie Solum noted the novelty of its inclusion.

27. Also noted by James Clifton, "Gender and Shame in Masaccio's Expulsion from the Garden of Eden," *Art History* 22 (December 1999): 140.

28. Werner L. Gundersheimer, "Renaissance Concepts of Shame and Pocaterra's Dialoghi Della Vergona," *Renaissance Quarterly* 47 (Spring 1994): 48, 53.

29. Vives, "Instruction," 185. Also, for example, "Nature hath ordained in all good and virtuous women this affection of shamefastness, which serveth as a restraint." Barnaby Rich, *The excellencie of good women* (1613), 22 quoted in Kelso, *Lady of the Renaissance*, 43.

30. Gundersheimer, "Renaissance Concepts of Shame," 51, quoting Pocaterra, *Dialoghi*,155.

31. Gundersheimer, "Renaissance Concepts of Shame," 40; James Cleland, *Hero-Paideia: Or the Institution of the Young Nobleman* (Oxford, 1607), 65, reprinted in *Institution of a Young Noble Man*, ed. Max Molyneux (New York: Scholars' Facsimiles and Reprints, 1948).

32. Cited in Kelso, *Lady of the Renaissance*,101.

33. Castiglione, *Book of the Courtier*, 214; Kelso, *Lady of the Renaissance*, 50–51, 100–101.

34. *Literary Works*, 1: 345, no. 594. For "disputation," see John Bulwer, *Chirologia and Chironomia* (1644), ed. James Cleary (Carbondale: Southern Illinois University Press, 1974), 201, Canon XI. About copies, see *Dynasties: Painting in Tudor and Jacobean England 1530–1630*, exhibition catalog (London: Tate Gallery, 1995), 128–29.

35. Campbell, "Renaissance Portraits," 141.

36. Burke, "Presentation of Self," 157–58. For other examples, see Campbell, "Renaissance Portraits," 98–99.

37. Lionardo Bruni, *De studies et litteris*, trans. Williams Harrison Woodward in *Vittorino de Feltre and Other Humanist Educators* (Cambridge: Cambridge University Press, 1897), 124.

38. Garrard, "Leonardo da Vinci," 64–65.

39. Quoted in Campbell, *Renaissance Portraits*, 220. Mary Rogers, "Sonnets on female portraits from Renaissance North Italy," *Word and Image* 2 (October–December 1986): 291–305.

40. The planet dominant at birth added its humoral influence to that existing since conception. For the thesis that Leonardo pictured all women with "phlegmatic features," see Gloria Vallese, "Leonardo's Malinchonia," *Achademia Leonardo Vinci* 5 (1992): 49.

41. Elias, *History of Manners*, 76. A woman should not "walk lustilye like a man" but should have "a slowe and mincing pace, like a woman" wrote Guazzo, *Civile conversation*, 80. See also Richard Brathwaite, *The English Gentlewoman* (London: Alsop and Fawsett, 1631), 82–93. By making motion easy or cumbersome, fashionable clothing promoted the difference in stride that the decorum of gender specified. For classical precedents, Jan Bremmer, "Walking, Standing, and Sitting in Ancient Greek Culture," in *A Cultural History of Gesture*, 20–21.

42. Michael Kwakkelstein, *Leonardo da Vinci as a Physiognomist: Theory and Drawing Practice* (Leiden: Primavera Press, 1994), 31–32.

43. Joaneath Spicer, "The Renaissance Elbow," in *A Cultural History of Gesture*, ed. Jan Bremmer and Herman Roodenburg (Ithaca, N.Y.: Cornell University Press, 1992), 84–128.

44. For an example of a woman pictured as a virago, see George de la Tour, *The Old Woman* (De Young Memorial Museum, San Francisco). For one referring to a male profession or activity, see Judith Leyster, *Self-Portrait* (National Gallery, Washington, c.1635).

45. E.g., Jan Vermeer, *Lady Writing a Letter with her Maid* (Beit Coll. Blessington, Ireland); Frans Francken, *Seven Works of Mercy* (Hermitage, Leningrad). With a servant or a peasant, the folded hands suggested a moment of waiting or rest.

46. Thanks to E. J. Johnson for this interpretation.

47. Bulwer, *Chirologia*, 99, diagram K, identified intertwined fingers as "tristi animi signo."

48. Betty Bauml and Franz Bauml, *Dictionary of Worldwide Gestures* (Lanham, Md.: Scarecrow Press, 1997), 270; Moshe Barasch, *Giotto and the Language of Gesture* (Cambridge: Cambridge University Press, 1987), 91–95; Francois Garnier, *Le Langage de l'image au Moyen Age* (Paris, Léopard d'Or, 1982), 1: 198. Renaissance examples include Donatello, *Tomb of John XXIII* (Battisterio, Florence, ca. 1425); Fra Angelico, *Betrayal of Christ* (silver chest door, San Marco Museum, ca. 1455–61, catalog p. 59). Holding someone else by the wrist meant to "impede," according to Bulwer, 177, *Chirologia*, figure H.

49. Crossing hands in male portraits for religious reasons might constitute an exception. Since Christ's hands were pictured as similarly crossed during his mocking, taking this pose could be another way of applying the doctrine of *Imitatio Christi* then popular in Germany and the Netherlands. The most highly influential male portrait with crossed hands was Albrecht Dürer's *Elector of Saxony, Frederick the Wise* (Gemaeldegalerie, Berlin, 1496), who wished to present himself as God's chosen leader (I thank the historian Peter Starenko for that information). For *Imitatio Christi*, see Erwin Panofsky, *The Life and Art of Albrecht Dürer* (Princeton, N.J.: Princeton University Press, 1971), 39 and Joseph Koerner, *The Moment of Self-Portraiture* (Chicago: University of Chicago Press, 1993), 76.

50. Willem Goeree, *Schilderkonst, verligterie, teykenkonst* (Amsterdam: Goeree, 1682), 297–98, 309 quoted in Roodenburg, "How to Sit," 179; Richard Weste, "Booke of Demeanor with the Allowance and Disallowance of certain Misdeameanors in Companie" (1619), reprinted in Frederick Furnivall, *Early English Meals and Manners* (London: Treubner, 1969), 213: "To hang the head on any side, / doth shew hypocrasie."

51. Neroccio de'Landi, *Lady* (National Gallery, Washington, ca. 1490) exceptionally portrays an unidentified woman with a tilted neck.

52. Leonardo did not mention eyes in his guidelines for depicting women as modest, but others repeatedly urged women to keep their eyes lowered. In portraiture lowered eyes never became standard practice because that would have lessened recognizability. Also, other means existed to suggest modesty.

53. Zoellner, "Leonardo's Portrait," 123.

Chapter 4. Compassion in the Public Sphere of Milton and King Charles

I would like to thank Mary Floyd-Wilson, Gail Kern Paster, Katherine Rowe, and Heather Ruland Staines for their helpful comments on earlier drafts of this essay.

1. Marshall also engraved the portrait of Milton that served as the frontispiece to his *Poems* of 1645. Milton hated the likeness, which undoubtedly fed into his animus towards *Eikon Basilike*. Yet, as Elizabeth Skerpan-Wheeler shows, Milton largely ignores the engraving and concentrates on the written text of the book, failing to realize that the entire, integrated text (word and image together) generates the book's powerful effect. "Authorship and Authority: John Milton, William Marshall, and the Two Frontispieces of *Poems* 1645," *Milton Quarterly* 33 (1999): 105–14.

2. *Eikon Basilike: The Povrtraictvre of His Sacred Maiestie in His Solitvdes and Svfferings*, 1st ed., 2nd issue (London, 1648/49), 67.

3. *Eikon Basilike*, 36.

4. John Milton, *Eikonoklastes*, in *Complete Prose Works*, 8 vols. (New Haven, Conn.: Yale University Press, 1953–82), 3.452.

5. Milton, *Eikonoklastes*, 3.576.

6. Jürgen Habermas, *The Structural Transformation of the Public Sphere: An Inquiry into a Category of Bourgeois Society*, trans. Thomas Burger with Frederick Lawrence (Cambridge, Mass.: MIT Press, 1989), 99, 97. See also Habermas's essay "The Public Sphere," trans. Shierry Weber Nicholsen, in *Jürgen Habermas on Society and Politics*, ed. Steven Seidman (Boston: Beacon Press, 1989), 231–36.

7. Habermas, *Structural Transformation*, 27. Although not translated into English until 1989, this work (his doctoral dissertation) appeared in German in 1962 and represents an early stage in his career. For a useful introduction to the work and its reception, see Craig Calhoun, "Introduction: Habermas and the Public Sphere," in *Habermas and the Public Sphere*, ed. Calhoun (Cambridge: MIT Press, 1992), 1–48.

8. Habermas, *The Theory of Communicative Action*, 2 vols., trans. Thomas McCarthy (Boston: Beacon Press, 1984), 1.285–86.

9. Habermas, "An Alternative Way out of the Philosophy of the Subject: Communicative versus Subject-Centered Reason," in *The Philosophical Discourse of Modernity: Twelve Lectures*, trans. Frederick Lawrence (Cambridge: MIT Press, 1987), 295–96, 315.

10. Habermas, "Alternative Way," 317.

11. Habermas, "Alternative Way," 325–26.

12. Victoria Kahn, *Machiavellian Rhetoric: From the Counter-Reformation to Milton* (Princeton, N.J.: Princeton University Press, 1994), 241.

13. Because of the limitations of space, this essay will concentrate on the ethical and political implications of rhetorical theory and practice but largely leave aside the issue of imitation in early modern rhetoric and poetics. Nonetheless, it is important to acknowledge that underlying many of the debates about the role of the passions in political rhetoric is the problematic nature of imitation and the image in a reformed Christian culture. The image or icon produces a passionate response, without which there can be no rhetoric or poetry, yet fears about the seductive nature of imitative fiction haunt all Protestant writing. Most pertinently, the cultural anxiety over imitation and its effects generates some of the most inflammatory passages in *Eikonoklastes*' attack upon the royal image.

14. Kahn, though, makes a strong case for such a reading of Aristotle, Renaissance humanism, and Habermas in "Habermas, Machiavelli, and the Humanist Critique of Ideology," *PMLA* 105 (1990): 464–76.

15. Norbrook, "*Areopagitica*, Censorship, and the Early Modern Public Sphere," in *The Administration of Aesthetics: Censorship, Political Criticism, and the Public Sphere*, ed. Richard Burt (Minneapolis: University of Minnesota Press, 1994), 8. I would add, we need a history of the citizen as well as of the *subject*. For Habermas's critique of the history of the subject, see his essays in *The Philosophical Discourse of Modernity*.

16. On Wright's life as a context for his treatise, see Thomas O. Sloan, "A

Renaissance Controversialist on Rhetoric: Thomas Wright's *Passions of the Minde in Generall*," *Speech Monographs* 36 (1969): 38–54; Sloan, Introduction to *The Passions of the Minde in Generall*, (Urbana: University of Illinois Press, 1971) xi–xlix; William Webster Newbold, Introduction to *The Passions of the Mind in General* (New York: Garland, 1986), 3–16.

17. On English Catholic attempts to gain toleration under Elizabeth and James despite the opposition of Rome and the Jesuits, see Peter Holmes, *Resistance and Compromise: The Political Thought of Elizabethan Catholics* (Cambridge: Cambridge University Press, 1982), especially 90–98, 186–223.

18. Thomas Wright, *The Passions of the Minde in Generall* (London, 1630), I.i.3–4. I am quoting from the reprint edition edited by Thomas O. Sloan. He reproduces the 1630 text, which is a corrected version of the second edition of 1604.

19. This notion of persuasive moving is derived from Cicero's *movere*; see Debra K. Shuger, *Sacred Rhetoric: The Christian Grand Style in the English Renaissance* (Princeton, N.J.: Princeton University Press, 1988), 120.

20. Wright, *Passions*, I.i.4.

21. Wright, *Passions*, I.ii.8.

22. Wright, *Passions*, I.iv.15.

23. Sloan, *Passions*, Introduction, xxii.

24. See Caroline M. Hibbard, *Charles I and the Popish Plot* (Chapel Hill: University of North Carolina Press, 1983).

25. Habermas, *Structural Transformation*, 89–102, quotation 91.

26. Kahn gives a subtle account of the attempts by Civil War writers, both royalist and republican, to come to terms with religious conscience by distinguishing between persuasion and coercion. Hobbes, she argues, makes religious conscience legitimately subject only to persuasion, but makes all public actions subject to the state's legitimate powers of coercion. Kahn, *Machiavellian Rhetoric*, 144–65.

27. Habermas's initial formulation of his theory tends to follow a Marxist economic determinism, leaving relatively little room for the influence of religion or other cultural factors. David Zaret gives a critique of such blind spots in his "Religion, Science, and Printing in the Public Spheres in Seventeenth-Century England," in *Habermas and the Public Sphere*, 212–35; and, more generally, his *Origins of Democratic Culture: Printing, Petitions, and the Public Sphere in Early-Modern England* (Princeton, N.J.: Princeton University Press, 2000), especially 3–43; see also Norbrook, "*Areopagitica*," 3–33.

28. On print technology and the public sphere in the sixteenth century, see Alexandra Halasz, *The Marketplace of Print: Pamphlets and the Public Sphere in Early Modern England* (Cambridge: Cambridge University Press, 1997). On the origins of the eighteenth-century public sphere in the conflicts between crown and parliament under the early Stuarts, see Zaret, *Origins of Democratic Culture*.

29. Habermas, *Structural Transformation*, 32, and, generally, 27–67.

30. Habermas, "The Public Sphere," 231.

31. On the reach of Reformation printed texts to all strata of society, see Tessa Watt, *Cheap Print and Popular Piety, 1550–1640* (Cambridge: Cambridge University Press, 1991). In addition, see the work of Christopher Hill, especially *The World Turned Upside Down: Radical Ideas During the English Revolution* (1972; reprint

London: Penguin, 1991), and David Underdown, *Revel, Riot, and Rebellion: Popular Politics and Culture in England 1603–1660* (Oxford: Oxford University Press, 1985).

32. The thrust of revisionist scholarship has been to deny long-term causes to the English Civil War and the development of democratic institutions in England. Although the questioning of teleological Whiggery and reductive Marxism was needed, it is not possible to deny the existence of ideological conflict in a society divided along religious and other lines. For useful correctives to revisionism, see the essays in Richard Cust and Ann Hughes, eds., *Conflict in Early Stuart England: Studies Religion and Politics 1603–1642* (London: Longman, 1989); and in Kevin Sharpe and Peter Lake, eds., *Culture and Politics in Early Stuart England* (Stanford, Calif.: Stanford University Press, 1993); and, most recently, Zaret's argument in *Origins of Democratic Culture*. Unlike Zaret, however, who places the origins of a public sphere largely in the publication of Parliamentary debate during the early stages of the Civil War, I would chart out the earliest origins of the modern public sphere in the print of Renaissance humanism and the sixteenth-century Reformation.

33. For useful accounts, see Victoria Kahn, *Rhetoric, Prudence, and Skepticism in the Renaissance* (Ithaca, N.Y.: Cornell University Press, 1985); Kahn, "Humanism and the Resistance to Theory," in *Literary Theory/Renaissance Texts*, ed. Patricia Parker and David Quint (Baltimore: Johns Hopkins University Press, 1986), 373–96; Kahn, "Habermas, Machiavelli"; Kahn, *Machiavellian Rhetoric*; Norbrook, "Areopagitica," especially 8–11. These works are all indebted to J. G. A. Pocock, *The Machiavellian Moment: Florentine Political Thought and the Atlantic Republican Tradition* (Princeton, N.J.: Princeton University Press, 1975).

34. Quoted in Lawrence Green, "Aristotle's *Rhetoric* and Renaissance Views of the Emotions," in *Renaissance Rhetoric*, ed. Peter Mack (New York: St. Martin's, 1994), 6.

35. This assessment has been confirmed by recent studies of *The Rhetoric*. Aristotle's theory of rhetoric, they have shown, does not aim to teach the reader how to become an effective or persuasive public speaker, but by instead focusing on deliberation or prudence, it reveals the role that the practical art of persuasion plays in the civic life of the polis. As Eugene Garver argues, "Aristotle's originality in the *Rhetoric* extends to making deliberation the center, and therefore to the idea of rhetoric as *civic* activity." *Aristotle's "Rhetoric": An Art of Character* (Chicago: University of Chicago Press, 1994), 45–46. Garver's powerful reinterpretation of the *Rhetoric* argues that Aristotle addresses not the professional orator, who only wants to know how to persuade effectively, but the citizen or legislator, who wants to understand rhetoric's role in the civic polity. His approach to the *Rhetoric* shares many of the principles of Kahn's *Rhetoric, Prudence, and Skepticism*. See also George A. Kennedy's recent translation and commentary, *Aristotle "On Rhetoric": A Theory of Civic Discourse* (Oxford: Oxford University Press, 1991). Quotations will be from that translation.

36. Aristotle himself opens his *Rhetoric* by expressing his objections to teachers who treat rhetoric as mere emotional manipulation (I.i.3–6 1354a). Yet, once he has divided persuasion into three parts—*logos* or the argument behind the speech, *ethos* or the character of the speaker expressed in the speech, and *pathos* or the emotions moved in the audience of the speech (I.ii.1–7 1355b–56a)—he devotes much of the remainder of his treatise to describing the various passions and how they are moved.

37. Renaissance humanists turned to the *Rhetoric* for its investigations into the psychology of an audience's emotions (Green, "Aristotle's *Rhetoric*," 1–26), and some early modern writers on the passions even treat the book as a handbook on the emotions. For example, Edward Reynolds' *Treatise of the Passions* omits a full discussion of the various forms of grief such as sympathy and mercy by simply telling readers to turn to Aristotle's *Rhetoric*—and not to his *Ethics* or *De Anima*: *A Treatise of the Passions and Faculties Of the Soul of Man* (London, 1650), 232–33.

38. See Alexander Nehemas, "Pity and Fear in the *Rhetoric* and the *Poetics*," in *Aristotle's "Rhetoric": Philosophical Essays*, ed. David J. Furley and Alexander Nehemas (Princeton, N.J.: Princeton University Press, 1994), 257–82. For some Renaissance treatments, see Green, "Aristotle's *Rhetoric*."

39. Nehemas, "Pity and Fear," 264–67.

40. There are, of course, important differences between Aristotle's ethics and the Christian moralism of Wright and Senault, but the early modern writers would have understood their projects as being essentially the same. In fact, some Calvinist writers, like David Papillon, were disturbed by the omission of God's predestined grace from such Aristotelian notions of character and ethics (see n. 69). For a useful discussion of Aristotelian *ethos* and ethics, see Francis Sparshott, *Taking Life Seriously: A Study of the Argument of the "Nicomachean Ethics"* (Toronto: University of Toronto Press, 1994). Kathy Eden's work follows such issues through rhetoric and poetics: *Poetic and Legal Fiction in the Aristotelian Tradition* (Princeton, N.J.: Princeton University Press, 1986); *Hermeneutics and the Rhetorical Tradition: Chapters in the Ancient Legacy and Its Humanist Reception* (New Haven, Conn.: Yale University Press, 1997).

41. Susan James, *Passion and Action: The Emotions in Seventeenth-Century Philosophy* (Oxford: Clarendon Press, 1997).

42. James, *Passion and Action*, 208–52; Shuger, *Sacred Rhetoric*, 118–53.

43. Aristotle, *Rhetoric*, II.viii.2 1385b.

44. Aristotle, *Rhetoric*, II.viii.14 1386a.

45. Caussin, *The Holy Court in Five Tomes* (London, 1650), I.iii.83.

46. Aristotle, *Rhetoric*, II.viii.13 1386a.

47. My understanding of the ethical and moral debates over mercy and pity are indebted to conversations with Shawn Smith.

48. Seneca, *De clementia*, II.v.1. On the contrast between *clementia* and *misericordia*, see also II.iii–vi. I am following the Loeb text, but altering the translations freely.

49. Seneca, *De clementia*, I.ii.3.

50. Calvin is quoting Pliny the Younger. *Calvin's Commentary on Seneca's "De clementia,"* ed. Ford Lewis Battles and André Malan Hugo (Leiden: E.J. Brill, 1969), 360, note to *De clementia*, II.iv.4, my translation. This commentary was Calvin's first printed work, which suggests the importance of the problem of compassion to Christian ethics.

51. Nicolas Coeffeteau, *A Table of the Humane Passions* (London, 1621), 356–57.

52. J.-F. Senault, *The Use of Passions*, trans. Henry Carey Earl of Monmouth (London, 1649), 508. Augustine is the ultimate source of most early modern Christian attacks upon the Stoic conception of the passions. See, for example, *City of God*, IX.4–5; XIV.2, 8–10.

53. Wright, *Passions*, I.iv.17.

54. Coeffeteau, *Table*, 374.

55. Senault, *Use of Passions*, 508.

56. *Cour Sainte* was a very popular work, appearing in numerous, ever-expanding editions from the 1620s through the 1660s. Its lives of biblical, historical, and contemporary figures served as source material for several French dramas of the period. For a brief life of Caussin, see George Drew Hocking, *A Study of the "Tragoediae Sacrae" of Father Caussin (1583–1651)*, Johns Hopkins Studies in Romance Literatures and Languages, vol. 44 (Baltimore: Johns Hopkins University Press, 1943), 9–19.

57. I am quoting from the first complete English translation, *The Holy Court in Five Tomes* I.i.1.

58. Caussin, *Holy Court*, I.iii.90; IV.98.

59. John Young first identified for me the source of Caussin's image. I am quoting from the following editions: *Biblia Sacra* (Paris, 1642), *The Bible* (Geneva, 1560), *The Holy Bible Translated from the Latin Vulgate[Douay-Rheims]* (Baltimore: John Murray, 1914). Tyndale's 1534 New Testament is the original source for all of these phrases from the Geneva Bible. See *Tyndale's New Testament*, ed. David Daniell (New Haven, Conn.: Yale University Press, 1989). The Authorized, King James Version does restore the visceral imagery to the last three examples, though it stops short of actually imagining a God with bowels as the Vulgate does in Luke 1:78. In the passage from the first letter of John, "bowels *of compassion*" refers not to God or Christ but to a human being (I John 3:17; italics added in the original to note the interpolated phrase). Likewise, the two from Paul's letter to the Philippians do not directly speak of God's bowels of compassion but of Paul finding refuge and love in the "bowels and mercies" of Christ (Phil. 2:1). *The Holy Bible: Authorized King James Version* (New York: Meridan-Penguin, 1974).

60. David Hillman, "Visceral Knowledge: Shakespeare, Skepticism, and the Interior of the Early Modern Body," in *The Body in Parts: Fantasies of Corporeality in Early Modern Europe*, ed. Hillman and Carla Mazzio (New York: Routledge, 1997), 80–105.

61. Hillman, "Visceral Knowledge," 85.

62. Hillman, "Visceral Knowledge," 85–86. Hillman does acknowledge this problem in a footnote (101–2 n. 33), but the changing nature of communion is much more central to the changing nature of compassion than he admits.

63. For example, see the Catholic bishops' interrogation of Anne Askew and her final confession that the mass is "the most abhomynable ydoll that is in the worlde. For my God wyll not be eaten with tethe, neyther yet dyeth he agayne." *The Examinations of Anne Askew*, ed. Elaine V. Beilin (New York: Oxford University Press, 1996), 144.

64. On Monmouth's career and political allegiance, see *DNB*. The publisher of the Senault translation was Humphrey Moseley, known not only for his edition of Milton's *Poems* (1645)—published with Marshall's engraving of the poet—but for a wide range of cavalier poetry and royalist texts such as William Sanderson's *A Compleat History of the Life and Raigne of King Charles from His Cradle to his Grave* (London, 1658).

65. Senault, *Use of Passions*, sigs. b5r–v.

66. Senault, *Use of Passions*, sig. A2v.

67. Wright, *Passions*, II.iv.69.

68. Senault, *Use of Passions*, sig. A3v.

69. Senault, *Use of Passions*, 2. Indeed, some of Monmouth's readers wanted to circumscribe reason's place even further than Senault wishes. For instance, when David Papillon sets out to publish a version of Senault aimed at a more popular audience, he acknowledges Monmouth's translation but asserts that his version will correct the original book's account of reason and grace. Papillon recognizes that Senault's praise of reason contains an implicit Catholic defense of free will against predestination. He counters that salvation, and hence all virtuous action, comes only through the "Free-grace of God, and that the Principles of true Christianity have more power to make men obtain the mastery over their passions then the Principles of Morality can have." *The Vanity of the Lives and Passions of Men* (London, 1651), sig. A3v. In other words, ethics will get you nowhere without grace. See also Shuger, *Sacred Rhetoric*, 133–35.

70. Senault, *Use of Passions*, 4.

71. Senault, *Use of Passions*, 8.

72. Senault, *Use of Passions*, 510.

73. Francis F. Madan, *A New Bibliography of the Eikon Basilike* (Oxford: Oxford University Press, 1950).

74. On the authorship question, see Madan, *New Bibliography*, 126–63.

75. *Eikon Basilike*, 24–25.

76. See the essays in the recent volume, *The Royal Image: Representations of Charles I*, ed. Thomas N. Corns (Cambridge: Cambridge University Press, 1999), especially Elizabeth Skerpan Wheeler, "*Eikon Basilike* and the Rhetoric of Self-Representation," 122–40.

77. *Eikon Basilike*, 227.

78. *Eikon Basilike*, 55.

79. *Eikon Basilike*, 67.

80. Roy Strong, *Van Dyck: Charles I on Horseback* (New York: Viking, 1972), 29–31.

81. *Eikon Basilike*, 231.

82. On the publication of *Eikonoklastes*, see the introduction in *Complete Prose Works*, 3.147–67. Once largely ignored as a sub-literary work, *Eikonoklastes* has received attention recently as a formative moment in Milton's intellectual development. David Loewenstein, *Milton and the Drama of History: Historical Vision, Iconoclasm, and the Literary Imagination* (Cambridge: Cambridge University Press, 1990), 51–73, emphasizes the tract's anti-theatricality, while Stephen Zwicker, *Lines of Authority: Politics and English Literary Culture, 1649–1689* (Ithaca, N.Y.: Cornell University Press, 1993), 39–59, emphasizes its anti-poetic argument. Sharon Achinstein, "Milton and King Charles," in *Royal Image*, 141–61, gives a thorough account of *Eikonoklastes'* anti-Catholic politics.

83. Milton, *Eikonoklastes*, 3.342.

84. Milton, *Eikonoklastes*, 3.601.

85. *Eikon Basilike*, 34, 39.

86. Kevin Sharpe reads Charles's claim to have an authoritative conscience that speaks for the entire nation within the context of other Tudor and Stuart royal writings that created a royal discourse of authority. "The King's Writ: Royal Authors and Royal Authority in Early Modern England," in *Culture and Politics*, 117–38.

87. *Eikon Basilike*, 65.

88. Milton, *Eikonoklastes*, 3.447.

89. Habermas, *Structural Transformation*, 89–102.

90. Sharon Achinstein gives a strong reading of some of the logical problems Milton encounters when he distinguishes between true and false conscience in "Milton Catches the Conscience of the King: *Eikonoklastes* and the Engagement Controversy," *Milton Studies* 29 (1992): 143–63.

91. Milton, *Eikonoklastes*, 3.601.

92. Milton, *Eikonoklastes*, 3.601.

93. Wright, *Passions*, III.iv.98.

94. Wright, *Passions*, III.iv.99.

95. Wright, *Passions*, III.iv.99.

96. Wright, *Passions*, IV.i.105.

97. Milton, *Eikonoklastes*, 3.342.

98. Kahn compares Machiavelli and Habermas on this issue, "the attempt to formulate a nontranscendental notion of practical reason that will permit both a rational critique of ideology and the practical arbitration of conflicting but equally valid demands." "Habermas, Machiavelli," 472.

99. The precise status and amount of free debate that Milton allows for in *Areopagitica* is one of the most enduring debates in Milton studies. Those who argue against a liberal reading of Milton include Stanley Fish, "Driving from the Letter: Truth and Indeterminacy in Milton's *Areopagitica*," in *Re-membering Milton: Essays on the Texts and Traditions*, ed. Mary Nyquist and Margaret W. Ferguson (New York: Methuen, 1987), 234–54; and John Illo, "*Areopagiticas* Mythic and Real," *Prose Studies* 11 (1988): 3–23. The best defense of the liberal *Areopagitica* is Michael Wilding, "Milton's *Areopagitica*: Liberty for the Sects," *Prose Studies* 9 (1986): 7–38. For readings in the light of Habermas's theory, see Norbrook, "*Areopagitica*"; Donald Guss, "Enlightenment as Process: Milton and Habermas," *PMLA* 106 (1991): 1156–69.

100. Milton, *Areopagitica*, in *Complete Prose Works*, 2.565

101. See Norbrook, "*Areopagitica*," 23–24. On Milton's ambivalent attitudes towards rhetoric in *Eikonoklastes*, see my "Charles's Grandmother, Milton's Spenser, and the Rhetoric of Revolution," *Milton Studies* 41 (2002): 139–71.

102. Habermas, *Structural Transformation*, 57–67. For a useful account of capitalism and the passions, see Albert O. Hirschman, *The Passions and the Interests: Arguments for Capitalism Before Its Triumph* (Princeton, N.J.: Princeton University Press, 1977).

103. Milton, *Samson Agonistes*, 270–71, in *Complete Poems and Major Prose*, ed. Merritt Y. Hughes (New York: Macmillan, 1957).

104. Milton, *Paradise Lost*, 12.648, in *Complete Poems and Major Prose*.

Chapter 5. Melancholy Cats, Lugged Bears, and Early Modern Cosmology: Reading Shakespeare's Psychological Materialism Across the Species Barrier

1. Here and throughout I follow the *Riverside Shakespeare*, ed. G. Blakemore Evans, 2nd ed. (Boston: Houghton Mifflin, 1997).

2. I have been influenced in my thinking about Hal and Falstaff's speech acts by Harry Berger, Jr., "The Prince's Dog: Falstaff and the Perils of Speech-Prefixity," *Shakespeare Quarterly* 49 (1998): 40–73.

3. For an introduction to the early modern schema of human life, see Nancy G. Siraisi, *Medieval and Early Renaissance Medicine: An Introduction to Knowledge and Practice* (Chicago: University of Chicago Press, 1990), 97–114.

4. On the proverbial melancholy of cats (Tilley C 129), see the entry for melancholy in the *Oxford Dictionary of English Proverbs*, ed. F. P. Wilson, 3rd ed. (Oxford: Clarendon Press, 1970), 524. The gib cat was not necessarily castrated, Herbert and Judith Weil point out in the New Cambridge *1 Henry IV* (Cambridge: Cambridge University Press, 1997), note to 1.2.58. The "hare is melancholy meat" (*ODEP*, 354). The association of hares and old, or more precisely dead lions was also proverbial, says the *ODEP*: "Hares may pull dead lions by the beard."

5. On the baiting of animals, see Stephen Dickey, "Shakespeare's Mastiff Comedy," *Shakespeare Quarterly* 42 (1991): 255–75, esp. 264–65 and Erica Fudge, *Perceiving Animals: Humans and Beasts in Early Modern English Culture* (New York: St. Martin's, 2000), 13–18. See also Keith Thomas's magisterial study, *Man and the Natural World: A History of the Modern Sensibility* (New York: Pantheon, 1983), esp. 114.

6. In addition to the Weils' edition, see David Bevington's edition of *Henry IV, Part I* for the Oxford Shakespeare (Oxford: Clarendon Press, 1987), notes to 1.2.69–78.

7. On the use of dung as rhetorical endpoint, see my *The Body Embarrassed: Drama and the Disciplines of Shame in Early Modern England* (Ithaca, N.Y.: Cornell University Press, 1993), 147–49. Editors seem to think the line means "the melancholy [people] of Moor-ditch," that is, that the Prince names Moorditch here because lepers and mad folk (both of whom were associated with melancholy) were allowed to beg there; see, for example, Bevington, *Henry IV, Part I*, note to 1.2.74.

8. Katharine Park, "The Organic Soul," in *The Cambridge History of Renaissance Philosophy*, ed. Charles B. Schmitt, Quentin Skinner, and Eckhard Kessler (Cambridge: Cambridge University Press, 1988), 469.

9. On Aristotle's distinction between blooded and non-blooded creatures, see G. E. R. Lloyd, *Science, Folklore and Ideology: Studies in the Life Sciences in Ancient Greece* (Cambridge: Cambridge University Press, 1983), 32–33.

10. On Aristotle's definition of the soul, see Katharine Park, "The Concept of Psychology," in *The Cambridge History of Renaissance Philosophy*, 455. On the faculties of the soul, see Park, "The Organic Soul," 464–84; a helpful diagram appears on 466.

11. *The Passions of the Mind in General* (I.2) (Urbana: University of Illinois Press, 1986), 9. For a general introduction to the early modern view of the passions, see Susan James, *Passion and Action: The Emotions in Seventeenth-Century Philosophy* (Cambridge: Cambridge University Press, 1997), 1–16.

12. Michael C. Schoenfeldt, *Bodies and Selves in Early Modern England: Physiology and Inwardness in Spenser, Shakespeare, Herbert, and Milton* (Oxford: Cambridge University Press, 1999), 3.

13. Katharine Eisaman Maus, *Inwardness and Theater in the English Renaissance* (Chicago: University of Chicago Press, 1995), 195.

14. See Gail Kern Paster, "Nervous Tension," in *The Body in Parts: Fantasies of Corporeality in Early Modern Europe*, ed. David Hillman and Carla Mazzio (London:

Routledge, 1997), 111. A similar case is made in the same volume by David Hillman, "Visceral Knowledge," 83.

15. I am quoting here from *The Body Embarrassed*, 8.

16. Shigehisa Kuriyama, *The Expressiveness of the Body and the Divergence of Ancient Greek and Chinese Medicine* (New York: Zone Books, 1999), 237.

17. Charles Taylor, *Sources of the Self: The Making of the Modern Identity* (Cambridge, Mass.: Harvard University Press, 1989), 188–89 (emphasis added). See also Susan Bordo, *The Flight to Objectivity: Essays on Cartesianism and Culture* (Albany: State University of New York Preas, 1987), 8.

18. There is a succinct discussion of the qualities in Lester S. King, "The Transformation of Galenism," in *Medicine in Seventeenth Century England*, ed. Allen G. Debus (Berkeley: University of California Press, 1974), 17–24.

19. Francis Bacon, "Of the Wisdom of the Ancients (*De Sapientia Veterum*)," in *Works*, ed. James Spedding, Robert Leslie Ellis, and Douglas Denon Heath, 14 vols. (London: Longmans, 1868–90), 6: 710–11.

20. I am quoting from Thomas Moffett, *Health's Improvement* (London, 1655), 234, but the thought is a commonplace.

21. For a diagrammatic representation of these linkages, see Londa Schiebinger, *The Mind Has No Sex?: Women in the Origins of Modern Science* (Cambridge, Mass: Harvard University Press, 1989), 162.

22. The classic treatment of melancholy remains Raymond Klibansky, Erwin Panofsky, and Fritz Saxl, *Saturn and Melancholy: Studies in the History of Natural Philosophy, Religion, and Art* (London: Thomas Nelson, 1964); but see also Juliana Schiesari, *The Gendering of Melancholy: Feminism, Psychoanalysis, and the Symbolics of Loss in Renaissance Literature* (Ithaca, N.Y.: Cornell University Press, 1992).

23. "Terrors of the Night," in *The Unfortunate Traveller and Other Works*, ed. J. B. Steane (Harmondsworth: Penguin, 1971), 217.

24. See Edward H. Sugden, *A Topographical Dictionary to the Works of Shakespeare and His FellowDramatists* (Manchester: Manchester University Press, 1925), 352. Apparently the fetid waters of Moorditch did not usually move at all, since in *Lenten Stuff* Nashe mentions the wonder of the "common people about London, some few years since . . . at the bubbling of Moorditch"; see *The Unfortunate Traveller and Other Works*, 442. Sugden speculates that this led in 1592 to the cleansing and broadening of the ditch (352), but John Stow complains that it was "neuer the better"; see *A Survey of London*, ed. Charle Lethbridge Kingsford, 2 vols. (1908; reprint Oxford: Clarendon Press, 1971), 2: 20.

25. Edward Topsell, *The Historie of the Four-Footed Beastes* (London: William Jaggard, 1607), 103.

26. On the relation of heat to blood in Aristotle, see Lloyd, *Science, Folklore and Ideology*, 32–33.

27. Topsell, *Historie of the Four-Footed Beastes*, 105.

28. For a related argument on the ramifications of temperature, see my "The Unbearable Coldness of Female Being: Women's Imperfection and the Humoral Economy," *ELR* 28 (1998): 416–40.

29. See the *OED* entry (4a) for *bagpipe*, quoting Henry Crosse, *Vertues Commonwealth* (1603): "The Seruingman, the Image of sloath, the bagge-pipe of vanitie,

like a windie Instrument, soundeth nothing but prophanenesse." Interestingly, Falstaff asks Hal to "trouble me no more with vanity" (1.2.81–82).

30. Discussion of animals' characters is to be found in Aristotle's *Historia Animalium* passim; see Lloyd, *Science, Folklore and Ideology*, 18–26.

31. Sir Philip Sidney, *The Countess of Pembroke's Arcadia (The Old Arcadia)*, ed. Katherine Duncan-Jones (Oxford: Oxford University Press, 1985), 223.

32. The point of origin for this critical commonplace is probably C. L. Barber, *Shakespeare's Festive Comedy: A Study in Dramatic Form and Its Relation to Social Custom* (Princeton, N.J.: Princeton University Press, 1959), 197.

33. William B. Ashworth, Jr., "Natural History and the Emblematic WorldView," in *Reappraisals of the Scientific Revolution*, ed. David C. Lindberg and Robert S. Westman (Cambridge: Cambridge University Press, 1990), 306. Ashworth refers, with qualified admiration, to Michel Foucault, *The Order of Things: An Archaeology of the Human Sciences* (New York: Pantheon, 1970): "Foucault may not have been a good historian, or a historian at all, but he somehow managed to see a feature of the Renaissance that proper historians have somehow overlooked" (325–26).

34. Thomas Wilson, *The Arte of Rhetorique*, ed. Thomas J. Derrick (New York: Garland, 1982), 375. I owe this reference to Mark Breitenberg, *Anxious Masculinity in Early Modern England* (Cambridge: Cambridge University Press, 1996), 43.

35. John Sutton, *Philosophy and Memory Traces: Descartes to Connectionism* (Cambridge: Cambridge University Press, 1998), 36.

36. Moffett, *Health's Improvement*, 22.

37. In this, I wish to counter the argument put forward by Erica Fudge that virtually all early modern thinking about animals is anthropomorphic at bottom; see *Perceiving Animals*, 1–10. The issue is not, as anthropologist Richard Tapper has pointed out in a more general context, that ways of categorizing animals simply derive from human social classifications. Rather, a society's ways of classifying the natural order inform categories describing the relation of the individual to the group; see "Animality, Humanity, Morality, Society" in *What Is An Animal?*, ed. Tim Ingold (London: Unwin Hyman, 1988), 50–51.

38. For astute comments on the complexity of attitudes toward bears, see David Wiles, *Shakespeare's Clown: Actor and Text in the Elizabethan Playhouse* (Cambridge: Cambridge University Press, 1987), 168–72, especially on the interchangeability of actors and bears in other Shakespearean references.

39. Dickey comments: "this simile registers Macbeth's increasingly bitter awareness that he has become a beast whose sole function is to perform in the spectacle of his own execution"; see "Shakespeare's Mastiff Comedy," 264–65.

40. Moffett, *Health's Improvement*, 45. Patricia Fumerton has discussed this practice and similar cooking practices as torturing animals: "torture is the tasty seasoning that flavors the otherwise plain meat." See "Introduction: A New New Historicism" in *Renaissance Culture and the Everyday*, ed. Patricia Fumerton and Simon Hunt (Philadelphia: University of Pennsylvania Press, 1999), 1–3, esp. 2. The analogy between human and animal flesh allows us to think differently about the meaning of this enforced tenderization while not denying the reality of the animals' suffering.

41. Wright, *Passions of the Mind*, 97.

42. Quotations from contemporary documents appear in Dickey, "Shake-speare's Mastiff Comedy," 257; in contrast to Dickey's implication that Elizabethans could not imagine or care about animal suffering, there is Thomas Moffett's comment in *Health's Improvement* (30) about sympathy for beasts about to be slaughtered: Moffett describes the pain and suffering of beasts about to be slaughtered—a sight he says only hard-hearted butchers can see—"the hearing of heavy sighs, sobs, and grones, the passionate strugling and panting for life." Also see Wiles, *Shakespeare's Clown*, 168–69.

43. Within the context of the Elizabethan public theater, the image of the baited bear, by calling up audience memories of the pleasures of watching blood sports, encourages spectators to acknowledge their own emotional investment in prolonging Macbeth's defiant last moments and delaying their own anticipated gratification at his death. See Cynthia Marshall, *The Shattering of the Self: Violence Subjectivity, and Early Modern Texts* (Baltimore: Johns Hopkins University Press, 2002).

44. Gilles Deleuze and Félix Guattari, *A Thousand Plateaus: Capitalism and Schizophrenia*, trans. Brian Massumi (Minneapolis: University of Minnesota Press, 1987),154.

45. Deleuze and Guattari, *A Thousand Plateaus*, 153.

46. Park, "The Organic Soul," p. 469.

47. Wright, *Passions of the Mind*, 8.

48. Wright, *Passions of the Mind*, 16–17.

49. Wright, *Passions of the Mind*, 45.

50. Wright, *Passions of the Mind*, 24.

51. Wright, *Passions of the Mind*, 12; on the heart as the receptacle of feelings, see Robert A. Erickson, *The Language of the Heart, 1600–1750* (Philadelphia: University of Pennsylvania Press, 1997), 11–15.

52. Wright, *Passions of the Mind*, 7.

53. As quoted by Tapper, "Animality, Humanity, Morality, Society," 47–62.

54. Wright, *Passions of the Mind*, 23.

55. Wright, *Passions of the Mind*, 23–24.

56. For a summary of environmental appraisal by animals as part of what anthropologists call ecological psychology, see Edward S. Reed, "The Affordances of the Animate Environment: Social Science from the Ecological Point of View," in Ingold, ed., *What Is an Animal?*, 110–26.

57. In this respect, as in others, the early modern account of cognitive function is remarkably like that of some current cognitive science; see Antonio Damasio, *The Feeling of What Happens: Body and Emotion in the Making of Consciousness* (New York: Harcourt Brace, 1999), 35–38 and passim; and Sutton, *Philosophy*, 13–20.

58. Damasio, *The Feeling of What Happens*, 168–94; see tables 6.1, 6.2 on 174–75 for a diagram of the differences.

59. Wright's neutrality may be a function of his own distance from the pastoral life or the fact that no wolves remained in England; Topsell is far less neutral: "it had been a shameful misery to indure the tyranny of such spoiling beastes without labouring for resistaunce and reuenge," *Historie of the Four-Footed Beastes*, 741. Richard Tapper argues that animal behavior serves as a natural basis

for human morality because animals can be seen to act like humans but do so without the imposition of rules, here against the theft and devouring of another's property.

60. Suddenness is, for Paul Ekman, a defining attribute of the onset of emotion; see "Biological and Cultural Contributions to Body and Facial Movement in the Expression of Emotions," in *Explaining Emotions*, ed. Amélie Oksenberg Rorty (Berkeley: University of California Press, 1980), 81.

61. Wright, *Passions of the Mind*, 144–45. The nouns in this sentence are drawn from the subheadings of Book 2, Chapter 4, entitled "*The fourth effect of Passions, which is, disquietnesse of the minde.*"

62. I am quoting Tim Ingold, "Introduction," in *What Is An Animal?*, 6.

63. Sutton, *Philosophy*, 16–17.

64. "The First Epistle of Dr. Conradus Gesnerus before his History of Fourefooted Beastes," in Topsell, *Historie of the Four-Footed Beastes*, sig. ¶ 1v.

65. Linda Charnes, *Notorious Identity: Materializing the Subject in Shakespeare* (Cambridge, Mass.: Harvard University Press, 1993), p. 75.

Chapter 6. English Mettle

1. All Shakespeare references are to *The Norton Shakespeare*, ed. Stephen Greenblatt (New York: W.W. Norton, 1997). Ian MacInnes's paper, "Decocting Cold Blood: Climate Theory and Military Science in *Henry V*," delivered at the 1995 Shakespeare Association of America conference in Chicago, was my introduction to the humoral complexities of this passage. MacInnes contends that *Henry V* "attempts to challenge the most disturbing aspect of climate theory, its determinism, by suggesting that Henry's value lies in his ability to translate his own transcendence of humoral norms into a national transcendence that will allow the English to replace the vagaries of climate with discipline and leadership." MacInnes has since developed his ideas further in a paper he delivered at the 2000 MLA Convention in Washington, D.C., "'The Men Do Sympathize with the Mastiffs': English Dogs and National Identity," which questions whether English valiance is represented in the play as a production of "conscious intervention," as in the breeding of dogs. Though our interests and conclusions differ, my thinking about this passage and the play as a whole owes a general debt to his fine work.

2. In a scene that anticipates *Henry V*, the Persians marvel at Tamburlaine's martial prowess, wondering of "what mould or mettle he be made" (I.2.6.17). Christopher Marlowe, *Tamburlaine Parts One and Two*, ed. Anthony B. Dawson (New York: W.W. Norton, 1997).

3. Gail Kern Paster has discussed the implications of Hamlet's claim that he is a "muddy-mettled rascal" (2.2.544) in "'Roasted in Wrath and Fire': The Ecology of the Passions in *Hamlet*," paper delivered at the 2002 meeting of the Shakespeare Association of America in Minneapolis.

4. Philip Massinger, *A Very Woman* (London, 1655): 3.1.86.

5. Entry 1f under "Metal" in the second edition of the *Oxford English Dictionary Online* (1989).

6. Gail Kern Paster, "The Body and Its Passions," *Shakespeare Studies* 29 (2001): 44.

7. Thomas Wright, *The Passions of the Minde in Generall* (1604), ed. Thomas O. Sloan (Urbana: University of Illinois Press, 1971), 37.

8. In a discussion that focuses on the stirring of physical movement, Paster has addressed how in early modern physiological discussions "the forceful behaviors of minerals would compare, analogically, with forceful behaviors in animate life. This means that like the explosions of air, fire, and gunpowder in the containing barrel of a gun, so growth, motion and other life-sustaining operations would result from explosions of air and fire within the body's dense liquidity." "Nervous Tension: Networks of Blood and Spirit in the Early Modern Body," in *The Body in Parts: Fantasies of Corporeality in Early Modern Europe*, ed. David Hillman and Carla Mazzio (London: Routledge, 1997), 109.

9. On the complexities of "courage" as a virtue, ideology, emotional temperament, or psychology in Western culture, see William Ian Miller, *The Mystery of Courage* (Cambridge, Mass.: Harvard University Press, 2000).

10. Wright, *Passions of the Minde*, lviii–lxiii.

11. I make this argument in "*Othello*, Passion, and Race," in *Writing Race Across the Atlantic World, 1492–1763*, ed. Philip Beidler and Gary L. Taylor (New York: Palgrave, 2003).

12. On the non-naturals, see Nancy G. Siraisi's *Medieval and Early Renaissance Medicine: An Introduction to Knowledge and Practice* (Chicago: University of Chicago Press, 1990), 101 and Andrew Wear, "Making Sense of Health and the Environment in Early Modern England," in *Health and Healing in Early Modern England*, ed. Andrew Wear (Aldershot: Ashgate, 1998), 131. On geohumoralism, see Mary Floyd-Wilson, *English Ethnicity and Race in Early Modern Drama* (Cambridge: Cambridge University Press, 2003).

13. See John Sutton, *Philosophy and Memory Traces: Descartes to Connectionism* (Cambridge: Cambridge University Press, 1998), 25–49, esp. 40–41. See also Ernst Cassirer, *The Individual and the Cosmos in Renaissance Philosophy* (New York: Harper and Row, 1963), 145–46.

14. *Hippocratic Writings*, ed. G. E. R. Lloyd (London: Penguin, 1983), 164.

15. Juan Huarte, *Examen de ingenios: The Examination of Mens Wits* (1594), trans. Richard Carew (Gainesville, Fl.: Scholars' Facsimiles and Reprints, 1959), 244.

16. Mikhail Bakhtin, *Rabelais and His World*, trans. Helene Iswolsky (Bloomington: Indiana University Press, 1984), 27.

17. See Peter Stallybrass's "Patriarchal Territories: The Body Enclosed," in *Rewriting the Renaissance: The Discourses of Sexual Difference in Early Modern Europe*, ed. Margaret W. Ferguson, Maureen Quilligan, and Nancy J. Vickers (Chicago: University of Chicago Press, 1986), 123–42. Gail Kern Paster's *The Body Embarrassed: Drama and the Disciplines of Shame in Early Modern Europe* (Ithaca, N.Y.: Cornell University Press, 1993) draws on Bakhtin's figurations of grotesque and classical bodies to demonstrate how humoral discourse in the early modern period is inflected and generated by distinctions in class and gender. My own thinking about the ethnological implications of humoralism is deeply influenced by Paster's work.

18. Hippocrates, *Writings*, 166.

19. Bakhtin, *Rabelais*, 355.

20. In "Transmigrations: Crossing Regional and Gender Boundaries in *Antony and Cleopatra*," I consider how hot climates were understood to challenge the conventional opposition between dry men and wet women. In *Enacting Gender on the English Renaissance Stage*, ed. Anne Russell and Viviana Comensoli (Urbana: University of Illinois Press, 1998), 73–96.

21. For some commonplace characterizations of the phlegmatic, see Ruth Leila Anderson, *Elizabethan Psychology and Shakespeare's Plays* (New York: Russell and Russell, 1966), 34.

22. On the melancholic's fantastic fears, see chapter XIII of Thomas Walkington's *The Optick Glasse of Humors* (1631) (Delmar, N.Y.: Scholars' Facsimiles and Reprints, 1981).

23. Wright, *Passions of the Mind*, 37.

24. Michael C. Schoenfeldt, *Bodies and Selves in Early Modern England: Physiology and Inwardness in Spenser, Shakespeare, Herbert, and Milton* (Cambridge: Cambridge University Press, 1999), 74.

25. I am quoting Schoenfeldt quoting Shakespeare's Sonnet 94.

26. Jean Bodin, *Method for the Easy Comprehension of History* (1565), trans. Beatrice Reynolds (New York: Columbia University Press, 1945), 104. At the same time, Bodin recognizes Hippocrates as the "highest authority" (86).

27. On classical environmental theory, see Richard F. Thomas, *Lands and Peoples in Roman Poetry: The Ethnographical Tradition* (Cambridge: Cambridge Philosophical Society, 1982); Clarence Glacken, *Traces on the Rhodian Shore: Nature and Culture in Western Thought from Ancient Times to the End of the Eighteenth Century* (Berkeley: University of California Press, 1967); and Frederick Sargent, II, *Hippocratic Heritage: A History of Ideas About Weather and Human Health* (New York: Pergamon Press, 1982). Jean Bodin, Giovanni Botero, Pierre Charron, Thomas Walkington, and Levinus Lemnius are among the early modern writers who understand climatic effects in Aristotlelian terms.

28. Walkington, *The Optick Glass*, 24–25.

29. Levinus Lemnius, *The Touchstone of Complexions*, trans. Thomas Newton (London, 1581), 13.

30. See for example, Bodin, *Method*, 93. See also Samuel Kliger, *The Goths in England: A Study in Seventeenth and Eighteenth Century Thought* (Cambridge, Mass.: Harvard University Press, 1952), 244.

31. Appealing to climate theory, Giovanni Botero observes in his *Relations of the Most Famous Kingdoms and Commonwealths Throwout the World* (1616), trans. R. I. (London, 1630) that northern armies are often compared to "swarmes of bees. And most true it is, that Jordanes and Olaus terme the North, the Store-house of Mankind"; quoted in Kliger, *The Goths in England*, 244.

32. Lemnius, *The Touchstone of Complexions*, 18.

33. Demonstrating that the process of civility penetrated early modern representations of internal physiology, Gail Kern Paster has shown how spirits "are themselves important signifiers of social difference." "Nervous Tension," 120.

34. Bodin, *Method*, 114.

35. Pierre Charron, *Of Wisdome* (n.d., before 1612), trans. Samson Lennard

(Amsterdam: Facsimile, 1971), 174. Bodin observes that northerners "accomplish everything by force of arms like slaves and in the way of wild beasts" (*Method*, 115).

36. Schoenfeldt, *Bodies and Selves*, 1. On regional mind/body oppositions, see Bodin, *Method*, 98.

37. Bodin, *Method*, 133. Moreover the "best soldiers always are chosen from the farmers and plebes, whose abilities are in manual work" (121). And so it goes that rulers and politicians thrive in the middle regions, priests and prophets in the south. Giovanni Botero, noting that northerners do best as soldiers or tradesmen, states that their "wits consist in their hands." *Relations of the Most Famous Kingdomes*, p. 15.

38. Botero, *Relations*, 14.

39. Most critics, as David J. Baker has observed, see the play as propaganda for an ideal incorporation of these disparate nations, yet they overlook, as he rightly contends, how the "multiple allegiances and identifications—as 'Englishmen,' 'Irishmen,' 'Welshmen,' and/or as hybrids of these various designations" may "trouble any sense of sturdy Englishness the play might promote." *Between Nations: Shakespeare, Spenser, Marvell, and the Question of Britain* (Stanford, Calif.: Stanford University Press, 1997), 24–25.

40. Stephen Greenblatt, *Shakespearean Negotiations: The Circulation of Social Energy in Renaissance England* (Berkeley: University of California Press, 1988), 63, 57.

41. Baker observes that MacMorris is a character who "veers wildly between barbarism and civility, and who thus intimates all of the mutability that Spenser decried among the Old English," *Between Nations*, 40.

42. J. O. Bartley, quoted in Baker, *Between Nations*, 54. My understanding of how the play represents—through Fluellen—the Welsh's vexed relationship to England and Englishness is indebted throughout to Baker's extensive discussion of these issues, 44–62.

43. Baker, *Between Nations*, 61; see also Phyllis Rackin, *Stages of History: Shakespeare's English Chronicles* (Ithaca, N.Y.: Cornell University Press, 1990), 238–41.

44. Rackin, *Stages of History*, 240.

45. For a nuanced reading of this scene, see Baker, *Between Nations*, Baker, 57–58.

46. Norbert Elias, *The Civilizing Process: The Development of Manners*, trans. Edmund Jephcott (New York: Urizen Books, 1978), 56. The Erasmus quotation is cited by Ari Wesseling, "Are the Dutch Uncivilized?: Erasmus on the Batavians and His National Identity," *Erasmus of Rotterdam Society Yearbook* 13 (1993): 88.

47. Wesseling, "Are the Dutch Uncivilized?" 71, 74.

48. Desiderius Erasmus, "On Good Manners for Boys," trans. Brian McGregor, ed. J. K. Sowards, *Collected Works of Erasmus* (Toronto: University of Toronto Press, 1985), 25: 289. My emphasis.

49. Elias, *The Civilizing Process*, 200.

50. I take up this subject in *English Ethnicity and Race in Early Modern Drama*. Though she does not stress the "tension" or "ambivalence" in England's subscription to the civilizing process, Debora Shuger's essay "Irishman, Aristocrats, and Other White Barbarians" broaches many of the issues at play here, noting for example that with the "publication of [William] Camden's *Britannia* in 1586, a radically different model of English prehistory replaces [the former] legitimizing myths." A "devolutionary scheme, which portrays early British history as the gradual decline of an

advanced civilization" is succeeded, Shuger contends, by the "slow and bloody civilizing process that followed Roman colonization," and this shift in perspective eventually led to an admiration for the "manly virtues of the [northern] barbarian." *Renaissance Quarterly* 50 (Summer 1997): 496, 520.

51. Richard Helgerson, *Forms of Nationhood: The Elizabethan Writing of England* (Chicago: University of Chicago Press, 1992), 243.

52. Quoted in R. F. Jones, *The Triumph of the English Language* (Stanford, Calif.: Stanford University Press, 1953), 18.

53. Lemnius, *Touchstone*, 16v.

54. Hamlet's disdain for his native inclination forms a kind of kinship with the English anxiety that their nation has already absorbed this Danish trait. It is, in fact, an early modern commonplace to identify English drinking as a practice learned from the Danes. But the English writers' exertion to designate drunkenness as a foreign custom—a recognizably Danish (or German or Dutch) habit, is motivated by their concern that such customs eventually become "rooted" in the body. Considered from another angle, English and Danish national distinctions dissolve in the heated blood and fleshy appetites common to all northerners. On drinking as an English trait inherited from the Danes, see William Camden *Remains Concerning Britain* (1605), ed. R. D. Dunn (Toronto: University of Toronto Press, 1984), 21; George Gascoigne, *A Delicate Diet* (London, 1576), 18; *A Warning-Piece to All Drunkards* (London, 1682).

55. We may be reminded that in *The Hystorie of Hamblet*, Belleforest describes Hamlet as a man whose sober virtues mark him as unique among the "barbarous and uncivill" denizens of Denmark; F. DE. Belleforest, *The Hystorie of Hamblet* (1608), in *The Sources of Hamlet* (London: Oxford University Press, 1926), 179.

56. In a paper entitled "Hamlet's Mirth," presented in the seminar "Scripting Behavior" directed by Frank Whigham at the 2000 meeting of the Shakespeare Association of America in Miami, I extended this discussion to consider how the vogue of melancholia in England exemplified the conflict between class aspirations and ethnic identity. Celebrated as elite refinement and condemned as foreign infection, melancholy was simultaneously perceived by the English as the perfect counter to their humoral imbalances and as a willful alienation from one's nativity. See also *English Ethnicity and Race in Early Modern Drama*, ch. 3.

57. *Markets of Bawdrie: The Dramatic Criticism of Stephen Gosson*, ed. Arthur F. Kinney (Salzburg, Austria: Salzburg Studies in English Literature, 1974), 90–91. That the theater, foreign fashions, feasting, etc. have brought about the degeneration of the English people's warlike qualities is also a discernable theme in John Northbrooke, *A Treatise wherein Dicing, Dauncing, Vaine Playes or Enterluds . . . are reproved* (1577), Phillip Stubbes, *The Anatomy of Abuses* (1583), and William Rankins, *The Mirror of Monsters* (1587). See Jean E. Howard's discussion of degeneracy in antitheatrical discourse, which she reads as effect of rising class tensions. *The Stage and Social Struggle in Early Modern England* (London: Routledge Press, 1994), 26. See also Robert Matz, "Sidney's *Defence of Poesie*: The Politics of Pleasure," *English Literary Renaissance* (Spring 1995): 131–47.

58. As historian Herwig Wolfram explains, northern humanists challenged the Italian historians' characterization of the barbaric invasions by reinterpreting them

as migrations of "healthy, strong, youthful" peoples that reinvigorated a declining civilization. "Gothic History and Historical Ethnography," *Journal of Medieval History* 7 (1981), 312. See Robert Burton's articulation of this idea in *The Anatomy of Melancholy*, ed. Holbrook Jackson (New York: Vintage, 1977): 1.2.1.6. In a reading of *Henry V* that is sympathetic in many ways with my own, David Glimp has argued that King Henry "preside[s] over a transformation of Englishmen into what Debora Shuger would perhaps call 'white barbarians,' but he does so strategically, not in order to destroy England, but to augment it and extend its dominion." In their shared appeals to providence, Glimp contends, the play's representation of England's invasion parallels Edmund Spenser's characterization of the barbaric migrations in *A View of the Present State of Ireland. Increase and Multiply: Governing Cultural Reproduction in Early Modern England* (Minneapolis: University of Minnesota Press, 2003), 94.

59. See Wendy Wall's characterization of *Henry V* as a "play that obsessively returns to cultivation, farming, weather, and eating as crucial elements for forging national distinctions, [and that] meditates explicitly on the claims and limits of a national husbandry." "Renaissance National Husbandry: Gervase Markham and the Publication of England," *Sixteenth Century Journal* 27 (1996): 784.

60. On the humoral implications of this passage, see Jurgen Schafer, "When They Marry, They Get Wenches," *Shakespeare Quarterly* 22 (Summer 1971): 203–311. See also David Glimp, who argues that this "defense of an ethics of unregulated self-indulgence . . . informs Falstaff's account of his own surrogate paternity of Hal," *Increase and Multiply*, 84. Intriguingly, to reinvent indulgence as regulation, Falstaff relies on the language of husbandry, which in *Henry V* is associated with the degeneration of martial prowess.

61. Thomas Heywood, *Apology for Actors* (1612), in *The English Stage: Attack and Defense 1577–1730*, ed. Arthur Freeman (New York: Garland, 1973), Book I, B4. Baker invokes this same passage in posing the very question I am addressing here: "when *Henry V* held up the purebred Englishman as the national ideal and urged all men of 'grosser blood' to model themselves on him, would [an aristocratic Irish-/Welsh-/Scots-man] have thought of himself as the original or the epigone?" *Between Nations*, 42–43. For another perspective on how this play may have aimed to channel the audience's emotional energies, see Joel B. Altman, "'Vile Participation': The Amplification of Violence in the Theater of *Henry V*," *Shakespeare Quarterly* 42 (1991): 1–32.

Chapter 7. Hearing Green

Epigraph: Noam Chomsky, *Syntactic Structures* (The Hague: Mouton, 1957), 15.

1. William Shakespeare and John Fletcher, *The Two Noble Kinsmen*, 1634 quarto text, in *Shakespeare's Plays in Quarto*, ed. Michael J. B. Allen and Kenneth Muir (Berkeley: University of California Press, 1981), 67. The line is numbered 4.3.3 in William Shakespeare, *Complete Works*, ed., Stanley Wells and Gary Taylor (Oxford: Clarendon Press, 1989), 1249. Quotations from Shakespeare's scripts hereafter are given with original spelling and punctuation, from quarto or folio texts as noted, with act, scene, and line references supplied from the Oxford edition. After

the first citation in each case, further quotations from a given play are cited in the text by act, scene, and line numbers.

2. Thomas Wright, *The Passions of the Minde in Generall*, rev. ed. (London: Valentine Simmes for Walter Burre, 1604), 45. Further references are cited in the text.

3. F. P. Wilson, ed., *The Oxford Dictionary of English Proverbs*, 3rd ed. (Oxford: Clarendon Press, 1970), 412, 337.

4. *Romeo and Juliet*, 3.5.219–21, 1623 folio text, in *The First Folio of Shakespeare*, ed. Charlton Hinman (New York: W.W. Norton, 1968), 686.

5. Marsilio Ficino, *Three Books on Life*, trans. Carol V. Kaske and John R. Clark (Binghampton, N.Y.: Medieval and Renaissance Texts and Studies, 1989), 203. Further references are cited in the text.

6. Helkiah Crooke, *Microcosmographia: A Description of the Body of Man*, 2nd ed. (London : Thomas and Richard Cotes for Michael Sparke, 1631), 687. Further references are cited in the text.

7. James VI and I, *The Poems of James VI of Scotland*, ed. James Craigie, vol. 1, Scottish Text Society 3rd ser. 22 (Edinburgh: Blackwood, 1955), 80. Further references are cited in the text.

8. Francis Bacon, *Silva Silvarum: Or a Natural History* (London: J. H. for William Lee, 1626), 177.

9. John Donne, *Collected Sermons*, vol. 5, ed. George R. Potter and Evelyn M. Simpson (Berkeley: University of California Press, 1959), 55.

10. Hippocrates, "Airs, Waters, Places," in *Hippocratic Writings*, ed. G. E. R. Lloyd (Harmondsworth: Penguin, 1978), 165–66.

11. *The Faerie Queene* 2.12.72.6 in Edmund Spenser, *The Faerie Queene, Book Two*, ed. Edwin Greenlaw (Baltimore: Johns Hopkins University Press, 1933), 177. Further references are cited in the text by book, canto, stanza, and line numbers.

12. Andrew Marvell, "The Garden," in *The Poems and Letters*, ed. H. M. Margoliouth, 3rd ed. rev. Pierre Legouis and E. E. Duncan-Jones (Oxford: Clarendon Press, 1971), 1: 226.

13. Andrew Marvell, *Andrew Marvell*, ed. Frank Kermode and Keith Walker (Oxford: Oxford University Press, 1990), 299.

14. *The Reign of King Edward III*, 2.1.1–2, in *The Shakespeare Apocrypha*, ed. C. F. Tucker Brooke (Oxford: Clarendon Press, 1908), 73. Further references are cited in the text.

15. Claude M. Simpson, *The British Broadside Ballad and Its Music* (New Brunswick, N.J.: Rutgers University Press, 1966), 268–78.

16. *Hero and Leander*, 1.11–14, in Christopher Marlowe, *Complete Works*, ed. Fredson Bowers, 2nd ed. (Cambridge: Cambridge University Press, 1981), 2: 431.

17. Linda Woodbridge, "Green Shakespeare," in *The Scythe of Saturn: Shakespeare and Magical Thinking* (Urbana: University of Illinois Press, 1994), 152–205; David Wiles, "Robin Hood as Summer Lord," in *The Early Plays of Robin Hood* (Cambridge: D. S. Brewer, 1981), 7–30; Thomas Wright, ed., *Songs and Ballads with Other Short Poems, Chiefly of the Reign of Philip and Mary* (London: J. B. Nichols, 1860), 119–24.

18. Simpson, *The British Broadside Ballad*, 269.

19. Phillip Stubbes, *The Anatomy of Abuses* (London: Richard Jones, 1583), sig. O4v. Further references are cited in the text.

20. Plutarch, *Lives of the Noble Grecians and Romans Compared Together*, trans. Sir Thomas North (London: Thomas Vautroullier and John Wright, 1579), 211–12.

21. *The Merry Wives of Windsor*, 2.1.58–60, 1623 folio text, in *The First Folio*, 62.

22. Willi Apel, *Gregorian Chant* (Bloomington: Indiana University Press, 1958), 208–26.

23. Francis Proctor and Christopher Wordsworth, *Breviarum ad Usum Insignis Ecclesiae Sarum*, 3 vols. (Cambridge: Cambridge University Press, 1879–86), 1: mlxvii, 2: 39.

24. Walter Howard Frere, *The Use of Sarum*, 3 vols. (Cambridge: Cambridge University Press, 1898–1901), 2: 69.

25. Maurice Frost, *English and Scottish Psalm and Hymn Tunes c. 1543–1677* (Oxford: Oxford University Press, 1953), 3–15.

26. Frost, *Psalm and Hymn Tunes*, 11.

27. Noam Chomsky and Morris Halle, *The Sound Pattern of English* (New York: Harper and Row, 1968), 1–55; Stephen Handel, *Listening: An Introduction to the Perception of Auditory Events* (Cambridge, Mass.: MIT Press, 1989), 147–60; John Laver, *Principles of Phonetics* (Cambridge: Cambridge University Press, 1994), 95–118; Ian R. A. MacKay, *Phonetics: The Science of Speech Production* (Boston: Allyn and Bacon, 1987), 125–52; John Laver, "Linguistic Phonetics," in *The Handbook of Linguistics*, ed. Mark Aronoff and Janie Rees-Miller (Oxford: Blackwell, 2001), 150–79.

28. Abigail Cohn, "Phonology," in *The Handbook of Linguistics*, 180–212.

29. MacKay, *Phonetics*, 129–30; Kenneth N. Stevens, *Acoustic Phonetics* (Cambridge, Mass.: MIT Press, 1998), 48.

30. M. B. Parkes, *Pause and Effect: An Introduction to the History of Punctuation in the West* (Berkeley : University of California Press, 1993), 9–19.

31. Roy Harris, *Rethinking Writing* (Bloomington: Indiana University Press, 2000), 136–37. See also Paul Saenger, *Space Between Words: The Origins of Silent Reading* (Stanford, Calif.: Stanford University Press, 1997).

32. D. B. Fry, *Homo Loquens: Man as a Talking Animal* (Cambridge: Cambridge University Press, 1977), 83.

33. MacKay, *Phonetics*, 290–91.

34. John Hart, *An Orthography* (London: William Seres, 1569), sigs. 9–9v. Further references are cited in the text.

35. Thomas Dekker, *A Strange Horse Race* (London: Nicholas Okes for Joseph Hunt, 1613), sig. C4v.

36. Robert Robinson, *The Art of Pronunciation* (London: Nicholas Oakes, 1617), sig. B2.

37. E. J. Dobson, *English Pronunciation 1500–1700*, 2nd ed., 2 vols. (Oxford: Clarendon Press, 1968),1: 200–14; Laver, "Linguistic Phonetics," 166.

38. George Puttenham, *The Art of English Poesie*, ed. Gladys Doidge Willcock and Alice Parker (Cambridge: Cambridge University Press, 1936), 73.

39. Thomas Campion, *Observations in the Art of English Poesie*, in *Campion's Works*, ed. Percival Vivian (Oxford: Clarendon Press, 1909), 36. Further references are cited in the text.

40. Samuel Daniel, *A Defence of Ryme*, in *Poems and A Defence of Ryme*, ed. Arthur Colby Sprague (Chicago: University of Chicago Press, 1965), 132. Further references are cited in the text.

41. *The Vnder-wood* 29.1–6, in Ben Jonson, *Ben Jonson*, ed. C. H. Herford, Percy Simpson, and Evelyn Simpson, vol 8 (Oxford: Clarendon Press, 1947), 183. Further references are cited in the text.

42. Wesley Trimpi, *Ben Jonson's Poems: A Study of the Plain Style* (Stanford, Calif.: Stanford University Press, 1962), ix, 6.

43. Stevens, *Acoustic Phonetics*, 248–49.

44. *Timber* in *Ben Jonson*, 8: 584.

45. *Sonnets*, 85.5–8, in William Shakespeare, *Shakespeare's Sonnets*, ed. Stephen Booth (New Haven, Conn.: Yale University Press, 1977), 74.

46. "To the Memory of My Beloved, the Author, Master William Shakespeare, and What He Hath Left Us," 68, in *Ben Jonson*, 8: 392.

47. D. B. Fry, *The Physics of Speech* (Cambridge: Cambridge University Press, 1979), 126–27.

48. Joel Fineman, "The Sound of O in *Othello*: The Real of the Tragedy of Desire" in *The Subjectivity Effect in Western Literary Tradition: Essays toward the Release of Shakespeare's Will* (Cambridge, Mass.: MIT Press, 1991), 143–64.

49. Thomas Nashe, *A Pleasant Comedy, Called Summer's Last Will and Testament* (London: Simon Stafford for Walter Burre, 1600), sigs. B3–B3v. Further references are cited in the text.

50. Garrett Stewart, *Reading Voices: Literature and the Phonotext* (Berkeley: University of California Press, 1990), 7–8. Further references are cited in the text.

51. Stephen Booth, "Poetic Richness: A Preliminary Audit," *Pacific Coast Philology* 19: 1–2 (1984): 76. Further references are cited in the text.

Chapter 8. Humoral Knowledge and Liberal Cognition in Davenant's Macbeth

1. Quotations from William Shakespeare's *Macbeth* follow *The Riverside Shakespeare*, 2nd ed., ed. G. Blakemore Evans (Boston: Houghton Mifflin, 1997). I read 4.2.22 after Dover Wilson.

2. Sir William Davenant, "A Proposition for Advancement of Moralitie" (London, 1653), attributed and reprinted by James R. Jacob and Timothy Raylor, "Opera and Obedience: Thomas Hobbes and 'A Proposition for Advancement of Moralitie by Sir William Davenant,'" *Seventeeth Century* 6, 2 (Autumn 1991): 244. Quotations from "A Proposition" cite this reprint.

3. Thomas Browne, *Pseudodoxia Epidemica* (London, Printed by T. Harper for E. Dod, 1646), 8.

4. Steven Shapin, *A Social History of Truth: Civility and Science in Seventeenth-Century England* (Chicago: University of Chicago Press, 1994), 219.

5. Jacob and Raylor explore Davenant's involvement with two groups of reformers, the Marquis of Newcastle (in Paris, in the 1650s, including Hobbes and René Descartes) and the Samuel Hartlib circle ("Opera and Obedience," 233).

6. Shapin discusses this trend and Boyle's comments (from Robert Boyle's Papers, Royal Society of London, vol. 38. f. 154), *A Social History*, 219.

7. Jacob and Raylor, "Opera and Obedience," 214, discussing Davenant's work in the 1650s.

8. Keith Wrightson, "Estates, Degrees, and sorts: Changing Perceptions of society in Tudor and Stuart England," in *Language, History and Class*, ed. Penelope Corfield (Oxford: Blackwell, 1991), 30–52.

9. Michael C. Schoenfeldt, *Bodies and Selves in Early Modern England: Physiology and Inwardness in Spenser, Shakespeare, Herbert, and Milton* (Cambridge: Cambridge University Press, 1999). Norbert Elias, *The Civilizing Process*, vol. 1, trans. Edmund Jephcott (New York: Urizen Books, 1978).

10. Reid Barbour, *English Epicures and Stoics: Ancient Legacies in Early Stuart Culture* (Amherst: University of Massachusetts Press, 1998).

11. Jacob and Raylor outline the Cavendish circle debates on Cartesian "obedience training" ("Opera and Obedience," 217–19).

12. John Sutton, *Philosophy and Memory Traces: Descartes to Connectionism* (Cambridge: Cambridge University Press, 1998), 41. Sutton draws on Gail Kern Paster's study of the humors, *The Body Embarrassed: Drama and the Disciplines of Shame in Early Modern Europe* (Ithaca, N.Y.: Cornell University Press, 1993), and Nancy G. Siraisi, *Medieval and Early Renaissance Medicine: An Introduction to Knowledge and Practice* (Chicago: University of Chicago Press, 1990).

13. See Locke's discussion of the ethical procedures of assent and dissent that characterize a rational, executive consciousness. John Locke, *An Essay Concerning Human Understanding* (1690), ed. Peter Nidditch (Oxford: Clarendon Press, 1975), 4.15–16.656.

14. Charles Taylor, *Sources of the Self: The Making of the Modern Identity* (Cambridge, Mass.: Harvard University Press, 1989). Of the intellectual historians cited here, Taylor makes the broadest claims for a shift to "radical reflexivity" and inwardness, arguing that proprietary models of cognition and emotion converged in a distinctively modern self, derived from common strains of sixteenth- and seventeenth-century political and social thought, theology, and physiology.

15. Sutton, *Philosophy and Memory Traces*, points out how deeply Cartesian physiology remains embedded in the body. William Miller observes that radical reflexivity is a mode of inwardness available to Western subjectivity as early as the Icelandic sagas. "Deep Inner Lives: Individualism and People of Honour," *History of Political Thought* 16, 2 (Summer 1995): 190–207.

16. On the relation between affect and consent in early theories of contract, see Victoria Kahn, "'The Duty to Love': Passion and Obligation in Early Modern Political Theory," in *Rhetoric and Law in Early Modern Europe*, ed. Victoria Kahn and Lorna Hutson (New Haven, Conn.: Yale University Press, 2001).

17. Catherine Lutz, *Unnatural Emotions: Everyday Sentiments on a Micronesian Atoll and their Challenge to Western Theory* (Chicago: University of Chicago Press, 1988), 5.

18. Anna Wierzbicka, "Emotion, Language, and Cultural Scripts," in *Emotion and Culture: Empirical Studies of Mutual Influence*, ed. Shinobu Kitayama and Hazel Rose Markus (Washington, D.C.: American Psychological Association, 1994), 189–90. Arlie Russell Hochschild analyzes modern "emotion rules" in *The Managed Heart: Commercialization of Human Feeling* (Berkeley: University of California Press, 1983).

19. The difficulties of extrapolating early modern emotion in the theater are explored in Thomas Cartelli, *Marlowe, Shakespeare, and the Economy of Theatrical*

Experience (Philadelphia: University of Pennsylvania Press, 1991); Theodore Leinwand, *Theatre, Finance, and Society in Early Modern England* (Cambridge: Cambridge University Press, 1999), esp. 144ff.; and Andrew Gurr, *Playgoing in Shakespeare's London*, 2nd ed. (Cambridge: Cambridge University Press, 1996). Barbara H. Rosenwein calls for a more complex reception theory and a renewed attention to local conventions and contexts for parsing emotion. See "Worrying About the Emotions in History," *American Historical Review* 107, 3 (June 2002). <http://www.historycooperative.org/journals/ahr/107.3/ah0302000821.html> (7 Jan. 2003). Examples of such local work can be found in Lorraine Daston and Katherine Park, *Wonders and the Order of Nature, 1150–1750* (New York, Zone Books, 1992), and Carol Clover, *Men, Women and Chain Saws: Gender in the Modern Horror Film* (Princeton, N.J.: Princeton University Press, 1992). In "Dido's Ear: Tragedy and the Politics of Response," *Shakespeare Quarterly* 52, 3 (2001): 360–82, Heather James explores emotional receptivity, and the Shakespearean construction of what Rosenwein might call "emotional communities" (para. 35).

20. As Katharine Eisaman Maus, *Inwardness and Theater in the English Renaissance* (Chicago: University of Chicago Press, 1995); Francis Barker, The Tremulous Private Body: Essays on Subjection (London: Methuen, 1984); and others have shown, we recognize "modernity" in rhetorical structures that mirror our own emotion scripts. Margareta De Grazia critiques this interpretive practice in "The Motive for Interiority: Shakespeare's Sonnets and Hamlet," *Style* 23, 3 (Fall 1989): 430–44.

21. See Steven Mullaney, "Mourning and Misogyny: Hamlet, The Revenger's Tragedy, and the Final Progress of Elizabeth I, 1600–1607," *Shakespeare Quarterly* 45 (1994): 144; also Leinwand, Theatre, Finance, and Society, Introduction. Linda Williams ascribes similar functions to twentieth-century popular film, "Discipline and Distraction: Psycho, Visual Culture, and Postmodern Cinema," in *"Culture" and the Problem of the Disciplines*, ed. John Carlos Rowe (New York: Columbia University Press, 1998), 87–120.

22. Joseph Roach, *The Player's Passion: Studies in the Science of Acting* (Newark: University of Delaware Press, 1985), 44. Roach reminds us that the player's contagious passions and spectator's response are among the most important tropes for the management of emotion in the period.

23. Michel Serres with Bruno Latour, *Conversations on Science, Culture, and Time*, trans. Roxanne Lapidus (Ann Arbor: University of Michigan Press, 1995), 45.

24. Renato Rosaldo argues broadly that cultural processes should be theorized as "heterogenous processes" not "self-contained" wholes, in *Culture and Truth: The Remaking of Social Analysis*, 2nd ed. (Boston: Beacon Press, 1993), 20–21.

25. Rosenwein, para. 36. Rosenwein cites John Baldwin's study, *The Language of Sex: Five Voices from Northern France Around 1200* (Chicago: University of Chicago Press, 1994), as one example of the varied voices that make up the emotion discourse of a given community and period. The essays in the present volume, which track the many conflicting versions of stoic and anti-stoic thought in Renaissance Europe, offer later examples.

26. Humoral structures of feeling resonate still in modern emotion discourse, as Schoenfeldt notes, *Bodies and Selves*, 169–70.

27. Antonio Damasio, *Descartes' Error: Emotion, Reason, and the Human Brain* (New York: Putnam, 1994). See also Michelle Z. Rosaldo, "Toward an Anthropology of Self and Feeling," in *Culture Theory*, ed. Richard A. Shweder and Robert A. LeVine (Cambridge: Cambridge University Press, 1984), 137–57.

28. The *OED* (sb. 3) dates the earliest modern use of confusion as a cognitive condition ("mental perturbation or agitation such as prevents the full command of the faculties") to the late sixteenth century.

29. Thomas Wright, *The Passion of the Minde in Generall* (1604), ed. Thomas O. Sloan (Urbana: University of Illinois Press, 1971), 334.

30. Lorraine Daston, "Fortuna and the Passions," in *Chance, Culture and the Literary Text*, ed. Thomas M. Kavanagh (Ann Arbor: University of Michigan Press, 1994), 24–47.

31. Early modern humors are socially embedded phenomena, "relat[ing] the body to its environment, and explain[ing] the literal influences that flow into it from a universe composed of analogous elements" (Schoenfeldt, *Bodies and Selves*, 3). "At each meal," Schoenfeldt reminds us, the humoral individual was remaking himself in Taylor's terms, "by methodical and disciplined action" (11; quoting Taylor, *Sources of the Self*, 159).

32. *Treatise of the Passions and Faculties of the Soule of Man* (London: Robert Bostock, 1640), reprinted in facsimile with an introduction by Margaret Lee Wiley (Gainesville, Fl.: Scholars' Facsimiles and Reprints, 1971), 296.

33. Sutton reminds us that cognitive processes like memory serve a critical forensic function for the contractarian subject. In Locke, for example, individual memory allows for a rigorous backward accounting of affective life, providing the "sameness of self through time" required to make contracts. Such extension of self occurs only in consciousness, as a feature of its self-reflexive processes rather than the (discontinuous and unstable) affective states reflected on. See Locke, *An Essay Concerning Human Understanding*, 2.27.10–16; also discussed in Taylor, *Sources of the Self*, 172–73. For a survey of the separation of passions and cognitive processes in seventeenth-century natural philosophy, from Descartes to Rousseau, see Amélie Oxenberg Rorty, "From Passions to Emotions and Sentiments," *Philosophy* 57 (1982): 159–72.

34. On antitheatrical anxieties about social hierarchy and affective contagion, see Jean Howard, *The Stage and Social Struggle in Early Modern England* (London: Routledge, 1994).

35. This perceptual division of labor anticipates the privileged role of the eye in eighteenth-century aesthetics, as well as the turn away from "audition" to "spectation" as the dominant idiom of performance in later periods. Jacobean audiences went to "hear" a play; we go to "see" a band. See Gurr, *Playgoing*, ch. 4.

36. On the Baroque career of curiosity, from vice to elite intellectual art, see Lorraine Daston, "Curiosity in Early Modern Science," *Word and Image* 11, 4 (October–December 1995): 391–404.

37. Jacob and Raylor, "Opera and Obedience," note that this formulation draws on Hobbes and adumbrates the economic passions later theorized by Bernard Mandeville and David Hume (232–33).

38. William Davenant, *The First Dayes Entertainment at Rutland House*. London (1657), 23–24.

39. On the critical role of face to face practices of authentication in early modern science see Shapin, *A Social History*, 305. Shapin describes these practices as a counterdiscourse that supplements the Lockean and Cartesian emphasis on internal assessment, judgment and assent.

40. Lorraine Daston, "Fortuna" (27) describes hope and fear as increasingly significant "passions of uncertainty"—part of a late seventeenth-century repudiation of chance and fortune, and embrace of probabilistic theory. When "uncertainty was no longer absolute, but relative to our state of knowledge," passions that inform deliberation and move the will to act take center stage, as they do in Descartes's *Passions de l'âme* (1649).

41. *The Complete Works of Aristotle*, 2 vols., ed. Jonathan Barnes (Princeton, N.J.: Princeton University Press, 1984), 2: 2202–4.

42. Reynolds echoes concerns about fear that go back to Plato, who dismissed "rashness and fear, foolish counsellors both." *Timaeus; Critias; Cleitophon; Metaxenus; Epistles*, trans. R. G. Bury, vol. 9 of *Plato*, Loeb Classical Library (Cambridge, Mass.: Harvard University Press, 1975), 181.

43. Thomas Elyot describes the effects of illness as "horrour or shrovelynge of the body myxt with heate" (*Castle of Helthe* [1541], 52b). Horror retains its use as an environment and landscape term well into the eighteenth century, even as passions theory shifts towards more privatized descriptions of emotion. Thus, the atmospheric "horrors" of Gothic fiction create a particularly intense perception of affinity between external and internal phenomena, in the humoral mode, well into the Enlightenment. See Pope's extended use of pathetic fallacy in the landscape of "Eloisa to Abelard."

44. According to Wright, "Passions are not only, not wholy to be extinguished (as the Stoicks seemed to affirme) but sometimes to be moved, & stirred up for the service of vertue" (*Passions of the Minde*, 17). Similarly, Reynolds: "For as in Religion, a Feare that is governed by the Word of God, so proportionably in Morality: a Feare grounded by the Word of Reason, is the Principle of Wisedome" (*Treatise of the Passions*, 298).

45. Michael Macdonald, "*The Fearefull Estate of Francis Spira*: Narrative, Identity, and Emotion in Early Modern England." *Journal of British Studies* 31 (1992): 32–61.

46. I am indebted to Mary Floyd-Wilson's study, *English Ethnicity and Race in Early Modern Drama* (Cambridge: Cambridge University Press, 2003), which describes this pattern of affective translation as a particularly English preoccupation of the period.

47. Elizabeth Fowler discusses the "political habituation of the passions of the subject" in the topoi of counsel in "The Rhetoric of Political Forms: Social Persons and the Criterion of Fit in Colonial Law, *Macbeth* and the Irish Masque at Court," in *Form and Reform in Renaissance England: Essays in Honor of Barbara Kiefer Lewalski*, ed. Amy Boesky and Mary Thomas Crane (Newark: University of Delaware Press, 2000), 70–104.

48. See Sally Mapstone, "Shakespeare and Scottish Kingship: A Case History," in *The Rose and the Thistle: Essays on the Culture of Late Medieval and Renaissance Scotland*, ed. Mapstone and Juliette Wood (East Lothian: Tuckwell Press, 1998), 158–89, for a detailed comparison of the source texts from the fourteenth century

on. On the Stuart politics of Shakespeare's 4.3, see Arthur Kinney, "Scottish History, the Union of the Crowns, and the Issue of Right Rule: The Case of Shakespeare's Macbeth," in *Renaissance Culture in Context: Theory and Practice*, ed. Jean R. Brink and William F. Gentrup (Brookfield, Vt.: Scolar Press, 1993), 18–53; and David Norbrook, "Macbeth and the Politics of Historiography," in *Politics of Discourse: The Literature and History of Seventeenth Century England*, ed. Kevin Sharpe and Steven N. Zwicker (Berkeley: University of California Press, 1987), 78–116.

49. Mary Floyd-Wilson, this volume.

50. Lady Macbeth and Macbeth provide a particularly horrifying vision of the destructive effects of fear on courtly counsel. Macbeth is tyrannical specifically in murdering potential counsellors, such as Banquo. By the end of the play he explicitly associates counsel with cowardice and humoral pressure: "Go prick thy face and over-red thy fear, / Thou lily-livered boy. What soldiers, patch? / Death of thy soul, those linen cheeks of thine / Are counsellors to fear" (5.3.14–17).

51. For one example, see John O. Whitney and Tina Packer, *Power Plays: Shakespeare's Lessons in Leadership and Management* (New York: Simon and Schuster, 2000).

52. See David Norbrook, "The Reformation of the Masque," in *The Court Masque*, ed. David Lindley (Manchester: Manchester University Press, 1984), 94–110; also Lois Potter, "Reformed Stage," in *The Revels History of Drama* (London: Methuen, 1981), 4: 294–301.

53. As Jacob and Raylor note ("Opera and Obedience," 239 n. 94) Hobbes's primary division of passion is between humans and animals, particularly in the case of curiosity, "the care of knowing causes." Thomas Hobbes, *Leviathan*, ed. Michael Oakeshott (New York: Collier Books, 1962), ch. 6, 51. Hobbes's relative neutrality to questions of estate may be less representative of contemporary English passions theory than Davenant's care.

54. Richard Kroll, "Emblem and Empiricism in Davanant's *Macbeth*," *English Literary History* 57, 4 (Winter 1990): 835–64.

55. Jean Marsden explores parallel scenes of feminine counsel in *The Re-Imagined Text: Shakespeare, Adaptation, and Eighteenth-Century Literary Theory* (Lexington: University Press of Kentucky, 1995), ch. 1, 24–25.

56. Quotations from Davenant's *Macbeth* follow *Five Restoration Adaptations of Shakespeare*, ed. Christopher Spencer (Urbana: University of Illinois Press, 1965).

57. Folger ms. W.b. 537. "The Musick in Mackbeth," attr. "Math. Lock."

58. This revision complicates the play's royalist ethos, but it is consistent with other Restoration versions of the Scottish story. Peter Heylyn's widely reprinted *Cosmography*, for example, which supplies the "Argument" to Davenant's *Macbeth*, cuts the testing scene completely. Heylyn makes Malcolm's restoration the work of Macduff and "some few patriots," "assisted with Ten Thousand English" and all moved by a natural abhorrence of Tyranny. Malcolm doesn't appear until the last line, to be "Seated in his Throne" (Spencer, *Five Restoration Adaptations*, 36).

59. David Marshall explores the structures of passionate exchange emerging in the medium of prose in this period; see *The Figure of Theater: Shaftesbury, Defoe, Adam Smith, and George Eliot* (New York: Columbia University Press, 1986). Alexandra Halasz explores early print readership in *The Marketplace of Print: Pamphlets*

and the Public Sphere in Early Modern England (Cambridge: Cambridge University Press, 1997).

60. John Bulwer, *Pathomyotomia: or a Dissection of the Significative Muscles of the Affections of the Minde* (London: W. W. for Humphrey Moseley, 1649), f8v.

61. Francis Kirkman, *The Wits, or, Sport upon Sport: In Select Pieces of Drollery, Digested into Scenes by Way of dialogue: Together with Variety of Humors of Several Nations* (London: Printed by Henry Marsh, 1662); also Thomas Jordan, *Pictures of Passions, Fancies, & Affections, Poetically Deciphered* (London: Printed by R. Wood, 1641).

62. A late seventeenth-century commonplace book records the "history of Macbeth" verbatim from either Heylyn or Davenant's play, testifying to the circulation of this version of the story in print. See Folger ms F. 910 H 51.

63. Kevis Goodman richly accounts for the trope of affective labor in "'Wasted Labor'? Milton's Eve, the Poet's Work, and the Challenge of Sympathy," *ELH* 64, 2 (Summer 1997): 415–46.

Chapter 9. Five Pictures of Pathos

1. See E. H. Gombrich, *Aby Warburg: An Intellectual Biography, with a Memoir on the History of the Library by Fritz Saxl*, 2nd ed. (Chicago: University of Chicago Press, 1986); Konrad Hoffmann, "Angst und Methode nach Warburg: Erinnerung als Veränderung," in *Aby Warburg: Akten des internationalen Symposions Hamburg 1990*, ed. Horst Bredekamp, Michael Diers, and Charlotte Schoell-Glass (Weinheim: VCH, Acta Humaniora, 1991), 261–67; Carlo Ginzburg, "From Aby Warburg to E. H. Gombrich: A Problem of Method," in *Clues, Myths, and Historical Method*, trans. John Tedeschi and Anne C. Tedeschi (Baltimore: Johns Hopkins University Press, 1989), 17–59; and Gertrud Bing, "Editorial Foreword" to Aby Warburg, *The Renewal of Pagan Antiquity*, trans. David Britt (Los Angeles: Getty Research Institute, 1999), 82.

2. See Warburg, *The Renewal*, 89, 271, 553–58.

3. Warburg, *The Renewal*, 556.

4. Warburg, *The Renewal*, 82.

5. See Hermann Usener, *Götternamen: Versuch einer Lehre von der religiösen Begriffsbildung* (Bonn: Friedrich Cohen, 1896), 3–5; for Warburg's notes from Usener's lectures concerning similar topics see Gombrich, *Aby Warburg*, 29.

6. Hermann Usener, "Mythologie," in *Vorträge und Aufsätze* (Leipzig: Teubner, 1907), 37–65, esp. 57–59.

7. Quoted in Gombrich, *Aby Warburg*, 77.

8. For Warburg's lecture, see Aby M. Warburg, *Images from the Region of the Pueblo Indians of North America*, trans. Michael P. Steinberg (Ithaca, N.Y.: Cornell University Press, 1995); for the quotations, 50, 17.

9. See for instance Hoffmann, "Angst und Methode," 264; and Anthony Grafton, Introduction to Giambattista Vico, *New Science* (London: Penguin, 1999), xiii.

10. Usener, "Mythologie," 57.

11. When in *Middlemarch* George Eliot named her antiquarian scholar Isaac

Casaubon, she knowingly recalled a real scholar of the early seventeenth century; the universalizing project her character pursued, however, described by Eliot with a mixture of fascination and disdain, was pure Vico.

12. Giambattista Vico, *The New Science*, trans. Thomas Goddard Bergin and Max Harold Fisch (Ithaca, N.Y.: Cornell University Press, 1984), 76–77, paragraphs 225–26. Citations to the *New Science* will hereafter be given in the text and employ the now-standard paragraph numeration. For Vico's Italian original I use Giambattista Vico, *Opere*, 2 vols., ed. Andrea Battistini (Milan: Mondadori, 1990). For a more extended account of the Vichian topics summarized here, see Gary Tomlinson, "Vico's Songs: Detours at the Origins of (Ethno)Musicology," *Musical Quarterly* 83 (1999): 344–77.

13. Or at least it usually is so. There are occasional moments when he seems to glimpse Vico's broader view, as in the Pueblo Indian lecture, where he describes dance, with its drumming and chanting, itself as a magical, causal symbol (*Images,* 16–17, 48); or in his article on Dürer, where he writes, with an aphoristic genius that brings to mind Benjamin, that "The true voice of antiquity, which the Renaissance knew well, chimes with the image" (*The Renewal,* 555).

14. Warburg, *The Renewal*, 386, 543–44.

15. Katharine Park, "The Organic Soul," in *The Cambridge History of Renaissance Philosophy,* ed. Charles B. Schmitt, Quentin Skinner and Eckhard Kessler (Cambridge: Cambridge University Press, 1988), 465–84, esp. 481.

16. For more detailed accounts of Ficinian song, see D. P. Walker, *Spriritual and Demonic Magic from Ficino to Campanella,* 2nd ed. (Notre Dame, Ind.: University of Notre Dame Press, 1975) and Gary Tomlinson, *Music in Renaissance Magic: Toward a Historiography of Others* (Chicago: University of Chicago Press, 1993).

17. Ficino, *De vita coelitus comparanda,* 3: 21: quoted from Tomlinson, *Music in Renaissance Magic,* 111–12.

18. Al-Kindi, *De radiis,* quoted from Tomlinson, *Music in Renaissance Magic,* 122–23.

19. Pomponazzi, *De incantationibus,* and Diacceto, *De pulchro,* quoted from Tomlinson, *Music in Renaissance Magic,* respectively 201, 126–27.

20. The account here of Monteverdi's late style recalls and elaborates that in Gary Tomlinson, *Monteverdi and the End of the Renaissance* (Berkeley: University of California Press, 1987); for the first two quotations see 205, 219. For the preface to the *Madrigali guerrieri et amorosi,* see *Strunk's Source Readings in Music History,* rev. ed., ed. Leo Treitler, vol. 4, *The Baroque Era,* ed. Margaret Murata (New York: W.W. Norton, 1998), 157–59.

21. Ellen Rosand, "The Descending Tetrachord: An Emblem of Lament," *Musical Quarterly* 65 (1979): 346–59.

Chapter 10. The Passions and the Interests in Early Modern Europe: The Case of Guarini's Il Pastor fido

1. Albert Hirschman, *The Passions and the Interests: Political Arguments for Capitalism before its Triumph* (Princeton, N.J.: Princeton University Press, 1977), 9.

The present chapter builds on a lecture I gave as Visiting Chair of Italian Studies at the University of California, Berkeley, in 1996. I am grateful to Louise George Clubb for this invitation, for her intellectual example, and for her hospitality during my stay. Thanks are due as well to the editors of this volume, Catherine Gimelli Martin and Lawrence Rhu, for comments on an earlier draft.

2. See, for example, Cicero, *De oratore*, trans. E. W. Sutton and H. Rackham (Cambridge, Mass.: Harvard University Press 1967), 2.53.216: "appeals, whether mild or passionate, and whether for winning favour or stirring the feelings, must be swept aside by exciting the opposite impressions, so that goodwill may be done away with by hate, and compassion by jealousy." Aristotle's discussion of catharsis was also read as a theory of countervailing passion. See the account of these debates in Bernard Weinberg, *History of Literary Criticism in the Italian Renaissance*, 2 vols. (Chicago: University of Chicago Press, 1961).

3. On the reception of Horace in the Renaissance, see Marvin T. Herrick, *The Fusion of Horatian and Aristotelian Criticism, 1531–55* (Urbana: University of Illinois Press, 1946), and Weinberg, *History of Literary Criticism*, 1: 71–249. For Castelvetro's argument about pleasure as the goal of poetry, see Lodovico Castelvetro, *Poetica d'Aristotele vulgarizzata e sposta*, ed. Werther Romani, 2 vols. (Bari: Laterza, 1978). In his commentary on Aristotle's *Poetics*, Guarini's friend Antonio Riccoboni also argued that pleasure—"fabulosa delectatio"—was the primary end of poetry, while moral instruction was an ancillary effect. For Riccoboni, poetry was an art, and in this respect like rhetoric. See Weinberg, *History of Literary Criticism*, 1: 604.

4. See Nicholas Perella, *The Critical Fortune of Battista Guarini's "Il Pastor Fido"* (Florence: l.S. Olschki, 1973), 6.

5. Guarini defended *Il Pastor fido* in his *Compendio della poesia tragicomica*. I quote the *Compendio* from Giambattista Guarini, *Il Pastor fido e Il Compendio della poesia tragicomica*, ed. Gioachino Brognoligo (Bari: Laterza, 1914). Part of the *Compendio* is translated by Allan H. Gilbert in *Literary Criticism: Plato to Dryden* (New York: American Book Company, 1940). *Il Pastor fido* was composed between 1580 and 1585, and circulated in manuscript before being published in 1590. Giason Denores published his *Discorso di Iason Denores intorno à que' principii, cause, et accrescimenti, che la comedia, la tragedia, et il poema heroica ricevono dalla philosophia morale & civile, & dai governatori delle republiche* in 1586. The text is reproduced in *Trattati di poetica e retorica del cinquecento*, ed. Bernard Weinberg, 4 vols. (Bari: Laterza, 1970–74), 3: 375–419. Guarini responded with *Il Verrato* in 1588. Denores responded to this in 1590. In 1593 Guarini published *Il Verrato secondo*. The two are published in Battista Guarini, *Opere*, ed. G. A. Tumermani, 4 vols. (Verona, 1737–38), vol. 3. The *Compendio* combines the two replies to Denores in a somewhat less vitriolic form than the originals.

6. See Weinberg, *History of Literary Criticism*, 2: 1103. According to Weinberg, the polemic surrounding *Il Pastor fido* "poses . . . the issues of Renaissance practical criticism more clearly and in a more concentrated way" than any other Italian polemic of the sixteenth century. This opposition between didacticism and aesthetic autonomy has informed modern readings of *Il Pastor fido* as well. Here critical opinion is divided over whether *Pastor fido*'s emphasis on providence and natural law is simply a disingenuous cover for a celebration of earthly pleasures; or whether

Guarini is genuinely concerned to reconcile pleasure and virtue, natural and divine law, free will and providence in accordance with the dictates of the Counter-Reformation Church.

7. For an earlier defense of the innovations of romance, see C. B. Giraldi Cinzio, "Discorso . . . dei romanzi," in *Scritti critici*, ed. Camillo Guerrieri Crocetti (Milan: Mazorati, 1973). An English translation exists in *Giraldi Cinthio on Romances*, trans. Henry L. Snuggs (Lexington: University Press of Kentucky, 1968). Cinzio's treatise was completed in 1549 and published in 1554.

8. Torquato Tasso, *Discourses on the Heroic Poem*, trans. Mariella Cavalchini and Irene Samuel (Oxford: Clarendon Press, 1973), 30.

9. Cited in Perella, *The Critical Fortune*, 11. See also Denores, *Discorso*, in Weinberg, *Trattati*, 3: 375–76: "essendo la poetica, come è anco la retorica, soggetta alla filosofia morale e civile, e da essa ricevendo ogni sua più regolata produzione, que' più svegliati governatori delle republiche . . . hanno con prudentissime ordinazioni procurato . . . che tutte però finalmente risultassero a lor beneficio et a conservazione di quella tal ben formata republica."

10. Denores, *Discorso*, in Weinberg, *Trattati*, 3: 405, 418.

11. Denores, *Discorso*, in Weinberg, *Trattati*, 3: 413.

12. Vittorio Rossi, *Battista Guarini ed Il Pastor Fido* (Torino: E. Loescher, 1886), 250 n. 1: "quelle due infelici sorelle, le prime che lessero una tal famosa tragicommedia pubblicata pur allora alle stampe [*Il Pastor Fido*], fatte alla prima lezione sì buone maestre di impurità che ne aprirono subito scuola, mutando la casa in postribolo e publicando sè per meretrici; non le tante maritate, che, udita recitare la medesima pastorale (ed è osservazione di molto tempo), dove pudiche andarono, di là partirono impudiche, e praticando quella sciolta scienza d'amar chi piace, di che udirono colà i precetti, scoperta l'infedeltà e con gli adulteri uccise, dalla finte lascivie di una tragicommedia riportarono per sè il vero riuscimento di una tragedia."

13. As Belisario Bulgarini argued, rather than effecting a catharsis of the passions and inspiring in us a hatred of sin, Francesca seduces her readers just as she was herself seduced: the aesthetic pleasure of reading displaces any moral considerations. For Bulgarini this meant that, pace the Counter-Reformation defenders of Dante, poetry was an art, not subordinate to practical philosophy. See Giuseppe Toffanin, *Il Cinquecento* (Milan: F. Vallardi, 1954), 601.

14. Cited by Rossi, *Battista Guarini*, 249.

15. See Guarini, *Compendio*, 245: "se le pubbliche rappresentazioni sono fatte per gli ascoltanti, bisogna bene secondo la varietà de' costumi et de' tempi si vadano eziando mutando i poemi"; and 272–74 on the new genre of tragicomedy. I quote here from Weinberg, *History of Literary Criticism*, 2: 1104; see also 1078–79.

16. As Weinberg comments in *History of Literary Criticism*, "Against the old thesis that the precepts of art determine the poet's practice is set the new thesis that the poet's practice determines the precepts of art. More moderately stated, the contention is that practice and precepts are in constant interaction, with no fixity or permanence on either part" (2: 1104–5).

17. Guarini, *Il Verrato*, cited in Weinberg, *History of Literary Criticism*, 2: 656–57.

18. See Guarini, *Verrato secondo*, quoted in Perella, *Critical Fortune*, 342–43. See also Weinberg, *History of Literary Criticism*, 2: 680: "According to Guarini, this is an

Aristotelian distinction . . . between the error *per se* (which consists in a bad imitation) and the error *per accidens* (which consists in imitating an object in itself bad or untrue)." Guarini could also have found this distinction between the philosophical and rhetorical treatment of the passions and of the supreme good in Cicero, *De oratore*, 1.51.222–1.52.225. See also *Il Verrato secondo* (in Guarini, *Opere*, 3: 93; quoted in Perella, *Critical Fortune*, 347), where Guarini points up difference between Aristotle's definition of happiness in *Nicomachean Ethics* and in the *Rhetoric*: in the former, "la felicità esser operazione dell'animo virtuosamente prodotta nella vita perfecta"; "Ma nella retorica, dove la considera, secondo l'opinione de' più, ce la descrive molto alterata. La felicità, dice egli, è una fortuna prospera accompagnata con la virtù, ovvero una vita, che non ha bisogno di nulla, una vita lieta e secura, un possedere di molte facoltà, un esser gagliardo della persona, un'aver modo, e di fare, e di conservare, d'accrescere tutte le dette cose. . . . Quando Aristotile dice, che la favola è azione di felicità, e d'infelicità, non intende della morale, ma di quella della retorica."

19. On these two ends of poetry, see Weinberg, *History of Literary Criticism*, 2: 657, quoting Guarini, *Il Verrato*. On the way in which poetry tempers and purges the passions, see 2: 658. In his discussion of purgation in his *Compendio*, Guarini adopts the medical interpretation of catharsis, according to which the "purifying and cleansing of the emotions" moderates them and ultimately makes them more serviceable to virtue (*Compendio*, 235–37).

20. The phrase "signor del mondo" comes from Battista Guarini, *Trattato della politica libertà* in *Opere*, ed. Marziano Guglielminetti (Turin: UTET, 1971), 866; "l'umana cupidità [che] non ha termine" (865). The *Trattato* was composed in 1589 but not published until the nineteenth century, when it was criticized by Foscolo for celebrating despotism. See Luigi Fassò's Introduction to his edition of *Il Pastor fido* (Turin: Einaudi, 1976).

21. Perella, *Critical Fortune*, 349; *Verrato secondo* in Guarini, *Opere*, 3: 101. Few critics have noted the political dimension of Guarini's defense of *Il Pastor fido*. An exception is Giuseppe Toffanin, *La fine dell'umanesimo* (Milan: Fratelli Bocca, 1920), 154ff. See also Jane Tylus Klein, "Purloined Passages: Giraldi, Tasso, and the Pastoral Debates," *MLN* 99 (1984): 101–24, esp. 114, who focusses on the links Guarini establishes between his pastoral characters and mythical legislators at the beginning of civilization. For Machiavelli's censure of ideal republics, see chapter 15 of *The Prince*.

22. Niccolò Machiavelli, *The Prince*, trans. Robert M. Adams (New York: W.W. Norton, 1977), 27.

23. The sixteenth-century Englishman John Hoskins argued in a similar vein in his manual of rhetoric, *Directions for Speech and Style* (c. 1599–1600), and here the connection between Aristotle and Machiavelli is explicit. According to Hoskins, the teaching of Aristotle's *Ethics* is unfit for the real world because, "as Machiavel saith, perfect virtue or perfect vice is not seen in our time . . . therefore the understanding of Aristotle's *Rhetoric* is the directest means to move, to please, or to present any motion whatsoever." Quoted in Wayne Rebhorn, *The Emperor of Men's Minds* (Ithaca, N.Y.: Cornell University Press, 1995), 127–28.

24. See Terence Cave, *Recognitions: A Study in Poetics* (Oxford: Clarendon Press, 1988), Introduction. In Aristotle's *Rhetoric*, probable reasoning is an interested

activity in two senses: it is in the interest of the orator to persuade his audience by means of probable arguments and he determines what is probable by accommodating his arguments to the passions and interests of his audience.

25. See Cave, *Recognitions*, 246. In book 1 of the *Rhetoric* Aristotle classifies as atechnical proofs signs such as "laws, witnesses, contracts, torture, and oaths"—atechnical because the orator finds them ready-made: they are not a product of his rhetorical art although he may draw on them to make his case. In chapter 16 of the *Poetics* Aristotle tells us that recognition (one of three elements of the tragic plot) involves probable reasoning about similarly atechnical signs of identity; and in chapter 24 he relates such inartistic proofs to paralogism, that is, to probabilistic or faulty reasoning: "Paralogism, which consists in inferring an antecedent from an inadequate consequent, is the name in logic for the procedure by which contingent clues are made to yield positive identifications. In logic, it is a dubious procedure; in practice, it works often enough to secure its survival. . . . paralogism is both the means by which characters in fictions deceive other characters (the tactic of the impostor) and the means by which the writer induces the reader to credit his fiction" (Cave, *Recognitions*, 249).

26. Sixteenth-century Italian critics of *Il Pastor fido*, such as Giovanni Malacreta and Fausto Summo, objected to various improbable elements of the plot, implicitly linking Guarini's violation of artistic decorum with a similar offense to ethics. For example, they criticized Aminta's prayer to Diana for revenge. For Guarini's defense, see *Compendio*, 284; though see 285 where Guarini points out that, pace Aristotle, *Oedipus Rex* does involve the sign of Oedipus's pierced feet, which corresponds to the cradle and the cessation of miracles in the temple in *Il Pastor fido*; in both, however, these are signs "nascenti dall'intima necessità della favola," and in any case are rather motives for crediting the ensuing account rather than material evidence themselves (285: "sono più indizi che segni"). For Guarini's critics, see Weinberg, *History of Literary Criticism*, 2: 1096. Fausto Summo similarly complained that the comic parts of Guarini's plot were "vile, dishonest, cold, and not very probable" (Weinberg, 2: 1095).

27. See Guarini, *Compendio*, 280.

28. By interest here I mean both self-interest and political interest, as well as the relationship between them. I quote from Battista Guarini, *Il Pastor fido*, ed. Fassò, and, unless otherwise indicated, from the seventeenth-century translation by an acquaintance of Edward Dymocke (or by another Dymocke), reprinted in *Three Renaissance Pastorals: Tasso, Guarini, Daniel*, ed. Elizabeth Story Donno (Binghamton, N.Y.: Medieval and Renaissance Texts and Studies, 1993). See also the seventeenth-century translation of Richard Fanshawe, *A Critical Edition of Sir Richard Fanshawe's 1647 Translation of Giovanni Battista Guarini's "Il Pastor Fido,"* ed. Walter F. Staton, Jr., and Willam E. Simeone (Oxford: Clarendon Press, 1964). The Fanshawe translation is more accurate, but the Dymocke translation (which omits a substantial part of the original) is often more readable.

29. Critical opinion is divided on the relationship of virtue and pleasure, as well as divine fate and human action in this play. In "Fate, Blindness, and Illusion in the *Pastor Fido*," *Romanic Review* 49 (1958): 252–68, Nicholas Perella argues that the message of *Il Pastor fido* is skeptical and naturalistic: the weakness of human reason

and the obscurity of divine will justify focussing on this worldly pleasure, though "sanctioned" by providential oversight (265). In "The Moralist in Arcadia: England and Italy," *Romance Philology* 19 (1965): 341–52, Louise George Clubb stresses in contrast the genuinely ethical dimension of the play: "anti-natural reason and law are proved false; true reason and true law are found to be in accord with heaven, fate, and nature" (348). Similarly, whereas postlapsarian art (Corisca) corrupts nature, true art is in conformity with nature (349). Thus, "while it is impossible to disagree with Perella that the erotic effect dominates in the *Pastor Fido*, it is equally impossible to agree that the praise of *onestà* is only a conventional pretext" (350). I know of no argument, however, that reads the play in terms of the political interest of aesthetic and rhetorical form as I do here.

30. Terry Eagleton, *The Ideology of the Aesthetic* (London: Blackwell, 1990), 34. Eagleton is anatomizing the ideology of the aesthetic as it develops in eighteenth-century European culture but the description he offers also describes the Arcadian world of *Il Pastor fido*.

31. Good and evil turn out to be the result of what we might call good or bad aesthetic force. Here it's interesting to note that Guarini's predecessor Giraldi—alias Cinthio—derived the term romance etymologically from Roma, and Roma from the Greek for strength or power. See *Cinthio*, ed. Snuggs, 5.

32. *Il Pastor fido*, 4.2.89–91; I quote Fanshawe, 4.2.3238–39; Dymocke, 4.2.26–27. This rhetoric of the passions could also be called an art. See Louise George Clubb's tracing of the use of "arte" in *Il Pastor fido* in *Italian Drama in Shakespeare's Time* (New Haven, Conn.: Yale University Press, 1989), 133. As she points out, "the word is most often on the lips of the deceitful Corisca"; but it also used by Carino in reference to "l'arte del poetar" (5.1.189) and the art of medicine.

33. *Il Pastor fido*, 3.1.23–29; Fanshawe, 3.1.2103–8 (from whom the translation is taken); Dymocke, 3.1.16–20.

34. *Il Pastor fido*, 3.2.73–74; Fanshawe, 3.2.2139–40 (from whom the translation is taken); Dymocke, 3.2.7–8.

35. *Il Pastor fido*, 3.2.92–95; Fanshawe, 3.2.2155–58 (from whom the translation is taken); Dymocke, 3.2.17–20.

36. In the second *Verrato*, Guarini distinguished poetry from rhetoric and politics by arguing that "poetry is unique in being concerned simultaneously with both vice and virtue, since both are objects of imitation" (Weinberg, *History of Literary Criticism*, 2: 1085, paraphrasing Guarini).

37. *Il Pastor fido*, 3.3.367–70; Fanshawe, 3.3.2382–83 (from whom the translation is taken); Dymocke, 3.3.130–32.

38. *Il Pastor fido*, 3.3.456–57; Fanshawe, 3.3.2446–47; Dymocke, 3.3.188–89 (from whom the translation is taken).

39. *Il Pastor fido*, 4.8.980–81, 1023; Fanshawe, 4.8.387–80, 3909; Dymocke, 4.8.10, 33.

40. *Il Pastor fido*, 4.8.1056–58; Fanshawe, 4.8.3932–33; Dymocke, 8.4.54–55.

41. *Il Pastor fido*, 5.6.1207–8; Fanshawe: 5.6.5223–24; Dymocke, 5.6.155–57.

42. On Boccalini, see Friedrich Meinecke, *Machiavellism*, trans. Douglas Scott (1924; Boulder: University of Colorado Press, 1984), 70–89. I quote from Henry Carey's translation of Boccalini, *News from Parnassus* (London, 1656), citing volume and number from *I Ragguagli di Parnasso*, and then page number in Carey.

43. Robert M. Adams translates this section of the *Ragguagli* in his edition of Machiavelli, *The Prince*, 262–64.

44. Roger Ascham, *The Scholemaster*, ed. Lawrence J. Ryan (Charlottesville, Va.: Folger Shakespeare Library and University Press of Virginia, 1967), 68.

45. Ascham, *The Scholemaster*, 73–74.

46. Ascham, *The Scholemaster*, 66. Ascham mentions Machiavelli on p. 72.

47. Arthur F. Marotti, "'Love Is Not Love': Elizabethan Sonnet Sequences and the Social Order," *ELH* 49 (1982): 396–428, 399. On the political dimension of Elizabethan pastoral, see also Louis A. Montrose, "Of Gentlemen and Shepherds: The Politics of Elizabethan Pastoral Form," *ELH* 54 (1987): 415–39.

48. Lorna Hutson, *The Usurer's Daugher: Male Friendship and Fictions of Women in Sixteenth-Century England* (London: Routledge, 1994): "both humanistic *novelle* and neoclassical drama were considered to be formally instructive in the forging of ambiguous contractual relations which, based in merely local acts of persuasion, might gain a man credit with his interlocutor, without rendering himself legally obliged or accountable. As 'schoolmasters' of such subversive ethics, these fictions were perceived by men like Gosson and Ascham to be threatening to the traditional forms of alliance-friendship, which depended on unambiguously signalled 'assurances' (sworn promises, gifts, acts of hospitality) of allegiance and fidelity between houses" (118). See also Jean-Christophe Agnew, *Worlds Apart: The Market and the Theater in Anglo-American Thought, 1550–1750* (Cambridge: Cambridge University Press, 1988); and Joan Pong Linton, *The Romance of the New World: Gender and the Literary Formations of English Colonialism* (Cambridge: Cambridge University Press, 1998), who discusses how anxiety about the new market economy is displaced onto sixteenth-century popular romance.

49. On affect, see Hutson, *Usurer's Daughter*, 13, and chapter 6.

50. Lois Potter, *Secret Rites and Secret Writing: Royalist Literature, 1641–1660* (Cambridge: Cambridge University Press, 1989), 107. On the political dimension of seventeenth-century prose romance in England, see also Annabel Patterson, *Censorship and Interpretation* (Madison: University of Wisconsin Press, 1984); and my "Reinventing Romance, or the Surprising Effects of Sympathy," *Renaissance Quarterly* 55 (2002): 625–66.

51. Potter, *Secret Rites*, 73; Christopher Hughes, "Romance, Probability, and Politics in England, 1650–1720," Ph.D. dissertation, Princeton University, 1995, cites this passage in a discussion of the Puritan use of romance to suggest the improbability of the royal cause (75).

52. This and the following paragraphs on Fanshawe draw on a footnote to my article, "Margaret Cavendish and the Romance of Contract," *Renaissance Quarterly* 50 (1997): 526–66.

53. See M. M. Bakhtin, *The Dialogic Imagination*, ed. Michael Holquist, trans. Caryl Emerson and Michael Holquist (Austin: University of Texas Press, 1981), on the Greek "adventure novel of ordeal," in which "from the very beginning, the love between the hero and heroine is not subject to doubt; this love remains *absolutely unchanged* throughout the entire novel" (89). Bakhtin remarks on the relevance of this "chronotope" to the seventeenth century: "In the seventeenth century, the fates of nations, kingdoms and cultures were also drawn into this adventure-time of

chance, gods and villains, a time with its own specific logic. This occurs in the earliest European historical novels, for example in de Scudéry's *Artamène, or the Grand Cyrus*, in Lohenstein's *Arminius and Tusnelda* and in the historical novels of La Calprenède. Pervading these novels is a curious 'philosophy of history' that hands over the settling of historical destinies to an extratemporal hiatus that exists between two moments of a real time sequence" (96).

54. *The Faithful Shepherd*, trans. Fanshawe (London, 1647), 304, 221.

55. Fredric Jameson, *The Political Unconscious* (Ithaca, N.Y.: Cornell University Press,1981), 115–16. Jameson argues that the romance opposition between good and evil is itself an ideological construction, one best analyzed by Nietzsche in *The Genealogy of Morals*: "we have forgotten the thrust of Nietzsche's thought and lost everything scandalous and virulent about it if we cannot understand how it is ethics itself which is the ideological vehicle and the legitimation of concrete structures of power and domination" (114). For Jameson, tragedy is an example of a generic mode which is not predicated on such an ethical binary opposition: to the extent that the characters of a tragedy are perceived to be absolutely good or evil, the tragedy slides toward melodrama (116).

56. See Northrop Frye, *Anatomy of Criticism* (Princeton, N.J.: Princeton University Press, 1957).

57. Eagleton, *Ideology of the Aesthetic*, 3, 9, 27.

Chapter 11. Sadness in The Faerie Queene

1. Edmund Spenser, *The Faerie Queene*, ed. A. C. Hamilton (1977; reprint London: Longman, 1995), Book 1, Canto 1, stanza 2, line 8. Subsequent references to the poem will be made parenthetically, noting book, canto, stanza, and line numbers. I am grateful to the editors of this volume for their helpful and thoughtful comments on this essay.

2. Spenser, Appendix I: "A Letter of the Author's," in *The Faerie Queene*, 737–738.

3. When, for example, Brutus questions Casca in *Julius Caesar* (1599) as to why the unknowing subject of an assassination plot "looks so sad," Casca responds by describing the aspiring emperor's occasion for great joy, not depression: "Why, there was a crown offered him; and being offered him, he put it by with the back of his hand, thus, and then the people fell a-shouting." William Shakespeare, *Julius Caesar*, ed. David Daniell (Walton-on-Thames, Surrey: Thomas Nelson and Sons, 1998), 1. 2. 217, 220–22.

4. *OED*, 346. Pre-1628 usages of "sad" to name unhappiness abound. For example, see Shakespeare, *Tragedy of Antony and Cleopatra*, ed. Michael Neill (Oxford: Oxford University Press, 1994), 1.3.3–4; 1.5.50–60.

5. According to Katharine Park, nominalists in the late fifteenth century began to argue that the soul was not separated out to different parts of the body—as Aristotle had argued—but rather contained *in toto* throughout its tissues, membranes, bloodvessels, and extremities. "The Organic Soul," in *The Cambridge History of Renaissance Philosophy*, ed. Charles B. Schmitt, Quentin Skinner, and Eckhard Kessler (Cambridge: Cambridge University Press, 1988), 464–84. Galenists in the

sixteenth century increasingly argued for a similarly material dispensation of the soul, as when, for example William Vaughan argues that if "the soule is in the bloud, and dispersed through euery part of the same, (as God is wholy in the world, and wholy in euery part the same) then surely must it follow, that the variety of the bloud doth change and diuersifie the vnderstanding, and also that the actes of the vnderstanding soule doth change the humours of the body: so that out of these diuersities of tainted humours there are ingendred strange and wandring phantasies, caused by reason of such blacke bloud, smoake and sweat, which is crept into the humour of melancholy" *Approved Directions for Health* (London, 1612), 101–2. See also the opening chapter of André du Laurens's *A Discourse of the Preservation of Sight: of Melancholike Diseases; of Rheumes, and of Old Age,* trans. Richard Surphlet (London, 1599), 1–9: "That the braine is the true seate of the Soule, and that for this occasion all the instruments of the sences are lodged round about it."

6. Michael MacDonald, "*The Fearefull Estate of Francis Spira*: Narrative, Identity, and Emotion in Early Modern England," *Journal of British Studies,* 31, (January, 1992: 32–61, 46–49.

7. See Thomas Wright, *The Passions of the Minde in Generall, and with Sundry New Discourses Augmented* (1601), facsimile of the 1604 edition (Urbana: University of Illinois Press, 1971); Thomas Walkington, *The Optick Glasse of Humors* (London, 1639).

8. Paul Slack, "Mirrors of Health and Treasures of Poor Men: The Uses of the Vernacular Medical Literature of Tudor England," in *Health, Medicine, and Mortality in The Sixteenth Century,* ed. Charles Webster (Cambridge: Cambridge University Press, 1979), 237–73, 255.

9. Noel Brann, "The Problem of Distinguishing Religious Guilt from Religious Melancholy in the English Renaissance," *Journal of the Rocky Mountain Medieval and Renaissance Association* 1 (1980): 69. Quoted by Donald Beecher in "The Anatomy of Melancholy in Book I of the *Faerie Queene*," *Renaissance and Reformation,* New Series 12, 2 (1988): 85–99, 87.

10. MacDonald, "*Fearefull Estate of Francis Spira,*" 59–60.

11. Owsei Temkin, *Galenism: Rise and Decline of a Medical Philosophy* (Ithaca, N.Y.: Cornell University Press, 1973), 171.

12. I am not the first to suggest a link between these two texts. See, for example, Susan Snyder, "The Left Hand of God: Despair in Medieval and Renaissance Tradition," *Studies in The Renaissance* 12 (1965): 18–59, 38–39; Donald Beecher, "Spenser's Redcrosse Knight: Despair and the Elizabethan Malady," *Renaissance and Reformation,* New Series 1, 1 (1987): 115–17. Unlike Beecher, however, who argues that Redcrosse could not be suffering from religious melancholy "because the concept no longer existed *per se*" (114), I contend instead that Spenser deliberately resuscitates a Medieval model for religious sadness so as to counter the Galenic category of the dispositional melancholic.

13. See Robert Burton, *The Anatomy of Melancholy,* 3 vols., ed. Thomas C. Faulkner, Nicolas K. Kiessling, and Rhonda L. Blair (Oxford: Clarendon Press, 1989), 1: 372.

14. Timothy Bright, *A Treatise of Melancholie,* facsimile of the 1586 edition (New York: Columbia University Press, 1940), "The Epistle Dedicatorie," iii verso.

15. See Juan Huarte, *Examende ingenios: The Examination of Mens Wits* (Oxford: Clarendon Press, 1594).

16. Sukanta Chaudhuri, *Infirm Glory: Shakespeare and the Renaissance Image of Man* (Oxford: Clarendon Press, 1981), 63.

17. Walter Ralegh, *The Works of Sir Walter Ralegh*, 8 vols (New York: Burt Franklin, 1829), 8: 571–91, 571, 572. As Sukanta Chaudhuri explains Ralegh's schema, "The highest element of the soul, in which the divine image inheres, does not really belong to man. It is not an organic part of his humanity but merely an addition made by God, testifying to his mercy rather than man's power. It enables man to guide and fulfil the potential of his own nature; but the motive force is God's free and arbitrary goodness" (*Infirm Glory*, 62).

18. Stanley W. Jackson, "Acedia the Sin and Its Relationship to Sorrow and Melancholia," in *Culture and Depression: Studies in the Anthropology and Cross-Cultural Psychiatry of Affect and Disorder*, ed. Arthur Kleinman and Byron Good (Berkeley: University of California Press, 1985), 53–54. While there were also negative connotations attached to tristitia, not every manifestation of such sorrow was considered sinful, whereas acedia had a uniformly sinful reputation. See Morton W. Bloomfield, *The Seven Deadly Sins* (Lansing: Michigan State College Press, 1952), 356 n. 25.

19. See, for example, Hamlet's exonerating self-description at the end of Act 2: "The spirit that I have seen / May be a devil, and the devil hath power, T'assume a pleasing shape, yea, and perhaps, / Out of my weakness and my melancholy, / As he is very potent with such spirits, / Abuses me to damn me." Shakespeare, *Hamlet*, ed. Harold Jenkins (London: Methuen, 1982), 2.2.594–99.

20. Jonathan Goldberg, *Endlesse Worke: Spenser and the Structures of Discourse* (Baltimore: Johns Hopkins University Press, 1981), xi.

21. As Judith Anderson has noted, Redcrosse "does not fully possess the virtues which Fidelia, Speranza, and Charissa represent, and so these figures are bound to be abstract or disembodied. In fact, because Redcrosse neither possesses nor embodies the condition of Holiness at the outset of Canto 10, he, too, is bound virtually to disappear from sight." "The July Eclogue and the House of Holiness: Perspective in Spenser," *Studies in English Literature* 10 (1970): 17–32, 24–25.

22. Spenser's description of Contemplation here approaches Marsilio Ficino's definition of the state, described by Nesca A. Robb as one in which "the soul's grasp on essential truth [is] brought about by the full and harmonious exertion of reason and love," *Neoplatonism of the Italian Renaissance* (London: Allen and Unwin, 1935), 69.

23. Edgar Wind, *Pagan Mysteries in the Renaissance* (1958, reprint New York: Norton, 1968, 45.

24. John R. Maier, "Sansjoy and the Furor Melancholicus," *Modern Language Studies* 5: 1 (1975): 78–87, 84. For Ficino's account of genial melancholy see his *De Vita Libri Tres* (*Three Books on Life*), trans. Carol V. Kaske and John R. Clark (Tempe, Ariz.: Medieval and Renaissance Texts and Studies, 1998), 109–23. I follow Juliana Schiesari who argues that "the regime of the body that comprises book I [of the *De Vita*] is finally directed to an elision of the body, to its being forgotten so that the disappearance of the body implies its disappearance as an obstacle to philosophical contemplation." *The Gendering of Melancholia: Feminism, Psychoanalysis, and the Symbolics of Loss in Renaissance Literature* (Ithaca, N.Y.: Cornell University Press,

1992), 134. Spenser nowhere offers even a provisional endorsement of genial melancholy. Even in the House of Alma (2.9), the figure Melancholy's powers of insight are described as "idle thoughts and fantasies, / Deuices, dreames, opinions vnsound, / Shewes, visions, sooth-sayes, and prophesies; / And all that fained is, as leasings, tales, and lies" (2.9.51.6–9). This does not mean that Spenser rejects Ficino's high estimation of rapture, but rather underscores how multifaceted and contradictory Ficino's accounts of inspiration were. According to Paul Oskar Kristeller, Ficino developed two contradictory views on internal experience, one predicated on "the medieval Christian conception as given by St. Augustine" whereby "restlessness of consciousness . . . is inserted into a great metaphysical or theological context" and the other, in which, "when we speak of melancholy, the state of mind is conceived within itself and without any metaphysical background." *The Philosophy of Marsilio Ficino*, trans. Virginia Conant (New York: Columbia University Press, 1943), 213. "In spite of a common foundation and of a recognizable affinity," Kristeller goes on to say, "they [i.e. these two theories of internal experience] lack entirely a conceptual bond" (214).

25. Precise source-material studies supporting a specifically limitable, "Neoplatonic" range of ideas for Spenser, or any other poet in the sixteenth century, would flounder amidst what Don Cameron Allen termed, nearly seventy years ago, the sixteenth century "struggle towards eclecticism and harmonies." "The Degeneration of Man and Renaissance Pessimism," *Studies in Philology* 35, 1 (January, 1938): 202–27, 208. As Alastair Fowler has pointed out more recently, "the single orthodox Neoplatonic system, to which many Renaissance scholars have found it convenient to refer, has never had any real existence: differences, even between the systems of Pico and Ficino, obstinately divide the parts of the chimera." "Emanations of Glory: Neoplatonic Order in Spenser's *Faerie Queen*," in *A Theatre for Spenserians*, ed. Judith M. Kennedy and James A. Reither (Toronto: University of Toronto Press, 1973), 53–82, 7n. 3. Cf. Jon A. Quitslund, "Platonism" entry in *The Spenser Encyclopedia*, general editor A. C. Hamilton (Toronto: University of Toronto Press, 1990), 546–48.

26. See, for example, Andrew Hadfield, *Edmund Spenser's Irish Experience: Wilde Fruit and Salvage Soyl* (Oxford: Clarendon Press, 1997), esp. 113–45.

27. Gordon Teskey, *Allegory and Violence* (Ithaca, N.Y.: Cornell University Press, 1996), 17.

28. Teskey, *Allegory*, 17. As Susanne Wofford has argued, Spenser "presents his allegorical narrator as a hierarchizer, someone who will sort out the meanings for us, perhaps after hinting at a wider range of meanings that will not be pursued in his interpretation." *The Choice of Achilles: The Ideology of Figure in the Epic* (Stanford, Calif.: Stanford University Press, 1992), 223. See also Elizabeth Bieman, *Plato Baptized: Towards The Interpretation of Spenser's Mimetic Fictions* (Toronto: University of Toronto Press, 1988), 134–39.

29. Slack, "Mirrors of Health" 241.

30. J.-P. Pittion, "Scepticism and Medicine in the Renaissance," in *Scepticism from the Renaissance to the Enlightenment*, ed. Richard H. Popkin and Charles B. Schmitt (Wiesbaden: Otto Harrassowitz, 1987), 103–32, 117.

31. Hardin Craig, "Introduction" to Timothy Bright's *A Treatise of Melancholie*, v–xxii, xi–xii.

32. Referring to the *De Temperamentis*, Beecher argues that although this text was "well-known to Medieval thinkers ... with the general rise in prestige and influence of Galenic medicine in the sixteenth century came a correspondingly wider claim by physicians that the passions of the soul belonged to the sphere of medical authority in a clinical sense." "Anatomy of Melancholy," 89.

33. On Spenser's treatment of acedia in the poem, see Janet Spens, *Spenser's Faerie Queene: An Interpretation* (1934, reprint New York: Russell and Russell, 1967), 122–38. On the early modern period's conception of despair as paradoxically marking the first step either toward salvation or loss of faith, see Snyder, "The Left Hand of God," esp. p. 20. See also Thomas P. Roche's fine close-reading of the scene in "The Menace of Despair and Arthur's Vision, *Faerie Queene* I.9," *Spenser Studies* 4 (1984): 71–91.

34. Winfried Schleiner, *Melancholy, Genius, and Utopia in the Renaissance* (Wiesbaden: Otto Harrassowitz, 1991), 70.

35. Martin Luther, *Letters of Spiritual Counsel*, ed. and trans. Theodore G. Tappert (Philadelphia: Westminster Press, 1955), 93. "God created man for society and not for solitude," he says elsewhere. "Solitude produces melancholy. When we are alone the worst and saddest things come to mind" (95). Spenser, by contrast, requires of Redcrosse a period of fasting and seclusion in the House of Holiness before he is cured of his despair (1.10.25–26).

36. Schleiner suggests, in opposition to Luther's negative appraisal of melancholy, Melanchthon's positive appreciation of sorrowfulness, particularly as evidenced in his *Commentarius de Anima* (1540), noting that there is little in this reformer's assessment of melancholy that draws on "traditional humoral physiology" (*Melancholy, Genius, and Utopia*, 97). Unlike Melanchthon's model, however, Spenserian sadness asserts a dispositional-like—although humorless—quality, as it is an intrinsic part of Redrosse and Una's personae, not a state of mind that arises during certain activities.

37. Wright, *Passions of the Minde*, 17.

38. Thomas More, *De Tristitia Christi*, in *The Complete Prose Works of St. Thomas More*, ed. and trans. Clarence H. Miller (New Haven, Conn.: Yale University Press, 1976), vol. 14, part 1, 3, 19–21.

39. More, *De Tristitia*, 51, 55–57, 101.

40. Other studies that have probed Spenser's indebtedness to a wide range of Christian source materials include Harold L. Weatherby's "What Spenser Meant by Holiness: Baptism in Book One of *The Faerie Queene*," *Studies in Philology* 84, 3 (Summer, 1987): 286–307; and Carol V. Kaske, "Spenser's Pluralistic Universe: The View from the Mount of Contemplation (F.Q. I.x)," in *Contemporary Thought on Edmund Spenser*, ed. Richard C. Frushell and Bernard J. Vondersmith (Carbondale: Southern Illinois University Press, 1975), 121–49, in which the author maintains that—in the House of Holiness—"Spenser's stand is with the Catholics in the current faith-versus-works controversy" (135). Arguing from a more Protestant perspective, Darryl J. Gless contends that we need to broaden our theological understanding of sixteenth-century Calvinist doctrines, which he argues do not unambiguously reject the merit of good works. *Interpretation and Theology in Spenser* (Cambridge: Cambridge University Press, 1994), esp. 9.

41. See Linda Gregerson, *The Reformation of the Subject: Spenser, Milton, and the English Protestant Epic* (Cambridge: Cambridge University Press, 1995), 5. See also Kenneth Gross, *Spenserian Poetics: Idolatry, Iconoclasm, and Magic* (Ithaca, N.Y.: Cornell University Press, 1985), 19. Gross goes on to describe Spenser as an "ardently decentered" Protestant who, in *The Faerie Queene*, offered "no clear types of church, formal ritual, or priesthood" (49).

42. Barbara Lewalski, *Protestant Poetics and the Seventeenth-Century Religious Lyric* (Princeton: Princeton University Press, 1979).

43. The House of Holiness manifests, we might say, one key instance in which, in the words of Huston Diehl, "the iconophilia so characteristic of the traditional religion in the fifteenth century continues to manifest itself in the sixteenth century." *Staging Reform, Reforming the Stage: Protestantism and Popular Theater in Early Modern England* (Ithaca, N.Y.: Cornell University Press, 1997), 13. In his reading of the scene, Gless suggests that the surprisingly Catholic elements of the scene contribute to "a broad humanist effort to employ reading to provoke active thought rather than to instill unquestioned ideas." *Interpretation and Theology*, 146).

44. On the post-Spenserian "softening" of the "cosmic hierarchy" for allegory, see Angus Fletcher, *Allegory: The Theory of a Symbolic Mode* (1984, reprint Ithaca, N.Y.: Cornell University Press, 1995), 237–38.

Chapter 12. "Par Accident": The Public Work of Early Modern Theater

1. *A History of Literary Criticism in the Italian Renaissance* (Chicago: University of Chicago Press, 1961), 2: 1104.

2. Montaigne, *Essais* 2:6 "De l'exercitation." Quotations in French are from *Essai* 2.6 in Michel de Montaigne, *Essais*, ed. Maurice Rat (Paris: Garnier Frères, 1962), 1: 414. English translation from Donald Frame, *Complete Essays of Montaigne* (Stanford, Calif.: Stanford University Press, 1965), 272.

3. Annabel Patterson, *Censorship and Interpretation: The Conditions of Writing and Reading in Early Modern England* (Madison: University of Wisconsin Press, 1984). For Patterson, the predominance of "ambiguity and interpretive difficulty, in which texts and historical events are equally resistant to simple, settled meanings" (56) is the period's most salient feature with regard to defensive gestures against censorship.

4. Jean Howard's important work, *Theater and Social Struggle* (New York: Routledge, 1996), is a document to the effects exerted on the English theater by women's massive audience presence. For the phenomenon of the actress there is a growing body of material, particularly on the continent; see for example Kathleen McGill, "Women and Performance: The Development of Improvisation by the Sixteenth-Century Commedia dell'Arte," *Theater Journal* 43 (1991): 59–69. For English reactions to the actress, see Stephen Orgel's *Impersonations* (Cambridge: Cambridge University Press, 1996), 1–11.

5. Citations from Shakespeare will be from *The Riverside Shakespeare*, ed. G. Blakemore Evans et al. (Boston: Houghton Mifflin, 1974).

6. Alberti is quoted in Ferruccio Marotti, *Lo spettacolo dall'Umanesimo al Manierismo* (Milan: Feltrinelli, 1974), 49; Machiavelli's treatise can be found in

his *Teatro e tutti gli scritti letterari*, ed. Franco Gaeta (Milan: Feltrinelli, 1965), 196. De'Sommi's remarks, from *Quattro dialoghi in materia di rappresentazioni sceniche*, are in the edition of Marotti, 243.

7. Roland M. Frye, *The Renaissance Hamlet* (Princeton, N.J.: Princeton University Press, 1984), 286; the first Appendix to the work contains a number of references to sixteenth-century English drama's investment in the "mirror" as a useful theatrical tool. In particular, Frye cites Skelton, Wager, Fulwell, Jonson, Randolph, Thomas Lodge and Robert Greene as adapting Donatus's preface to Terence for their own works. *Hamlet*'s engagement with the "inner man" has been the subject of a plethora of studies that have argued for the play as the first drama of modern subjectivity, with Hamlet himself as the first modern subject. Thus Francis Barker, in one of the more influential studies of the last twenty years finds the prince to be a passive, reflective harbinger of the bourgeois individual who as of yet has no properly bourgeois world to live in. His interiority is only "gestural" (36) and there can be "little that remains ultimately opaque." Yet as this essay goes on to argue, the real "opacity" lies elsewhere, in the female figure Hamlet fails to reveal to us; Hamlet himself, in all of his posturing and engagement with the relentlessly public world of the stage, looks back rather than forward to a theater that persistently engages with, and refuses to respect as alien, others' interiority. On the "crisis of mimesis" staged by the play—"*Hamlet* . . . can be seen to rehease one basic contradiction in the history of the Elizabethan theater: the precariously achieved synthesis, maturing in Kyd and Marlowe, between humanist learning and native spectacle"—see, among many others, Robert Weimann, "Mimesis in *Hamlet*," in *Shakespeare and the Question of Theory*, ed. Patricia Parker and Geoffrey Hartman (London: Methuen, 1985), 275–91.

8. The characterization is that of Christine Smith, in "The Winged Eye: Leon Battista Alberti and the Visualization of the Past, Present, and Future," in *The Renaissance from Brunelleschi to Michelangelo: The Representation of Architecture*, ed. Henry A. Millon and Vittoria Magnago Lampugnani (Milan: Bompani, 1994), 452.

9. See, among others, M. Christine Boyer, *The City of Collective Memory* (Cambridge, Mass.: MIT Press, 1996), who comments apropos Alberti: "Borrowing lessons from the Greeks, the Renaissance humanists of the fifteenth century tried to instill a sense of composition and clarity into the chaotic disorder of their urban environments by projecting illusions of harmony and moral significance onto its fabric" (77).

10. *De re aedificatoria*, ed. Giovanni Orlandi and Paolo Portoghesi (Milan: Polifilo 1966), 2: 710.

11. Even the house, as Alberti discusses it in a key passage early on in his *De re aedificatoria*, becomes the site for a privileged form of visibility, as he instructs the architect to put windows at ground level, not only so that it will permit breezes to fill hot Italian homes—Alberti rarely works on the level of an abstract theorist—but so that it will enable the inhabitants of the house to "see and to be seen."

12. *Della pittura*, translated as *On Painting*, John. R. Spencer (New Haven, Conn.: Yale University Press, 1966), 77.

13. Alberti's own, and only play, a Latin comedy entitled *Philodoxus* and passed off by the young author as a play by one of Plautus's contemporaries, is based on a stock situation in Roman theater, albeit invested with an allegorical significance

that is strictly medieval: the lusting of a young man for a woman and his abduction of her (as Roman decorum demanded, she rarely appears in the play, and only has several lines as she is being abducted—"Heu, heu!") While Alberti's play was not staged—the first known reenactment of a Latin new comedy would not happen until 1475 in Ferrara, after Alberti's death—Alberti himself was largely sensitive to the unrelenting publicness of the Latin comic stage, in which all events took place in the intersection of several streets. Unwelcome participants in public life, women were largely banned from that space unless they were prostitutes or aging wives.

14. Cited in Marotti, *Lo spettacolo*, 46, where Alberti quotes the appropriate passage from Ovid's *Ars amatoria*.

15. *An Apology for Actors*, ed. Richard H. Perkinson (New York: Scholars' Fascimiles and Reprints, 1941), GG.

16. See his treatise, "Spectacula," excerpted in Mariotti, *Lo spettacolo*, particularly 53, in which he writes, "essendo l'homo sopra tuti li altri gregali animali maximamente nasciuto a la societate. . . . In veritate, poche altre cose et operatione in le citate sono piú apte a tal dolce et naturale desiderio del homo che epsi spectaculi."

17. *The Arte of English Poesie* (1589), introduction by Baxter Hathaway (Kent, Ohio: Kent State University Press, 1970), I, xiii, 46.

18. Gelli and Grazzini are cited in Arnaldo Momo, *La crisi del modello teatrale* (Padova: Marsilio, 1974), 41, 74.

19. Guarini wrote two long treatises defending his play from Denores, both of them extremely polemical and very long; both are found in his collected *Opere*, (Verona, 1737). Robert Henke's *Pastoral Transformations: Italian Tragicomedy and Shakespeare's Late Plays* (Newark: University of Delaware Press, 1997) has an insightful discussion of Guarini's theory and its impact on Shakespeare.

20. The five volumes edited by Philippe Ariès and Georges Duby, *A History of Private Life* (Cambridge, Mass.: Belknap Press, 1987–91), are among the most historically oriented works in recent years to take up the question of privacy, although the focus in the later periods is primarily on France.

21. "La Tragicomica purga dunque la maninconia, affetto nocivo che bene spesso conduce l'uomo a darsi la morte"; cited in Guarini, *Opere* 2: 247.

22. As a result of the attacks, both Corneille and Guarini in turn would launch their own spirited defenses: Guarini's two pamphlets to Denores between 1587 and 1590, culminating in his final, and mercifully brief, "Compendio della poesia tragicomica" in 1602; and Corneille's embroilment in the "Querelle du Cid" launched by Georges de Scudéry and taken up by the French Academy in one of their first cultural "missions." Most of the documents from the quarrel are available in *La Querelle du Cid*, ed. Armand Gasté (Paris: Welter, 1898).

23. "Lesson in Writing," in *A Barthes Reader*, ed. Susan Sontag (New York: Hill and Wang, 1982), 308.

24. The late sixteenth and early seventeenth centuries are also significant for the history of performance insofar as they witness the birth of opera: a public form that relies heavily on erotic desire and the musical delineation of "the feminine" and "the masculine." Susan McClary comments in *Feminine Endings: Music, Gender, and Sexuality* (Minneapolis: University of Minnesota Press, 1991): "Opera emerges and continues to function as one of the principal discourses within which gender and

sexuality are publicly delineated—are at the same time celebrated, contested, and constrained" (36–37).

25. Citations from *Le Cid* are from the edition of Georges Couton, *Oeuvres complètes* (Paris: Gallimard, 1980–87), volume I.

26. I elaborate the scene in the court and its relationship to Corneille's career in my chapter on "The Example of Corneille" in *Writing and Vulnerability in the Late Renaissance* (Stanford, Calif.: Stanford University Press, 1993), 174–204.

27. From the numerous verses addressed to *commedia* actresses such as Virginia Ramponi or Orsola Cecchini that focus on their *blushing*, it would seem that male spectators were intrigued by this sudden lack of control on the part of the actress which such a spontaneous act assumes. "Quel vago rosseggiar del casto viso / che voi scopriste al'hora / ch'il finto sposo vostro il bacio colse" (["thus I observed] the delicious blush that you revealed on your chaste features, when the man who played your husband collected a kiss") writes an "admirer" of Cecchini. The citation is in Ferdinando Taviani, "Un vivo contrasto: seminario su attori e attrici della Commedia dell'arte," *Teatro e storia* 1 (1986): 66, who suggests that the actress's blushing represents for the male spectators the limits of theater and performance. For in these apparent examples of an actress's loss of control, the male spectator experiences the sudden joy of conquest, as in the course of his rigorous scrutinizing of his adversary's many masks he suddenly finds a gap, a space where she is *no longer acting*. See also Roberto Tessari, "Sotto il Segno di Giano: La Commedia dell'Arte di Isabella e di Francesco Andreini," in *The Commedia dell'Arte from the Renaissance to Dario Fo*, ed. Christopher Cairns (Lewiston, N.Y.: Edwin Mellen, 1988), 1–31.

28. Chimène is for the academician a "monstre," a "fille désnaturée," and a "parricide"; from *Observations sur le Cid*, in *La Querelle du Cid*, 72. George Dukore has also published portions of the *Observations* in English, in *Dramatic Theory and Criticism* (New York: Holt, Rinehart, and Winston, 1974), 211–17.

29. All citations from the *Pastor fido* are from the edition of Luigi Fassò (Turin: Einaudi, 1976).

30. Timothy Murray's *Theatrical Legitimation: Allegories of Genius in Seventeenth-Century England and France* (Oxford: Oxford University Press, 1987) is an account of other such strategies for defending theater in early modern Europe.

31. Or, as he writes in 1589, tragicomedy produces beneficial effects in the body of the individual spectator as well as that of the theatrical community: it aims "di levarne sol quella parte che, traboccando fuor de' termini naturali, corrompe la simmetria della vita, onde poi nasce la 'nfermita" ("to remove only that portion which, having trespassed beyond its natural limits, corrupts the symmetry of life and causes sickness"); *Opere* 3: 198.

32. Robert Ornstein's classic *Moral Vision of Jacobean Tragedy* (Madison: University of Wisconsin Press, 1965) makes the case that Jacobean tragedy is preoccupied with the declining role of ethics in contemporary society; unlike *Hamlet*, for example, in which "the question [of the ethical attitude towards blood revenge] is quite simply ignored, although Shakespeare has many opportunities to raise it" (23). The argument that follows suggests that Shakespeare does in fact question the moral nature of revenge tragedy, largely by diverting or displacing Hamlet's revenge onto his violent treatment of his mother.

33. It is also a scene where, as Stephen Greenblatt has recently commented, Hamlet is allied for a brief moment with Fortinbras; *Hamlet in Purgatory* (Princeton, N.J.: Princeton University Press, 2001), 221.

34. *The First Quarto of Hamlet*, ed. Kathleen O. Irace (Cambridge: Cambridge University Press, 1998).

35. William Kerrigan, *Hamlet's Perfection* (Baltimore: Johns Hopkins University Press, 1994), 115.

36. Speaking of Iago's "assertion of inscrutability, the refusal to be accountable or to recount," Jonathan Goldberg calls attention to the power that inheres in the refusal to enter the sphere of speech. Gertrude, of course, does not take Iago's oath of silence. But in the Folio and Q2 she neither discloses her innocence nor explicitly confesses; and, to that extent, she withholds her own responsibility in the play's events. "Shakespearean Inscriptions: The Voicing of Power," in *Shakespeare and the Question of Theory*, ed. Patricia Parker and Geoffrey Hartman (New York: Methuen, 1985), 132.

Chapter 13. Strange Alteration: Physiology and Psychology from Galen to Rabelais

I would like to thank Patricia Parker and François Rigolot for their helpful comments on a very early and very rough version of this essay, written some years ago. I am also grateful to Robin Einhorn, Leslie Kurke, Celeste Langan and Michael Lucey, who read a somewhat later draft and offered good feedback. Colleagues and friends at the University of Washington, Seattle, listened to a lecture drawn from this material and helped me clarify some of my terms. Their questions were especially rigorous and useful. Special thanks go to the editors of this volume for their bibliographical suggestions, and for their patience.

1. "No hubo bien nombrado a don Fernando la que el cuento contaba, cuando a Cardenio se la mudó la color del rostro, y comenzó a trasudar, con tan grande alteración, que el cura y el barbero, que miraron en ello, temieron que le venía aquel accidente de locura que habían oído decir que de cuando en cuando le venía." Miguel de Cervantes Saavedra, *Don Quijote de la Mancha*, 2 vols., ed. Martín de Riquer (Barcelona: Editorial Juventud, 1971), 1: ch. 28, 280. Unless indicated otherwise, all translations into English in this article are by me.

2. Pontus de Tyard, *Solitaire premier*, ed. Silvio Baridon (Geneva: Droz, 1950), 6.

3. Friedrich Nietzsche, "On the Genealogy of Morals," *Basic Writings of Nietzsche*, trans. and ed. Walter Kaufmann (New York: Modern Library, 1968), 565. This is from section 16 of the second essay in the "Genealogy."

4. The citation is from Greenblatt's essay "Psychoanalysis and Renaissance Culture," in *Literary Theory/Renaissance Texts*, ed. Patricia Parker and David Quint (Baltimore: Johns Hopkins University Press, 1986), 215. It is quoted in Michael G. Schoenfeldt, *Bodies and Selves in Early Modern England: Physiology and Inwardness in Spenser, Shakespeare, Herbert, and Milton* (Cambridge: Cambridge University Press, 1999), 17.

5. Schoenfeldt, *Bodies and Selves*, 17.

6. Certainly, Nietzsche makes the point that one can suscribe to his own theory of the preeminence of physiology and still be "the sternest opponent of all materialism." See Nietzsche, *Basic Writings*, 565.

7. I should note that because of the eccentricities of spelling in Renaissance French the term "altération" (as it would be written in modern French) will often appear in my text without an accent. Rabelais, for example, is completely inconsistent in his spelling. I have generally reproduced the orthography of the editions I cite.

8. Galen, *On the Natural Faculties*, trans. A. J. Brock (Cambridge, Mass.: Harvard University Press, 1963), II.8, 179. The Latin is from the translation of Thomas Linacre, *De Naturalibus Facultatibus Libri Tres* (Venice: Iuntas, 1586), vol. 1: 300.

9. Galen, *Natural Faculties*, 211. On Galen's understanding of physiology, see Margaret Tallmadge May's introduction to her edition and translation of Galen's *On the Usefulness of the Parts of the Body* (Ithaca, N.Y.: Cornell University Press, 1968), 52ff. On the Renaissance survivals of this tradition, see Nancy Siraisi, *Medieval and Early Renaissance Medicine: An Introduction to Knowledge and Practice* (Chicago: University of Chicago Press, 1990), 78–114, as well as Owsei Temkin, *Galenism: Rise and Decline of a Medical Philosophy* (Ithaca, N.Y.: Cornell University Press, 1973), chapter 3.

10. "L'affection risifique donc est mise sous la passion de l'ame nommée joye, laquelle, comme dit est, procede du coeur, lequel estant frappé de ce qui luy est agréable, se dilate et eslargit soüefuement, comme pour embrasser l'object présenté: et en cest dilatation il espand beaucoup de chaleur naturelle avec le sang, et encore plus d'esprits, desquels en est envoyé bonne portion à la face." Ambroise Paré, "Introduction à la chirurgie," *Oeuvres complètes d'Ambroise Paré* (Paris: Chez Gabriel Buon, 1585), ch.21, 36. For another canonical Renaissance discussion of the same processes, see the massively influential *Examen de ingenios para las ciencias* by the Spanish doctor Juan Huarte de San Juan (1594); on alteration in specific, see the digression on fire which follows part 4. I have consulted the edition of Guillermo Serés (Madrid: Cátedra, 1989).

11. Paré, *Oeuvres complètes*, 8, 35: "S'il est immoderément, chaud, froid, humide ou sec, il altere et change la temperature du corps en semblable constitution que la sienne."

12. It is in this context that Montaigne, for example, uses the term repeatedly. However, it appears to become a part of the general jargon of political theory. Thus, in an Italian context, the Venetian diplomat Lorenzo Bernardo writes in 1592 that the Turkish state is falling into ruin, "al presente tutto questo ordine si va alterando e corropendo." Cited in Lucette Valensi, *The Birth of the Despot: Venice and the Sublime Porte*, trans. Arthur Denner (Ithaca, N.Y.: Cornell University Press, 1993), 70. In a future essay I hope to explore the deployment of Galenic alteration in late-Renaissance political theory.

13. Quoted from the anthology *Poesía lírica del Siglo de Oro*, ed. Elías Rivers (Madrid: Cátedra, 1990), 37.

14. François Rabelais, *Oeuvres complètes*, ed. Pierre Jourda, 2 vols. (Paris: Garnier, 1962), 1: 411.

15. Rabelais, *Oeuvres complètes*, 1: 562. The entry comes as part of a list of attributes describing the fool. It directly follows, of course, "fou collateral."

16. Marsilio Ficino, *In Convivium Platonis sive de Amore*, cited from the French edition of Raymond Marcel, entitled *Commentaire sur le banquet de Platon* (Paris: Les Belles Lettres, 1956), 146.

17. Ficino, *In Convivium Platonis*, 184.

18. Ficino, *In Convivium Platonis*, 163.

19. Michel de Montaigne, *Oeuvres complètes*, ed. Thibaudet and Rat (Paris: Bibliothèque de la Pléiade, 1963), 870. The passage comes from Montaigne's essay on sexuality, "On Some Verses of Virgil" (3.5). The currency of Ficino's work even as late as Montaigne may be demonstrated by the appearance in Paris in 1585 of a French version of the commentary on the Symposium, under the title *De l'honneste amour*. I have consulted this text with help from the Gallica Website at the Bibliothèque Nationale de France.

20. Montaigne's heterodox claim that the breakdown of discipline is what makes the human being most human is, of course, a very modern moment in his text. Perhaps it is no coincidence that this claim brings him into line with the assertions about desire and the self set forth by Greenblatt and cited, along with Schoenfeldt's counterclaim, in my opening paragraphs.

21. For these nuances, see: Edmond Huguet, *Dictionnaire de la langue française du seizième siècle* (Paris, Champion 1925), vol. 1; the *Dictionnaire du moyen français*, by A. J. Greimas and T. M. Keane (Paris: Larousse, 1992), 22; Randle Cotgrave's *A Dictionarie of the French and English Tongues* (London, 1611, repr., Columbia: University of South Carolina Press, 1950), s.v.; and Jean Nicot, *Trésor de la langue française* (Paris, 1606), s.v. On the Latin/French interface, see Jehan Thierry's *Dictionnaire françois-latin* (Paris, 1564), s.v. In a nuanced and elegant reading of the thematics of thirst in Rabelais, Thomas M. Greene discusses the use of the term "alteration," which, he notes, generally contains a hint of corruption. In fact, suggests Greene, the modern "neutrality" of the term may be the effect, in part, of Rabelais's influence. My argument would be the contrary, that the "neutrality" of the term is rooted in its Galenic context. My own reading, in any event, tries to account for Greene's insistence on the negative connotations of the term, while noting, as we shall see, that in texts from different genres "around" Rabelais the word functions differently and demonstrates a striking polyvalence. Moreover, Greene suggests that the meaning "to excite thirst" "may not have been one of [the] readiest meanings" of "altérer." He may be inferring too much from Huguet's modern *Dictionnaire*, since the connection with thirst is listed as primary by Thierry and among regularly accepted meanings by Cotgrave and Nicot. See Greene's essay, "The Hair of the Dog That Bit You: Rabelais' Thirst," in *The Vulnerable Text: Essays on Renaissance Literature* (New York: Columbia University Press, 1986), 80–82.

22. It is worth stressing that I do not have in mind here something like Freud's notion of the antithetical meanings of primal words, but rather, as Ficino's circle image suggests, a set of displacements, a movement along a line as the soul makes its journey to God.

23. The phrase "altération et corruption" renders, imperfectly, Leone Ebreo's "mutazione et alterazione." I quote Pontus de Tyard, *Leon Hébreu, Dialogues d'Amour*, ed. T. Anthony Perry (Chapel Hill: University of North Carolina Press, 1974), 270. For alternate mentions of "soif" and "altération" see, for example, 263.

The Italian is from Leone Ebreo, *Dialoghi d'Amore*, ed. Santino Caramella (Bari: Laterza, 1929), 325. Curiously, the puns on alteration that one finds in French and Spanish vernacular literature during the period seem to be much less frequent in Italian. However, it is tantalizing to recall, especially given my discussion of Rabelais, below, that the Italian word "alterazione" also carries with it a connotation of drunkenness.

24. Louise Labé, *Oeuvres complètes*, ed. François Rigolot (Paris: Garnier-Flammarion, 1986), 99.

25. Pontus de Tyard, *Les Erreurs amoureuses*, ed. John A. McClelland (Geneva: Droz, 1967), 3. 33, p. 296.

26. Greene, in "The Hair of the Dog" mentions the importance of Neoplatonic thirst, but, obviously, given the topic of his essay, focuses on Rabelais, to the exclusion of the lyric texts that interest me here.

27. Joachim du Bellay, *Oeuvres poétiques*, edited by Daniel Aris and Françoise Joukovsky (Paris: Garnier, 1993), vol. 1, 35.

28. Maurice Scève, *Délie, object de plus haulte vertu*, ed. Eugène Parturier, introduction by Cécile Alduy (Paris: Société des Textes Français Modernes, 2001), #152, p.112.

29. See Labé's *Oeuvres complètes*, 145.

30. William Shakespeare, *Shakespeare's Sonnets*, ed. Stephen Booth (New Haven, Conn.: Yale University Press, 1977), 100.

31. For a good elaboration of the ways in which the *Sonnets* concern themselves with the management of the passions, see Schoenfeldt, *Bodies and Selves*, Chapter 3. In a well-known discussion of the Renaissance sonnet, Joel Fineman draws a distinction between the continental tradition of lyric desire, which, in his view, is tied to the rhetoric of vision, on the one hand, and, on the other hand, the model of lyric subjectivity found in Shakespeare's *Sonnets*, which is linked to the dynamics of writing. Shakespeare's invention of modern subjectivity, in Fineman's words, "thinks itself through, presents itself *as*, its difference from such erotic orthodoxy." *Shakespeare's Purjured Eye* (Berkeley: University of California Press, 1986), 19. I would want to insist, against Fineman's homogenizing summary of the Continental tradition, that desire and subjectivity are bound tightly to the semantic resources of the national vernaculars. In French that seems to involve a model of selfhood which can only escape the disequilibrium of the body through an act of reading (or misreading) the very terms through which passion afflicts the self. In this context, the notoriously slippery thematic of writing in the *Sonnets* presents the potentially welcome option of a kind of scriptural fixity through which the self can recast physiological imbalance as moral or epistemological dilemma.

32. William Shakespeare, *The Winter's Tale*, ed. J. H. P. Pafford (London: Methuen, 1963), 1.2. 369–86.

33. Pierre de Ronsard, *Le Bocage, les meslanges*, ed. Françoise Joukovsky (Paris: Garnier-Flammarion, 1995), 33.

34. Rabelais, *Oeuvres complètes*, vol. 1, 48. Further references to Rabelais will include page numbers in the text.

35. On the importance of purgation as an element in the humoral tradition, see Gail Kern Paster, *The Body Embarrassed: Drama and the Disciplines of Shame in Early Modern England* (Ithaca, N.Y.: Cornell University Press, 1993), 130–38.

36. See Cotgrave, *A dictionarie*, s.v.

37. On the importance of thirst and Pantagruel's birth, see Greene, "Rabelais' Thirst," 82. On the theme of thirst in Rabelais and its relationship to Christian iconographic traditions, see Florence M. Weinberg, *The Wine and the Will: Rabelais's Bacchic Christianity* (Detroit: Wayne State University Press, 1972).

38. See note 23, above.

39. David Quint, *Origin and Originality in Renaissance Literature* (New Haven, Conn.: Yale University Press, 1983), chapter 6. My account of the end of the *Third Book* is drawn from Quint's fine discussion. On the ways in which later depictions of thirst in Rabelais (specifically, at the end of the *Fifth Book*) respond to or "correct" the corrupting power of alteration see, again, Greene, "Rabelais' Thirst." On the redemptive dimension of Rabelais's narratives more generally see the several interesting studies by Edwin M. Duval, *The Design of Rabelais's Pantagruel* (New Haven, Conn.: Yale University Press, 1990), and *The Design of Rabelais's Tiers Livre de Pantagruel* (Geneva: Droz, 1997).

40. John Milton, *Paradise Lost*, ed. Merritt Y. Hughes (New York: Macmillan, 1985), 2: 1024. The passage is echoed, seven books further on in *Paradise Lost*, when Satan tells Eve of the sensual and intellectual pleasure he himself felt upon eating the apple: "Sated at length, ere long I might perceive / Strange alteration in me, to degree/ of Reason in my inward Powers, and speech / Wanted not long, though to this shape retain'd" (9. 598–60). For a good discussion of Milton's insistence on the gustatory nature of the fall see Schoenfeldt, *Bodies and Selves*, chapter 5. On Milton's relationship to vitalist materialism see the fascinating study by John Rogers, *The Matter of Revolution: Science, Poetry, and Politics in the Age of Milton* (Ithaca, N.Y.: Cornell University Press, 1996). esp. Chapters 1 and 4. Rousseau's uses of alteration are noted via citation, by Jacques Derrida, in *Of Grammatology*, trans. G. Spivak (Baltimore: Johns Hopkins University Press, 1976), 200ff. Rousseau is drawing both on the contexts I have explored in this essay and on another tradition, beginning, so far as I can tell, in the seventeenth century in France, which links the notion of alteration as corruption to the action of "altering" texts and thus to the thematics of writing. A further study would be needed to connect Rousseau's uses of the term to its earlier histories.

Contributors

ZIRKA Z. FILIPZCAK is Professor of the History of Art at Williams College. Her publications include *Picturing Art in Antwerp, 1550–1700*; *Hot Dry Men, Cold Wet Women: The Theory of Humors in Western European Art*; and articles on diverse topics, such as Leonardo's optical knowledge, depictions of miracles, and the absence of old women in scenes of heaven.

MARY FLOYD-WILSON teaches English at the University of North Carolina at Chapel Hill. She is the author of *English Ethnicity and Race in Early Modern Drama* and has published essays on early modern racial discourse, Shakespeare, and Ben Jonson.

TIMOTHY HAMPTON is Professor of French, Comparative Literature, and Italian Studies at the University of California, Berkeley. He is the author *of Writing from History: The Rhetoric of Exemplarity in Renaissance Literature* and *Literature and Nation in the Sixteenth Century: Inventing Renaissance France*. He is also editor of *Baroque Topographies: Literature/Philosophy/History*. He teaches and writes widely on early modern European culture.

VICTORIA KAHN is Professor of Rhetoric and Comparative Literature at the University of California, Berkeley. She is the author of *Rhetoric, Prudence, and Skepticism in the Renaissance* and *Machiavellian Rhetoric: from the Counter-Reformation to Milton*, and coeditor of *Machiavelli and the Discourse of Literature* and of *Rhetoric and Law in Early Modern Europe*. She is currently completing a book on the literature and political theory of the English civil war, entitled *Contract and Artifice: The Crisis of Political Obligation in England, 1640–1674*.

GAIL KERN PASTER is Director of the Folger Shakespeare Memorial Library and editor of *Shakespeare Quarterly*. Her publications include *The Idea of the City in the Age of Shakespeare*, *The Body Embarrassed: Drama and the Disciplines of Shame in Early Modern England*, the Revels Plays edition of

Middleton's *Michaelmas Term* (2000), and articles on the body in early modern drama.

KATHERINE ROWE, Associate Professor of English, Bryn Mawr College, is the author of *Dead Hands: Fictions of Agency, Renaissance to Modern*, as well as articles on Renaissance anatomies, tragic emotions, Shakespeare on film, and early modern drama.

MICHAEL SCHOENFELDT is Professor of English at the University of Michigan, and Director of the Program in Medieval and Early Modern Studies. He is the author of *Prayer and Power: George Herbert and Renaissance Courtship, Bodies and Selves in Early Modern England: Physiology and Inwardness in Spenser, Shakespeare, Herbert, and Milton*, and essays on Spenser, Shakespeare, Jonson, Donne, Herrick, Milton, and Amelia Lanyer.

BRUCE SMITH is Professor of English at Georgetown University. He is the author of four studies of early modern English culture: *Ancient Scripts and Modern Experience on the English Stage 1500–1700, Homosexual Desire in Shakespeare's England, The Acoustic World of Early Modern England*, and *Shakespeare and Masculinity*.

JOHN STAINES teaches English at Earlham College. His research focuses on appeals to the passions in the political rhetoric of the early modern public sphere. He has presented his work at several national conferences, including meetings of the Modern Language Association, the Renaissance Society of America, the Arizona Center for Medieval and Renaissance Studies, and the Sixteenth Century Studies Conference. "Elizabeth, Mercilla, and the rhetoric of Propaganda in Spenser's *Faerie Queene*," *Journal of Medieval and Early Modern Studies* 31, 2 (2001): 283–312.

RICHARD STRIER is Frank L. Sulzberger Professor in the College and the Department of English at the University of Chicago. He is the author of *Love Known: Theology and Experience in George Herbert's Poetry* and *Resistant Structures: Particularity, Radicalism, and Renaissance Texts*. He has co-edited a number of collections of essays, most recently, *Writing, Reading, and Political Engagement in Seventeenth-Century England*, with Derek Hirst, and has published essays on Shakespeare, Donne, religious poetry, and critical theory. He is currently editing the Quarto *King Lear* with contextualizing historical materials, and gearing up for books on Shakespeare's skepticism and Donne's development.

GARY TOMLINSON, Annenberg Professor in the Humanities and Chair of the Department of Music at the University of Pennsylvania, is a specialist in music of the late Renaissance and early Baroque, opera, music and cross-cultural contact, and cultural history and historiography. He has been awarded the Alfred Einstein prize of the American Musicological Society, a Guggenheim fellowship, and a MacArthur fellowship, He is the author of *Monteverdi and the End of the Renaissance, Metaphysical Song: An Essay on Opera,* and *Music in Renaissance Magic: Toward a Historiography of Others.* His current work concerns Aztec song and theories of European colonialism.

DOUGLAS TREVOR teaches English at the University of Iowa. He is coeditor, with Carla Mazzio, of *Historicism, Psychoanalysis, and Early Modern Culture,* and has published essays on Donne, Herbert, and Thomas More. He wrote the introduction to the new Pelican edition of *Julius Caesar,* and is currently working on a book entitled *The Reinvention of Sadness: Scholarly Melancholy and the Pain of Learned Life.*

JANE TYLUS, Professor of Italian Studies at New York University, is author of *Writing and Vulnerability in the Late Renaissance,* coeditor with Margaret Beissinger and Susanne Wofford of *Epic Traditions in the Contemporary World: the Poetics of Community,* and author of articles on Renaissance Classicism and Italian drama.

Index

Acknowledgments

It is with the truest of emotions that the editors of this volume wish to thank those who brought it to life. The first and largest portion of thanks must go to the Folger Institute and the Andrew Mellon Foundation, who asked Gail Paster to direct four weekend seminars in 1999–2000 on basic issues in the humanities. The result was "Reading the Early Modern Passions," from which title the present book takes its name. The faculty and graduate student participants—some of whom are also authors of essays herein—brought to every weekend's discussion an extraordinary energy and the highest standards of responsiveness and learning. As one of our guest faculty commented after a morning session, "This is the best two hour discussion I've heard in years." We were blessed as well with an inspired and provocative guest faculty—Catherine A. Lutz, Steven Mullaney, William Ian Miller, Zirka Z. Filipczak, and Gary Tomlinson. We are grateful to Cathy and Steven for presenting the overarching questions so brilliantly, to Bill for insisting on answers to the hardest and most provocative questions, to Zirka and Gary for their disciplinary breadth and wisdom and for returning as contributors to this volume. Barbara Mowat and Kathleen Lynch of the Folger Institute spurred us along from seminar to anthology with their enthusiasm and belief in the importance of the topic, while Owen Williams and Lisa Meyer, also of the Folger Institute, were the presiding organizational spirits providing key tactical and logistical support. We are also grateful to the Folger Reading Room staff, especially Camille Seerattan, for ever-gracious help to seminar members. We are grateful to Werner Gundersheimer, then director of the Folger, for agreeing to use Folger publication funds to support this volume's publication. Thanks go, as well, to the Madge Miller Fund at Bryn Mawr College and the University Research Council at the University of North Carolina, Chapel Hill for its financial support in preparing the manuscript for publication.

The generous counsel of many friends made editorial collaboration on this volume an exhilarating and rewarding process. We owe particular thanks to Scott Black, Lynn Enterline, Steven Mullaney, Kristen Poole, Patricia

Reilly, Lauren Shohet, Garrett Sullivan, Lyn Tribble, and Julian Yates for their cogent responses to the introduction as it matured. Each of us has individual debts to acknowledge as well. Mary Floyd-Wilson owes thanks also to David Glimp, Ian MacInnes, and Garrett Sullivan—all readers of proven mettle—whose expertise, rigor, and enthusiasm were indispensable. Audiences at the 2002 SAA meeting in Minneapolis and at a session on "Land, Property, and Space in the Early Modern World" at Penn State improved her essay with their thought-provoking questions and responses. For intellectual help of a very high order on the subject of animal passions, Gail Paster wishes to thank Jeffrey Jerome Cohen, Julie Solomon, Garrett Sullivan, and Ian MacInnes. The late and much-missed Susan Snyder was, as always, an encyclopedic fount of knowledge. Linda Woodbridge and Richard McCoy provided wonderful audiences—at Penn State and the CUNY Graduate Center respectively—at crucial early moments of research. For Katherine Rowe, many of those listed above have been a source of sustaining intellectual community, as well as specific counsel on the history of emotions on and off stage. To these she would add, with equal warmth, Edmund Campos, Tom Cartelli, Jane Hedley, Heather James, Nora Johnson, Kate Levin, Joseph Roach, and Michael Tratner.